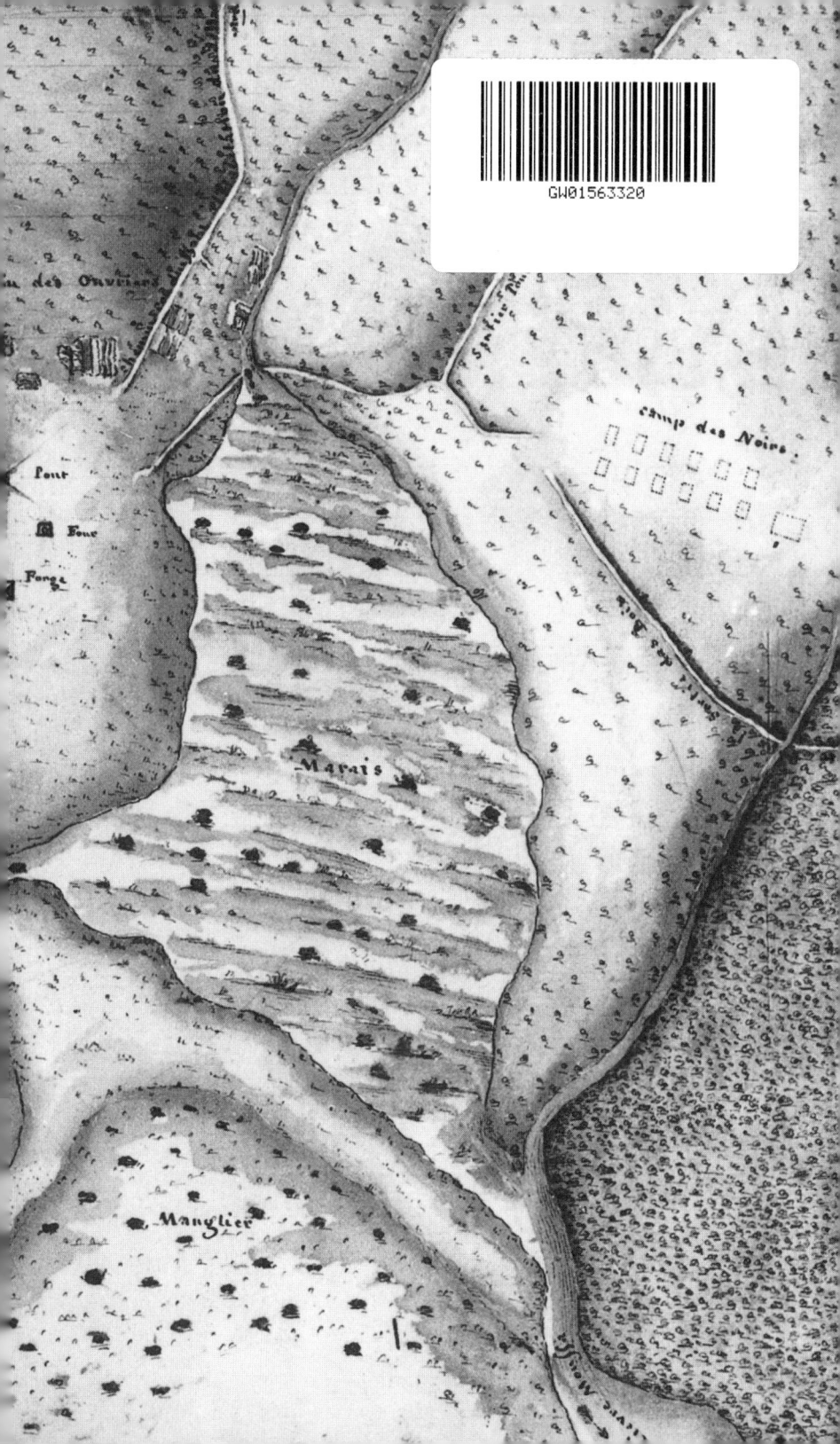

Rivals in Eden

Front Endpaper:
Map of Romainville's Établissement du Roi (Bibliothèque Nationale, Paris).

Back Endpaper:
Sainte Anne island, site of the first French settlement (Author).

By the same author

*Hard Times in Paradise: The History
of Seychelles 1827-1919*

Rivals in Eden

THE HISTORY OF SEYCHELLES
1742 - 1827

William McAteer

PRISTINE BOOKS
Mahé : Seychelles

To
JULIETTE
whose idea it was

First published in 1991 by
The Book Guild Ltd, Lewes, East Sussex.

This revised edition is published by
PRISTINE BOOKS
PO Box 158, Mahé,
Seychelles
2002

Copyright © William McAteer 2002
email: wmcateer@seychelles.net

All rights reserved.
No part of this publication may be reproduced by any process
without the written permission of the copyright owner.

Printed in Great Britain
by The Cromwell Press
Trowbridge, Wiltshire

ISBN 99931-809-0-4

CONTENTS

List of illustrations and maps		6 & 7
Introduction		9
Chapter 1	*Three Brothers*	11
Chapter 2	*Crocodiles and Coconuts*	28
Chapter 3	*Short Cut to India*	44
Chapter 4	*First Settlement*	61
Chapter 5	*Collapse of a Colony*	71
Chapter 6	*The King's Officer*	83
Chapter 7	*Revolutionary Interlude*	101
Chapter 8	*Honourable Surrender*	119
Chapter 9	*Envoys from India*	134
Chapter 10	*Exiles from France*	152
Chapter 11	*Death at Anjouan*	175
Chapter 12	*The Rivals*	198
Chapter 13	*Human Bondage*	219
Chapter 14	*Rule Britannia!*	231
Seychelles Roll-Call		250
Sources and Notes		264
Bibliography		290
Seychelles Capitulation		292
Index		294

ILLUSTRATIONS

BETWEEN PAGES 64 AND 65

Jean Moreau de Séchelles (Bibliothèque Nationale, Paris).
Château de Séchelles (Author).
Marie-Jean Hérault de Séchelles (Bibliothèque Nationale, Paris).
Château de Montgeoffroy (Author).
Plan of Isle Seychelle, 1778 (Bibliothèque Nationale, Paris).
Arms of the Compagnie des Indes Orientales (Musée de la Compagnie des Indes, Lorient).
Sketch by Morphey of Isle Seychelle, 1756 (Archives de France, Paris).
Plan for Gillot's spice garden (Archives de France, Paris).
Decorative title-piece, Seychelles chart, 1777, (Bibliothèque Nationale, Paris).
Coco de mer nut (Author).
Giant tortoises on Curieuse island (Ian McAteer).
Crocodile (from water-colour by Claude-Nicolas Billerey, 1751-52 (Bibliothèque Municipale, Besançon).
Duc de Praslin (Bibliothèque Nationale, Paris).
Mahé de la Bourdonnais (Bibliothèque Nationale, Paris).
Pierre Poivre (Bibliothèque Nationale, Paris).
Comte de La Pérouse (Bibliothèque Nationale, Paris).
Louis-Antoine Bougainville (Bibliothèque Nationale, Paris).
Antoine Sartine, Duc d'Alby (Bibliothèque Nationale, Paris).
Sketch map of Isle Séchelle (Archives de France, Paris).
Letter from Grenier to friend (Archives de France, Paris).
Alexis-Marie de Rochon (Bibliothèque Nationale, Paris).

BETWEEN PAGES 160 AND 161

Chevalier de Ternay (Musée de la Marine, Paris).
Magallon de la Morlière (Bibliothèque Nationale, Paris).

Jean-François Hodoul (Hodoul family).
Robert Surcouf (Bibliothèque Nationale, Paris).
Demand by Captain Henry Newcome of H.M.S. *Orpheus* for surrender of Seychelles, 1794 (Seychelles National Archives).
Captain Charles Magon (Musée de la Marine, Paris).
Tippu Sultan (British Library, London).
View of Pondichéry (British Library, London).
Explosion in Rue St Nicaise, Paris: illustration and street plan (Bibliothèque Nationale, Paris).
Napoleon Bonaparte as First Consul (Christie's Images).
Letter by deportee Bertrand Guilhémat to Captain Guieysse (Guieysse family papers).
Battle of *Sybille* and *Chiffonne* (National Maritime Museum, Greenwich).
Captain Charles Adam (Blair Adam collection).
Captain George Collier (National Maritime Museum).
Blair Adam house, Kinross-shire, Scotland (Author).
General Decaen (Bibliothèque Nationale, Paris).
Admiral Linois (Musée de la Marine, Paris).
Quéau de Quinssy (photo: Author, Seychelles National History Museum).
Quinssy's tomb (Author).

MAPS

Mahé island	8
Praslin group	34
Amirantes, Mascarene islands, and Madagascar	48
Maldives, Chagos archipelago, and India	178

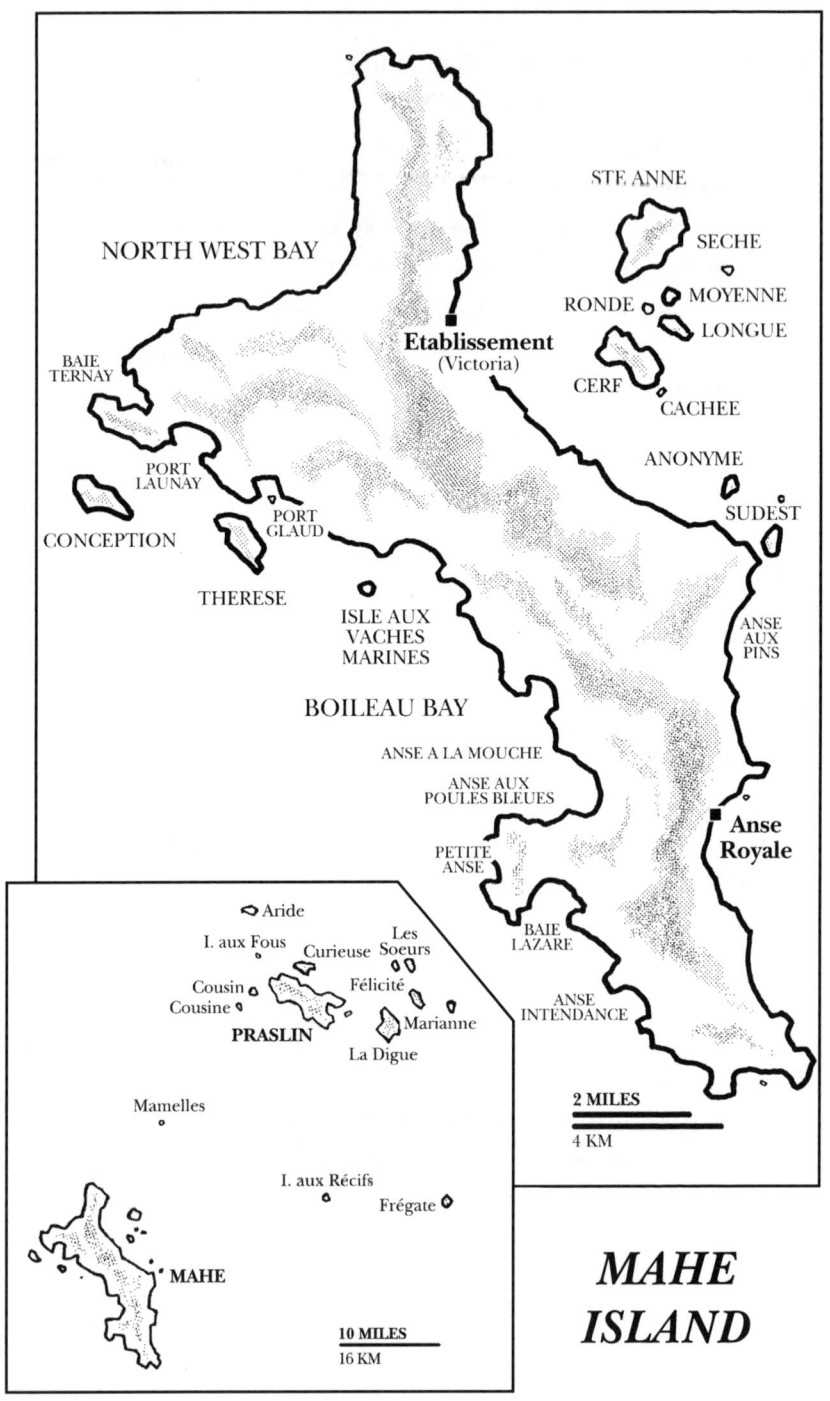

INTRODUCTION

Some eighty kilometres north of Paris, amid the fields and forests and gentle streams of Picardy, stands the Château de Séchelles, built in 1740 by Jean Moreau, who had acquired some years previously the *seigneurie* of the lands of Cuvilly and Séchelles.

Moreau de Séchelles is not totally unknown to history. A successful civil and military administrator, he served as Louis XV's Finance Minister for two years until his retirement in August 1756. That same year the name Séchelles was given, first, to one and subsequently to a group of uninhabited islands that had been discovered by France in the western Indian Ocean.[1]

With time the name of the islands changed to Seychelles, and it was as such that they passed at the end of the Napoleonic wars from French to British rule. A century and a half later, in June 1976, the original colony, together with other widely scattered clusters of sand, coral and palms — totalling more than one hundred islands in all — became the independent Republic of Seychelles.

In this account of the French settlement of the islands the varied spelling of Seychelles is retained, as well as the old names for the other French outposts in the Indian Ocean: the Isle de France — today's independent Mauritius — and the the Isle Bourbon, or Réunion. France's principal rival in the East was Great Britain, although the French almost always referred to their enemy as England, and the English. In these pages it had been found convenient to follow French style.

Material for this book came mainly from archives in Paris, London, and Mauritius, although research also involved inquiry at other places, notably in northern France at the privately owned Château de Séchelles and the adjoining village of Cuvilly, and at Caen, in Normandy; also in Scotland, at Blair Adam, Kinross-shire; at Réunion; and in Seychelles, where the national archives have in recent years acquired several documents relating to the French period that were previously held elsewhere. At all those places the author found ready, often generous assistance.

To past and present historians of Seychelles

acknowledgements are due for much valuable material consulted by the author in the preparation of this book.

Doha, Qatar, 1991

REVISED EDITION

This revised and re-titled edition of *Rivals in Eden* forms part of a History of Seychelles of which part two, *Hard Times in Paradise*, was published in 2000. In addition to the change of title there are a number of corrections to the text, and several illustrations have been replaced.

Mahé, Seychelles, 2002   William McAteer

1

Three Brothers
1742-1756

> These ilands ... ought very diligently to be
> sought of by them that shall travaile hereafter.
> *English seaman, January 1609*

Throughout the morning the ship had stood in towards the island, her approach so leisurely it seemed as if she were reluctant to reach the deserted shore. Had a watcher been present he would have noted her sturdy Dutch build and, if inquiry had been possible, might have learned that she was the *Charles*,[1] of 50 tonnes, commanded by Jean Grossin, of the French Compagnie des Indes.

When about a quarter-league from the shore – the time by then being past one o'clock – the *Charles* came to anchor; an entry in the log would record that she lay "in 25 fathoms of water, on a fine sandy bottom".

Two hours later a second ship glided into the bay. She, too, had appeared out of the south-west, and although her large lateen sail might have suggested she was an Arab trader homeward bound to the Gulf the tartane *Elisabeth* was French like her companion; together, they were on a voyage of discovery for the governor-general of the island colonies of Isle de France and Bourbon. The *Elisabeth's* captain, Lazare Picault, named the anchorage Port St Lazare.[2] The date was Wednesday, 21 November 1742.

More than three months had elapsed since Picault's departure from Isle de France to explore the waters to the north-east of Madagascar. During that time he had come across several islands, for the most part negligible strands of sand and coral, partially covered by thick bush, their only inhabitants birds and giant tortoises.

It had been on the last and largest of these, on the low, serrated expanse of the Jean de Nove atoll, that they had found tortoises bigger and more numerous than they had ever seen, some so large that six men together had been unable to load them into the boats. For the Frenchmen tortoise stew was common enough fare; like turtle, it was an agreeable substitute for beef, which was often scarce at the Isle de France. They noted that the tortoises of Jean de Nove were not only larger than those of Rodrigues island, the usual source of supply, but they were tastier as well[3].

Picault had hoped to find water. The many birds indicated that there was fresh water somewhere on the island, but although he sent a party tramping more than ten miles round the atoll none was found. Early the next day, the thirsty Frenchmen sailed away north-eastwards into unknown seas. Three weeks would go by before they again sighted land. Their cargo of live tortoises provided food, but soon the only relief from thirst was the rainwater they managed to collect. Despair lay ever heavier on their hearts as each day passed without a hint of land until, in the afternoon of Monday, 19 November, the crew of the *Elisabeth* was roused by a cry from the lookout.

"It is a very high island, which lies 15 leagues to the north-east-quarter-north of us," wrote Picault. During the night they continued to sail towards it and, at daylight, observed that there were more than one island. "The new island is to the west of the first, one or two leagues distant," Picault noted. "It is high, round and rugged. The first is also mountainous, and has white patches in the south."

Picault was sure they had reached the islands known to the Portuguese as Tres Irmãos, or Three Brothers, although according to his sailing directions they should have been the Amirantes. At that moment, however, his main concern was not where he was, but whether he would find fresh water.

Although only a few hours of daylight remained, Picault ordered two parties ashore, and soon the *Elisabeth's* long boat, powered by its great sweeps, was cutting solidly through the clear green water. Once safely within the reef, the boat's crew could see huge coral heads below the surface as they raced a boat from the *Charles* to the shore. There, on a gently sloping beach, a landing was made without difficulty.

The wind had now freshened, rustling the fronds of the coconut palms, which stretched back some way across flat terrain before the land rose abruptly in an impenetrable barrier of rock and vegetation. From this forest came the call of birds and a pervasive chorus of unseen insects, as if warning of a stranger's approach.

The seamen, who had unloaded several empty water casks on the beach, moved off in groups in search of a stream. Further up the coast from where the two ships were anchored the islet of white rock, which had at first appeared like a marker to the anchorage, was turning dark against the evening sun. Away in the hazy distance, broken off from the main island's western promontory, were two small islands — or was it three? Suddenly, breaking into nature's reverie, there was a shout. Someone had found water — a small brook flowing out of the undergrowth and spilling over on to the sand. It was to be the first of several streams they would find.

Picault named one of the streams Rivière au Caïman, after the crocodiles they encountered there. These creatures, which he misnamed caymans,[1] seem to have kept their distance, for Picault recorded in his journal that he had found no *mauvaise bette* on the island. There were also in the forest many giant tortoises, although not as large nor as numerous as those on Jean de Nove, and a great variety of birds: pigeons, doves, guinea fowl, parrots, and sea birds. There were also bats, and an abundance of fish both in the streams and the sea. Truly, remarked Picault, it could be called the Island of Plenty.

Picault did not sail round the island, and the other side remained unknown to them. However, Grossin, with a fair degree of accuracy, estimated that the island was as high as the Isle de France (at 2,969 feet it is only 283 feet higher), with a circumference of between 15 and 20 leagues. He noted that the trees were much straighter than those of the Isle de France, and that they would make beautiful masts for ships. There were also many fine bays where ships could be careened, and in the mountain gorges the earth appeared fertile. They saw no sign of human habitation, or even that anyone had passed that way.

By now it was almost the end of November and Picault, who had been instructed by the governor-general to call at Rodrigues for a cargo of tortoises and be back at the Isle de France by 15 January, decided it was time to leave. At daybreak on Monday, 26 November, the *Elisabeth* and the *Charles*, laden with 33 tortoises and 600 coconuts, sailed from their anchorage on a light breeze. Before they could clear the land, however, a calm set in and, for fear of drifting on to rocks, they had to lie at anchor for the rest of the day.

The following morning, as they passed the southern tip of the island, they sighted for the first time a group of smaller islands to the north-east. With this final fragment of information to add to his report, Picault bent course for the island of Rodrigues. He still had doubts about the position and identity of the islands he had discovered, but it was not until some weeks later that the full extent of his navigational errors became apparent. At six in the evening of 6 January 1743 the *Elisabeth's* look-out sighted land eight to ten leagues away in the north-west. This had to be Rodrigues, which lay some 250 miles east of the Isle de France, yet Picault was perturbed to find the coastline unfamiliar.

"In this uncertainty we sailed along the coast during the night," he wrote. "At six in the morning we saw the land, five to six leagues away, which we recognised perfectly as being Madagascar." Even allowing for the difficulty at that time of estimating longitude at sea without an accurate chronometer, Picault could hardly be excused for finding himself 1,000 miles off course. In the words of a contemporary, he was "more fortunate than wise".[5]

* * *

The Portuguese navigators who first explored the western Indian Ocean at the beginning of the 16th century found the mid-ocean islands east of Madagascar inhabited only by giant reptiles, small mammals, and birds. There were no signs that man had ever lived there, although it is certain the islands were known by some of those who sailed the ocean in ancient times: Arabs, Indians, and Chinese among others, including the Phoenicians, who are reputed to have rounded the Cape from east to west 2,000 years before the Portuguese.[6]

Many of the islands are coral atolls or waterless rocks, where no one would voluntarily make his home, and even the larger islands, their slopes covered with exotic forest and cruelly slashed by deep gorges, would not be particularly attractive to a people on the move, who could be expected to push on towards the shores of India or Africa.

France's interest in the islands dates from the early 17th century, when several unsuccessful settlements were made on the Madagascar coast. In 1662 the French moved to the most westerly of the Mascarene islands, which they named Isle Bourbon, and when the Dutch, who had been occupying the neighbouring island of Mauritius[7] off and on since 1638 finally abandoned it in 1710 the French settled there, renaming it the Isle de France. The two islands, with agricultural economies based on slave labour from Madagascar and Africa, were administered for the Crown by the Compagnie des Indes. Possessing good natural harbours, the Isle de France quickly gained in importance over Bourbon, and in 1735 a governor-general responsible for both islands was appointed, with his headquarters in the Isle de France.

Bertrand François Mahé de La Bourdonnais was 36 when he was made governor-general. Like so many of the illustrious figures in French maritime history he was a Breton from St Malo, and already had a colourful career behind him as a sailor and trader in the East. The energy and enthusiasm he brought to his new post was soon to shake the two islands out of their tropical lethargy.

Within a year he had totally reorganised the island administration, introduced new crops and industries, consolidated Port Louis as the capital and main port on the favourable north-west coast of the Isle de France, and begun construction of barracks, hospitals, aqueducts, mills, and canals. Because there was a lack of skilled manpower he himself undertook the training of young artisans, for he was both engineer and shipbuilder.

La Bourdonnais's eldest daughter by his second marriage, Madame de Montlezun, left a brief description of her father which confirms the portraits that exist of him. "My father had handsome black eyes, as well as dark eyebrows. His nose was long and his mouth a little large. He was not at all stout: of middling height, being only slightly taller than five feet six inches, and holding himself very well. He had an alert, lively mind, and was very cheerful. His principal virtue was his humanity." [8]

La Bourdonnais's humanity prompted him to improve conditions for the slaves, although he was ruthless enough dealing with runaway slaves, or *marrons,* who roamed the islands in bands, often terrorising the inhabitants. One of his measures was to form commandos of armed slaves to hunt them down.

In creating a prosperous island colony La Bourdonnais never lost sight of the ultimate aim, to maintain and expand French power in India. He recognised the value of having a powerful base in the Indian Ocean, especially as the main settlement in India, Pondichéry, possessed only an open anchorage. Yet he must have wished that the Isle de France had been closer to India, for it took ships many weeks to reach there, particularly as long detours had to be made to avoid the multitude of islands and reefs that supposedly barred the direct route.[9]

In the favourable monsoon season, between April and October, with the wind from the south-east, ships leaving the Isle de France would first make for Cap d'Ambre, at the northern tip of Madagascar, before joining the traditional route pioneered by the Portuguese, which, after skirting north of the Maldives, brought them safely to the Malabar coast. During the contrary monsoon, the voyage to India could take all of three months, with ships sailing south as far as 30 degrees of latitude, where they would be blown eastwards by the prevailing winds until they turned north towards Sumatra and then reached across the Bay of Bengal to the Coromandel coast.

By 1740, however, several mariners were questioning the existence of all the hazards marked on the old charts which barred the way to India. It was to resolve that issue and, if possible, shorten the sailing time to India, that La Bourdonnais selected a young navigator from Toulon, Lazare Picault, to chart the islands lying north-east of Madagascar.[10] For this mission he gave Picault his own ship, the *Elisabeth*, and sent with him a company vessel under the command of Jean Grossin.

The early exploration of the Indian Ocean is not a straightforward story. French historian Eugène de Froberville, writing in 1848, noted that the most inextricable confusion persisted for more than two centuries over the geography of the ocean's archipelagos. "The sketchy portulans (sailing directions), being notoriously inexact, each navigator corrected the position of land according to his whim," he wrote. As a result genuine discoveries were recorded inaccurately on the charts, while new names were arbitrarily given to islands that were already known.

The Portuguese, first of the western nations to cross the Indian Ocean in their quest for the riches of the East, tried to keep secret what they knew of the route. Sometimes their charts were designed deliberately to mislead, and it suited their purpose if an imaginary string of islands and reefs across the ocean dissuaded others from following them to the Indies.

For the final stage of his historic voyage to India in 1498, Vasco da Gama sought the assistance of an Arab pilot-astrologer to see him safely across the ocean from Malindi, on the East African coast, to Calicut.[11] On his second voyage to India four years later he followed the same outward route, but on the return took a more southerly course and, as a result, made a first sighting of what are today the Seychelles islands.

In the early Portuguese charts there appears the Inscription *Ilhas que achou de segun vez almirante Dom Vasco* (Islands seen the second time by admiral Dom Vasco), and from this evolved the name Amirantes, given to the 20 or so coralline islands lying south-west of the main granitic group of the Seychelles. Although Vasco da Gama is thus associated with those smaller islands (which are now part of the Republic of Seychelles), it has been argued that his fleet probably sighted the larger granitic islands as well.[12] The *Roteiro,* or sailing directions of the voyage, makes no mention of any sightings, but an anonymous Flemish seaman recorded in his journal that two islands were seen on 26 March 1503. They saw a fire and people on the shore trying to attract attention, but if these were survivors of a shipwreck the Portuguese were not sufficiently interested to find out. They sailed on.[13]

Three years later the Portuguese navigator Fernão Soares, returning from India with four fully laden ships, sighted islands to the north-east of Madagascar, and subsequently the inscription Sete Irmas (Seven Sisters) appeared on the Portuguese charts in the approximate position of the

Seychelles. In the copying of names, however, Sisters could be confused with Brothers (Irmas and Irmãos), and in time the two seemed to be almost interchangeable, their number, also, varying from seven to three.[14]

Today the names of many Indian Ocean islands recall Portugal's pioneering role: Peros Banhos, Diego Garcia, Agaléga, the Chagos archipelago, Rodrigues, and the Mascarene islands. Of the 100 or so islands that comprise the Seychelles republic, however, only a few still indicate a Portuguese connection. In addition to the Amirantes, there is Cosmoledo, named after a Portuguese pilot, and Aldabra, a name that is probably Arabic in origin.

Of the others, however, there is no trace. The Baixos da Patram, São Francisco,[15] Corpo Sancto, and Sete Irmas have all disappeared, along with Roquepiz, Espirítu Sancto and the numerous *Albreolhos* that warned navigators to keep their eyes open. As Portugal's eastern empire collapsed before the growing resistance of Omani Arabs and the expansionist ambitions of the Dutch, English, and French these names were erased from the maps.

* * *

La Bourdonnais could hardly have been satisfied with Picault's sketchy report of his discoveries. News had reached him that the war which had begun in Europe three years previously over the Austrian Succession was likely to spread to India despite the reluctance of the French and English trading companies to be involved. If hostilities did break out in the East, Picault's island could become an important staging post on the way to India. It was essential, concluded La Bourdonnais, that Picault should return and thoroughly reconnoitre the archipelago.

On 7 December 1743 Picault - this time unaccompanied - sailed in the *Elisabeth* for Rodrigues, from where he took a bearing back along the route he had imagined he was following on his return voyage the previous year. On 16 April 1744 he fetched up a few leagues west of the Chagos archipelago, where the old Portuguese charts located the islands of the Three Brothers. After surveying the archipelago, he sailed west, until on 28 May he reached one of the outer islands of the group he had visited with Grossin 18 months previously. Picault anchored half a league from the shore, but a heavy sea prevented him from landing.[16] In the south-west he could see the large island he was now to refer to as "the former Three Brothers" and which he would rename, in honour of his patron, Isle Mahé, giving the island group the name Isles de La Bourdonnais.

The next day Picault sailed for his former anchorage off Mahé, but finding he could make no progress against wind and current he elected to anchor on the east coast. Manœuvring close to the shore and sounding repeatedly, he finally sailed into a large natural harbour "formed of eleven islands, all bordered with reefs". Here, on Mahé's north-east coast, the French would eventually form their settlement. Picault called the place Port Royal.

"This harbour is sheltered from all winds except that from the north-north-west, which blows there unhindered," he wrote, "but as it has three entrances and, consequently, three exits, one can stand out to sea in any wind."

Picault spent more than two weeks on the island, drawing up a report which was much more detailed than his first. He considered that the earth was good in places for sugar-cane cultivation, and that rice could be grown in the large areas of marshy ground he had found. He referred to the flat tops of some of the mountains and envisaged about 300 "pleasant estates" being established on the island. He also visited the surrounding islands and found tortoises everywhere although they were not in large numbers except, perhaps, in the interior, and he did not have time to hunt them there. He also reported seeing many turtles along the beaches.

Before leaving on 15 June for the Malabar coast of India, Picault sailed to the second largest island of the group, which he named Isle de Palme, on account of what he took to be great cotton-bearing latans growing there. These were, in fact, the mysterious coco de mer palms that from ancient times had been thought to grow under the sea, and whose double-lobed nuts, washed up on eastern shores, were much in demand on account of their supposed medicinal and aphrodisiac properties. It is not known if Picault collected any of the nuts, but if he did he left it to another to record the significance of his discovery.[17]

On 1 September 1744, two months after Picault's arrival back at the Isle de France, La Bourdonnais received news from France that the war had spread to all colonial outposts, and that even now an English squadron was on its way to the East. If he had been considering forming a settlement at Mahé he put the idea aside for the more urgent business of forming a fleet to carry the fight to the English in India.

Two years were to elapse, however, before La Bourdonnais, with naval reinforcements from France, set sail for India, where he would bring glory to France, the high point of his campaign being the capture of Madras. Later came the bitterness of repudiation, his recall to France and imprisonment in the Bastille on charges of corruption. He was eventually acquitted, but Mahé de La Bourdonnais died a broken man, in 1753.

By then Picault, too, was dead, and the *Elisabeth* had been lost in combat against the English. The islands he had discovered were all but forgotten. The direct route to India continued to beckon the adventurous few, including the English admiral Boscawen, who, in 1748, after a brief blockade of the Isle de France, sailed his fleet safely that way, arriving off the Coromandel coast just before the war ended and eliciting the admiration of the French for his achievement.[18]

* * *

During the early 16th century the English had contributed little to Europe's voyages of discovery, and it was only with the opening of Elizabeth's reign that they began seriously to seek a passage to the Indies. In 1577-80 Drake sailed round the world, forming, on the way, the first English colony in the Moluccas. By the end of 1599 the Queen had granted a charter to the East India Company, and within a year the company's first fleet had been dispatched to the East.

Those early voyages were separate undertakings financed by individual subscription, and from the first three rich profits were made from the sale of pepper and spices brought back from the Moluccas.[19] However, the ruthless determination of the Dutch to keep a tight grip on the spice trade, which they had themselves wrested from the Portuguese, induced the English to switch their interest from the Spice islands to mainland India, where the decay of the Mogul empire was invitation enough for European traders. Consequently, the company's Fourth Voyage, by the ships *Ascension* and *Union*, under the overall command of Alexander Sharpeigh, was directed towards Arabia and India.

The ships sailed from Woolwich on 14 March 1608, and after spending two months at the Cape, where another, smaller ship, the *Good Hope*, was built, Sharpeigh's fleet sailed on into the Indian Ocean. Almost immediately the three ships were separated by a storm. When it abated the *Ascension*, having lost sight of the others, continued alone up the Mozambique channel. On 25 November they put in at the island of Grande Comore, where the bosun Thomas Jones noted: "We were used of the king and people with all the kindnesse that might be; but could get no fresh water, yet had marvellous good refreshing of limes and some hennes and cocker nuts, which was a great comfort unto us."[20]

Their next call was at Pemba island, north of Zanzibar, where water was available. At first all went well. On the 18th day, however, as Jones and a party of seamen were completing the watering ashore they were ambushed by some of the inhabitants. "Praise be God, wee did escape their hands," Jones wrote, "onely my servant John Harrington excepted, whom they tooke and murthered most cruelly, I not being able to rescue him."

The Englishmen were now not well disposed towards Arabs, and when they overtook three dhows sailing up the coast they easily persuaded themselves that these were the same people who had treacherously attacked them at Pemba. The Arabs were invited on board, where, despite hostile feelings, all might have passed without incident had it not been for the ship's Flemish master, named Grove.

John Jourdain, travelling in the *Ascension* as a company factor, put the blame for the ensuing massacre squarely on Grove. "Our hardie master," he wrote, "with some others which I ommit, made foolish signes unto them shewinge the yarde arme, that they should there be hanged, which putt them in desperate feare, although there was noe such matter ment." Later, in the main cabin, an attempt was made to disarm an Arab who was seen to have a knife, and a fight broke out. "The reste (of the crew) tooke such armes as weare next to hand," recounted Jourdain, "and beganne to kill as faste as they could, soe that in very shorte time they weare all overboard ... which were slaine in the water by those (of the crew) that weare in our boats, so that I thinke not one of them escaped."

Afterwards there was a general pillage of the Arab ships, before the Englishmen, deeming it unwise to delay in these waters as the Portuguese would certainly seek to avenge their allies (the Arabs were, in fact, from Malindi and not Pemba), set course for Socotra island. Many days passed as they beat to and fro against the north-east monsoon, before they reached far out into the south-east in the hope of finding a more favourable wind.

On 19 January 1609, at about nine in the morning, the lookout sighted "high land", and as they approached, other islands came into view, which they took to be the Amirantes. By the afternoon they were five leagues off, and for the rest of the night stayed under slack sail. In the morning they stood in to seek water and "other refreshing".

"It is a very good roade betwixt two islands about a mile and a halfe distant from iland to iland," wrote Jourdain, "and there lyeth ... other three ilands about three leagues of the place where wee ankored, soe that wee weare in a manner land locked, except towards the east-north-east and east."[21]

The next day (21 January), the *Ascension* was warped to within a pistol shot of the shore, where she lay "as in a pond" while the crew busied themselves getting water and wood on board. To the bosun Jones the place seemed an earthly paradise, with plenty of water, fish and bird life. However, he regretted the absence of people in this paradise, dubbing it "the desolate islands, because there are not any inhabitants upon them".

Jourdain explored several of the islands. "We found many coker nutts, both ripe and green, of all sorts," he remarked, "and much fishe and fowle and tortells (giant tortoises), but our men would not eate any of them, but the tortells (turtle doves) wee could kill with staves at our pleasure ... it is a very good refreshing place ... without any feare or danger, except the allagartes, for you cannot discerne that ever any people had bene before us."

He remarked on the fine timber. "On one of the ilands within two miles where wee roade, there is as goode tymber as ever I sawe of length and bignes, and a very firme tymber. You shall have many trees of 60 to 70 feete, without sprigge except at the topp, very bigge and straight as an arrowe."

The crew's reluctance to eat the tortoises — "of so huge a bigness which men will think incredible"[22] — arose not from the taste of the meat, which they likened to fresh beef, but because of the creatures' appearance. "They did look so ugly before they were boiled," remarked Jourdain, noting, however, that the men were seized of their aversion only after they had had two or three helpings of the tortoise stew.

On 1 February the *Ascension* sailed for Socotra and Aden.[23] The Englishmen, having made no claim to their earthly paradise, left the islands unnamed. Soon the sea and forest would obliterate all sign of their stay. Only the birds and reptiles, sovereign once more, remained witness to the unrecorded passage of the years. A century and a half almost had to elapse before the arrival of the Frenchmen Picault and Grossin, but it would be wrong to conclude that in that long interval the islands had no visitors. The ships of Europe, sailing in increasing numbers across the ocean, must have occasionally been carried into these waters, while pirate ships, too, found temporary refuge among the small uninhabited islands.

Those sea robbers, driven out of the Caribbean towards the end of the 17th century, made their principal base on Isle Sainte Marie, off the east coast of Madagascar, and it was to there that Long Ben Avery, Tom Tew, William Kidd, and other kindred figures repaired to live "in a great deal of dirty state and royalty".[24] Their favourite hunting grounds were at the approaches to the Red Sea and the Persian Gulf, where Arab and Moslem shipping could be ravaged at will. On the way back, laden with booty, the pirates would sometimes call at the islands north of Madagascar to replenish their water, careen their ships, and take on tortoises and coconuts; and when the authorities mounted punitive expeditions against them, they could lie low, with their treasure safely buried on one of the islands, until the return of better times.

Several of the Seychelles islands are reputed to be the sites of pirate treasure: Aride, Frégate, Praslin, Astove, and Mahé itself.[25] Much fantasy has been mixed with fact in the accounts of buried treasure, but sufficient evidence has been unearthed at different times to indicate a pirate presence.[26]

Of those who terrorised the Indian Ocean in the early 18th century one in particular, Olivier le Vasseur, known as La Buse, has had his name directly linked with the Seychelles. The fabulous treasure he supposedly buried there has prompted several attempts to locate it, first in the 1920s and again in the 1950s. Unlikely as the story is, Le Vasseur is said to have offered a clue to the whereabouts of the treasure as he was about to be hanged on Bourbon island. He threw to the crowd a piece of paper, shouting "Find my treasure who can", or words to that effect. The marks on the paper have been deciphered, but no one, so far as is known, has yet succeeded in finding the hidden hoard.[27]

* * *

The War of the Austrian Succession ended in 1748. Six years later, French and English troops were skirmishing in North America and, by 1756, the two countries were again formally at war. For want of a better name, the conflict became known as the Seven Years' War.

At the Isle de France, where the security of the route to India was always a matter of concern, maps and dossiers left by Picault and others were retrieved and pondered over, and the question asked as to what should be done about the uninhabited islands lying to the north-east of Madagascar. It was argued that it would be foolish and dangerous to allow the Isle Mahé to fall uncontested into English hands, especially as the islands in the vicinity appeared to be a rich source of wood and tortoises. Consequently, the governor-general, René Magon de la Villebague, gave orders for an expedition to be sent to lay formal claim to the island. For the task he chose a Company officer, Corneille Nicolas Morphey.

Son of an Irish father and French mother, Morphey was more experienced than Picault. He was also a conscientious officer, who was determined to return with as accurate an assessment as possible of the value of the island to France. The result was the first comprehensive description to be made of Mahé island.

Morphey sailed on 16 July 1756 in the frigate *Cerf*, accompanied by the sloop *Saint Benoît* (commander Préjean), arriving off Mahé's Port Royal on 6 September. Only after reconnoitring the entrance and putting down markers to indicate the reefs, did Morphey risk bringing the *Cerf* into the harbour. As the wind was unfavourable, he had to tow her in. The date was 9 September, feast day of Saint Anne. Morphey described the anchorage as the most beautiful he had ever seen.

While he settled down to making a detailed survey of the harbour, two officers and a party of men were sent into the interior. They returned three days later, reporting that they had seen many fine trees and good black earth for cultivation. The same day, Morphey sent off another party under his second-in-command, to make a complete tour of the island and report further on the nature of the soil and on the animals they found. This second group returned after two weeks. It had been an exhausting journey, as the men had to climb and scramble along steep slopes and hack their way through thick bush. They reported having crossed many streams, where they found carp, trout and other fish, although the numbers suggested depletion by crocodiles, which roamed everywhere on the island, reaching even to the mountain tops in search of food.

Still not satisfied with the information gathered, Morphey dispatched a third party, under what he described as "an intelligent officer". This final excursion into the interior lasted five days. On his return the officer leading the party reported that, contrary to Picault's findings, there was no flat land, and that the soil was much the same everywhere, yellow and gravelly. In the centre of the island he found the trees to be much sparser than elsewhere, and not of such good quality.

It must have been clear from the differing reports that the soil of the island varied considerably, but Morphey concluded anyway that the ruggedness of the terrain made the island unsuitable for habitation, a view that for many years was to dissuade the Isle de France government from actively encouraging settlement there. His forecast that it would be difficult for settlers to make roads along the steep mountain sides proved to be accurate, and until well into the next century the most convenient mode of travel from one part of the island to another was by boat.

Strategically, Morphey saw two main advantages for France in holding the island. First, there was its fine harbour, where he estimated that 200 vessels could be accommodated; secondly, there was an abundant supply of excellent timber, useful not only for ships but also for renewing the fortifications of the French settlements in India. He envisaged the setting up of a small outpost of from three to ten men, with about 100 slaves to cut and load wood for India.

His plan of the port now complete, Morphey took possession of the island for Louis XV and the Compagnie des Indes. On 1 November 1756, as the sun slowly rose over Sainte Anne island, the royal standard broke out from the mast that had been erected on a large fan-shaped rock at the head of the harbour, while the assembled company three times gave the cry *Vive le Roi,* to the accompaniment of nine discharges of cannon from the *Cerf* and the *Saint-Benoît.*

A large stone, the *pierre de possession,* carved with the arms of France and the name Isle de Séchelles, was left at the foot of the flagstaff.[28] In time, the name Séchelles would designate the whole group of islands, while the main island would revert to the earlier name of Isle Mahé.[29]

Morphey had intended visiting Picault's Isle de Palme, which lay 25 miles to the north-east, "but various circumstances and, in particular, lack of bread, did not permit him to prolong his voyage". According to instructions, he renamed the island Isle Moras.[30] The name did not survive; within a few years it had become the Isle Praslin.

Other names given by Morphey to the islands clustered round Port Royal proved more permanent. In addition to the largest of these, Sainte Anne, commemorating the feast day of Morphey's arrival, there is Cerf island, named after his ship, while the smaller ones received the rather unimaginative names of Longue, Petite (later Ronde), Moyenne, and Isle Sud-Est.

Morphey's acquisition of the Isle Séchelles did not result in any rapid colonisation of the island. Having staked its claim, France, or rather the Compagnie des Indes, lost interest. Morphey's report, like that of Picault's 15 years earlier, was filed away.

An anonymous manuscript, undated but written probably towards the end of the 1760s, noted: "In consequence of this negligence, perhaps brought about by two successive wars, these islands, known collectively as the Isles Mahé, were left forgotten, their position almost uncertain; one contented oneself with knowing that they existed and that the French flag, having once been planted, was an assurance of the property rights of the nation."

2

Crocodiles and Coconuts
1767-1769

> ... palmiers et doubles cocos; il n'y a aucun
> arbre qui mérite la moindre considération.
>
> *Officer of the Curieuse, November 1768*

It was hardly surprising that the directors of the Compagnie des Indes showed little interest in the Isle Séchelles; enough was happening elsewhere to engage their attention. Hostilities against the English in North America had spread to Europe, where England and Prussia confronted an alliance of France, Austria, and Russia. In India, too, English and French were again battling for supremacy.

The year after Morphey's *prise de possession* Chandernagore, the French trading post upriver from Calcutta, fell. This was soon followed by Clive's victory at Plassey, effectively ousting the French from Bengal. In January 1760 Lally was defeated at Wandiwash, and the following year Pondichéry surrendered. On the Malabar coast, France's only settlement, Mahé, was also lost to the English.[1] These reverses were matched by similar misfortune in North America and in Europe, where at Rossbach Prussia had soundly defeated the French in what was to prove the decisive battle of the war. By 1763 Louis XV was ready for peace.

Under the Treaty of Paris, which concluded the Seven Years' War, France lost all of Canada as well as other fragments of its colonial empire. Although Pondichéry and the other settlements in India were given back France's position there was never to be the same. The war sealed the fate of the

Compagnie des Indes. Weakened by apathy and debt, it was wound up in 1767, and French affairs in India and the Indian Ocean islands were put under the control of the Minister of Marine at Versailles.

The passing away of the company meant substantial changes in the administration of the Isle de France and Bourbon, where executive power was now to be shared by a governor-general and an intendant, the latter responsible for finance, police, justice and economic development, while the governor-general concerned himself with matters military. Unfortunately, it was soon apparent that the two men chosen to fill these positions were ill-fitted to work in tandem. The governor-general, Colonel Jean-Daniel Dumas, who had served with distinction in Canada, was an able enough administrator, but fixed in his opinions and lacking in diplomacy. His intendant, Pierre Poivre, was brilliant, adventurous, and unorthodox.

In the inevitable clash of wills Poivre had the advantage of being known and respected in the Isle de France. As a young man he had served in the East; he had been with La Bourdonnais at the capture of Madras and had lost an arm in a sea battle. When news of his public wrangling with Dumas reached Versailles, Poivre was severely admonished, while the unfortunate Dumas, with little more than a year's service as governor-general, was replaced.

During his early years in the Far East Poivre had observed at close quarters the workings of the Dutch spice monopoly, and had decided then that France should share in this lucrative commerce. Despite the danger of the undertaking – the Dutch having ordained death for anyone found cutting a spice plant – he succeeded in transporting to the Isle de France several clove and nutmeg seedlings. Unfortunately the project went sour. The plants died, there was lack of official support for continuing, and Poivre retired to France in disgust. He never relinquished, however, his dream of creating spice islands for France in the Indian Ocean, and on his return there as top civil administrator ten years later, he determined once more to try to break the Dutch spice monopoly.

Poivre served as intendant – at first in an acting capacity – from July 1767 to August 1772, during which time he strove to restore the island's economy, which had suffered greatly during the war. The effect was as if La Bourdonnais had returned – new buildings went up, water conduits were laid, a programme of reafforestation was begun and new crops and fruits were introduced.

He also encouraged a renewed search for a shorter route to India, and sought more information on the islands discovered by Picault and Morphey. He was convinced that if France did not extend its claim over the whole of that archipelago the ambitions of the English would prompt them to seize the islands.

An opportunity to confirm French sovereignty came towards the end of 1768, with the fitting out of an expedition by a former captain of the Compagnie des Indes, Marc Joseph Marion Dufresne, who planned to cut timber on the Isle Séchelles and bring back a cargo of tortoises, of which there were hardly any now on Rodrigues island.

As a result of Poivre's interest, Marion Dufresne was given the use of a king's ship, the *Digue*, under the command of Jean Duchemin, of St Malo, with as escort the schooner *Curieuse*, commanded by Lieutenant Lampériaire. The expedition, which remained at the Seychelles from October to December 1768, is described in a lengthy journal that not only gives a clear picture of the islands and the animal and bird life, but also offers glimpses of the hardship and dangers encountered by the crews.

Like all tropical islands the Seychelles receives ample rainfall, but unfortunately for Duchemin the last quarter of 1768 was exceptionally wet, the journal recording rain almost every day. This seriously delayed the cutting and loading of timber into the *Digue*. There was one small, but important consolation. Despite the soaking they all received no one fell ill, "which is sufficient proof that the rain is not unhealthy, and does not occasion any form of illness, as occurs in certain countries with a similar climate", he noted. Other observers were to confirm that the Seychelles islands enjoyed one of the healthiest climates in the tropics.

If rain was a problem for Duchemin, getting the slaves to work was another. He complained bitterly that the Isle de France settlers had lent him their most troublesome slaves, who continually escaped despite, remarked Duchemin, being fed "fish, tortoise, game birds ... which never a black has had before". Some of those who escaped returned the next day, considering even slavery preferable to being abandoned on an uninhabited island. The others became an additional hazard to the Frenchmen, on one occasion making a half-hearted attack on a party from the ships. Although Duchemin tried to hunt them down, five had to be left behind when the *Digue* sailed. The journal records their names as François, La Violette, Casse Marteau, Alexandre, and La Ramée.

The main threat to the seamen, however, came from the crocodiles, especially at night. A tented camp had been set up near Morphey's stone of possession for those working ashore, and on one occasion a sailor awoke to find his hand gripped by a crocodile. Fortunately it was a young animal and he was able to break free. After that few slept on the ground, choosing instead to sling a hammock between the trees, at least six feet from the ground. Even that did not ensure complete security.

The journal describes a raid by seven crocodiles on the camp at night. "One bit at a hammock and severed the rope. Someone fetched it several blows with an axe and it retreated, but without us being able to catch it or any of the others. We have been seeing greater numbers of these animals lately, and especially of an enormous size, since there are some 18 to 20 feet in length (about 19 to 21 English feet)."

The Frenchmen took pot shots with their muskets at the creatures, but Duchemin noted that to kill them the ball had to strike the neck joint, otherwise "they go off slowly, all the time alert with their jaws wide open, ready to devour whatever they come across". Yet generally, as Picault had noted, the crocodiles were wary of men. "I have noticed now that they are afraid when on land," Duchemin observed. "I went ashore several times and found them stretched out on the rocks, and they crawl away as soon as they see you. They are to be feared in the woods, however, where there are many leaves and where, if surprised by someone, they will bite. I believe, though, that they are most dangerous in the sea."

That the Seychelles crocodile was a monster is not surprising. As the only predator of any size, it had nothing to fear and could grow to a ripe old age. Only when it took to the sea, which was frequently, did it meet a powerful adversary, the shark. Reports by early visitors to the Seychelles agree that sharks around the islands were extremely aggressive, attacking small boats and snapping at oars, a behaviour pattern happily absent today. Froberville, who listed eight different types of shark around Mahé, reported that when a shark and a crocodile fought the noise could be heard from afar.

Like Picault and Morphey, Duchemin found that the giant tortoises were not numerous on Mahé. They had to be sought in the woods and there were barely enough to satisfy the daily needs of the crew. He noted that there were few young ones — presumably they were easy victims of the crocodiles — while some of the larger tortoises had one foot missing, evidence of a lucky escape. There were so many crocodiles on the island that Duchemin wondered how long it would take to destroy them all. In the event, within 30 years of a settlement being formed on Mahé, the crocodile was virtually extinct there, and it survived for only a few years more on outlying islands.[2]

Destruction of the crocodile did not mean a reprieve for the giant tortoise. Despite efforts by various administrations to restrict hunting, the giant tortoise was to disappear over the same period, remaining in substantial numbers only on distant Aldabra atoll. Its meat formed the basic diet of the settlers, and ships visiting the islands loaded hundreds at a time.

The green turtle suffered the same fate, particularly the females, as they were vulnerable when they came up on to the beach to lay their eggs. Many would be turned on their backs even before they had got rid of their eggs in the sand. Duchemin noted, however, that no green turtles were seen during their stay, only the smaller hawksbill, known to the French as *caret,* whose carapace provides tortoiseshell. A particularly cruel fate was reserved for the hawksbill turtle, which would be heated over a fire while still alive so that the plates of its shell could be easily removed.

The journal described how baby turtles, once hatched from the eggs in the sand, would instinctively make their way down the beach to the sea, where they would float for several days on the surface of the water. Many never reached the sea, being picked off by birds and crabs. Those that did were easily devoured by crocodiles, fish, and birds.

Another marine animal mentioned in the journal was the *vache-marine,* or dugong, although the description given suggests that the animals the Frenchmen found were seals, although none exists today in Seychelles waters.[3] Duchemin reported that about 20 vaches-marines were seen on a sandy strip between the twin rocks of Mamelles by two officers who had been sent to take sightings from this small island, which lies eight miles from Mahé. They apparently surprised the creatures asleep, and promptly killed them. They were from seven and a half to ten feet in length.

Sea cows, or dugongs, are purely aquatic. They never leave the water and would have been unable to haul themselves on to the shore as described in the journal. Also, Duchemin recorded that their skins were "very beautiful", an inappropriate description for a sea cow, whose skin is rough and only sparsely covered by hair. Duchemin was unsuccessful in his attempt to preserve the skins, but the animal fat gave 38 pots of good cooking oil. "They could have other properties I do not know of," he added.

The vache-marine, though a misnomer like the Seychelles cayman, is recalled in the names of two of the islands.

The journal was the first to record the presence of wild goats, said to have been the size of sheep and apparently so tame that they could be easily approached and killed. It was not uncommon for ships to abandon animals on uninhabited islands, so that they might eventually provide a source of food. It is not known when the first goats, or *cabris,* were introduced into the Seychelles, but it is recorded that the crew of the *Curieuse* left behind a billy goat and two females on Praslin island.

Parties traversing the interior of the main island came across small snakes, of which there were two species. Smaller reptiles such as lizards were also found; they were apparently twice the size of those in the Isle de France. The journal mentions the tiger chameleon, as well as the green toad of Seychelles; also a spider that was mistaken for a tarantula. Of other insects, mosquitoes were noted as formidable biters and flies as a great nuisance. Some large fruit bats were killed, but it is not recorded whether or not they were eaten. Only later, perhaps, did the bat become a culinary delicacy of the islands.

Many of today's place names recall the various animals, birds and insects which impressed, favourably or otherwise, the first visitors, such as Anse aux Poules Bleues,[4] Rivière Caïman, Île Chauve-Souris and, as already noted, Île aux Vaches-Marines. Remarking on the abundance of fish in the sea, the

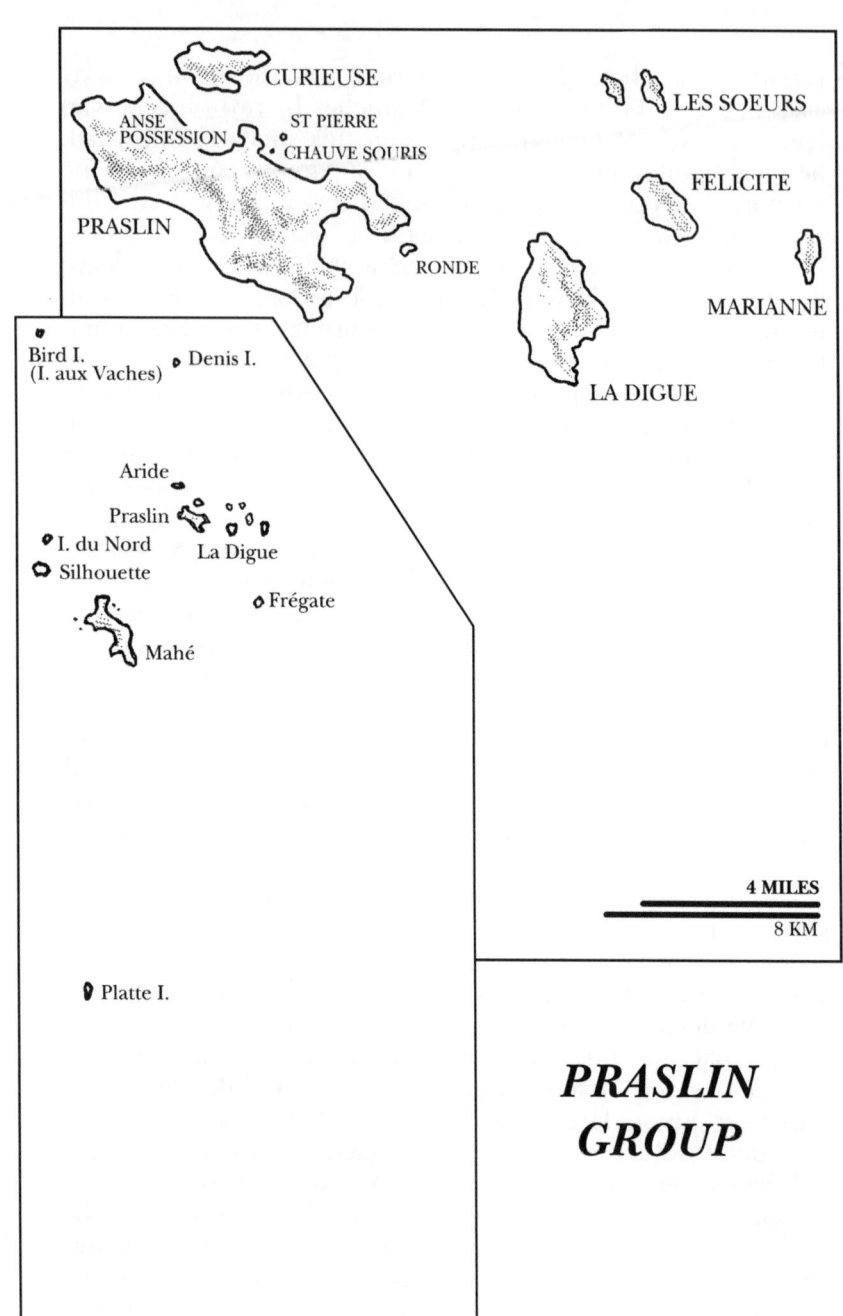

journal suggested that a small fishing industry might be established. Two hundred years later, under British colonial administration, the possibility of commercial fishing in the Seychelles was still being discussed.

On 1 November work began loading the cut timber into the *Digue*, and on the following day the *Curieuse* left to explore Isle Moras and the other islands in the north-east. Duchemin, who considered that Isle Moras merited "the greatest attention", gave instructions to Lampériaire to record the nature and quality of the soil, how the island was watered, and collect as much information as he could on the trees, grasses, shrubs, animals, birds, insects, fresh-water fish, stones and minerals. He was especially interested in the red, hard wood known as *bois de tec,* and he wanted an estimate of the number of coconut trees on the island.

Finally, Lampériaire was instructed to annex the island for France under the name Isle Praslin in honour of the then Minister of Marine, the Duc de Praslin.

What was to make the voyage of the *Curieuse* especially noteworthy, however, was not the acquisition or renaming of the second largest of the Seychelles islands but the discovery that the island was the home of the mysterious coco de mer palm, whose fruit, the double-lobed coconut, had given rise centuries before to the legend of an underwater tree. With Lampériaire and his men making the best of their way to Praslin, it may be an appropriate moment to consider the coco de mer legend.

* * *

It is related that long ago a nut of magical properties was from time to time washed up on the shores of India and the Maldives islands, and it was thought that it must come from an underwater tree. References to trees growing under the sea appear in various works of European literature. Antonio Pigafetta, in his account of Magellan's circumnavigation of the world in 1519, said he had been told that "below Java the Great, towards the north of the Gulf of China", there grew a large tree in which lived birds so big and strong that they could carry away an ox or elephant. One day a small boy, survivor of a shipwreck, climbed the tree, and, unknowingly, ensconced himself under the wing of one of the giant birds, which flew him back home, so that "neighbouring peoples knew that the fruits which they found in the sea came from this tree".

Pigafetta's bird was similar in size to the roc, mentioned by that earlier traveller in the eastern seas, Marco Polo,[5] although the fruit of his fabled tree was of relatively modest proportions, being "larger than a cucumber".

The Portuguese were more specific about the submarine tree. The chronicler João de Barros referred to the medicinal properties of the *côco do mar,* while Garcia de Orta located the tree in the Maldives islands. In a dissertation on the drugs used in India, published in Goa in 1563, he claimed that the *côco do mar* came from trees that had been submerged when the Maldives were separated from the Indian sub-continent. As a result the nut became known as the coco de Maldives and, duly latinised, was included under that name by the Dutch botanist Rumphius in his monumental *Herbarium Amboinense.*[6] The scientific name for the palm today, *Lodoicea maldivica,* retains the Maldives as its official source.[7]

However it was a Frenchman, François Pyrard de Laval, who, at the beginning of the 17th century, spread most effectively the story of the fabulous nut of the Maldives. Pyrard had sailed from St Malo in 1601 for the East Indies, but his ship ran aground on the Maldives and he and fellow survivors stayed on the islands for ten years as virtual prisoners. He later wrote a book about his travels, and described what he had learned about the coco de mer.

Pyrard recounted that during his stay the king of the Maldives had twice sent ships to look for a certain island named Poulloys, which was unknown to them but which they believed to be the home of the mysterious coconut that, like ambergris, was so highly prized that anyone finding one washed up on the beach had to surrender it to the king. Failure to do so meant having a hand cut off.

Pyrard described the nut as big as a man's head, and said it could be compared to two large melons stuck together. "They call it *Tauarcarré,* believing that it comes from some trees that are under the seas ... the king's men and officers ill-treat poor people they suspect of having found any, and when they want to annoy someone he is accused of this, as is the case with counterfeit coins; and when someone suddenly becomes rich it is usually said that he must have found *Tauarcarré* or ambergris, as if it were a treasure." It was the nut's reputed curative and stimulative properties that made it valuable. The kernel was supposed to be a powerful aphrodisiac as well as being a cure for a variety of ailments ranging from venereal disease to scurvy. The shell itself was said to be a complete antidote to any poison, and was therefore a safe drinking vessel. The nut's reputation eventually reached Europe, where the Hapsburg emperor Rudolph II (1576-1612) offered 4,000 gold florins for one nut.

The nut's mysterious origin was matched by its remarkable shape. Pyrard's description of two melons joined together is not particularly apt. Some other writers were equally coy in describing it. To the French traveller and scientist Rochon it had a "strange shape"; modesty prevented him from being more precise. Almost 100 years later, Froberville wrote that the shape was "as indecent to describe as to display", but a few pages further on risked scandalising his readers by likening the nut to "two thighs".

Bernardin de Saint Pierre, author of *Paul et Virginie,* the famous love story set in the Isle de France, was anatomically more accurate. To him it resembled "the anterior and posterior parts of the body of a negress at its bifurcation". Indeed it did, and does, with an attention to detail that has given rise to cheerfully unabashed names as *cul de négresse, coco fesse, coco indécent,* and *coco nu*; and, as pointed out by a more recent observer, the nuts, like the relevant part of the human anatomy, offer an infinite variety of shapes, no two nuts being exactly the same.[8]

This then was the mysterious nut, the riddle of whose origin the Frenchmen of the *Curieuse* were about to solve. The discovery, as sometimes happens, was rather an anticlimax.

* * *

On leaving the Isle Séchelles, Lampériaire first bent course for Frégate island, but wind and current prevented him reaching there, and several more days elapsed before the *Curieuse* eventually dropped anchor in the channel between Praslin and the island of La Digue. An officer who was sent ashore to reconnoitre the main island came back with a report that was not encouraging. "He told me that the mountain rises straight from the sandy beach," wrote Lampériaire, "and that he had seen nothing but some sort of palmiste which covered the mountains; not a single tree suitable for anything other than firewood."

Like Picault 22 years earlier the officer had seen the coco de mer palm without noting anything remarkable about the nut. It is surprising, however, that the sight of such a gathering of vegetable giants should have left anyone unmoved. Others were to be more suitably impressed. This is how Froberville described his first view of the palms:

"On the flat strips of sand, along the edges and in the middle of marshy ground, among the steepest rocks and on the highest summits of the mountains, everywhere one sees them standing erect, their majestic heads in the air, while the leaves, stirred by the breeze, produce a continual clatter like that of the paddles of a water mill.

"The tree rises, often, to 60 or 80 feet and it is as straight as a mast. Maximum diameter is of 15 to 18 inches, which hardly changes from base to summit. The head is normally crowned with ten to a dozen leaves of 20 feet in length, which form the shape of a fan. The wind frequently breaks them near the tip, so that they droop towards the ground. The leaves have a hard, leathery feel, and one notices on their axils a rather heavy down, similar to that which one finds on the latans of the western colonies. As the tree grows so the leaves fall, and are soon replaced. Their colour is olive green, but they yellow when dried."

Like other Borassoid palms, the coco de mer has male and female trees, the male being taller by some 20 feet. The female carries a cluster of five or six heart-shaped nuts which can weigh up to 50 pounds. As if to complement the suggestive shape of the nut once the husk is removed, the male tree, which bears no fruit, displays a prominent inflorescence that has been likened to a huge penis.

Lampériaire, who was not happy with where he was anchored, sent the officer ashore again to find a more secure roadstead, and it was in a small bay on the north coast, between the Isle Moras and a smaller island that had been named Isle Rouge by Picault on account of its red soil, that the *Curieuse* eventually anchored.

"This bay is without doubt the most beautiful place on the island," remarked Lampériaire. He named it Anse Possession. The next day, while one party explored Isle Moras or Praslin, another rowed across to the smaller island, which Lampériaire renamed Curieuse after his ship. Soon, the first discouraging reports were confirmed. Both islands were steep, rising almost straight from a narrow sandy shore, with huge rocks scattered about. The soil was poor, and the islands seemed to have been subjected to great fires at some time, the rocks showing signs of intense heat. As on the Isle Séchelles, many crocodiles were seen, and on one occasion Lampériaire's men abandoned their water casks on the shore and ran from them.

There were few trees that interested anyone. "I have yet to see a beautiful one," was Lampériaire's verdict. There were, of course, plenty of palms — "the type with the double coconut". For by now the nut of the coco de mer palm had been examined. Yet Lampériaire's journal evinces little enthusiasm. "There are many here," he noted. "The sandy bays, as elsewhere, are covered with them."

Perhaps because there were so many coco de mer palms no-one thought that the nuts could be valuable. Only one person in the expedition, a surveyor named Barré, seems to have had an inkling that they had stumbled on something important. If we are to believe Rochon, this was how he made his discovery:

"The surveyor Barré ... found on the Isle of Palms, at the water's edge, a fruit which he took at first for a coco de mer. He hid it carefully, but having pushed on into the forest he saw regretfully that the ground was covered with these fruits and the trees that bore them ... Looking closely at this forest Barré was persuaded that the coconut of this island could not be the true coco de mer. He contented himself with collecting, out of pure curiosity, about 30 of these nuts, which the celebrated Poivre formally declared to be the fruit so sought after in India and throughout Asia."

Given Lampériaire's lack of interest in the unusual nut, it was perhaps fortunate that Barré had sufficient curiosity to bring a quantity of the nuts away with him.

During his stay Lampériaire named the smaller islands in the Praslin group. There was to be Félicité, Marianne, Ronde, and the rocky islets of Ave Maria, Rocher Caché, and Baleine. Two tiny islets near where the Curieuse was anchored were named Saint Pierre and Juliette (now Chauve-Souris).⁹ Others named for the first time were, to the north and west, Aride, Isle aux Fous (usually referred to today as Booby island, after the Booby seabird, or *l'oiseau fou*), Cousin and Cousine. La Digue, the second largest of the Praslin group, had been named earlier by Duchemin as his ship passed close to it on his approach to the Isle Séchelles.

Of the other islands, Lampériaire noted: "To the north of the island La Digue there are, about four to five leagues away, three small isles, divided one from the other and which appear to be separated by a small channel. We named them the Three Sisters, because they appeared to us to be of the same shape. All three are a little higher than Isle Marianne ..." Here is one of the minor mysteries of the voyage of the *Curieuse* for there are only two Sisters. As for "all three" being higher than Marianne, the highest, East Sister island, is about 50 feet lower.

One of Lampériaire's last tasks was to raise the French flag over the island, henceforth to be known as Isle Praslin. At first light on Sunday, 20 November 1768, an officer and detachment rowed ashore and, with simple ceremony, unfurled the standard from a flagstaff, 46 feet high, that had been erected at Anse Possession. As the golden lilies of France fluttered in the morning breeze there were cries of *Vive le Roi*, while from the ship came the dull, intermittent voice of her cannon. At the base of the flagstaff, a small cairn of stones had been built on which a lead plaque proclaimed the acquisition of the island by the French Crown.

Later that day, in a small stream near the Anse Possession, a bottle filled with coarse sand was found. "It seems to have been there a long time," Lampériaire wrote.

Although the southern part of Praslin had not been explored, Lampériaire decided to conclude his visit as the weather had worsened. Two days after the flag-raising he left the anchorage by way of the north-west channel and, thanks to a favourable wind, was moored off Sainte Anne by five the same evening. In his log Lampériaire recorded seeing close to the ship "a monster similar in shape to a huge shark". It was dark grey with white spots, with many small fish in attendance. Undoubtedly this was a whale-shark, known in the Seychelles as *chagrin*, which can attain a length of 60 feet. Although harmless, it has a reputation of overturning small boats.

Duchemin had been waiting impatiently for Lampériaire's return, and he immediately sent a boat to bring him aboard the *Digue* to make his report. The journal reflects Duchemin's disappointment that the Isle Praslin "does not correspond to the agreeable aspect that it offers from afar". If he showed any interest — as he was to do later — in the strange double coconuts that had been found there, the journal ignores the fact. Duchemin was, it seems, more concerned about finding a good supply of tortoises, and within days of Lampériaire's return Duchemin had sent him off to the Jean de Nove atoll to load with tortoises. He was then to sail the *Curieuse* back to the Isle de France.

Duchemin stayed on for another month, completing the survey of the main island. His final, formal act was to raise the French flag on the new flagstaff that had been erected near Morphey's *pierre de possession* and proclaim the annexation of the whole Seychelles archipelago.

The ceremony took place on Christmas Day, 1768. Duchemin's declaration renewed French sovereignty over the Isle Séchelles and extended it to cover Isle Praslin and "all the islands that are adjacent, within sight and out of sight of these two principal islands; generally, all that exists on this bank". Three days later the *Digue* sailed for the Isle de France. The French had annexed the Seychelles; as will be seen, they were just in time.

The coco de mer nuts discovered on Praslin were immediately identified by Poivre as the mysterious coconut of ancient legend, and realising that its value lay as much in its rarity as in any medicinal use it might have he decided that the location of the palm should remain secret. Unfortunately Duchemin did not share Poivre's concern, for he returned to Praslin in another ship the following year to load a cargo of nuts for the Indian market. According to Froberville, this attracted the attention of the English, who very soon dispatched a corvette from Bombay to the islands.

As Rochon was to comment sourly: "The English were the only ones who knew how to make a new branch of commerce out of this find." They subsequently sent two ships a year from India to load with nuts, until the French put a stop to the trade by establishing a military outpost on Praslin.

* * *

A remarkable feature of the coco de mer palm is its restricted habitat. Not only did it grow exclusively in the Seychelles, but only on two islands, Praslin and Curieuse (the small isles of Saint Pierre, Chauve-Souris, and Round, where there are traces of the palm, can be conveniently regarded as part of Praslin). It has been suggested that the palms were relics of a much larger distribution and were isolated in geological times when the supposed continent of Gondwanaland joining Africa and Asia was submerged, to leave protruding above the sea the granitic peaks of the Seychelles. This isolation would be absolute, for, unlike the ordinary coconut, which floats easily and can survive in salt water for up to four months without the growing seedling being destroyed, the coco de mer is heavier than water and, if dropped in the sea, simply sinks to the bottom. This must, therefore, rule out the notion of whole coco de mer nuts floating away from Praslin island to be washed up on the shores of the Maldives.

First to propound this theory seems to have been Rochon, who, by way of confirmation, observed that as he left Praslin at the end of his visit in 1769 the current was running towards the Maldives, a remark he might have omitted after becoming aware of the complexity of the pattern of currents in the Indian Ocean.

Rochon's theory, to be tenable, requires that the coco de mer nut lie on the seabed until the husk has rotted. Only then, when, according to Froberville, the decomposed kernel gives off "an odour of urine", could it float away across the ocean to some distant shore. One can only marvel that on such decayed detritus of the sea there arose the legend of a fabulous nut sold throughout the East as a cure for flagging sexuality and a host of other bodily deficiencies.

Early writers on the Maldives offer little information on the coco de mer, and much of it seems hearsay. Pyrard de Laval's description of the nut is sketchy and, despite his ten years' enforced residence in the Maldives, it can be assumed he never saw one washed up on the shore. Other writers, like the Dutchman John Huyghen van Linschoten, refer to the huge nut of the Maldives as more esteemed than all the nuts of India, "for that they are good against all poison, which are fair and great and blackish". It is a description that would fit the coco de mer, although there is no mention of the double lobe.

The 13th century Arab writer and traveller Ibn Battuta, who, like Pyrard de Laval, spent many years in the Maldives, wrote about the coconut of Dhibat-al-Maha (Maldives), which had "the size of a man's head (the same dimension given by Pyrard de Laval) and is supposed to strengthen the body and add colour to the face". Ibn Battuta, who took a wife during his stay on the islands, added: "As for its aphrodisiac powers, its action in that respect is wonderful." Neither Ibn Battuta nor Van Linschoten refer to the nuts coming from the sea.

It is conceivable that the coco de mer palm once grew in the Maldives, as Garcia de Orta claimed, but in the absence of hard evidence the likeliest explanation for the double-lobed nuts being known widely in the East must be that they were brought back by sailors who had visited the Seychelles. As these distant islands remained virtually unknown, however, the legend of an underwater tree that bore strange fruit would have gained ready acceptance. Half-decayed nuts from the mysterious tree may or may not have been occasionally washed up on Asia's shores; it is immaterial. The rich reputation of the coco de mer would have been sufficient to keep the legend alive.

* * *

In 1775, seven years after Barré's discovery of the coco de mer, the Minister of Marine at Versailles received a letter with the following comment: "These nuts have, in truth, lost their value since becoming so common; one has even claimed, perhaps falsely, that those of Seychelles are inferior in quality to those that India has acquired from elsewhere."

3

Short Cut to India
1769-1771

L'expérience confirme chaque jour
mon système des courants.
Jacques Raymond de Grenier, July 1774

Early in June 1769 more than 100 astronomers waited at some 60 points around the world to observe the planet Venus pass in front of the sun. From their different timings of this rare phenomenon it was hoped to calculate accurately a basic measurement of the universe, the distance of the earth from the sun.

The English astronomer Halley[1] had the previous century proposed Venus as the most suitable planet for this purpose, but it was not until 1761 that the planet's orbit brought it into position for the first worldwide sightings to be made. The results had been unsatisfactory. Now, eight years later, there was to be a second chance. As Venus makes its transit only twice every 113 years, and would not pass directly across the sun again until the year 1874, it would also be the last chance for all those present.

Some big scientific names of the day were taking part in the exercise and there were others as yet relatively unknown. The Royal Society in London had appointed a newly commissioned naval officer, James Cook,[2] to record the transit from the Pacific island of Tahiti after their first choice, the Scots hydrographer Alexander Dalrymple, had withdrawn.[3] Among the intending observers from France was a naval astronomer, Alexis-Marie de Rochon.

Rochon, who was later to gain some fame for his work in optics, was in 1769 still in his late twenties and seeking to make his mark in the world of science. Born in Brest, Brittany, he had been intended for the Church, and although he had never gone beyond his noviciate he liked to be known as the abbé de Rochon.

After leaving the Church, Rochon was for a time librarian at the Royal Marine Academy at Brest before his appointment, in 1766, as a naval astronomer. In that capacity he made a voyage the following year to Morocco. On his return he was directed to join the corvette *Heure du Berger*, then getting ready to sail for the Isle de France under the command of Lieutenant Jacques Raymond Grenier.

The voyage of the *Heure du Berger* is famous in the annals of French exploration, not least for the bitter dispute that developed between Grenier and Rochon over the route they reconnoitred together from the Isle de France to India. It was perhaps inevitable that they should quarrel, for Grenier was no ordinary naval officer. Of similar mould — if not of equal fame — to Bougainville and La Pérouse, Grenier had a fertile and inquiring mind that turned easily to the problems of navigation. He was ambitious, confident in his ability, and intolerant of criticism, a feature of his character that could hardly endear him to the irascible and equally ambitious Rochon, who resented particularly the notion that it was to Grenier that he owed his official position of scientist to the expedition.

In his *Mémoires* Grenier recalled that he had first looked on his appointment to the *Heure du Berger* with dismay, for his ship was going out as a normal reinforcement to French naval strength in the East and it seemed unlikely he would have an opportunity "to satisfy my curiosity and widen my knowledge of the conditions of the Indian Ocean".

On his insistence, it was agreed with the Minister of Marine that he could carry out any exploration of the ocean he found time for. The question was, what should he explore? Grenier turned for assistance to the ultimate authority on the Indian Ocean, D'Après de Mannevillette, director of Charts and Plans for the Navigation of the Indies. D'Après responded by sending him a chart with the areas of the ocean that were not well known coloured in yellow.

Grenier also sought the views of others, commenting afterwards: "The more I attempted to instruct myself, the more I realised how much ignorance there was. Convinced at last that no one had ventured on the discovery of these seas because of the dangers that one imagined there, and assured besides of the advantages nature had placed there through the disposition and variation of the winds that blow there, I set myself a task of exploration: to find a shorter route in all seasons from the Isle de France to India, confronting all hazards with a combination of daring and prudence."

It was typical of Grenier that he should summarily dismiss the voyages of earlier navigators who had successfully followed the direct route to India. However, it was not his intention simply to sail along the route; he would also fix accurately the positions of all the islands and reefs about which there was still a lot of uncertainty despite efforts by D'Après to update his charts.

According to Grenier, he asked the Ministry of Marine for Rochon's services so that the dangers of the route could be surveyed and their positions confirmed by expert astronomical observation. To Rochon the expedition appeared to be an excellent opportunity for him to view the expected transit of Venus from some convenient island in the Indian Ocean, and thereby make his contribution to an international scientific endeavour.

The *Heure du Berger* left France early in 1768. Rochon had sailed some weeks before, having chosen to travel in the royal storeship *Normande*, commanded by his friend Boudin de Tromelin.[1] In view of Rochon's subsequent quarrel with Grenier it was perhaps fortunate that the two men did not share each other's company during the long voyage round the Cape.

Disappointment awaited Grenier at the Isle de France. The governor-general, Dumas, did not share his enthusiasm for reconnoitring the short route to India, and Grenier was ordered instead to sail for Madagascar to make a detailed survey of the north-east coast and to examine the possibility of setting up a French trading post there.

France's attempts to colonise Madagascar had so far met with little success. The Malagasy were generally hostile to the white invader, and after years of intermittent warfare and massacres, along with frequent epidemics, the French had abandoned the settlements they had formed in the previous century. Madagascar was still regarded, however, as part of the royal domain, and in 1750 France gained an important foothold on the north-east coast when Queen Betia formally conceded the former pirate stronghold of Isle Sainte Marie.[5]

By the time of Grenier's arrival at the Isle de France the French were again tentatively considering Madagascar for settlement, as it was an important source of cattle and slaves for the Mascarene islands. This renewed attempt at colonisation, however, was to be made with the iron fist suitably covered, and Grenier was enjoined particularly to make friends with the Malagasy. A similar policy was already under way in the south of the island, where Comte Laurent de Maudave was trying to restore a French presence near the site of the old Fort Dauphin.

The *Heure du Berger* spent four and a half months at Madagascar, charting the coast from Foulepointe southwards to the mouth of the Mananjary river. Grenier travelled inland as far as Lake Alaotra, where he found "a delightful country, very fertile and inhabited by friendly people who desire nothing else than to trade with the French". Other tribes, however, were less friendly.

In a letter to the Minister of Marine, Grenier warned that if France wanted to re-establish itself in Madagascar, "we will be able to succeed only by adopting bold measures, and by knowing how to employ to this end gifts, kindness, and severity". The iron fist, although suitably concealed, could not be dispensed with.

Rochon, who accompanied Grenier to Madagascar, was highly critical of European methods of colonisation. "There is not one of those civilised nations which boast of having conceded some significant trading advantage in the interest of natural justice," he wrote. "All have been unjust and barbarous; almost all have carried steel, fire, and disease into those places where hope of gain has beckoned them. How can they be oblivious to the fact that the land where these savages live is as much their country as the land where we live is ours?"

He accused the Europeans of having introduced slavery into Madagascar, and argued that if the Malagasy had adopted the practice eagerly it was not really surprising, considering that

AMIRANTES, MASCARENE ISLANDS & MADAGASCAR

man had to ponder deeply on the matter before he could realise that liberty for others was essential to his own dignity. Rochon's commendable attitude on human rights was, in the 1760s, in advance of the accepted thinking of the time, although as these observations did not appear in print until 1791, at the height of the Revolution in France, most readers would have been receptive to his egalitarian concepts.

Rochon and Grenier brought back to the Isle de France a Malagasy chief, described as "very intelligent and very honest", who was clothed and fêted by the administrators before being sent back to Madagascar laden with presents. However, their efforts to win friends were already too late. Versailles was again losing interest in Madagascar, and not long after Grenier's expedition the Comte de Maudave abandoned his struggling settlement on the south coast.

During Grenier's absence Dumas — as a result of his rows with Poivre — had been replaced. The new governor-general was a naval captain, the Chevalier Desroches, but as he had not yet arrived to take up his appointment the administration was in the hands of Brigadier-General Jean Guillaume Steinauer. It was Grenier's good fortune that Steinauer was interested in the proposal to confirm a short and sure way to India.

Grenier also had an eager ally in Poivre. Duchemin's report on the Seychelles had only recently been received, and Poivre was anxious that Grenier should get more information about the islands and bring back additional samples of the coco de mer palm. As work was hurried on to make the *Heure du Berger* ready for sea, Grenier was given as escort a small corvette, the *Vert Galant*, that had recently arrived from France under the command of Lieutenant Lafontaine. On 30 May 1769, the two ships were ready to sail.

Grenier claimed later that he had been undecided on the exact course he would follow until, the day before departure, he was given a chart that traced Picault's voyage to the Seychelles in 1744. "I drew in on my own chart the route of this navigator and saw that he had run along the five degree parallel for a distance of four hundred leagues from east to west until reaching the Isles Séchelles, and I decided that if this parallel was likewise as clear between the 87th and 88th lines of longitude east of Paris, I would be rendering an important contribution to navigation by proposing to sail north as far as this parallel and follow it until one had traversed far enough east to raise Achen Point" (north-west Sumatra).

Briefly, Grenier had two aims: to show that during the favourable monsoon from May to October ships bound for India were being unnecessarily cautious in making first for the Cap d'Ambre at the northern extremity of Madagascar before sailing northwards to cross the equator as there was a perfectly safe and more direct route by way of the Seychelles; and, secondly, that during the contrary monsoon, from November to April, when a north-east wind blew above the equator, vessels bound for the Bay of Bengal could take advantage of the westerly wind below the equator and sail from Seychelles eastwards along the five degree line as far as Sumatra, from where they could fetch up to the Coromandel coast. As the usual route in this season involved a long detour into southern latitudes in search of the ever-present westerlies, Grenier's alternative would mean an even greater saving in sailing time.

As it was the end of May when the *Heure du Berger* and the *Vert Galant* left the Isle de France, Grenier decided to sail to Pondichéry by the direct Seychelles route suitable for the season, and on the return voyage sail westwards along the five degree south line until he had overlapped the track followed by Picault.

Meanwhile, Rochon had problems of his own. All his astronomical instruments were safely on board, but delay in the sailing of the *Heure du Berger* meant that the transit of Venus was now only three days away and if he were to make a worthwhile observation he needed something more stable than the deck of a ship under sail; a ship, moreover, whose exact position could only be a matter of conjecture. As it turned out, Rochon was able to attribute his failure to a moment of panic that gripped the ship when Grenier narrowly avoided running it on to an unseen reef.

"On that memorable day of the passage of Venus across the sun, in the month of June 1769," he wrote, "I was unable to make the important observation of the planet's transit, although the weather was clear and calm, because the corvette on which I was embarked was about to be shipwrecked on the Cargados; we had the choice of perishing, or making to windward round the most easterly point of that fearful reef."

At the last moment, Grenier succeeded in manoeuvring the *Heure du Berger* out of danger, and brought her into a protected bay of calm water. According to Rochon they could have made a landing there easily enough, "not only in order to determine its exact position but also to take off some tortoises that we could see on the beach", but he offered no explanation why they did not do so. Grenier, perhaps understandably, glossed over the incident, noting only in his *Mémoires* that at sunrise on 2 June they sighted the group of islands and reefs known as Saint Brandon (Cargados Carajos) more than one degree west of the position given them in D'Après's *Neptune Oriental*.

Lafontaine, following closely in the *Vert Galant*, logged: "Fresh breeze, good weather, the sea a little rough (contradicting Rochon's statement that it was clear and calm). The commander made us a signal for rocks, at the same moment he went about ... the said rocks are St Brandon, and were lying about one league off."

Grenier, always apologetic when he found errors in the charts of D'Après, reminded his readers that "this famous geographer" could record only what others told him. Rochon, however, spared neither D'Après nor Grenier.

Spilling out his bitterness over his failure to record the Venus transit, he dismissed Grenier as "a brave mariner, but at times too impetuous", accusing him of having almost shipwrecked them on two other occasions during the voyage. The Cargados incident was the beginning of an acrimonious relationship that was to reach its climax with the quarrel over Grenier's claim to have discovered the short route to India. It was a quarrel that simmered on for the rest of their lives.

It was on the distinguished head of D'Après, however, that Rochon was, publicly, to heap most of the blame. The basis of his accusation was that in drawing up his chart D'Après had confused the Cargados reefs with those of Saint Brandon and that, in an effort to reconcile differing reports on their positions, he had settled for a single, midway point between the two. Rochon argued that the two were at least 50 leagues apart and quite different in shape: Picault had indicated that the Cargados was crescent-shaped while the English chart based on the report of Captain Edward Ledger of the *Falcon* showed that Saint Brandon was like an equilateral triangle.

Rochon's criticism did not end there. Not only had D'Après confounded the Cargados with Saint Brandon he had also confused the widely separated islands of Astove and Agaléga, as well as committing "a multitude of other errors which, although less striking, were nevertheless of great importance". D'Après, he claimed, "lacked something of that readiness to discuss the findings brought back by various mariners, which is so necessary for the perfection of a marine chart".

More than 20 years elapsed before Rochon's criticisms of D'Après were published. By then the author of the *Neptune Oriental* had been dead for 11 years. But Rochon was unforgiving. In the index to *Voyages à Madagascar, au Maroc et aux Indes Orientales,* D'Après appears as the officer who confused the Astove reef with that of Agaléga, with a cross-reference to Astove as "the reef confused by M. D'Après with Agaléga".

In fact D'Après was right in thinking that the Cargados and Saint Brandon shoals were one and the same, a possibility that the Scotsman Dalrymple had also suggested. Dalrymple drew extensively on D'Après; he also made amendments when he thought the D'Après charts erred. "That I differ from my much respected friend," he wrote, "is no imputation; it is the misfortune not the fault of an hydrographer to be deficient in sufficient data."

Grenier attributed the many discrepancies in the reported positions of islands and reefs not only to the different winds and currents prevailing at certain times of the year, but also to the fact that ships making the same sighting were often sailing in opposite directions. A chart he made showing the principal currents of the Indian Ocean, was a notable contribution to navigational knowledge.

The *Heure du Berger* and the *Vert Galant* spent just over four weeks at Seychelles. Grenier explored the islands and careened his ship, a lengthy operation involving the removal of everything on board. Lafontaine reported that the crew of the *Vert Galant* helped in the unloading, transferring stores either into their own ship or on to the beach. Rochon, complaining about the unwieldy size of the quadrant the Academy of Marine had given him, busied himself ashore with his astronomical observations. "It is surprising that a place so close to the equator should have a temperate climate," he remarked, for this was the coolest time of the year. He found the terrain disappointing. "The view is picturesque, but once one lands the prospect is not so amusing; it is no more than a stretch of sand from which the mountains rise, difficult of access and cut by gorges so steep that one rarely finds a flat piece of land more than half a kilometre in length."

He deplored the presence of "these monstrous crocodiles that throw themselves on any man who is careless of where he is walking". But even more dangerous were the sharks and barracuda that patrolled the harbour waters. Of these Rochon had one nasty experience, when he had to wade ashore after his rowing boat foundered in the harbour. The fish came in to attack the men in the water, and several seamen were injured.

Rochon set up his observatory near the flagstaff overlooking the harbour and from there fixed the position of the main island, noting: "Of all the observations that I made on Séchelles to determine the longitude of this island, that on which I can count the most was that of the reappearance of the first satellite of Jupiter, which took place on 3 July at eight o'clock."

Rochon recorded the Seychelles latitude accurately, but it seems that he was some eight minutes too far east in his calculation of longitude. At one point in his account he gives the position of the flagstaff as 53 degrees 15 minutes east of Paris; Grenier recalls Rochon giving him almost the same reading. Elsewhere in his book, however, Rochon mentions the correct position of 53 degrees 7 minutes. At some later date, Rochon had taken the opportunity to correct his readings.

Grenier, in his *Mémoires,* has little to say about the Seychelles. In a note to the Minister of Marine, written the following year on his return to France, he explained: "I believe it is all to the good to leave even our own merchant fleet in ignorance of the important position of these islands, and the advantages that one could acquire from them, for fear that the enemy might get hold of this knowledge before France can establish herself there." He suggested that captains who were given his charts when sailing to the East should be required to return them to store after the voyage. Such was the policy which had been adopted 200 years earlier by the Portuguese in a vain effort to keep secret the routes to the Indies.

Grenier and Rochon also spent some time at Praslin, where they collected coco de mer nuts. Poivre, eager to transplant the coco de mer in the Isle de France, had also instructed Grenier to bring back some young plants. "We carried out this commission with zeal," says Rochon. "We did more, we brought back for the Natural History Museum in Paris a large palm 20ft high, and much information that was received with interest." Rochon also enthused over the great number of birds on Praslin, mentioning the black parrot, found today only on Praslin, and the *pigeon hollandais,* or fruit pigeon. He also made a large collection of shells.

It was while they were off the coast of Ceylon, nearing the end of their voyage to Pondichéry, that Grenier, again, almost ran his ship aground. According to Rochon, one of the officers – it was probably Duroslan, Grenier's first lieutenant – had pointed out to Grenier that if he maintained his course he would run aground on the Petite Basse. Grenier, instead of verifying his course on the chart, took objection to the remark and refused to hear more. Rochon claimed that, pretending not to know how the ship's course was plotted, he induced Grenier to show him how it was done. Almost immediately, Grenier realised his danger and gave orders to go about, signalling at the same time for the *Vert Galant* to stand by to give assistance. By this time the *Heure du Berger* had been caught in the large waves surrounding the Petite Basse, but fortunately in the evening they were tossed away from danger.

On the return voyage from Pondichéry, Grenier adhered to his proposed route, sailing westwards from near the Sumatra coast along the five degree south parallel until he crossed the track made by Picault in the same latitude. Grenier had now proved his point. His submission to the Marine Academy at Brest would proudly claim that "as neither he (Picault) nor I came across any sort of danger, it is my duty ... to point out to you that if, one day, this route is put to use, it is I who was fortunate enough to have proposed it and to have carried it through".

Back at the Isle de France, Grenier handed over copies of his report and charts to the governor-general, Desroches, before setting off for France. He had good reason to hasten back, guessing correctly that Rochon would do his best to discredit him and that it was essential his new route should be submitted to the judgment of the Academy at Brest before Rochon had time to marshal adverse arguments.

Although Rochon was to seek credit for contributing to the more direct route to India by fixing the positions of its principal dangers, he was not convinced of its safety, particularly for a squadron of ships. He expressed strong reservations about the advisability of sailing north to Seychelles because of "the reefs and shallow soundings which are little known in these waters", and he criticised Grenier, probably with justification, for not taking sufficient time to locate accurately all these dangers; he also doubted whether Grenier was correct (as he was) in assuming that the west winds along the five degree parallel were sufficiently constant between October and May to ensure swift and secure passage for shipping.

Perhaps most damaging to Grenier was Rochon's claim that the *Heure du Berger* had in fact been off course as she ran along the five degree parallel, this being the result of a ruse by Rochon to prevent Grenier running her aground during the night on Addu island, the most southerly of the Maldives chain.

Grenier, as might be expected, took the criticism badly. He charged that his critics were prompted by jealous prejudice, ill-will and that they were puffed up by self-esteem. He likened himself to Christopher Columbus, who had been considered a fool when he first returned from America.

In the end, the Marine Academy stood by Grenier. His *Mémoires* were ordered to be printed; he received the approbation of the Academy of Sciences in Paris — a blow for Rochon, who was one of its correspondents — and, as a final mark of honour, was summoned to the court at Fontainebleau, where he stayed for two months before eventually returning to the Indian Ocean in command of the frigate *Belle Poule*.

Rochon's reservations on the route were not altogether unreasonable. Nevertheless the honour of having pioneered the direct route to India belongs to Grenier. In subsequent years it was used regularly by those sailing to and from India, among them Suffren, who followed it without mishap to bring his squadron to battle off the coast of India.[6]

Rochon now disappears from our story. In 1771 he joined Kerguelen's expedition sailing from France to explore the southern ocean, but — one might almost say it was inevitable — he left the ship after a quarrel.[7] Then Poivre asked him to accompany Marion Dufresne who was about to leave on what was to be his ill-fated voyage to New Zealand, but Desroches, apparently tired of Rochon's petulance, refused permission.

In 1772 Rochon sailed for home in the *Indien*, accompanying Poivre, who was retiring after five years as intendant of the Isle de France and Bourbon. In 1774 he was appointed *garde du cabinet de physique et d'optique du roi*. It was during this period that Rochon carried out his remarkable work in optics. Among the instruments he developed was the micrometer (in making it he used quartz brought back from Madagascar), later described by Arago[8] as one of the most remarkable discoveries in astronomy, and he is also credited with having been the first to utilise in scientific research the principle of double refraction.

Rochon did not fare well during the Revolution. He lost all his positions and honours and was forced to retire to his native Brest. In those anti-clerical times poor Rochon must have regretted his assumed title of abbé. In the upheaval he also lost the manuscript for the first part of his projected book, but in 1791 he managed to publish a volume on Madagascar. Two further volumes, of his now rewritten account of his voyages to Morocco and to India with Grenier, appeared in 1801-02. In these Rochon allowed himself some words of praise for Napoleon,[9] which could well have been done with an eye to his rehabilitation for soon afterwards he and his wife were allowed back to Paris.

Rochon died in Paris in 1817. In a funeral oration, a member of the Academy of Sciences extolled his achievements, his work in optics and his services to navigation. It was not the occasion to speak of his irritability, his intolerance, his quarrels with Grenier and Kerguelen, his spitefulness. Rochon was a brilliant scientist, but the greatness he so eagerly sought eluded him.

Today, in the Seychelles, his visit there is recalled by the Rochon River, a small stream rising above the capital, Victoria, whose rushing waters are now conserved in the Rochon Dam, which was erected in 1969 to provide the beginnings of a piped-water supply to the island. It seems a pity that Grenier is not likewise remembered. He deserves to be for it was his voyage in 1769 that finally convinced France of the usefulness of the Seychelles as a port of call on the way to India and led, within a year, to the establishment of the first French settlement.

Grenier continued to sail the Indian Ocean, first as commander of the frigate *Belle Poule*[10] and later as captain of the *Boudeuse*, in which he fought during the American revolutionary war. His promotions in the navy raised him to the rank of commodore, while his reputation was further enhanced with the publication in 1787 of a manual of sea warfare, *L'Art de la Guerre sur Mer*. He died, as the Vicomte de Giron, in Paris in January 1803.

* * *

Before we turn to the establishment of the first French settlement in the Seychelles, mention must be made of two further voyages of exploration. The first, by Grenier's former second-in-command, Duroslan, saw the formal annexation by France of Silhouette and La Digue, the two largest Seychelles islands after Mahé and Praslin. The main purpose of the voyage, however, was to cap Grenier's achievement by sailing eastwards from Seychelles along that section of the five degree parallel that Grenier himself had not sailed.

Duroslan also aimed to answer Rochon's criticism that the dangers lying on the route from the Isle de France to Seychelles had not been sufficiently charted, by reconnoitring the islands known as the Amirantes. He found and named five of the islands or sand cays, although it required a further voyage the following year by Labiollière in the *Etoile du Matin* to complete the survey of the coral island chain.

Duroslan, who had assumed command of the *Heure du Berger* when Grenier left to return to France, sailed from Port Louis on 27 December 1770. He was accompanied by the *Étoile du Matin*, commanded on this first voyage by d'Hercé. On 8 January they passed what was probably Isle Platte, which lies 80 miles south of Mahé. Continuing on a north-westerly course, with favourable winds and a strong current carrying them swiftly westwards, they sighted towards the end of the following day an island which Duroslan named Isle du Berger. The next morning, when an officer and party went ashore, they found that high tide split the island in two. Crocodiles were seen, but to their disappointment there was no water, and the coconuts were small and disagreeable to the taste.

During the next few days Duroslan followed a zigzag course naming three more small islands, Étoile, Marie-Louise and Isle des Noeufs. At noon on the day they left Isle des Noeufs they passed a small cay which was named Boudeuse, probably after the ship in which Bougainville had circumnavigated the globe two years previously.

For the next ten days the two ships sailed north and northeast without sighting land until, on the evening of 22 January, Mahé came into view. Duroslan spent two weeks at Mahé, visiting the small French settlement that had recently been established on Sainte Anne and unloading the supplies he had brought. One of his officers, Oger, went by launch to Silhouette, where he took formal possession of the island.[11] He also carried out an extensive survey. Oger noted that the soil was good, but with only a thin layer covering the rock. More turtles were there than on the other islands; also many crocodiles and sharks. He considered that the water was better than that found on Mahé.

Oger went on another launch expedition when the two ships moved to Praslin to load with cocos de mer. He reported sailing along the shore of the Sisters. "They are arid and the soil appeared to me to be nothing but rocks, one heaped on the other," he logged. Trees were few, and very small and although there were plenty of palms none had the double coconut. "The island Félicité, which I also sailed along close to shore, seemed to me to be of the same type as the Three Sisters."

Oger had left the *Heure du Berger*, moored in Curieuse Bay, at half-past five that morning (Sunday, 10 February 1771). At nine o'clock he brought his boat into a sandy bay on the south-east shore of La Digue. The sea had been calm, but a small squall blew up and swamped them. To save the boat they had to sink it, and then struggle to the shore. Their supply of food was lost, as well as Oger's surveying instruments and plans he had made of the islands. The next day they managed to refloat the boat, but they found the rudder was badly damaged. Oger reported that the shape of La Digue had no resemblance to that given on earlier charts. The only place capable of being cultivated was opposite to where they had landed. The seamen killed a dozen crocodiles, some of which were nearly 15 feet long. Again, there were no double coconuts. Before leaving La Digue Oger "left on the island a document confirming our act of possession".

With the damage to the rudder, Oger found the boat being driven away by wind and current, and was forced to anchor between La Digue and Praslin. Eventually he and three others managed to land on Praslin, at the Baie Sainte Anne, and set off across the island to fetch provisions and assistance from the ship. It was a tiring journey, scrambling over rocks, cutting their way through the undergrowth, and keeping an eye open for crocodiles. But there were bright moments, too. "I saw one animal which was very similar to the cayman, but with a more pointed head and his colour more yellow," reported Oger. "He ran before us much faster than the lightest of us could run. He is a salamander."

Oger's return was recorded in the *Heure du Berger* log under the date 13 February 1771: "At one hour in the afternoon, M. Oger arrived with three persons; they had been wrecked on La Digue island and after having repaired the boat they landed in the bay on the south-east of Praslin. Lacking provisions, M. Oger came for supplies, which we intend sending tomorrow morning. Our people took five turtles on the reef in the bay on the north-east of Curieuse island." Four days later, with the launch back on board, Duroslan left Praslin, taking a north-easterly course to sound the extent of the Seychelles bank before setting off on Grenier's route eastwards and finally rounding off his voyages by surveying the positions of the islands of the Diego Garcia archipelago.

On his return to France Duroslan had his reward. Writing from Brest, where he had been laid low with a raging cold accompanied by several bouts of fever, he told D'Après that the Minister had found his reports useful and had cancelled half of his debts to the Crown, instructing Poivre to write off the remainder on Duroslan's return to the Isle de France.

Some months earlier, the *Étoile du Matin*, commanded now by Labiollière, had sailed again for the Seychelles. On board was an officer sent by Poivre to establish a spice garden on the islands. Labiollière had been instructed to carry out a further reconnaissance of the Amirantes, and as a result the Isle du

Berger was again visited — and renamed by Labiollière Isle Poivre, the name it retains today. Labiollière sailed on and named several other small islands lying to the north and northwest: St Joseph, D'Arros, after the naval commander at the Isle de France, and Desroches, after the governor-general. He also visited another island which he named Remire.

By fixing the positions of the main islands of the Amirantes group Duroslan and Labiollière had put the finishing touches to Grenier's mission of finding the shorter route to India. In years to follow individual ships would continue to report sightings in the waters around Seychelles — often identifying as discoveries islands that were already known — but by now the main hazards of the route had all been plotted.

4

First Settlement
1770-1772

> Comme je n'ai vu que ces commencemens
> si mal combinés, je ne peus juger de
> l'événemens qui en résultera.
> *Unsigned memoir on Seychelles, c.1774*

Having proclaimed sovereignty over the whole Seychelles archipelago, the French could hardly avoid for long the next step of forming a settlement. But who would be willing to finance a colony of such doubtful value?

The Isle de France administrators, mindful of their chronically depleted budget, were reluctant to incur more expense by fathering a new settlement, especially as reports by the various expeditions to the islands were contradictory on the quality of the soil and the amount of flat, cultivable land. Timber and tortoises, it seemed, were the only sure products, and these could be exploited by sending an occasional ship to the islands.

Versailles was equally unwilling to add to its colonial commitments. Half a century of domestic extravagance and European wars under Louis XIV, followed by another 50 years of free spending by the Regency and Louis XV had brought the government close to bankruptcy. Louis — by 1769 the Well-Beloved in name only — might still indulge his official mistress, Madame du Barry, but there were no funds for the Ministry of Marine to establish a new colony in the Indian Ocean.

Thus the Seychelles might have remained nominally French,

and uninhabited, until the end of the century or, as was more likely, until the English arrived and acquired the islands for themselves. That this did not happen was thanks to two men. One was Pierre Poivre, whose interest in the islands had been sharpened by a belief that they might prove the ideal site for growing spices. The other enterprising spirit was a Norman nobody, Henri François Charles Brayer du Barré, who sought to make his fortune by exploiting the natural resources of the islands, which would serve him also as a staging post for shipping slaves from Africa to the Isle de France.[1]

Neither Brayer du Barré's settlement on Sainte Anne island nor Poivre's spice garden at Anse Royale on Mahé survived for more than a few years, but it was enough to ensure that when the English came the islands were in French hands, and remained so until their eventual surrender to Britain at the end of the Napoleonic wars.

Poivre's first courageous attempts to break the Dutch spice monopoly have already been noted. When he retired to France in 1756 his campaign to cultivate spices in the Isle de France had been totally discredited, but 11 years later, on his return to the Indian Ocean as acting intendant, he carried specific instructions from the King to pursue once more "with the utmost diligence" the introduction of spices into the colony. It meant starting again from scratch, acquiring by stealth the necessary plants from the Dutch East Indies, but Poivre was as enthusiastic as before. Several voyages to the Moluccas were made, all unsuccessful. It was not until June 1770 that Poivre's agent, Simon Prévost, returned with a substantial quantity of plants and seeds. His two ships, the *Vigilant* and the *Etoile du Matin*, unloaded at Port Louis 400 nutmeg plants, 10,000 nutmeg seeds, and 70 clove plants.

Poivre did everything this time to ensure that the plants would succeed. An ordinance was passed fixing heavy penalties for stealing or damaging plants, a necessary measure as Poivre received almost no support for his scheme from the Isle de France settlers. Two gardeners of French parentage had been brought from the Celebes to care for the plants, but unfortunately they had little experience in the task and by the end of the year only 50 nutmeg and 14 clove plants remained.

Poivre did not give up easily. If, as was now clear, the Isle de France was unsuitable for spice growing he would try elsewhere. At neighbouring Isle Bourbon he found the settlers more receptive to his scheme, and as the soil also proved more suitable several successful plantings were made. Yet the island still fell short of Poivre's ideal, and when instructions came from Versailles telling him to send seeds to the Central American settlement at Cayenne he resolved he would make one more attempt to find a site for his spice plants in the Indian Ocean.

Poivre had, in fact, thought of the Seychelles many years earlier. In a conversation with Malesherbes[2] after his return to France in 1758 he pointed out that the Seychelles lay in a similar latitude to that of the Dutch spice islands, which could be a decisive factor for the success of a spice plantation. At that time the Seychelles islands were hardly known. Since August 1770, however, with a small settlement having been established there, Poivre may have considered he could use this as his base. If so, he soon abandoned the idea. Reports on the progress of the Saint Anne settlement, at first so encouraging, were not to his liking. Nor was the gentleman who had founded the settlement, Brayer du Barré.

Most writers of Seychelles history dismiss Brayer du Barré as a rogue. His correspondence certainly reveals him to have been ambitious and scheming, and not above employing fraud and deceit when things went wrong. Yet it is his naïvety that is most remarkable. Unsuited for the cut-throat business of colonial adventure, he looked constantly to Versailles for support, writing beseechingly to this notable or that. But all in vain; he remained without funds, heavily mortgaged to the government, swindled right and left by unscrupulous ship captains. Ill-managed, sabotaged, neglected, his settlement on Sainte Anne island was eventually to crumble.

When his detractors in the Isle de France challenged his integrity, he produced a certificate showing he had managed honestly and accurately the accounts of a Royal Military School lottery at Rouen for a period of three and a half years[3]. On leaving Rouen, Brayer du Barré had gravitated to Versailles, where, like others on the periphery of the court, he made proper obeisances to his betters and played on his Norman connection to ingratiate himself with those who might further his career.

At some point he became known to the Minister of Marine,

the Duc de Praslin, and as a result was given the loan of three ships, together with a government contract to transport troops and supplies to the East. On the face of it, it was a promising deal, for although the government was to pay him much less than the usual rate Brayer du Barré was to enjoy in future all the trading rights of the defunct Compagnie des Indes.

"It was," commented a Minister, "a unique circumstance in favour of the *sieur* Barré, and it is to be presumed that if he had had means appropriate to the importance of this speculation, it would have been for him infinitely advantageous." Unfortunately, the means was something Brayer du Barré did not have.

Unexpected expenses had arisen during the outward voyage of his three ships, the *Thélémaque*, the *Duc de Praslin*, and the *Comte de Saint-Florentin*. Long before they reached the Cape sickness broke out among the troops, and the ships had to put in there while the soldiers received treatment at Brayer du Barré's expense. Already heavily mortgaged to the government at Versailles, he had to start borrowing again as soon as he arrived at the Isle de France early in 1770. For someone who intended to create a new trading empire in the East it was an inauspicious start.

The earliest reference to Brayer du Barré's proposed settlement in Seychelles is his written authority from Desroches and Poivre to fit out an expedition for "the Three Brothers or Seychelles", although the project must have been discussed previously at Versailles, where it would have been made clear to Brayer du Barré that everything was to be at his risk. The authorisation stipulated that he would form a settlement of about 30 men "to cut wood for construction, fish, and provide enough food for nine months, tools and arms". Clearly, the government still thought the Seychelles was suitable only for temporary occupation.

The *Thélémaque* sailed from Port Louis at the beginning of August under the command of Captain Lecore, arriving at Seychelles, after a quick passage, on 27 August 1770. The officer in charge, Major Delaunay, decided to establish his camp on Sainte Anne instead of on the main island. His first concern was to grow food for his party of 28, almost half of whom were slaves, and the flat ground at the southern end of the smaller island seemed ideal for rapid cultivation.[4]

Two châteaux in France have links with the family name of Séchelles. Jean Moreau, who had acquired the seigneurie of Séchelles and Cuvilly in Picardy, built a château there in 1740.

Jean-Marie Hérault de Séchelles, grandson of Jean Moreau's elder daughter, Hélène, was brought up by his widowed mother and grand-mother at the Château de Montgeoffroy (below), the home in Anjou of the Marshal de Contades. Hérault de Séchelles, royalist lawyer turned revolutionary, died with Danton under the guillotine in 1794.

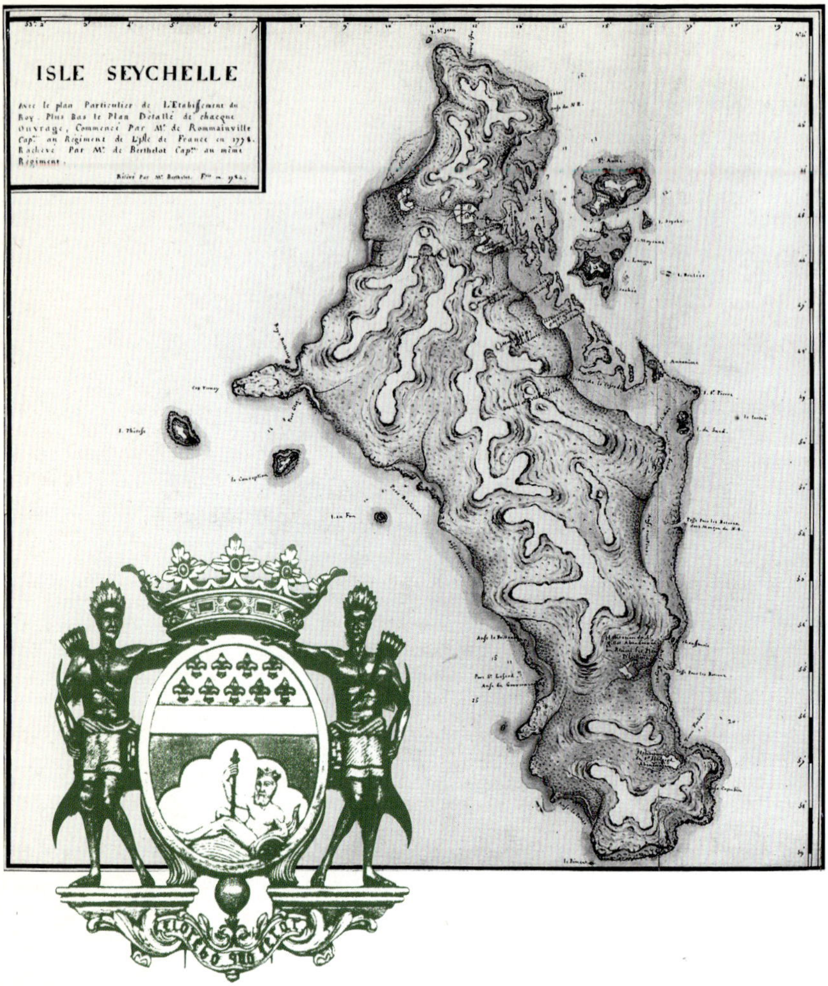

Plan of the Isle Seychelle at the time of the creation of the Établissement by Lieutenant Routier de Romainville in 1778. Inset: the arms of the Compagnie des Indes Orientales, which formed the first settlement in Seychelles. Below: the Isle Seychelle, from sketches made by Captain Corneille Nicolas Morphey in 1756.

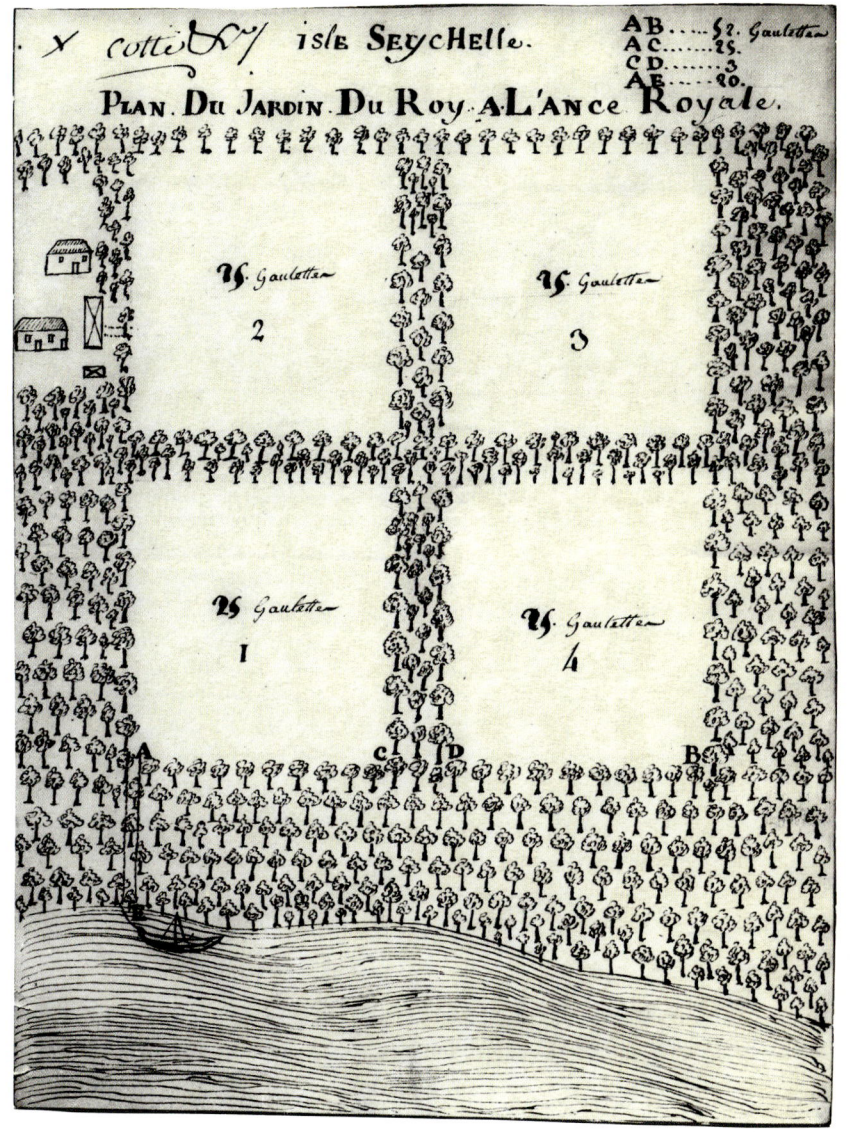

Plan drawn by Gillot for the King's Spice Garden at Anse Royale. In the four separate beds he was to grow cloves, nutmeg, pepper, and cinnamon. A 'gaulette' is an old French measurement.

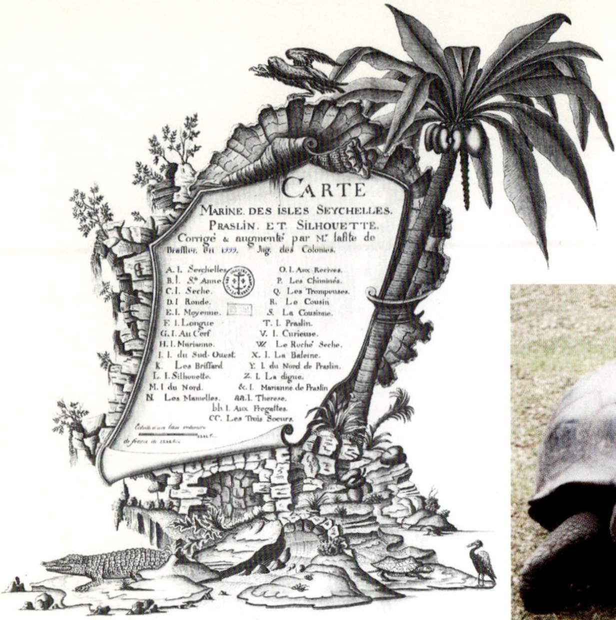

Top: Decorative title-piece of a chart of Isles Seychelles, dated 1777. Images include a crocodile, giant tortoise, and a Coco de Mer palm. After the husk of the Coco de Mer is removed, the suggestive shape of the double-lobed nut (above) is revealed. The giant tortoises (right) were photographed on Curieuse island. The crocodile (below) is from a water-colour by Claude-Nicolas Billerey, 1752.

César Gabriel de Choiseul-Chevigny, Duc de Praslin, Secretary of State for Foreign Affairs from 1761 to 1770, and Minister of Marine, 1766 to 1770.

*Bertrand Mahé de La Bourdonnais
Governor-general of Isle de France and
Bourbon 1735-46*

*Pierre Poivre, Intendant of Isle de France
and Bourbon 1767-72*

*Comte de la Pérouse
Mariner and explorer*

*Louis-Antoine Bougainville
Mariner and explorer*

Antoine de Sartine, lieutenant-general of police and later Minister of Marine (1774-80). In an attempt to win his favour, Brayer du Barré sent him a map of Mahé, with a bay on the west coast marked 'Port Sartine'.

qu'on vendra de moi a mon retour de cette campagne. en attendant ne m'oubli pas. mon ennemis l'abbé Rochon part en france par l'jourd'hui. s'il fait mouvoir contre moi quelque nouvelle cabale prenez ma cause en main, vous devez être assuré de ma reconnaissance autant que du sincere et inviolable attachement avec lequel.

j'ai l'honneur d'être

Monsieur

Votre très humble
et très obéissant serviteur
Le Chr. grenier

faits je vous prie agréer mes
respects a madame Rodier.

The abbé Rochon, naval hydrographer, made a pioneering voyage to Seychelles in 1769 in the Heure du Berger. He and Captain Grenier quarrelled frequently. In this letter Grenier warns a friend in Paris to beware of 'mon ennemi' l'abbé Rochon.

Delaunay's choice was approved the following year by the captain of a visiting English ship. He described it as "much the best of these islands for a settlement", and refused to believe Delaunay when told that the French planned to transfer to the main island as soon as more men and supplies arrived. The English had got wind of Delaunay's settlement through an engineer officer stationed at Madras, Captain Phillip Pittman, who had been given a French chart of the Seychelles by the Dutch during a stop-over the previous year at the Cape.

The chart indicated the anchorages of the *Digue* and the *Curieuse*, as well as the sites of the flagstaffs and stones of possession of the main island and Praslin. Pittman promptly sent it off to the East India Company headquarters at Bombay. "The chart bears such marks of authenticity that I thought a copy would not be unacceptable to you," he wrote in a covering letter. "You are the most capable judges and can best decide what political end such an acquisition can answer to the French, or if it can affect the security of our settlements."

As a result of Pittman's report the Bombay Council decided to send two company ships, the *Eagle* and the *Drake*, to reconnoitre the islands and the coast of Madagascar so "that we may be informed as fully as possible of the establishment lately made by the French thereon, and the force they may have at those places ..."

The *Drake* was sent to Madagascar, while the *Eagle*, under the command of Lieutenant Lewis, visited the Seychelles during July and August 1771. Lewis called first at Praslin, where the English were later to be accused of removing the plaque placed there by Lampériaire and substituting one of their own, as well as setting fire to the forest on Curieuse island.

From Praslin, Lewis sailed over to Sainte Anne, where, as the French and English were at the time in a rare period of peace, he was greeted in friendly fashion by Delaunay. By now the crops planted by the Frenchmen were flourishing, and the *Eagle*'s captain subsequently reported to Bombay that a large area of the island was producing maize, rice, tobacco (the *Eagle* took away a sample of this crop), coffee, cotton, and vegetables of different sorts. At Praslin, Lewis had also loaded coco de mer nuts to take back to India.

For the moment the French had forestalled any attempt by

the English to claim the islands, although in Bombay it had been noted that they would be excellent for refreshing ships' crews, information that was to be made use of in the future. The company ships had also visited the islands of the Chagos archipelago, and it was there, on the island of Diego Garcia, that the English were soon to form an outpost.[5]

News of the initial success of Delaunay's settlement had reached the Isle de France through Duroslan of the *Heure du Berger*, who, it will be recalled, had sailed in December 1770 to reconnoitre the Amirante islands. Poivre had instructed Duroslan that if he should find the Seychelles settlers starving he should not hesitate to bring them back.[6] Instead, an overjoyed Brayer du Barré was now clamouring for his settlement to be expanded.

"All that is needed now is to send men and supplies, and to set up a *grand établissement* on Séchelle," he wrote to a friend. To the Duc de Praslin he offered to go himself to the island to direct things personally. He urged Praslin to conclude an agreement with the King of Portugal for a regular supply of African slaves, and estimated that he could provide up to 1,800 slaves a year for the Isle de France.

To supplement slave labour in the Seychelles, he suggested recruiting farm labour from poorhouses and orphanages in France, for the soil was obviously ideal for agriculture. "The rice and maize are of very fine quality," he boasted, "as well as the cassava and vegetables of all kinds." The coffee, too, had surpassed all expectation. It would, he claimed, soon be as good as that of Mocha. What Brayer du Barré did not realise was that the soil, although fecund, was only a thin cover and would soon be exhausted.

He cited as possible industries the manufacture of coconut oil and fish oil, as well as salted fish and tortoiseshell for export. Poivre had promised him pepper, nutmeg, cinnamon, and vanilla plants, together with instructions for planting, but he intended going himself to the Philippines for additional plants, as well as to recruit workers for a coir rope industry.

He suggested establishing forts on the islands, and asked the Minister to send him a company of artillery. "I can assure Your Eminence," he wrote, "that with a little assistance I will be in a position within a year to put these islands into a state of defence, and the colony will be run to your satisfaction."

Duroslan's report on the new settlement also excited the curiosity — and jealousy — of the Isle de France business community. Some approached Brayer du Barré to see if they might share in its prosperity, one, the Chevalier de la Gonnevière, proposing to set up a plantation with 50 slaves. Others were irked that a newcomer should so quickly acquire a prosperous colony, and soon rumours were circulating about his dishonesty and indebtedness. At first, Brayer du Barré ignored them, but on 4 August 1771 he called a meeting in Port Louis to defend himself against "several ill-intentioned people (who) are attempting to besmirch his reputation and harm his credit worthiness".

Forty-eight signatories, including Marion Dufresne, attested to Brayer du Barré's good conduct, honesty and industry, and condemned "the injurious words and writings that he has told us have been spread about him, even as far away as Europe". However, the rumours continued, and less than two years later Brayer du Barré held another meeting, this time at the home of the apostolic prefect, M. de Contenor. Again he brought away a document as proof of his honesty.

Meanwhile his demands for assistance from the colonial government continued unabated. He asked for the loan of two ships so that he could send Delaunay the additional workers, slaves and supplies he needed to move the settlement from Sainte Anne to the main island. Eventually, the government gave him a small vessel, the *Marianne*, which sailed for the Seychelles with 60 workers. Brayer du Barré was later to complain that the workers were in the main "very bad characters" and, in the case of the blacks, had come straight from jail. He was also to complain about Poivre, who, having at first expressed satisfaction over the settlement, was now abandoning him.

What did it matter to the government if he failed or not, Brayer du Barré asked the Minister in a lengthy letter of recrimination. Everything was to his account. He was only helped with the transporting of supplies, while the produce of the islands was loaded into king's ships and sold at the Isle de France at a profit. If it were not for the fact that he realised the importance of the Seychelles to France he would let the whole scheme collapse. Unfortunately for Brayer du Barré, Poivre was now convinced that the founder of the Seychelles settlement lacked the business acumen, not to mention the financial resources, to carry through the ambitious schemes that kept passing through his head. Instead of supplying Brayer du Barré with the spice plants he had ordered from the Far East,[7] Poivre decided to send his own agent to the Seychelles to select a suitable site for a spice garden which would be independent of Delaunay's settlement. He chose a former officer of the disbanded Battalion de l'Inde, Antoine Nicolas Benoît Gillot, who for the past eight years had served as a captain in the Isle de France part-time militia. It was not, as we shall see, a particularly happy choice.

Gillot, who had first visited the Seychelles with Duchemin's expedition, sailed from Port Louis in October 1771 in the *Étoile du Matin*, under the command of Labiollière. Although he carried a letter from Poivre to Delaunay which requested the Seychelles commandant to give him every assistance, Gillot was not received kindly. Only with great difficulty did he manage to get a boat to travel round the islands, looking for the most suitable site for a spice garden. Even so he had to omit the southern and western areas from his survey. Of the main island and Praslin, which he visited later, he left a detailed report, containing his decision to site the spice garden at Anse Royale, on Mahé's south-east coast. The area, he noted, had a thick, black soil, with a sandy sub-soil, and a large marsh through which flowed two fine streams.

Having chosen the site, Gillot's task was to mark out the dimensions of the Jardin du Roi and, with the help of Delaunay's slaves, to start clearing the ground, ready for planting. The plan was for four beds, divided by standing trees and with banana trees to provide shade for the plants and retain moisture. In each of the four beds would be planted clove, nutmeg, cinnamon, and pepper.

Gillot had one of the beds cleared and then, giving as an excuse lack of time, he decided to return to the Isle de France. He left behind a sketch of the proposed garden with instructions to Delaunay to clear the rest of the garden by June or July. Gillot took passage in the *Marianne* (Captain Picard), which was returning to the Isle de France after having landed labourers for the Delaunay settlement. The *Marianne* called first at Praslin to load with cocos de mer, and during its visit there (22 February to 3 March 1772) Gillot visited several parts of the island. He noted that Praslin was in fact much larger than shown on the original plans, but that only a third of it was suitable for cultivation. "The other two-thirds," he wrote, "are nothing but mountains, ravines, piled high with rocks and practically impassable."

Like earlier visitors, Gillot marvelled at the giant coco de mer palms, in whose shade no other plant could survive. Gazing up at their swaying heads, 60 feet or so above him, he noted that, as far as he could tell, the trees bore both fruit and flowers. The other trees were similar to those of the main island.

Gillot remarked that the island's streams did not flow freely to the sea, being blocked at their mouths by sandbars through which the water seeped slowly until, with a downfall of torrential rain, the stream overflowed, breaking through the sand to the sea. He found no trace of the goats that had been left on the island by the *Curieuse*, and concluded that they had been devoured by the crocodiles, which were more numerous than on Mahé and "very large and hungry".

It was still the tail-end of the cyclone season when the *Marianne* left Praslin. For six long weeks she battled southwards against heavy seas and contrary winds. On 13 April, they were in sight of the Isle de France, but as the *Marianne* strove to reach the shelter of Grand Port, in the south-east corner of the island, a great storm hit them. Nothing could save the ship in the boiling cauldron of wind and water. With the sails ripped from the masts, the rudder gone, and mountainous seas crashing on her decks, the *Marianne* was thrown on to the reef and sank. Gillot was among the survivors, lucky to be alive but with all his possessions gone.

On shore more bad news awaited him. All his slaves had run away, or otherwise disappeared, and his house had been ransacked. Gillot estimated his losses at 9,000 livres, of which he was to get only 1,800 back in compensation from Poivre. Faced with ruin Gillot decided the only thing to do was to return to Seychelles. According to him, Poivre encouraged him to do so with promises "which he would certainly have honoured if he had himself not departed so suddenly".

Poivre's term at the Isle de France was finally running out. After five years of exceptional service to the colony he was tired of the continual squabbling with Desroches and the home government. He had asked for his recall, and it had been granted.

Shortly before his departure, one of the ships that he had been waiting for returned from the Moluccas with a cargo of clove and nutmeg plants. Poivre asked Gillot to sail with it to the Seychelles and begin immediately his planting at Anse Royale. According to Gillot the main inducement offered by Poivre was a salary of 2,400 livres, in addition to subsistence until such time as he could provide for himself. This open-ended benefit was before long to be disputed by Poivre's successors.

The *Nécessaire* sailed for Seychelles on July 1772. On board were Gillot, with two copies of printed instructions from Poivre on the correct manner of planting and caring for the spice plants, and Pierre Hangard, a former soldier whom Poivre had given permission to settle in the Seychelles.

In his instructions to Gillot, Poivre made it clear that the King's spice garden must be completely independent of the Brayer du Barré settlement, and that Gillot was in no way answerable to Delaunay, nominal commandant of the colony. Furthermore, Gillot was instructed to avoid as much as possible all communication with the other settlement.

The creation on a small island colony of two rival settlements under commandants who were not only independent but were officially directed not to co-operate or even communicate with each other was a recipe for disaster.

5

Collapse of a Colony
1772-1777

> Une société quelconque se détruit promptement
> par elle-même quand ceux qui la composent
> et la conduisent n'ont ni mœurs ni principes.
> *Memoir on Seychelles, c. 1774*

Pierre Hangard was not a gentleman. As Brayer du Barré liked to point out, not only had he served as a common soldier with the Compagnie des Indes, he had also for a time been responsible for looking after the company's pigs. Since leaving the army, however, Hangard had improved his status. Several profitable slaving expeditions to Madagascar had enabled him to buy property in Isle de France, and by 1772 he had made enough money to seek his fortune in the new colony of Seychelles.

Brayer du Barré tried to bar him from going, saying he had no authority from the King to allow anyone to settle in the islands, but Hangard appealed to Gillot, who persuaded Poivre to give permission for the ex-soldier to accompany him in the *Nécessaire*. Gillot regretted later having intervened. Although himself not above reproach in the matter of plundering the colony's resources, he was soon jealous of Hangard's ability to enrich himself. Hangard, according to Gillot, was like all the others, "wicked without honour or honesty".

The former soldier may have been unscrupulous, greedy, and capricious, as well as being continually at loggerheads with authority. He would certainly have been included in the sweeping condemnation by one French official, who deplored the fact that not enough care was taken to ensure that only the virtuous, the reliable, and the sober were allowed to settle in Seychelles. But if Hangard is singled out as a bad example among the settlers, it can only be because he lived longer than the others, a period of some 30 years, before dying, a blind, cantankerous old man.

On their arrival at Seychelles, Gillot and Hangard found Delaunay's colony in a sorry state. The harvest that had seemed so promising the previous year had failed, and most of the inhabitants had abandoned Sainte Anne to live on the main island, where they quarrelled continuously. Delaunay seemed no longer to exert control and, if Brayer du Barré is to be believed, spent his days wandering on the beach collecting shells.

Hangard was not slow to profit from this scene of disorder. He proposed to Delaunay that he should be allowed to settle on the vacant site on Sainte Anne, where he would grow food for the rest of the colony. Delaunay agreed. Later, when the commandant refused to pay Hangard for food supplied, the new proprietor of Sainte Anne compensated himself by seizing Brayer du Barré's possessions. "Was there anything more unjust than this?" complained the aggrieved party to Versailles.

The news the *Nécessaire* brought back about the chaotic state of the Seychelles colony alarmed the Isle de France administrators, and the new governor-general, the Chevalier Charles Louis d'Arzac de Ternay, decided on immediate evacuation. Orders were issued that the frigate *Belle Poule*, which was preparing to sail for the Malabar coast, should call at Seychelles on the way and embark as many of the inhabitants as possible. As neither Ternay nor the new acting intendant, Jacques Maillart Dumesle, shared Poivre's enthusiasm for spice culture, the *Belle Poule* was also ordered to bring back the King's slaves working at the spice garden at Anse Royale. Ternay was reluctant, however, to withdraw completely from the Seychelles. He realised that a French. flag was by itself not enough to keep the English out, and he advised Versailles that Brayer du Barré should be allowed to continue with a small settlement of about 20 workers.

He warned De Boynes, who had succeeded Praslin as Minister of Marine, that the English were sending two ships a year to Praslin island to collect coco de mer nuts, and that several Englishmen at Surat had announced that they were going to establish a colony in Seychelles. "It could have been wished, no doubt, that one had never discovered these islands," Ternay ruefully observed.

He suggested to the Minister that if, as was probable, the Brayer du Barré settlement again failed, "it would be appropriate to acquire this establishment for the account of the King". Several years were to pass before Versailles accepted this last piece of advice.

The *Belle Poule* left for Seychelles on 8 October 1772. In command was Grenier, who, back from France, welcomed the opportunity to sail once more the route to India he had pioneered with Rochon in 1769. This time, thanks to the westerly winds that blow below the equator from October to April, he would be able to make the outward voyage along the five degrees south line, and so silence for good critics like Rochon who were still maintaining that the route was not safe. He knew that Rochon, who had recently sailed for France in the same ship as Poivre, would keep trying to discredit him. "Do not forget my enemy the abbé Rochon," Grenier wrote to a friend in France. "If he starts to plot against me again, look after my interests. You will be assured of my gratitude."

On reaching Seychelles, Grenier embarked as ordered most of the workers of the settlement, including Delaunay, who left behind in charge of the depleted colony his second-in-command, Anselme. All the slaves at the spice garden were also put aboard the *Belle Poule*, but Gillot elected to remain, and was for the next two years to be virtually ignored by the Isle de France administrators.

The *Belle Poule* did not arrive back at the Isle de France until May 1773. Delaunay, still feeling bitter over the failure of his settlement, protested to Brayer du Barré at the way he had been treated. He claimed that the workers he had been sent were useless and had, in any case, been enticed away by Gillot to the spice garden. During a prolonged stay in the Isle de France Delaunay remained officially the Seychelles commandant. In July 1774 a notice in the Official Gazette announced that he was returning to resume his duties.[1] He never did, and at this point Delaunay disappears from our story.

Despite the setback he had suffered, Brayer du Barré had no intention of abandoning his enterprise. New demands were dispatched to Versailles for a ship or two and some workers, even slaves from the Port Louis chain gang would do. An advance of 150,000 livres would also be useful. With that he could refund all he owed to the government and prove his detractors wrong. Poivre had done nothing for him, and it was now reserved to De Boynes to reap the glory of establishing an important colony for France, If, as had been rumoured, it was the government's intention to take the colony over, he should be compensated. Perhaps he might be appointed commissioner for the islands, at a suitable salary.

To all these importunings and suggestions De Boynes remained impervious, even when Brayer du Barré sent him gifts of a talking parrot and a bird of paradise. In desperation Brayer du Barré wrote to the Comte d'Estaing,[2] sending him a chart of Seychelles and claiming the Admiral's protection and support. Since founding the colony, he informed d'Estaing, he had suffered "a thousand disagreements and misfortunes without number", all caused by the bad faith and jealousy of his enemies. "I have been the victim and dupe of all those I have employed," his letter concluded.

News of the disintegration of the colony continued to reach the Isle de France, brought by ships that had called at the islands to load with wood and tortoises. In June 1773 La Pérouse, commanding the *Seine*, put in at Seychelles on his way to Pondichéry. He reported finding the greatest disorder among the settlers. No cultivation was going on and people were dying of hunger as the only food supply was from the slaughter of turtles, he reported.

La Pérouse had to shelter from bad weather at Praslin, and he visited the cairn erected by Lampériaire almost five years earlier. He found that the lead plaque carrying the arms of France was no longer there, and concluded that it had become detached through corrosion and had fallen into the sea.

Another distinguished navigator to visit the islands, Bougainville, warned Versailles of the importance of the Seychelles, and urged that steps should be taken to curb the depredations of ships' crews.

In a memorandum to the Minister, he wrote: "The result of the government not giving to these islands the attention they merit is that vessels leaving the Isle de France for Pondichéry pass by these islands where they destroy large tracts of forest, loading with timber suitable for shipbuilding, which they sell at Madras. Not content with carrying away the tortoises, they make oil from them which results in enormous destruction and which will soon exhaust this important and nutritious commodity."

Bougainville also mentioned the "terrible things" done on the islands by military deserters who had escaped from a ship taking them to Pondichéry. It was reports such as this that were eventually to force the Crown to take direct control of the islands.

Two months after the visit by La Pérouse in the *Seine*, another French ship, the *Étoile*, under the command of Denis de Trobriand, called at Mahé. Sailing from there on a north-north-easterly course Trobriand sighted on 11 August 1773 a small coral island not marked on his chart. He named it Denis island. Going ashore with three officers, he found that the soil was excellent. The trees he considered too spongy for boat construction and although there were no signs of fresh water he concluded that it could be found below the surface.

The visitors were surrounded by thousands of birds, "so little accustomed to the sight of man that we would kill as many as we liked with sticks," Trobriand noted. As no-one seemed to have been there before him he claimed the island for France, burying in the soil a bottle containing the act of possession in the name of De Boynes. Thus was the last island of the main Seychelles group discovered and annexed to France. To verify his claim, Trobriand sailed off in a westerly direction to sight the neighbouring coral island of Isle aux Vaches (today's Bird island), before continuing his voyage to Pondichéry.

On 10 May 1774 Louis XV of France died of smallpox. He was succeeded by his 20-year-old grandson, the ill-fated Louis XVI, and his Austrian queen, Marie-Antoinette. In the reshuffle of the King's Council the elderly Comte de Maurepas was named Chief Minister, while De Boynes was replaced as Minister of Marine by the police chief of Paris, Antoine de Sartine.

When news of the change of government reached the Isle de France Brayer du Barré immediately redirected his quests for favours. Congratulating Maurepas on his appointment, he sent him a chart of Seychelles and reminded him of the efforts he had made to establish a colony there, including the assistance he had given for the development of the King's spice garden. He enthused over the produce of the islands reporting that there was not only timber, tortoises and coconuts, but also pearls, amber and birds' nests. He had planted trees of all types, he told Maurepas, as well as coffee, indigo, cocoa, even dates, and all would be producing within two years.

Of course, he had had disappointments, and had been deceived monstrously by everyone. As he had not been able to enjoy fully the rewards of his labour, he suggested that he might be given fishing rights in the waters surrounding the Seychelles and the Amirante islands. It might be appropriate, too, if he were to be given exclusive use of the islands of Sainte Anne, Cerf, and Silhouette, and first choice of land on Mahé, La Digue, and Curieuse; Praslin, too, where he wanted to set up a sugar-cane factory, for, as he pointed out with justification to Maurepas, it was important that the French should show that they were in possession of that island which interested the English so much.

Brayer du Barré also sought permission to exploit undisturbed any other islands that might be discovered in the vicinity. To conserve the resources of the Seychelles, he urged that the killing of tortoises and turtles be prohibited, as well as the hunting of small animals such as game birds, hares and rabbits.

If Maurepas felt any sympathy for Brayer du Barré, not so Sartine. After perusing the Seychelles correspondence, and noting Brayer du Barré's disclosure that he had received offers from the English to hand the settlement over to them (another of his fantasies, perhaps), Sartine determined that the Norman adventurer should be replaced.

On 23 January 1775 he wrote to Ternay. It was clear, he told the governor-general, that the security of the island was in danger as long as Brayer du Barré controlled the settlement. However, because of the costs involved, he could not agree to Ternay's suggestion that the King take over the islands. "It would appear to me to be much more convenient to give them for a certain number of years to some private individual who would undertake to exploit them at his own cost, without recourse to the government."

Sartine had in fact selected someone, a landowner of the Isle de France, Leroux Kermoseven,³ with whom he had made a tentative arrangement that the latter would have a free hand to exploit the Seychelles for a period of nine years.

Kermoseven was one of the richest men in the Isle de France and — what was all-important to Sartine — was willing to meet the total cost of the enterprise. All that he asked was the loan from the King of a small coasting vessel. He also wanted the authority to appoint his own commandant, who would have a detachment of four soldiers under a corporal.

Inhabitants of Isle de France would be established on the islands, and Kermoseven would ensure that new crops were introduced. At the end of the nine years the islands would be handed over to the Crown, Kermoseven retaining only those establishments he himself had set up. Sartine told Ternay that he supposed Brayer du Barré would not create any difficulties about losing his colony, and that if he did Ternay should intervene.

The scheme fell through. Kermoseven never acquired the Seychelles, nor did the other private individuals who put forward proposals for leasing the islands. One of those, named St Amant, arrived in Paris offering to go himself to Seychelles as governor if he could have sole rights to the islands' produce for a period of 12 years. St Amant's proposal is interesting in that he was opposed to the slave economies of the French Indian Ocean islands. "If one desires to create a strong and progressive colony," he wrote, "it is necessary to introduce as few slaves as possible." He suggested only the temporary loan of about 60 King's slaves to establish the colony, which would then be run exclusively by about ten or 12 families from France, good farmers, strong, sober and industrious. He thought some of those who had returned to France after the loss of Canada at the end of the Seven Years' War would make suitable settlers, but he refused to consider inhabitants from the Isle de France or Bourbon, whom he considered to be indolent, with a passion only for hunting and fishing.

He would require, too, a detachment of soldier-tradesmen, under a sergeant and corporal, and a shipload of provisions twice yearly from the Isle de France. St Amant was also anxious about the spiritual needs of the settlers, which seem to have been ignored despite the founding in December 1771 at Delaunay's settlement of the first Seychelles parish of Saint

Antoine of Padua. He insisted that the government should send a chaplain, chosen by him, to the islands, as well as a skilled surgeon.

St Amant's proposals had much to commend them, but the cost — estimated at about 242,000 livres — was not to Sartine's liking. Nor, with the example of Brayer du Barré in mind, could it be assumed that St Amant had the means to succeed in his venture, for, as a report drawn up for the Minister's consideration warned: "A project undertaken by a man who has nothing usually ends up with nothing." St Amant's proposal was rejected.

It was at about this time that Gillot decided to return to the Isle de France. For more than two and a half years he had been tending the spice garden at Anse Royale and, as he explained in a letter to Sartine, he could no longer accept the unjust treatment he was receiving from the Isle de France administrators. Not only had his slaves been taken away and never replaced, but his frequent letters to Ternay and Maillart Dumesle had been ignored. With no food supply from the Isle de France he had been reduced to a diet of maize and water.

He had also developed "a very dangerous illness", which required immediate medical attention, and therefore, having arranged for someone to look after what was left of the spice garden, he had decided to quit his miserable situation and present his complaints personally to the governor-general. Gillot was suffering from haemorrhoids, which were to become a recurring topic in his later correspondence from the Seychelles, doubtless evoking more amusement than sympathy in the Isle de France.

Gillot left Seychelles on 7 April 1775 in the brigantine *Quartier François*, bound for Bourbon. The voyage normally took 35 days, although a good ship with favourable winds could do it in 20 days or less. The *Quartier François* reached Bourbon after 48 days, disembarking what must have been a rather disgruntled Gillot at Sainte Suzanne on 25 May.

Before continuing his voyage to the Isle de France, Gillot called on the Bourbon commandant, Bellecombe, to whom he explained the medical reasons for his trip. He seems, however, to have said little about the deterioration of the Seychelles colony, and indeed spoke enthusiastically about the spice garden, for Bellecombe found him "so happy with the progress, that he is still very much determined to pursue spice cultivation and follow it through to the success that it appears to promise him". It is not surprising if Bellecombe was sceptical: after almost three years in Seychelles the extent of Gillot's spice garden was one clove bush, five nutmeg trees, four cinnamon bushes and several pepper trees. Bellecombe, who at the time was waiting for first reports on Bourbon's own spice trials, could only hope that his settlers would have more to show for their labours.

Gillot received a cool welcome on his arrival in the Isle de France. The administrators had not yet decided what was to happen to the Jardin du Roi once a successor to Brayer du Barré had been found, and Gillot's sudden appearance was embarrassing. Maillart Dumesle, who had served previously in Cayenne, favoured the American colony for spice growing and wanted to abandon the Seychelles garden. Ternay, however, counselled patience. There had as yet been no satisfactory results from spice cultivation either in the Isle de France, where the young botanist Jean-Nicolas Céré, who had taken charge of Poivre's garden at Pamplemousses,[4] waited for his clove trees to flower, or in Bourbon, where the secretiveness of the settlers made it difficult to know what was happening.

At least, as regards nutmeg and cinnamon, Gillot seemed to be doing marginally better than the others, and with an impatient Versailles offering a prize of two African slaves to the first settler in any of the islands who produced fruit on either a nutmeg or clove bush, it might be difficult to explain why they had abandoned the Seychelles garden. Better, and safer, to send Gillot back to Seychelles to continue with his garden.

Gillot claimed he returned to Seychelles reluctantly. He had already lost 9,000 livres on his first mission, and was down a further 10,000 livres as a result of his second stay in Seychelles. He had managed to get Ternay to agree to pay him the salary of 2,400 livres a year that had been promised by Poivre, and he had been given 12 slaves to tend the garden. Ternay, however, had warned him that the appointment would be for a limited period only, for, as Gillot bitterly noted, "the King could not be expected to pay and feed me for ever". As a final rebuff, the administrators had curtly turned down a request by Gillot for a small loan to purchase a personal slave — "the only means left to me to live and help repay my debts".

Brayer du Barré was also, by now, in a desperate situation. All his trading ventures had failed. The *Thélémaque* had been wrecked off Madagascar, and the crew had made off with most of the cargo.[5] He had been cheated out of the proceeds of another expedition which he had fitted out to trade between the East Indies and Martinique. Every shipload of his that arrived from the Seychelles was sold off at the Isle de France by his creditors.

In Seychelles, his property was at the mercy of people like Hangard, or Captain Glaud, who, aided and abetted by Gillot, had systematically denuded the islands of Thérèse and Conception of all their tortoises. When he complained to the administrators they turned a deaf ear. The government seemed determined to encompass his ruin. When he said he wanted to go to Seychelles to take control of the settlement he was told he would first have to pay back what he owed the government, Sartine having refused to write off his original loan.

In desperation, Brayer du Barré turned to fraud, spreading reports that a silver mine had been discovered there, and he presented Maillart with a piece of metal purporting to have come from the mine. Brayer du Barré's accomplice in this fraud was duly jailed, and Sartine warned Maillart Dumesle that it should "serve to put you on your guard against the tricks which greed can utilise to ensnare your zeal".[6]

Brayer du Barré switched next to flattery, writing to Sartine and enclosing a map of Seychelles showing a newly discovered anchorage on the west coast which he said he had named after the Minister. He suggested that he might go there to make "the most accurate observations" of this anchorage as he never had any confidence in those he employed.

Before receiving a reply Brayer inserted a notice in the Official Gazette announcing his decision to sail for Seychelles.[7] Maillart Dumesle reminded him that the conditions under which he could establish himself there would be the same as those of the original agreement with Poivre. He would not have exclusive rights to the islands' produce and although he might exercise certain police powers he would have to refer wrongdoers to the judgment of the administrators at the Isle de France. His request for the loan of a King's ship for six months was refused and, most important of all, he was ordered to repay the 174,000 livres he owed to the Crown. Brayer du

Barré complained bitterly to Sartine, invoking the goodwill of the Minister and the court to rescue him from his "cruel situation". A copy went to the governor-general, but the administrators were apparently unmoved. At the end of January 1776 an exasperated Brayer du Barré bundled up his unanswered letters to the administrators and sent them off to Sartine. Grenier, returning to France in the *Seine*, undertook to deliver them to the Minister.

Six months later Brayer du Barré was in Seychelles. Had Sartine relented, and given permission for him to leave the Isle de France his debts notwithstanding? There is a gap in the correspondence and one can only conjecture by what means Brayer du Barré reached his settlement.

On 1 August 1776 Maillart Dumesle received a letter from him complaining that the captain of the brig *Tonnant* had loaded a cargo of tortoises and wood in defiance of his express orders and requesting its confiscation when the *Tonnant* arrived at Bourbon. In this he failed, for Captain Boulet claimed that the tortoises had not been taken from the Seychelles at all, but from "an island about three to four leagues wide, which he had discovered north-north-east of the Seychelles".

Who was to say there was no such island, and, as the Bourbon ordonnateur, De Crémont, pointed out in his letter to the governor-general: "It is only the Isle des Trois Frères, otherwise known as Seychelles island, which is mentioned formally in the notice forbidding the taking of tortoises without the express permission of the government." He suggested that in order to prevent the complete destruction of the tortoises the government's ban should cover all islands within a distance of 30 leagues.

Writing to the Minister on 26 January 1777 Crémont reported that Captain Grosleau, of the *St Joseph*, with some 400 tortoises on board, had brought complaints from Seychelles that Brayer du Barré had formed a private army of military deserters and was attempting to exert authority over everyone by force. Crémont concluded: "I think it is essential, Monsieur, to have M. Brayer removed at the soonest."

If Brayer du Barré were removed, who would replace him? For Ternay there had been only one answer, the course he had been advocating since taking office, that the King should take over the colony. Having by now been replaced as governor-general by another naval officer, the Chevalier Guiran Labrillane,[8] Ternay was on his way home, a passenger in the *Belle Poule*, to press his opinion personally on Sartine, an opinion that, within a few months, was given added point by the news that Brayer du Barré had sailed from Seychelles for India on 18 May 1777.

Whether, as suggested by Crémont, the new governor-general had ordered Brayer du Barré's removal or whether he had departed of his own accord we do not know. Either way there must have been a feeling of relief in the Isle de France that the troublesome Brayer du Barré had not only left Seychelles but, if the rumours of his death were true, had departed permanently from the scene.

The confirmation of his death finally came. Brayer du Barré had died at Pondichéry on 3 June 1777, a few days after his arrival in India. As the founder of a colony he had not been a notable success. Chronically in debt and with no head for business, he had finally succumbed to the hostility and duplicity of the Isle de France trading establishment. In the end he and his Seychelles settlement had become an embarrassment to France. Now that he was gone, a fresh start could be made. This time, surely, the business of forming a colony would be done properly, by the King.

6

The King's Officer
1777-1787

> Ils mériteraient un homme dur, sévère, qui
> les punirait rigoureusement.
> *Antoine Nicolas Gillot, 1785*

For 15 years France had been at peace with England. The Treaty of Paris, which had ended the Seven Years' War in 1763, had shorn France of most of her overseas possessions and few doubted that, sooner or later, Versailles would take steps to expunge the humiliation of defeat.

The opportunity came with the rebellion in England's American colonies. French volunteers fought alongside the settlers almost from the start, but France officially stood aside until, in October 1777, with the surrender of the English general Burgoyne at Saratoga, it was clear to Versailles that a rebel victory was a possibility. France signed an alliance with the Americans, and in the following year Spain and Austria also entered the war against England.

The prospect of war had added weight to Ternay's advice to Versailles to send a military commandant and troops to the Seychelles. A small force on Mahé might not prevent the English from landing there, but its presence would dissuade the enemy from seizing the islands before war was declared, and it could also give warning of any enemy moves against the Isle de France. The French knew that the English were actively planning operations in the Indian Ocean as an English officer sent to spy on the Isle de France defences had been trapped by the island authorities into disclosing his country's plan to assemble a strong naval force at the Seychelles for an attack on the Isle de France as soon as war was declared.

Colonel Charles Frederick, of the Bombay army, had arrived at the Isle de France early in April 1777, in a French ship. He said he was on his way back to India, and hoped to find an onward passage to Pondichéry. The authorities were immediately suspicious, for it seemed strange that the English colonel had not found a berth in a ship sailing from the Cape directly to India. They refused to let him land, and invited him instead to cross to Bourbon and to wait there for a ship. At the same time a warning was sent to the Bourbon governor, the Vicomte de Souillac, to keep an eye on the Englishman and on no account allow him to view the island's defences.

During the brief voyage to Bourbon in the store ship *Bricole*, Frederick made friends with the bosun, an Englishman named Kitchin. The outcome of this encounter was a proposal to Kitchin that he should betray his adopted country and supply information to England. Kitchin reported the conversation, and was instructed to respond favourably, at the same time gleaning as much information as he could about the English colonel's intentions. At their subsequent meetings Kitchin claimed to be familiar with the waters around the Seychelles, which made Frederick even more eager to recruit him.

Frederick's reaction to Kitchin's supposed knowledge was understandable, as the islands and shoals lying to the north of Madagascar were still largely unknown to English ships. Grenier's advice of seven years earlier that France should keep secret the results of his pioneering voyages had been heeded, and it was not until the end of the Napoleonic wars in 1815 that the English acquired a full knowledge of the shorter route to India.

Frederick told Kitchin that on his return to Europe he should report to Lord Sandwich[1] in London or, failing that, contact the British ambassador in Paris. He declined to give Kitchin a letter of introduction, saying only that the authorities in England would be informed about him. With that, believing he had recruited a valuable agent, Frederick continued on his way.

It was not until 3 November 1778 — several months after the formal declaration of war with England — that a military detachment sailed for the Seychelles. Under the command of Lieutenant Charles Routier de Romainville, it consisted of a sergeant, corporal, and 13 soldier-tradesmen of the Isle de France Regiment. Also on board the corvette *Hélène* were a surgeon and two naval carpenters to see to the cutting of timber. Romainville's orders were to bring the colony back under control "and to procure for the inhabitants every means of preventing a foreign power forming a settlement there". He was also to supervise the distribution of land to the new settlers it was hoped to send from Bourbon. For the unruly remnants of Brayer du Barré's former colony, Romainville's arrival was a timely reminder that they were still under government authority.[2]

His first task was to construct living quarters for himself and his men, and it was at this *Établissement du Roi,* on the banks of the Rivière Saint Louis, that the present Seychelles capital, Victoria, was formed. The buildings consisted of a commandant's house, with, nearby, a store and, standing on higher ground, a hospital. Further off, nearer the stream, there were barracks, the stone foundations of which formed the prison, and a kitchen. A small wooden bridge across the stream led to the forge, huts for the slaves, and a vegetable garden.

The largest building was the store, measuring some 85 feet by 32 feet. The commandant's house was of modest proportions, about 32 feet by 12 feet. Although described by a later commandant as very small and very unhealthy, it was spacious in comparison to the barrack block which, of similar area, had to accommodate perhaps up to 15 men — or about 25 square feet per man. The buildings, except for the prison and kitchen, were constructed of unchosen timber, without interior panelling, ceilings or window panes. None of the buildings remains today, although some ruined masonry near the present State House (built in 1911) is believed to be the original stone prison.

An important part of Romainville's mission was to halt the settlers' destruction of the islands' natural resources, and to ensure a regular supply of tortoises for the King's ships and hospitals at the Isle de France. Soon after his arrival he sent back the *Hélène* to Port Louis with 600 tortoises, the first of several live cargoes. Romainville noted that the destruction of the tortoises was much worse than had been imagined. They were now so scarce on the main islands that it was necessary to travel to the smaller islands to find them. To restrict the settlers' movements, two small ships, the *Cheval-Marin* and the *Saint Denis*, were sent from the Isle de France to patrol off shore. Romainville also established a park at Isle au Cerf where tortoises could be safely kept until shipped to the Isle de France.

Romainville enjoyed the confidence of the governor-general of Isle de France and Bourbon, Souillac, who had succeeded Guiran Labrillane in the top post on the latter's death in April 1779. Commenting on the progress reports he had received from Romainville, Souillac observed to the Minister that "one could not have achieved a better profit than he did with the means at his disposal, and he employs them with an intelligence that can only confirm the good opinion that we have conceived of his talents".

Unlike Delaunay, with his liking for shell collecting, or Gillot and his desultory efforts to grow spices, Romainville was a man of action. Souillac's appreciation of his zeal for carrying out orders promptly received a blow, however, when it was learned that Romainville had destroyed the spice garden at Anse Royale. It was a misunderstanding, Souillac explained to Versailles. Ships that had appeared off Mahé in May 1780 had been assumed, mistakenly, to be English, and Romainville had immediately ordered the spice garden to be destroyed. It was true, wrote Souillac, that he had advised Romainville to prepare the spice garden for burning if it appeared that it would fall into enemy hands, but he had not meant him to act so precipitously.

"I made known to him my surprise and displeasure," Souillac assured the Minister. "He re-read my letter, confirmed that he had badly misunderstood it and offered me his sincere regrets. But the thing having been done, there was no means of remedying it". To allay the Minister's anger Souillac pointed out that as the Seychelles was so poorly defended, the spice plants would probably have fallen into English hands sooner or later, so perhaps it was just as well they had been destroyed.

Souillac might also have added that the spice garden had hardly been a success, and that in any case the plants were no longer the property of the King, the Jardin du Roi having been handed over three years previously by the Isle de France authorities to the keeper of the garden. It was the latter, Gillot, who had been the real loser when Romainville had ordered his men to uproot and burn the plants.

Since his return to Seychelles at Ternay's suggestion, Gillot had fared no better than before. Lacking any real interest in the Jardin du Roi, he had, before Romainville's arrival, attempted in foolish and impetuous ways to exert authority over his fellow settlers.

We find him forbidding a recent arrival, a former merchant navy captain from Bordeaux, Jean-Baptiste Quienet, from clearing ground at Anse à la Mouche, on Mahé's south-west coast. Gillot claimed he was acting in the interests of the Crown, although in reality he wanted the flat and fertile area for himself. Always ready to condemn the settlers, Gillot, like Brayer du Barré, was more upset about not sharing in their lucrative pursuits than in the destruction of the colony's resources.

In due course word reached the Isle de France that Gillot was neglecting the garden in favour of other interests. As a result his appointment was terminated, although, as a concession, he was allowed to keep the garden and its few spice plants. Deprived of the King's slaves, Gillot struggled on without notable success. In a letter to Céré, dated 16 March 1779, he complained that the clove and nutmeg trees had been planted in the wrong place, adding that it was Poivre who had "thrown him into error". "The clove tree, which does not like too much moisture, is in a humid place," he wrote, "while the nutmeg trees, which need to be in the vicinity of water, are in dry soil."

Céré agreed that the plants seemed to have been badly situated, and advised Gillot to transplant the clove tree to a drier area. He also told him that nutmeg trees of the same age as his were already producing at the Isle de France (the first nutmeg had been ceremoniously picked in December 1778), while more than two years had elapsed since the first clove had been gathered. "One would have thought that the climate of the Seychelles islands would have been more suitable for spice plants, but I see this is not so," Céré commented, adding tartly that the real reason might be Gillot's neglect of the garden.

Unfortunately Gillot was unable to derive any benefit from Céré's advice as shortly afterwards the garden was burned on Romainville's orders. Only the cinnamon escaped total destruction.

A year later Romainville was recalled to the Isle de France. In a letter from Souillac and the new ordonnateur and acting intendant, Étienne-Claude Chevreau, the Minister was informed that Romainville, if he had not been brought back, "would have died from lack of medicine and other treatment for a liver ailment caused by fatigue and overwork". His successor, Berthelot de la Coste, also a lieutenant in the Isle de France Regiment, was as indolent as Romainville had been industrious. His neglectful attitude angered the governor-general, who warned: "We are going to make it clear to him that he must carry out our orders, and bring his attention to bear on all those matters that appear to us to merit it."

One matter of concern to the Isle de France government was the war in India, where French arms had failed to score a decisive victory either on land or at sea. A fleet commanded by Sir Edward Hughes that had been sent by England to reinforce her naval forces in eastern waters was a constant threat to the security of the French islands, and it was with relief that the Isle de France welcomed in October 1781 the arrival of a powerful squadron under Suffren.

On his voyage out Suffren, in his flagship the *Héros* (74), had scored a notable success by preventing the English from seizing the Dutch settlement at the Cape. After leaving the Isle de France he was to keep Admiral Hughes heavily engaged in Indian coastal waters for the rest of the war.

Suffren's arrival in the East probably saved the Seychelles settlement from destruction by the English. In an exchange of letters between East India House in London and the Admiralty in November 1781, the company suggested that a force should be sent to destroy the French settlement. "We consider the importance of these islands to be very great," wrote the company directors. "We apprehend the French may from thence convey a military force to India with much greater facility than from Mauritius; and it must be evident that they can keep up a communication with Madagascar with less difficulty than from their other islands." The Admiralty agreed that the company might have the support of a ship of the line for an attack on the Seychelles, the only proviso being that nothing should be done that would upset the King's European allies.

In the event the Seychelles survived the war unscathed. Hostilities ended formally in January 1783. For France, other than the satisfaction of seeing the independence of the United States of America recognised, there were no great gains. Tobago was returned to her and some ports in Senegal, and there was an extension granted to her fishing rights off Newfoundland. Weighing the balance on the other side was the cost of the war, which ushered in a financial crisis that would within a few years prove fatal to the French Crown.

At the Isle de France the tightening of purse-strings once peace was declared meant that the cost of maintaining a Seychelles garrison was scrutinised anew. The supplementary wages paid to the soldiers when they worked at their trades had already been cut. As a further economy Souillac decided that instead of sending another military commandant to the islands — La Coste, predictably, had been dismissed — the post should be offered to Gillot. So began the most acrimonious governorship in the history of the colony.

Unlike the novelist, who confers on his fictional characters the colour and substance of real people, the historian frequently finds that his documentary sources have left him with a mere outline, a faceless, cardboard figure stubbornly devoid of passion or prejudice, without bowels or bile. It is then that the discovery of a small nugget of personal data like a medical report is doubly welcome, a reminder that the people of the past were indeed flesh and blood, prone to react not only to the unfolding of exterior happenings but also to the promptings of their own physical and psychological disorders. In such mundane matters as an upset stomach or a toothache frequently lies the clue as to why events took the course they did.

If, in Seychelles of the 1780s, one was to seek a single reason for the colony being brought near to rebellion it would undoubtedly be the governor's piles, the "frightful illness" that had prompted Gillot to sail to the Isle de France for treatment and which, nine years later, was still tormenting him.

From an 18th century standpoint "frightful" is an appropriate description not only for the ailment but also for the treatment the surgeon might offer. Gillot admitted that he feared an operation for his haemorrhoids more than the bloodiest battle; he would not have it, even though he felt at times that he would die "in the most painful manner". Manfully he bore his discomfort, and it is hardly surprising that he made life equally uncomfortable for those under his command.

The settlers, who had resented Gillot's superior attitudes from the time of his arrival to establish the spice garden, regarded with dismay his newly acquired power as colony commandant to interfere with their profitable enterprises, especially the sale of tortoises to visiting ships. As for the soldiers of the garrison, they were not inclined to be overly respectful to a militia captain. They recognised in the bluster and bad temper a weak commander, and became slack, scruffy, and unruly.

By January 1785 the garrison had been reduced by death and desertion from 15 to 11 and within a few months the soldiers of the Isle de France Regiment were withdrawn and replaced by ten fusiliers of the Pondichéry Regiment, under a sergeant and corporal. According to Gillot, they were worse than their predecessors.

"Bandits without discipline" was how he described them, while their sergeant was "a seditious rascal". He complained that none had a trade of any use, and that without carpenters, a mason, and locksmith he could not carry out repairs to the King's buildings. The store required re-roofing, the outside stairs were rotten, and the verandah of his office would inevitably collapse and kill someone.

Gillot's main problem, however, was lack of food. Ships arrived infrequently with provisions from the Isle de France — storm and shipwreck took their toll — and those coming from Africa or India were themselves short of supplies and, often enough, badly in need of repair. Gillot found that meeting their needs was something "I cannot honestly avoid, although this results in my starving when alone". Sometimes shipwreck survivors turned up, and months would elapse before they could be found a passage either to the Isle de France or India. It meant extra mouths to feed.

In a report to the administrators, Gillot recounted the ordeal of 27 survivors of a Portuguese ship who reached the

Seychelles after nearly 50 days at sea. The ship, with a crew of 12 Indians, 12 passengers, eight of whom were white, and about 50 black servants and slaves, was sailing from Tranquebar on the Indian coast to Trincomalee when it was hit by a storm off the coast of Ceylon. The vessel, its sails ripped away, was driven remorselessly by the current away from the land. Every piece of cloth on board, sheets, table cloths, even the women's skirts, were sewn together to make a sail, but by then the land had disappeared. Uncertain of his course, the captain steered to the west hoping to sight the coast of India.

Days passed. The little food on board was soon finished. The only water was from the occasional tropical downpour which was carefully collected, but there was never enough. One by one, those on board perished. Hope had long vanished when one morning, just after eight o'clock, a heavy shower of rain cleared, to reveal a high island on the horizon. All that day they made towards it until nightfall, when they lay off the island until morning. Daylight failed to disclose an easy landing place (on what was Silhouette island), so they sailed to a smaller island nearby (Isle du Nord). There, in a rough sea, the ship ran aground and broke up, but the survivors managed to struggle ashore.

For almost a month they stayed on the island, living off turtle meat until, tired of the monotony, they decided that an attempt should be made to reach the large island that lay to the south-east. Lacking tools to make a boat, they put together a crude raft, and on this two Portuguese and three Indian sailors set off.

After several days of paddling, the exhausted men reached the northern end of Sainte Anne. There, after resting at Hangard's settlement, they were taken across to Gillot, who, the same evening, sent two pirogues to bring back their companions from Isle du Nord.

It was two months before Gillot managed to have 20 of the survivors taken to India. The others, a trader, a merchant navy captain, a free black and four slaves, he intended putting on the first ship for the Isle de France. The slaves were particularly fortunate for, valuable as they might be as chattels, slaves were invariably the first to be abandoned to their fate in a shipwreck.

Rochon related a remarkable story of survival by a group of slaves on a small desert island in the Indian Ocean. The slaves were being taken from Madagascar to the Isle de France in July 1761 when the ship, the *Utile*, ran aground on the reef surrounding the Isle du Sable, or Tromelin island, about 50 miles off the eastern coast of Madagascar. An officer, 17 sailors and one black were drowned, but the rest of the crew and passengers and most of the slaves managed to reach the shore. Little more than a spit of sand in the ocean, the island offered the bare means of survival: there was water, if one dug deep enough into the sand, and an abundant supply of turtles. They stayed there for about a month, before the crew and passengers set off in the only available boat for Madagascar.

"Everybody with any human feelings will shudder when they think of these poor blacks left to perish," wrote Rochon. And in fact 15 years were to pass before eight survivors, out of the original 90 slaves, were rescued by the corvette *Dauphine*. All were women — one with a child — living in shelters made from turtle shells, and clothed in bird feathers. They told the *Dauphine's* commander, Tromelin, that the others had died of misery, or been lost in attempts to escape from the island by raft. They had sighted five ships during the 15 years, but none had been able to approach close enough to take them off. The *Dauphine* took them to the Isle de France, where, as some form of compensation for their ordeal, they were henceforth allowed to live freely at the State's expense.

Tromelin island was to remain a hazard for ships sailing to and from Madagascar, and the French would occasionally dispatch a vessel from the Isle de France to check whether any shipwreck survivors were stranded there. A vivid description of the desolate scene that greeted the visiting mariner has been left by Admiral Laplace, who, as captain of the *Favorite*, was sent on such a mission in 1830. Finding, like so many before him, that the reef prohibited any attempt at a landing he sailed round the island firing a gun to attract attention. The only response was from the seabirds that took to the air, screaming indignantly at being disturbed.

"The waves broke with a terrifying crash on the reef which surrounds the island like a shield against the assault of the ocean," wrote Laplace. "Along this barren stretch of sand, from which rebounded in blinding brilliance the full force of a fiery sun, our eyes sought for a trace that would announce the existence of some unfortunate shipwreck victim. On a little mound, which is the highest part of the island, a piece of wood, knocked askew by the wind, formed the shape of a cross. All around we saw the remains of huts and wells, made no doubt by the people from the *Utile*."

Shipwreck was one danger that sailors faced, disease was another, especially for those on slave ships. One, the *Belizair*, had to be helped by Gillot's men to a mooring off Isle au Cerf when it was found that the crew were too weak from scurvy to launch the ship's boats. In one report dated 8 May 1787, Gillot mentioned that the captains of three slavers recently arrived from Africa had died.

During their stay at Mahé, ships usually loaded with about 50 to 200 tortoises, although Gillot complained that most then called at outlying islands to load with more without his permission. "All that these people are after is wealth," he wrote. "They will devastate all the islands, which are already badly ravaged." It was the same warning that Brayer du Barré had given ten years earlier; but now the number of tortoises had dwindled rapidly, thousands having been slaughtered since the first days of the French colony. Gillot mentioned among the guilty captains Boileau, Gilbert, and Drancourt; also Praslin's sole white settler, Pierre Lambert, whom he suspected of secretly supplying ships that called there.

But it was on the head of his former protégé Hangard, that Gillot directed most of his bitterness. Hangard, from his modest beginnings on Sainte Anne, had moved first to Anse Forbans and then, three years later, he had acquired with the agreement of La Coste what Gillot described as "an immense piece of land" along North West Bay (today's Beau Vallon and Bel Ombre). He was now the most powerful settler in the colony, with 90 slaves and, according to Gillot, "an overwhelming insolence".

In one of his frequent letters of complaint to the Isle de France administrators, Gillot urged that Hangard should be forced to give up Sainte Anne. "So long as the Isle Sainte Anne is in the hands of this man, to whom it does not belong, it will be hidden from the vigilance of the commandant and used in secret trading with all ships," he wrote. "Hangard and Quienet go out to them scarcely before they have moored, to spread all sorts of odious calumnies against me, because I never give more than 60 tortoises at the most to any ship."

Gillot had to admit, to his chagrin, that Hangard knew all the best places to find tortoises, while he himself lacked the means of collecting enough for the King's ships and hospitals. His pirogue, which had never been big enough for the job, had been lost on the reef off Cap Ternay. He wanted to replace it with one about 18 feet long, but found that all the large trees suitable for constructing such a craft had been destroyed. He asked the administrators to send him one, preferably from Bourbon. He also asked for his "black rascals" to be exchanged, noting that "of the 11 slaves that I have of the King's, that is six blacks and five negresses, half of them are always on the run". Most troublesome was Domingue, also called Machabée, who had recently slipped away in a small pirogue to Silhouette with another slave and a negress. Gillot had dispatched soldiers to the island to hunt them down, but they had brought back only the woman. "I am going to send them back again with orders to fire on the runaways and to bring back the head of this Domingue, who is a rascal, an arsonist, and I will have it planted on the road to serve as an example to the other blacks," he wrote.

Gillot urged the administrators to send sober, hardworking families to Seychelles — the settlers from Bourbon had still not materialised — and he called for the expulsion of "certain inhabitants". He singled out Hangard and Lambert, the largest landowners, and Quienet as "people without morals, lost in vice and debauch", who were continually trying to displace him. Gillot deplored their unmarried state and the fact that they had mistresses from among their slaves. It is recorded that one of Hangard's daughters, Marie-Jeanne, was married by the chaplain of the ship *Marquis de Castries* (for Seychelles had no resident priest) to Jean-Marie Lebeuze, the son of a sailor living with Quienet. Gillot also made much of Quienet's "scandalous affair" with a freed slave from Madagascar, Volamaëffa. To her Quienet eventually bequeathed most of his possessions, and she was for a while to rival Hangard as one of Seychelles' largest slave-owners.

Gillot had little good to say about anyone; even Savy and D'Offay, whom he had considered as gentlemen — one a former colleague from his days in India — were dismissed in one outburst as "small dogs, content with barking from afar".

For three months now he had been confined to bed, tormented by his haemorrhoids and complaining about having no medicine or the milk that he needed. He had tried in vain to catch some of the 60 or so cows that wandered wild in the island, and in a letter to the Isle de France he asked whether the intendant would make him a gift of two or three cows and a bull. In a later letter he announced that he had decided to return to the Isle de France for treatment once more. "My state of health is so serious and dangerous that whatever repugnance I may have from doing something without the permission of my superiors, I intend taking the first vessel that comes to return so that I can acquire a cure for my ills."

He had almost agreed to be operated on by a visiting ship's surgeon, but decided against it. "Considering the lack of vegetables here for making the nourishing soup I would need — for I am always constipated — the lack of ointment for dressings, the fact that my peace of mind would be disturbed and a fit of anger might kill me, besides the fact that I would be under the care of two surgeons who know nothing about my illness, I did not think it likely I would survive."

The surgeons were Menez, who was waiting for a ship to return to the Isle de France, and his successor, Jacquin. To Gillot all surgeons posted to Seychelles were useless drunkards, but despite his lack of confidence in their professional abilities he seems in the end to have stayed on under their care, for we find him a few months later being attended to by Jacquin.

Accounts of what happened between Gillot and Jacquin early one morning in April 1785 differ in detail. Gillot said he had summoned the doctor to his house for ointment he needed for one of his servants; according to Jacquin he was called to attend to a boil that was aggravating Gillot's haemorrhoids. An argument developed between the two, and Gillot apparently ordered Jacquin to leave. The doctor did not move. "I repeated my command," reported Gillot, "and added that I would give him a taste of my stick if he did not go away. He then spoke familiarly to me, sneering defiance and telling me that if I gave him one blow he would give me a hundred."

Gillot said he then tried to put the doctor out of the room. "He seized me, because he is more powerful than I and accustomed to fight in this way. I got away from him, leaving the stick in his possession, to fetch a sabre which was on the other side of the room. Instead of leaving he followed me, wrested it from my grasp before I could withdraw it from the scabbard, and then beat me for ten minutes, during which time the sergeant and two soldiers arrived."

The soldiers' testimony gave a somewhat different account of the incident. They said that, hearing cries from the commandant's house, they entered to find Gillot "armed with a sabre in one hand and a stick in the other, and the king's surgeon, the *sieur* Jacquin, holding his wrists." It was obvious, they added, that Jacquin was trying to prevent Gillot from hitting him. As they separated the two men, "M. Gillot gave him (the doctor) a blow on the head with his stick".[3] Gillot then ordered them to take Jacquin to the prison, where he was detained for 15 days. After his release Jacquin wrote to the governor-general, seeking to bring an action against Gillot.

Gillot responded with paranoiac bluster. In a letter to Souillac he described Jacquin as "ignorant and lazy, a complete good-for-nothing" to whom he (Gillot) had shown a thousand kindnesses, getting nothing but insolence in return. Not only Jacquin, but Hangard, Quienet and the whole detachment were rogues.

Clearly, relations in Seychelles were deteriorating dangerously, and on 2 July 1785 Chevreau signed an order appointing Pierre-Louis Popequin, who had served previously with Benyowski's Volunteers in Madagascar,[4] as a replacement for Jacquin, who was given permission to return. By then, however, Jacquin was dead, his demise being attributed by Gillot to "debauchery with our inhabitants, soldiers and sailors of the *Castries*". It was the start of a chain of events that would result within a few months in Gillot's disgrace.

On Jacquin's death Gillot had sent soldiers to collect his belongings, but it was some hours before a sentry was posted to guard the dead surgeon's effects. Later, when he made an inventory, Gillot found that 500 piastres Jacquin was known to have were missing.[5] There were several suspects, but Gillot arrested only Jacquin's servant girl, Maugonette. The soldier apothecary who had assisted Jacquin, Renard, had also had an opportunity to steal the piastres but he was, according to Gillot, an honest young man completely above suspicion. Later, the

King's procurator at the Isle de France was to stress the irregularity of Gillot's conduct, for not only had he failed to secure Jacquin's possessions, he had also given coins, ornaments, and surgical instruments belonging to the doctor to Renard. One of the bracelets had been subsequently sold by the apothecary to a daughter of the Savys.

Even then the affair of the missing piastres might have blown over had Gillot not accused Quienet of being an accomplice in the theft. "The negress (Maugonette) ... would not have dared to steal without someone advising her," he wrote to the administrators. "In which case, if the negress is guilty, of which there can be little doubt, then Quienet is guilty of encouraging her and is therefore a rascal ... who should be judicially and publicly punished."

Gillot had allowed his dislike for Quienet to overcome caution and commonsense. His adversary was by this time at the Isle de France, where he had been sent by Gillot after a violent quarrel with his mistress Vola-maëffa, and on hearing of the accusation against him was ready to counter with a damning piece of evidence against Gillot. He told the administrators of an IOU for 400 piastres that he (Quienet) owed to Jacquin which had been torn up in front of witnesses by Gillot. Gillot, who told Quienet he was making him a present of it, had then tried to get him to agree to overlook the other items that had been taken from Jacquin's possessions. This he had refused to do. Quienet also complained to the administrators that since his departure from Seychelles Gillot, who had latterly allowed him to cultivate land at Anse à la Mouche, had seized it for himself and put his own slaves to work on it.

Quienet's statement confirmed the administrators' opinion of Gillot that he was dishonest as well as incompetent, and the sooner he was removed from command the better. There were external circumstances, too, that decided Souillac to intervene in the Seychelles administration. The English, who had formed a settlement on Diego Garcia, were thought to be planning the seizure of other islands. If this was the case it was imperative that the Seychelles should be made secure.

The problem of defending Mahé island had never been properly investigated, and if an officer was sent to assess the military needs of the colony he could, at the same time, investigate Gillot's conduct and the whole question of the Seychelles administration. Souillac appointed to this task an engineer who had been in charge of roads construction in the Isle de France, Jean-Baptiste de Malavois, who would be accompanied to the Seychelles by a surveyor, Bataille, to help in the allocation of land to new settlers and to undertake repairs of government buildings.

The part of Malavois's mission that concerned Gillot was contained in separate secret instructions, but Gillot, guessing that he was about to be the subject of an inquiry, prepared to resign. He pleaded with Souillac to spare him a public humiliation. It was true, he told the governor-general, that, "being very ill and preoccupied", he had agreed that Quienet should work the land at Anse à la Mouche, but he had immediately regretted it and withdrawn his consent. Pointing out that Quienet knew nothing about agriculture, he requested Souillac to allocate the land to him so that he could settle there, as a private citizen, with his wife and child. He urged the governor-general to deny Hangard and Quienet the pleasure of seeing him not only resigning as commandant but being forced to relinquish the land at Anse à la Mouche.

The administrators' reply gave Gillot little comfort. It described as a grave mistake Gillot's failure to make an inventory of all Jacquin's possessions after his death, and said that it was now improbable that Maugonette could be convicted of any offence. "What is worse, and what compromises you personally — if it is true, as rumoured here — is that you gave to the *sieur* Quienet, or rather tore up in his presence, a note of the 400 piastres he owed to Jacquin." The letter urged Gillot "to advise us of the truth of this matter", and warned him that a mission was to be sent to Seychelles to inquire into the theft of the surgeon's belongings.

On the question of the land at Anse à la Mouche, the administrators were equally critical. "We are unable to hide from you our regret that you should wish to take over that particular piece of land, after having allowed the *sieur* Quienet to work there, as he has assured us was the case ... It is this abuse of authority that alienates the people and causes them to rebel."

They concluded with a severe reprimand: "There exists within you a heatedness, not to say a passion, that goes to prove all that has been said and written to us about your conduct ... It is not surprising that such unbecoming conduct by a person in your position has embittered the feelings of the Seychelles inhabitants, and we greatly fear that you may have occasion to regret the decision you have taken to remain amongst them."

Confronted with the destruction of the promissory note, Gillot confessed. "But," he added plaintively, "why did Quienet, who saw better than I the mistake I was making, accept this money? Should he not have refused it, and put me back on the path of rightness from which he saw I was straying." And he offered to pay the 400 piastres "if this restoration is sufficient to extinguish the bad light in which I find myself". As for the land at Anse à la Mouche, he did not really want it. He was going to return to the Isle de France and the administrators could give the land to Quienet. He was indeed sorry he had accused Quienet of theft, he had only explained himself badly, for he believed that Quienet was innocent.

Malavois and Bataille arrived in the corvette *Éclair* on 27 November 1786; at about the same time a new detachment of troops arrived in the ship *Reine*. Despite his stated intention to go back with the *Éclair*, Gillot stayed on, uneasily, as commandant, ingratiating himself with Malavois as the latter began his inquiries.

"Our object in not to judge or condemn anyone," the administrators had told Malavois in the secret instructions, "but to inform ourselves so that we are able, in the proposals for the administration of the Seychelles island we intend to introduce, to take every measure to avoid the reappearance of these troubles." They directed Malavois to investigate not only claims against Gillot, but also to assure himself that the settlers' resentment was not prompted simply by their annoyance at being prevented from behaving in a manner prejudicial to the good of the colony. As regards the Jacquin affair, no legal action was contemplated — the commission of inquiry was being deferred "until a more favourable time" — although Malavois was asked to find out, as quietly as possible, whether or not Gillot was guilty of the theft of the missing piastres.

The final reference to Gillot appears in a letter dated 30 July 1787 to Malavois from Souillac and Chevreau's successor as intendant, Motais de Narbonne. In it they informed Malavois that "the case of M. Gillot is of little concern here. We are sending a successor for him, and we will have his antagonist, the *sieur* Quienet, sent back to Seychelles. In this way, we think that there will be nothing more heard of this affair."

Gillot, we may assume, returned to the Isle de France. His 16 years in Seychelles, first as creator of the spice garden at Anse Royale and then as commandant for the King, had been a dismal failure. He had at times been grossly neglected by the Isle de France government, although this hardly excuses his inept and erratic administration. He had presided over a community in which every base motive was indulged with little restraint. In the end it was, as he had feared, the Hangards, Quienets, and Lamberts who had triumphed.

7

Revolutionary Interlude
1787-1793

> Nous ne sacrifierons aux colons ni la Nation,
> ni les colonies, ni l'humanité entière.
> *Robespierre, 1791*

Malavois arrived in Seychelles armed with a list of regulations drawn up by the governor-general to tighten control over the colony. These had been set out on a large placard, which Malavois gave to Gillot with instructions that he should post it prominently at the Établissement so that everyone would be aware of the new laws.

Souillac's provisional regulations — there were altogether 14 articles, comprising what was in effect a draft constitution for the Seychelles — were read by the settlers with dismay. Clearly, their freebooting life was over. Almost all their profitable activities were banned or required the commandant's permission, which, it was obvious, would not be readily given. Not only was hunting of tortoises and turtles prohibited, but also the collection of coconuts and firewood.

The strict controls extended to visiting ships. There was to be no more happy bartering of tortoises for a bottle of brandy from the ship's store. From now on the settlers must forget their lazy, wasteful ways and, in the words of the Isle de France administrators, "occupy themselves exclusively with the cultivation of the land given to them".

Inhabitants such as Hangard, who held large tracts of land in different parts of the island, would have to settle on one, and surrender the rest. Even the land they owned would not be theirs to sell freely. Every transfer required in future the approval of the Isle de France administrators, and if a settler left Seychelles without finding an approved purchaser his land would be forfeited to the Crown. It was also decreed that the French flag would fly on Praslin at all times, guarded by a corporal's detachment, which meant that there would be difficulties in going there to load a boat with coco de mer nuts.

All the natural resources of the islands were henceforth a Crown monopoly, with the inhabitants confined to agricultural pursuits, growing enough food for themselves and a surplus for the King's troops and slaves. Settlers unwilling to accept these conditions would have to quit the Seychelles.

Malavois had also been instructed to recommend reforms in the colony's administration and defence, using the provisional regulations as guide lines. Never one to shirk his responsibilities, he produced the most comprehensive and detailed survey of the islands made during the period of French rule.

Among his major recommendations, Malavois urged the administrators not to send too many Bourbon inhabitants all at once to Seychelles. He pointed out that although life in Bourbon was frugal the hardships were even greater in Seychelles, where bare survival was about all one could expect. There were few, if any, provisions from Europe, and Seychelles settlers had to make their wine from sugar-cane, and cook their food with turtle or fish oil.

Malavois attributed the settlers' lack of interest in agriculture to the absence of proper land titles. Some only had the verbal authority of the commandant, with the result that "they do not regard themselves other than as strangers in the colony". He believed that with secure titles the settlers would stop ruining the soil by moving away to another area as soon as the land appeared exhausted and, instead, "take the necessary measures to maintain fertility and even improve it".

He noted that Mahé was well watered by streams, although none was big enough to justify the inhabitants' description of them as rivers. The soil, although variable in depth, was generally only a thin cover and consequently needed careful attention. It was of poorer quality in the north of the island, which, unfortunately, was the area favoured by the settlers because of easier access to the port. Overall, Malavois noted that there were "few places in the world where vegetation grows so rapidly" as in Seychelles. Fruit and vegetables that had been imported from the Isle de France, such as bananas, pineapples, and sugar-cane, grew well, although the settlers showed little interest in their cultivation. Cinnamon which had escaped the burning of the spice garden was flourishing. Other imported plants doing well were tobacco and cotton. Malavois correctly forecast that the latter would one day provide a small branch of commerce for the island.

Hangard was the only settler who grew crops in substantial quantity; as a result the detachment, the King's slaves and other inhabitants were dependent on him for food. Malavois, like others before him, remarked that the weather was cooler than one might expect so near the equator, and that the air was healthy. Despite the danger of infection from visiting slave ships "outside ailments never seem to spread".

He drew up detailed proposals on how the colony might be most effectively defended, estimating that it would cost about one million livres, excluding the necessary artillery, to do the job properly. His plan involved fortifying Sainte Anne, Cerf, Longue, and the other islands ringing the harbour, as well as constructing redoubts on the reef fringing the western entrance to the anchorage. These emplacements, bristling with cannon, would be manned by 1,000 white and Indian troops. As it would be difficult to defend Praslin successfully he suggested that only a small detachment should be stationed there, to warn Mahé of an approaching enemy. He also proposed lookouts on Silhouette, and similar outposts on Frégate and Récif islands to cover the eastern approaches. The other islands, he believed, "do not merit serious consideration, for the greatest harm an enemy could do would be to burn the forests and take away the tortoises".

Summing up, Malavois recognised the dilemma that the islands posed for France, echoing Ternay's view that it was unfortunate the Seychelles existed at all. From an agricultural or commercial aspect the colony was unlikely to become "very interesting", but Mahé's superb anchorage and its convenience as a recuperative stop-over for slave ships meant that there was "a very delicate balance in deciding whether to maintain or abandon this colony". France would not wish to see it fall to another; at the same time, could she afford to hold on to it?

Assuming the government could not afford the cost of defending the islands — which was the case — Malavois advised the withdrawal of the detachment of French soldiers, replacing them with a similar number of sepoys. White troops, he pointed out, easily lost their discipline when posted to an isolated colony, and Indian soldiers would in any case be more suitable in enforcing the regulations concerning wood, coconuts, tortoises, and in hunting down runaway slaves. "One would not need to trouble about subsistence for this detachment," he added, "and during a war they would not be essential for the defence of the Isle de France."

Souillac and Motais de Narbonne were well pleased with Malavois's report — illuminating, well compiled, and worthy of their attention" was how they described it — and on 30 July 1787 most of his recommendations, together with the provisional decrees, modified in certain instances but generally retaining, even elaborating, the original restrictions, were promulgated in a document of 30 separate articles.

This constitution, if one could call it that, was obviously not expected to have a long life. Its provisions were aimed at exploiting, exclusively for the government's benefit, the natural resources of the islands until they would inevitably be lost to the English in the next war. Any attempt at defending the islands was ruled out, and, as Malavois had advised, the detachment of the Pondichéry Regiment was to be immediately withdrawn and replaced by sepoys.

"Whatever one did to defend Seychelles would be a complete waste," noted Souillac's successor, Entrecasteaux.[1] "We must confine ourselves to profiting from the natural products of this archipelago and the advantages that these islands offer to our navigators."

One of the principal tasks given to Malavois had been to recommend how best to ensure adequate supplies of tortoises and turtles for the navy and the King's hospitals. Government attempts to curb private trading had been totally ineffective and the numbers of these creatures, even on the outlying islands, continued to drop alarmingly. Malavois estimated that during the four years of Gillot's command (1783-87), more than 13,000 had been taken, one captain, St Pé of the *Bons Amis*, having shipped more than 4,000 in two voyages.

Malavois's plan was to remove as many of the tortoises as

possible from the islands and collect them in two parks, one at Sainte Anne, the other at Cerf island, the site that had been chosen by Romainville for a park. Ships would be allowed to load only at these points, at a fixed price. Any cargo loaded elsewhere would be subject to confiscation. A particularly bitter blow for the Seychelles inhabitants was the decision that they, too, should buy tortoises for consumption at the parks at the same price as visiting ships, that is, six sols a pound.

Other major prohibitions contained in the provisional regulations — the collection of coconuts and wood — were confirmed. However, coconuts that fell on Crown land adjacent to a settler's habitation could be used by him, but this right was for a limited period only, and the settlers were advised to plant their own palms. They were also required to retain a quarter of their land for wood. Anyone found cutting firewood elsewhere, or causing other damage, would be liable to be shipped back to the Isle de France.

Malavois's proposal that land grants on Mahé should be of 112 acres was confirmed, although the administrators modified their original proposal by allowing those who already had more than this to retain it. No land, however, was to be granted "in the islands of the archipelago adjacent to that of Seychelles, which are to be set aside solely for the conservation and multiplication of tortoises and other natural produce". Land would be given only to those of good morals and reputation, married, natives as far as possible of the Isle de France and Bourbon or Seychelles, children of settlers, or men useful to agriculture and navigation.

The regulations required the inhabitants to supply a fixed amount of rice and maize to the King's store, in addition to feeding themselves and their slaves. Although the Seychelles climate had been proved ideal for spice cultivation, there was no mention of spices in the regulations. The administrators had, in fact, decided that the islands were too exposed to enemy attack and that there should be no repetition of Romainville's destruction of the Jardin du Roi. Poivre's dreams for the colony were — or so it was intended — finally shelved. Spice growing would be confined in future to the Isle de France and Bourbon, where, on the latter island especially, good progress with spices was being made.

Slave ships bound for Isle de France or on their way to the

Americas — about 30 were now calling each year at the Seychelles — were forbidden to use any island for reviving their human cargoes except those designated for the purpose by the commandant. Any ship in quarantine had to anchor off the small appendage to Cerf island known as Isle Cachée.

King's ships were to be provisioned in future only at Sainte Anne. This was intended to discourage the drunken parties that took place ashore not only between sailors and settlers but also frequently with slaves, and all the rowdiness that inevitably followed. "By means of this disposition, the crews will no longer be able to visit all parts of the island of Seychelles, nor distract the inhabitants from their labour by too frequent visits," explained the regulations. Exemplary punishment was to be meted out to any ship's captain who caused or allowed any damage to be done on the islands, this to include cutting of firewood. Conviction on such a charge could mean a sentence of three years' service as a sailor in a King's ship. If the culprit was a King's officer his actions were to be reported to the administrators.

"We require the commandant of the Isle Seychelles to carry out the execution of these articles with severity," the regulations warned, "and to render an account to us of any infractions."

It was, of course, one thing to make rules; another to enforce them. Entrecasteaux believed that Malavois was the man for the task of instilling some discipline in the Seychellois. He was efficient, upright in behaviour, a devoted family man and firm believer in authority. He had, in addition, assisted in the shaping of the regulations. Malavois was by now back in the Isle de France, and due to take up an appointment in Bourbon. Instead, towards the end of 1788, accompanied by his wife and children, he returned to Mahé to assume command from Gillot's successor, Caradec.[2]

Malavois did his best to enforce the new regulations and not surprisingly was soon in conflict with the settlers, as well as with visiting ships. He could not possibly keep watch on every bay where a ship might put in to take or barter for tortoises, and his requests to the Isle de France for more boats and other assistance to stamp out illegal trading were blandly turned down. Poor Malavois could not even obtain an advance of salary. The new governor-general, Conway,[3] who had replaced

Entrecasteaux in November 1789, told him: "It is only with difficulty, considering the small amount of piastres that remain, for us to meet the expenses of this year."

Whenever Malavois was able to catch a settler or ship breaking the regulations he dealt with them severely, so much so that instructions were soon coming from the Isle de France advising him to use less authority and more persuasion with wrongdoers. He was told to refrain from taking direct action against ships, and simply to send in a report of the captains' misdemeanours. As for the settlers, Malavois was reminded that he was dependent on them for food and that if he upset them he might find himself with insufficient provisions for his troops, slaves, and visiting ships. For the moment, at least, he would be wise to tread warily.

The administrators' concern at a possible outbreak of lawlessness may have been sharpened by news coming from France, where traditional authority was increasingly under pressure. Already the Estates-General, the supreme advisory body in the kingdom that had not met for almost 200 years, had been summoned by the King to Versailles to discuss the country's financial crisis. It was not long until this gathering of notables, having transferred its meetings to Paris and proclaimed itself a sovereign assembly, issued its stirring declaration on the right of every Frenchman to freedom and equality.

Within a year the King was a virtual prisoner of the people, his condition symbolised by the new Revolutionary cockade of Bourbon white sandwiched between the red and blue of Paris. The cockade travelled to France's overseas colonies where, although adopted at first as a piece of fashionable frivolity, it helped to communicate the spirit of reform that was sweeping France.

In the Isle de France posters appeared calling for citizens to meet in the church of Port Louis on 4 February 1790 to discuss the setting up of an assembly similar to that in Paris. When the governor-general attempted to ban the meeting disorders broke out. Reluctantly Conway gave way, a concession to popular feeling that was to become the standard response of colonial governors throughout the Revolutionary period. His action was officially endorsed by news from France that the National Assembly had decreed on 8 March that each colony should express its opinion on the constitution it should adopt, under its own elected assembly. The same month the National Assembly set up a committee to draft a model constitution which each colonial assembly could modify to suit its own particular circumstances. Colonial representation in Paris had already been assured by a decree for the election of overseas deputies to the National Assembly, two seats having been allocated to the Isle de France and Bourbon.

The wind of change that had stirred emotions in the Isle de France had a similar impact in Seychelles. But mixed with the settlers' hopes and expectations were tremors of alarm. Fear of a slave uprising, always at the back of a settler's thoughts, had assumed a more immediate dimension with talk of the Rights of Man, of freedom and equality without distinction of colour. There was no place for such ideas in a community based on slave labour, yet from what one heard of the Isle de France Assembly it seemed there were some there prepared, for the sake of principle, to destroy the economic and social fabric of the colony.

It was with such thoughts that the Seychelles settlers gathered at the commandant's house on Saturday morning, 19 June 1790. Malavois had called the meeting three days previously, for it took time for messengers to reach the more distant settlers and for them to make the journey to the Établissement by pirogue. Almost all had turned up for what was obviously to be an important meeting. Quienet and Hangard were there; also D'Offay, Lebeuze, and Lambert, the latter, now 72, having abandoned his home on Praslin to live on the main island.

Others were Audibert and Morel Duboil, and three newcomers to the Seychelles: Nageon de l'Étang, who held the post of keeper of the King's store; the colony's surgeon, Conan; and their father-in-law, Jorre de St Jorre. Two absentees, Savy and Drancourt, were represented by Quienet and D'Offay.

Malavois informed the settlers that he had called them together to hear the contents of a letter addressed to them by the Isle de France Assembly, which had been delivered to him by Captain Boileau of the *Achille*. Having satisfied everyone that the seal on the letter was intact, be insisted on withdrawing while the letter was read and discussed. Nageon, who had assumed the chair, then read the letter. First, there was an extract of an Assembly decree under which the Isle de France deputy to the National Assembly in Paris would represent the interests of the Seychelles. To this there was ready acceptance by the settlers, followed by immediate protests over the next proposal, that the Seychelles should become an integral part of the Isle de France.

Completely against the mood of the meeting Nageon had suggested that this proposal be accepted, but in the ensuing uproar hurriedly vacated the chair, explaining that his stay in Seychelles had been too brief for him to take the lead in discussing such important matters. The settlers then insisted that Malavois be recalled. The commandant came back, and, although he refused to resume the chair, agreed to give his opinion on the Assembly's letter. Removed from its wrapping of polite phrases, his advice was to reject the proposed merger with the Isle de France and to declare Seychelles an independent colony. It was a startling proposition. Yet Malavois was not speaking hastily. One suspects that he knew well beforehand what the sealed letter from the Isle de France Assembly contained and had carefully thought out what the response should be.

Disillusioned by the lack of support he had had from his superiors, he was determined to resign as commandant. Yet he had no wish to return to the Isle de France, where all traditional authority seemed to be crumbling, and had decided to stay on in Seychelles as a private citizen. It was essential, therefore, that these islands should not be contaminated by any libertarian ideas. He knew that the Seychelles settlers, disgruntled by Souillac's strict regulations, would readily support any move to free themselves from the Isle de France's authority. The letter from that island's Assembly had given him the opportunity to put forward a proposal for independence without having to compromise himself too openly.

"The decree which the most honourable Assembly ... is proposing to us has been drawn up in extremely flattering terms for you," he told the settlers, "and you would not hesitate to adopt it if you did not feel that, by such an unlimited delegation of power, certain inconveniences ... could arise from this excess of confidence."

One did not have far to look for inconveniences. Referring to the regulations which he himself had tried to enforce, and which were the sole constitutional instrument for the administration of the Seychelles, Malavois asked: "Would you consider, Messieurs, to continue under such a regime?". Was it not time, he suggested, for Seychelles to have a new constitution adapted to its own special needs. He did not need to remind his listeners that under the present law, land in Seychelles could be allocated to any inhabitant from the Isle de France or Bourbon, and he hinted that under the new revolutionary government Seychelles might "be obliged by your superior colony to receive from her as fellow citizens those who would be a charge on you". Insisting that he was speaking to them not as commandant but "as father of a large family whom I wish to settle in this colony", Malavois struck a responsive chord by referring to the settlers' wish to see their progeny inherit the land, protected from an influx of outsiders who would "without doubt appear to you as a threat against your liberty".

Despite the "pure intentions" of the Isle de France, the people there had only vague notions, often erroneous, about the Seychelles, which they sometimes regarded as a convenient place of quarantine for ships or as a dumping ground for undesirables. It would be safer, Malavois suggested, to have the colony's problems tackled "by educated men of the locality, directly interested in the welfare of this island".

This was what the settlers wanted to hear. After Malavois had again withdrawn, they formally declared themselves a General Assembly, with Quienet as president and Nageon and St Jorre as secretaries. The following Saturday, they assembled again and confirmed their status as "a body apart and absolutely separate from the general and other assemblies of other French colonies, to which they remained united by ties of fraternity — which should exist between all good citizens — and by the general wish to restore liberty in the French empire under the best of Kings".

Two decrees were then approved. One requested the Isle de France administrators to restore the right to hunt for tortoises and turtles; the other, which had been prompted by the settlers' difficulty in gathering every Saturday morning, gave Quienet, Nageon, and St Jorre full powers to act on behalf of the Assembly. During the next two days, this committee of three — with, one would imagine, the counsel of Malavois — got to work drawing up amendments to Souillac's regulations.

It was decided that not only were the main restrictions to be removed, those concerning tortoises, coconuts and the sale of land, but also that in future no land grants should be made without the concurrence of a majority of the settlers, and that the islands of Praslin, Silhouette, Frégate, and the Isle du Nord should, in any case, be set aside specifically for settlement by children of the present inhabitants. No more free blacks were to be sent to Seychelles, and land allocated to a black family of Bourbon called Ramalinga, who had not yet taken up residence in Seychelles, should be redistributed.

Instead of having to hand over their surplus crops to the King's store, the inhabitants would in future give only an amount sufficient to feed the troops and the King's slaves, plus one-tenth for wastage. The rest they might sell as they wished. Visiting ships would have to pay for any tortoises or turtles they took.

Anxious that the Seychelles should share in the growing success of spice cultivation in the Mascarenes, the settlers asked for clove, cinnamon, nutmeg, and cocoa seeds for the restoration of the Jardin du Roi. They also asked the administrators to supply them with several decked boats, and to send a parish priest to cater for their spiritual needs.

A covering letter to the Isle de France Assembly explained why the Assembly's offer to assume responsibility for the Seychelles had to be declined. "You will appreciate the motives that oblige us to consider our liberty a unique gift which cannot be confided to anyone but the Mother Country," it said. The Isle de France deputies were left in no doubt that nature's gifts to the Seychelles, its tortoises and turtles, were not common property to "be shared by rapacious speculators whose activities would soon lead to their destruction". The right to exploit the natural resources of the Seychelles belonged solely to the Seychelles settlers. Thus was the banner of liberty unfurled.

Continuing turmoil in the Isle de France meant that little immediate heed was paid to the smaller colony's bid for freedom. Conway, in constant conflict with the Isle de France Assembly, was forced to resign as governor-general a month after the Seychelles declaration. The policy of his successor, Charpentier de Cossigny,[4] who had previously been governor of Bourbon, was to avoid confrontation with the new revolutionary assemblies, who were introducing sweeping administrative reforms similar to those introduced by the government in Paris.

Municipal councils were being set up, with local responsibility for finance, police and the courts. In Seychelles the Assembly did likewise, electing in November of that year a five-man committee with full municipal powers. Because of the small number of settlers and the difficulty for some to travel to the Établissement, the Assembly met rarely, and now that Malavois had resigned as commandant effective power was exercised by the municipal committee, which could delegate day-to-day administration of the colony to one of its members. The committee was charged with drawing up a formal constitution. Another development was the election of a justice of the peace — a new office created by the Revolution — to deal with domestic and civil cases. The justice, sitting with assessors, was also responsible for charity and the affairs of the poor.

The Assembly retained supreme judicial power, decreeing that its judgments were subject only to the authority of the King. Any previous law relating to the Seychelles that was incompatible with its decrees was declared void.

It was during this brief period of self-assertion that Seychelles first laid claim to all the islands in the western Indian Ocean which today form the territory of the Seychelles republic. The yardstick adopted covered all "islands which are dependencies of this archipelago and which are more than 300 leagues from any other French colony" — a claim that incorporated the Amirante islands and the isolated, southerly islands of Platte and Coëtivy. This claim was to be rejected before long by the Isle de France government.

By April 1791 the Isle de France had approved its own constitution. Under it the governor had the power of veto over the Colonial Assembly, but it was a right Cossigny was reluctant to invoke. When confronted by the revolutionary fervour of the deputies he was conciliatory, aiming above all to maintain the semblance, if only that, of the Crown's authority.

Three months after the Isle de France constitution came into force an opportunity arose for Cossigny to bring

Seychelles back under formal control of the King and the Revolutionary government in France. Two officials, Louis Yvon, the Isle de France procurator-general, and Gautier, commander of the Pondichéry Regiment, had been appointed civil commissioners at Chandernagore, the French settlement in Bengal. Before they sailed for India Cossigny instructed them to call at Seychelles to raise the Tricolour there and, if they saw fit, give formal approval to the various measures that had been adopted by the Seychelles Assembly. He told them their mission was to "induce the inhabitants to live peacefully" until news of their future arrived from Europe. While he had "complete confidence in their sagacity and prudence", he advised the commissioners to remain as short a time as possible in Seychelles.

The two commissioners arrived at Mahé on Saturday, 30 July, in the corvette *Minerve*, which put in at North West Bay, this being the more sheltered anchorage during the south-east monsoon. A message was sent ashore informing Nageon and the Seychelles Assembly — if it existed and was in session — of their arrival. "We will land as soon as convenient to you," wrote Yvon and Gautier. "We will give you then a more ample knowledge of our instructions as far as they concern this colony, and we will concert with you, without delay, all means to proceed with their execution."

The Assembly could not be convened until the Monday, but Nageon invited the commissioners to stay at his house at the Établissement, where it was decided that the Tricolour would be raised with due ceremony on Monday morning. There was only one problem: the *Minerve*, out of sight in North West Bay, would be unable to salute the flag at the precise moment of its unfurling.

Shortly after dawn on Monday, a junior officer from the *Minerve* announced to Nageon and the waiting crowd at the Établissement that the flag was about to arrive. A small procession, composed of an armed detachment and a deputation of two Seychelles inhabitants sent to North West Bay the previous day, escorted the flag as it was borne over the mountain pass and down into the town. There, before handing it over, the *Minerve's* captain, Lieutenant Charles Magon, made a short speech in which he congratulated the inhabitants on their patriotism and peacefulness. Among those present were the commanders and officers of three merchant ships in the harbour, the *Licorne*, *Nautille*, and *Persan*. Then, the great moment having arrived, to shouts of *Vive la Nation, la Loi et le Roi*, and a discharge of cannon and muskets, the Tricolour of France was raised.

Later, the commissioners adjourned to the *Salle du Gouvernement* to discuss with members of the Assembly the future of the colony. In their report on this meeting, Yvon and Gautier expressed satisfaction at the apparent readiness of the inhabitants to amend any of their decrees that might be unconstitutional – which Yvon and Gautier considered was the case – but the end result was that everything remained as it had been. The settlers seem even to have stuck to their ban on Coloured immigrants, saying "they would return any that were sent by the Isle de France". Invoking the "invincible law of necessity", the compliant commissioners told Cossigny that they were sure the settlers would, in due course, iron out anything that was unconstitutional.

Much of the commissioners' time appears to have been spent discussing the personal problems of Nageon and the colony's surgeon, Conan. The commissioners urged Cossigny to give Nageon an increase on his salary of 1,200 livres, pointing out that he was "an honest man with a large family" and that, as acting commandant, he found himself forced to provide hospitality to all who arrived on the island. They told Cossigny that to offset the cost of their own brief stay in Seychelles they had given Nageon 100 piastres, a quantity of wine and some flour borrowed from the ship. As for Conan, they urged that his salary of 600 livres a year be raised. He, too, had a large family and, having to visit ships in quarantine, his life was frequently in danger. If it were not possible to make up his salary to 1,500 livres, they suggested he should receive additional rations of wine, oil, soap, and candles, "objects which it is impossible to procure here whatever the price might be".

The commissioners also backed a request by Nageon for the award of the Cross of St Louis. He was in bad health, they said, and there was a danger of disorders in Seychelles if he should die. They urged Cossigny to appoint a successor as commandant as soon as possible.

In a separate letter to the intendant, André Dupuy (whose

post under the Revolutionary administration was now reduced to that of financial controller),[5] Yvon and Gautier proposed that he should take a sympathetic view of "this fledgling colony, much more interesting than had previously been thought". Its tranquillity, they said, spoke much in its favour and made it deserving of assistance.

Although the Seychelles decrees had been endorsed by Yvon and Gautier there could be no final approval of constitutional changes in the colony until France had decided on its own form of government. This, a constitutional monarchy, was formally brought into being in September 1791, when the King — a discredited figure since his abortive flight to Varennes — put his signature to the National Constitution. For a brief moment, the newly elected Assembly in Paris could turn its attention to the task of bringing the colonies into line with the new political structure at home.

Civil commissioners were dispatched to correct on the spot any irregularities in the implementation of the National Assembly's wishes. Four commissioners who had been assigned to the colonies east of the Cape of Good Hope arrived at the Isle de France in June 1792, accompanied by the newly appointed governor-general, the Comte de Malartic. Before travelling on to their ultimate destinations, they drew up a series of regulations for their respective colonies. Seychelles was not overlooked in this exercise, and altogether 112 decrees for its administration were approved by the commissioners. Although, technically, these were open to discussion and endorsement by the Seychelles assembly, the commissioners considered that Seychelles was too small and insignificant to be endowed with the type of government suitable for other, larger colonies.

One commissioner, a naval administrator from Lyon named Daniel Lescallier,[6] explained: "One has attempted in this plan to reconcile the sacred principles of the Constitution and the rights of the citizen with the necessity of diverting only very few persons to the internal administration and exercise of justice in a colony which is still nascent, very lightly populated, and where one cannot, without harming its progress, establish a system of taxation for paying salaries to a large number of public functionaries."

In effect, full executive power was to reside in the hands of the commandant — now formally designated civil agent and commandant. It would be his duty not only to "maintain with all his power the parts of the French Constitution that have been adopted by the Seychelles for its internal government", but also to apply or refuse, according to his conscience, the effect of any decree passed by the Seychelles Assembly.

Although the Assembly was declared completely independent of the Isle de France most of its power was removed by the regulation that restricted its meetings to one a year. Almost all the earlier pretensions were rejected. The territory of Seychelles was confined to the main island groups of Mahé, Praslin, Silhouette, and Frégate, while the assembly's curb on immigrants, particularly free Coloureds, was summarily dismissed. By implication, the settlers' demands to full control of the islands' resources were denied, and they were invited to sell their food crops to the government and take steps to improve the quality of their produce.

The commissioners invited all citizens — a status which included Coloureds and Blacks if they were children of legitimate marriage between free parents — to live in harmony, peace, and brotherly union and "to cease all acts or pretexts for reciprocal hate and disagreement". Those who had erred in their interpretation of the aims of the Revolution or who had attempted to divert it from its rightful course were assured of amnesty.

Although the commissioners had not the time nor, perhaps, the inclination to see personally to the introduction of their regulations, it was decided that Lescallier, who was due to sail to Pondichéry, should accompany the new Seychelles commandant, a captain in the Pondichéry Regiment named Charles Joseph Enouf, to Mahé and, by his brief appearance, lend authority to the new regulations.

Unfortunately for the commissioners their arrival at the Isle de France had coincided with one of the island's intermittent outbreaks of smallpox. As a result, they found themselves barred from the other island colonies. Already the commissioner Tirol, who had left the Isle de France in the *Minerve* with the new Bourbon governor Duplessis to take up his post there, had been prevented from landing under a 40-day quarantine imposed by Bourbon on all ships coming from the neighbouring island. The *Minerve* then sailed to Seychelles where, equally unwelcome, it was forced to quarantine at La Digue.

When, some days later, on 5 September 1792, the frigate *Fidèle* arrived off Sainte Anne with Lescallier and Enouf aboard it was also put in quarantine. No-one was permitted to land and Lescallier had to suffer the indignity of communicating the purpose of his visit by shouting to a small boat that cautiously came within hailing distance of the ship. Only in this way could Lescallier notify Nageon that he was leaving Enouf at Seychelles with a set of regulations for the administration of the colony which he hoped, as he explained later to the Minister, would ensure the necessary tranquillity and prosperity of the islands "until such time as the commission can consider fully this part of our possessions". That done, Lescallier continued on his way to Pondichéry, with Enouf camped uncomfortably on Cerf island waiting to assume the duties of commandant once the quarantine period was over.

In addition to appointing a new commandant of the Seychelles Malartic also ordered a further, detailed survey of the colony. The task was allocated to an engineer officer, Jean-Baptiste Lislet Geoffroy, who was to have sailed at the same time as Enouf. However, being laid low by smallpox it was not until 19 November that he left the Isle de France in the *Euphrasie*. On his arrival he, too, was forced to spend two weeks quarantined on Cerf island before being allowed to cross to Mahé.

Enouf gave him lodgings, and on 22 December Lislet discussed the survey with Malavois, who was now living as a private citizen at Anse Royale. "On the 27th I started the necessary work on the survey of the state land," he wrote. "It rained continuously for the rest of the month. From the 2nd to 9th January 1793 there was continuous rain and from the 10th to 31st there were only three days when the weather allowed us to go out."

Lislet suffered from his legs, which made it impossible sometimes for him to go into the woods. He managed to make a complete tour of the island, however, mentioning well known places along the coast such as the bays Forbans, Intendance, Police, Lazare, Poules Bleues; also Bougainville, La Baleine, Boileau, Barbarons, Grand Anse, Port Glaud, Port Launay, and Cap Ternay. He had some pithy comments on the Seychelles landscape and the difficulties of his mission. The rocks, piled one upon the other, were as large as houses, and the wind was sometimes so strong that trees and rocks came tumbling down the mountainsides. "I am not surprised that the surveyor here before me was only able to mark the greatest number of his points on paper," he concluded. As for the wild life, he referred to three or four kinds of snake, crocodiles 33 feet in length, scorpions bigger than half a man's hand, as well as huge spiders and centipedes. "There, Sir, the *belle société* that one finds here," he wrote.

But of the human society, with unnamed exceptions, Lislet had no complaints, noting that when he came finally to leave the colony at the end of December 1793 "our goodbyes went on for more than eight days".

By then Enouf had relinquished his command and left the Seychelles. Like two of his predecessors, Romainville and Gillot, he suffered from ill health. Few documents relating to his term as civil agent and commandant appear to have survived, but there are indications that he wielded power with tact and fairness. The settlers were later to ask him to represent their interests at the Isle de France.

He was the last commandant to hold his commission from the King, although even before his arrival at Seychelles the monarchy had been suspended following the 10 August uprising in Paris and the sacking of the Tuileries palace. By the time Enouf's period of quarantine was over and he could assume his duties as commandant the monarchy had been abolished. Enouf served for only a year in Seychelles. When he came to hand over to his successor and brother officer in the Pondichéry Regiment, Jean-Baptiste Quéau de Quinssy, Louis XVI had been executed, France was a republic, and was once more at war with England.

8

Honourable Surrender
1793-1798

Je veux peindre un héros qu'on admire et qu'on aime,
Qu'un citoyen est grand, lorsqu'il sert sa patrie.
A.L. Thomas, 1756

The governor-general, Malartic, could hardly have made a better choice. Not only was Captain Quéau Quinssy[1] competent, diligent, and honest, unlike most of those posted to Seychelles he had the advantage of robust good health.

Quinssy's contemporaries spoke of his "frankness, good manners, and helpfulness",[2] qualities that were to endear him to the islands' inhabitants during his 18 years as commandant. Inevitably, he made enemies. Some were jealous of his position, thinking it should have been theirs; others resented the restraints he imposed on their plundering of the colony's natural resources.

During the war the settlers' main concerns were to protect their commerce from disruption by the English and their homes and possessions from pillage. They readily supported Quinssy in the policy he was to follow of negotiating surrender terms with the enemy but this did not prevent some of them from later accusing him of lacking courage and patriotism.

In the Seychelles museum there is a portrait of Quinssy, a painting of uncertain date and origin.[3] It is doubtful if the artist has done justice to his subject, for while the eyes give a hint of that stubbornness and resilience of character that was to make Quinssy a national hero, the mouth, twisted in a smirk, suggests more the foolish conceit of a courtier than the easy authority of a military officer. Quinssy had been a courtier as well as a soldier, having as a young man served in the household of Monsieur, the brother of Louis XVI, before entering on a military career. Throughout his life he was to retain the manners and fashions of the *Ancien Régime*. One English visitor to the Seychelles, in 1824, noted that Quinssy, then in his mid-70s, still walked with "the precise minuet step peculiar to that generation", while his demeanour and dress made him a "testimonial to the merits of his valet de chambre and the honour of *la Grande Nation*".[1]

Born in Paris on 9 November 1748, Quinssy began his military career as an ensign with the Corps des Volontaires Étrangers de la Marine, which was formed in 1778 for service in the colonies. During the War of American Independence he served in Suffren's devastating campaign along the Indian coast, seeing action against the English at Porto Novo (Madras), Cuddalore, Negapatam, where he was wounded, and at the capture of Trincomalee. Later he served under the Marquis de Bussy, transferring in 1784 to the Pondichéry Regiment.

The outbreak of the Revolution in France found Quinssy with his regiment in the Isle de France, holding the rank of captain. In 1791 he was appointed member of a delegation sent to Paris to petition the National Assembly on army pay, but for some reason he was recalled. On his return to the Isle de France, he was put in charge of the Grande Rivière district. Then on 7 August 1793, Quinssy was appointed military commandant and civil agent of the Seychelles.

His posting to what was a lonely and primitive exile, coincided with another major event in his life, the break-up of his seven-year-old marriage. Whatever the cause of his divorce from Marie Madeleine Duval, just over a year after his arrival in Seychelles Quinssy married again, to a recent divorcee from the Isle de France, Marie Joseph Dubail. Despite the difference in their ages — she was almost 20 years his junior — Quinssy's second marriage was a long and fruitful union.

The population of the Seychelles had by now increased substantially from the half-dozen or so white settlers and their families who, with about 200 slaves, had composed the colony at the end of Gillot's administration. The total of Whites had risen to about 70 men, women, and children, with 500 slaves.

There were also 30 free Blacks or Coloureds, in contrast to the one free black inhabitant, Laurence, and his son, who were recorded in the island census of 1785.

Quinssy realised on his arrival at Mahé that there was little money for the administration of the colony, and that he was uncomfortably dependent on the settlers for much of his food. He found that Gillot's spice garden was in remarkably good condition, and he wrote to Dupuy asking for funds to expand it. He also suggested that Dupuy send him plants from the well-stocked garden at Pamplemousses, and, by way of return, ordered that a case of shells, rock crystals from Praslin and two cocos de mer of unusual shape be sent to Dupuy.

News about France and of the war in Europe reached Seychelles only intermittently. The political upheaval in Paris which at first had so exhilarated the Indian Ocean colonies had, by 1793, become a chronicle of horror. Quinssy had learned of the execution of the King before leaving the Isle de France; also of the Terror that now gripped Paris, with the daily execution of aristocrats and others who were deemed to be opposed to the Revolution. It was all far away, however, and to Quinssy his duty to the Republic and its representatives was clear. England and Spain were now aligned against France, and it was inevitable that the Indian Ocean would once more be a theatre of war.

Quinssy's major worry was that there were no longer any troops in Seychelles with which he could make even a pretence of defence. The detachment of the Pondichéry Regiment that had been withdrawn on the advice of Malavois had not been replaced, as suggested, by either black militiamen from the Isle de France or Indian sepoys. To defend the colony he would have to rely on the settlers themselves, and the few slaves who could be trusted with arms. In the armoury Quinssy found eight small cannons, and about 60 muskets and pistols, and with those he tried to put the Seychelles on a war footing by arming the inhabitants and ordering that they drill every Sunday morning. The results were not encouraging, and at the end of a few weeks Quinssy was forced to admit that only about half of the 40 male inhabitants could be regarded as part-time soldiers.

With those he would have to do the best he could, and he issued instructions on the procedure to be followed if an enemy ship was sighted. During the day the alarm was to be sounded by the firing of three cannon at four-minute intervals and drumming to quarters, and the flag at the Établissement would be hoisted. At night rockets would be fired. On these signals every able-bodied inhabitant would report to Quinssy to draw arms and await further orders. Inhabitants who lived too far away to be aware of the alarm would be warned by letter, delivered by government slaves. All this preparation may have given some reassurance to the settlers, but it is unlikely Quinssy himself ever envisaged committing his feeble force to battle. Even a single enemy ship of modest size would have soon scattered his amateur troops with a few well-directed salvoes. When the time came, Quinssy used a different defensive strategy — with never a shot fired.

For many months the horizon had remained empty of enemy ships; undisturbed, the life of the settlers continued its daily routine, until, early in the morning of 16 May 1794, five three-masted ships were sighted approaching from the south. Quinssy, who had been on a tour of the island and was spending the night at the home of a settler, hurried to the Établissement, having sent a runner on ahead with orders that the alarm should be sounded. When he arrived he found that the brig *Olivette* had just entered port, and he went on board to discuss the situation with the captain, Jean-François Hodoul, soon to become renowned for his exploits against the English. By now the five strangers were lying off Sainte Anne, and although they wore no flag Quinssy was certain from their appearance that they were English. Hodoul told him he intended to run his ship on to the reef in an attempt to escape capture.

As settlers arrived at the Établissement to be issued with arms, Quinssy ordered a cannon to be fired and the flag raised, but the strangers failed to respond. Shortly before nine o'clock, after the surgeon Le Prédou had been sent out to inquire what the ships wanted, one was seen to lower a boat. It went first to the *Olivette*, where some of the Lascar crew had remained on board. Quinssy claimed later that he had been prevented from opening fire on the English party — his supposition as to their identity having been correct — because the *Olivette* was flying the French flag, an explanation aimed, perhaps, at forestalling criticism by the Isle de France of his subsequent conduct.

Having seized the brig, the boat party came on to land, and the officer in charge was taken to Quinssy. Through a French prisoner, he introduced himself as Lieutenant William Goate, of the 32-gun frigate *Orpheus*, commanded by Captain Henry Newcome, commodore of the squadron which had been blockading the Isle de France. It also included the 50-gun ship *Centurion* and the *Resistance*, of 44 guns.[5] The other two ships were prizes: the *Duguay Trouin*, formerly the East Indiaman *Princess Royal*, and a Danish merchantman, the *Dorothea Elizabeth*.

Goate told Quinssy that the commodore wanted water and provisions for his squadron and the prisoners. The latter, numbering several hundred, were in a particularly wretched state, having suffered from lack of food and sickness during a prolonged voyage in the *Duguay Trouin* before her interception by the English off the Isle de France. The *Duguay Trouin* had fought bravely as she tried to escape, sustaining heavy damage from the well-directed fire of the *Orpheus*. The chase lasted several hours and at the end 21 of her crew were dead and more than 60 wounded. Many of those had died before reaching Mahé.

In making the request for water and food Goate showed no hostility, yet he presented Quinssy with his first real problem of the war. Was he to rebuff the English and defend the colony with his part-time soldiers, or should he acquiesce to Newcome's request? The easiest course would have been to supply the English squadron, and there were, after all, good humanitarian reasons for succouring the French sick and wounded. But Quinssy resented the casual acceptance by Newcome that he should be given supplies. Telling Goate that he was surprised the commodore had not taken the trouble to put his request in writing, he informed the English officer that he could not assist the enemy of the Republic. He would, however, communicate the gist of Newcome's message to the inhabitants.

As most of the inhabitants had gone into hiding at the approach of the ships only a handful of the most valiant remained to endorse Quinssy's proposal that, having no means to oppose the enemy, they should surrender. But he insisted that this should be done with strict formality. Consequently one of the inhabitants, Captain Cornier Bellevaut, was sent to the *Orpheus* to tell Newcome that they would not turn traitor by voluntarily aiding him, but that if formally called on, under duress, to surrender, the colony was ready to capitulate as long as their property was respected. The offer, drawn up by Quinssy, was made "in the name of all the inhabitants".

There was nothing in Newcome's orders about seizing the Seychelles islands, but he readily complied with Quinssy's request. His written ultimatum, in suitably terse terms, gave the commandant one hour to decide to surrender the colony, and warned that if there was any resistance "you must abide by the consequences". Verbally, Newcome assured Bellevaut that he would take possession only for the length of his stay, and that he would not leave a garrison behind when he sailed.

The proprieties having been observed, Quinssy prepared to surrender the island. The terms of the capitulation were drawn up — one can visualise Quinssy carefully writing out the seven articles that he presented to Newcome for signature — and an appropriate ceremony was arranged for nine o'clock the following morning when the French flag would be lowered to the accompaniment of three discharges of cannon and muskets and replaced by the Union Jack. Newcome had readily agreed to this, but Quinssy's stipulation that government arms, ammunition, and other stores would be untouched was curtly refused. They would, Newcome noted on the document, "remain at my disposal", although Quinssy might retain two 2-pounders as signal guns in case of a slave uprising. Private property would be respected, but, added Newcome, "I take the brig *Olivette*".

Quinssy had also to accept being made a prisoner-of-war, although this would be only while the English were in possession of the island.

The next morning, Saturday, 17 May 1794, the surrender of Seychelles took place. Captain Osborn, of the *Centurion*, which supplied an officer and 30 marines for the ceremony on shore, noted in his log that the weather, which had been pleasant with moderate breezes, had turned squally, with rain. Ten land turtles had been received from the *Orpheus*, a supplement to the cask of salted beef that had been opened that day. A new main topsail was being bent on the yards, and the crew were also employed rounding the cables. Having recorded these important shipboard happenings, Osborn concluded: "Sent a party of marines to demand the Governor surrender; fired several guns, hauled down the French flag and hoisted an English Jack". Captain Newcome, on board the *Orpheus*, was equally succinct. His log reads: "AM at 8 the marines of the squadron, under Lieutenant Matthews, landed when the island capitulated."

During the following week work of provisioning the ships went on, with coopers making casks for water and boat parties bringing on board sacks of coconuts and vegetables, which Newcome told Quinssy would be paid for. The *Olivette* was also put to good use, and brought back tortoises from Praslin. The sick French prisoners, whom Newcome had decided to release, were landed on Sainte Anne. He later wrote to Malartic requesting that a similar number of British officers and men held in the Isle de France be released. Newcome also paroled about 140 French prisoners, who promptly disappeared into the woods once ashore.

Before sailing for Madras on 1 June the squadron made a further prize, a slaver from Africa which unwittingly entered the harbour thinking that the English ships, which had hoisted false colours, were a French squadron.

The *Centurion* log describes the taking of the *Deux Andrés*:

> Tuesday, 27 May ... *Resistance* made the signal for seeing a strange sail in the offing. AM at half-past 5 saw the above sail working to windward; at 11 the strange sail standing into the bay, but perceiving us to be English ships put about and stood to sea: the *Orpheus* made the *Resistance* signal to chase; at noon the *Resistance* in chase and several boats from the squadron ...
>
> Wednesday, 28 May ... Moderate breezes and clear weather. PM at half past twelve the aforementioned chase struck to the *Resistance*; a lieutenant from our boat took possession and brought her in; found her to be a French ship *le Deux Andre*, from Mosambeck (sic) to the Mauritius, with 400 slaves ...[6]

Quinssy had wanted Hangard to go out in a pirogue to warn the *Deux Andrés* of the presence of the English, but the sea proved too rough. French soldiers on Sainte Anne also tried to alert the approaching ship. Once the *Resistance* brought her forecastle guns to bear, the fleeing slaver quickly surrendered.

The loss of the *Deux Andrés* meant the confiscation of a valuable cargo, for the English took her slaves with them when they sailed five days later. Describing his departure, Newcome wrote: "Not thinking it of sufficient consequence to leave any force, I quitted the place, having taken the Republican flag and all the military and naval stores, also the brig *Le Olivete* (sic), leaving the implements of agriculture, for building houses etc, for the use of the poor inhabitants." The cannon that were not taken were spiked and the battery platforms broken, although Newcome gave Quinssy a receipt for the loss and damage.

Having satisfied the needs of the English, Quinssy was now desperately short of food, with only a small quantity of rice and some potatoes and vegetables to feed the 200 or so ex-prisoners left behind on Sainte Anne or who had escaped from the squadron and were now scattered over the main island. Detailing an officer named Collet from the *Duguay Trouin* to round up the ex-prisoners and set up a camp for them on Sainte Anne, Quinssy summoned the inhabitants to discuss the implications of the island's surrender and decide the next step.

From the start Quinssy had been careful to conform to the new democratic processes one would expect in a republic. The settlers, through their Assembly, had agreed to the surrender and the lowering of the French flag, and the question Quinssy now put to them was whether the flag should be hoisted again over the colony. The alternative was to remain without a flag until instructions came from the Isle de France.

Quinssy had no doubts on the matter. It was, he told the settlers, the natural desire of all good Frenchmen — which, of course, he knew the Seychelles inhabitants to be — to display their national flag, but because of the precarious position in which they found themselves, with no defences at all and the English likely to reappear at any time, it would be wiser before restoring the flag to seek guidance from the Isle de France. The settlers did not require much persuasion - better to play safe by remaining without a flag than run the risk of the English plundering their property on the pretext that they had broken the capitulation. From this it was only a small step to accepting the notion of a permanent neutrality, with Mahé an open port to French and English alike. As the war wore on, and the English tightened their blockade of the other Indian Ocean islands, the advantages of standing aside from the conflict became more and more apparent.

This was not, however, an attitude that recommended itself to the authorities in the Isle de France, with the result that a protracted dispute over the flag went on throughout the war between Quinssy and the settlers on one hand and the Isle de France on the other. For although Quinssy eventually complied with the order to rehoist the Tricolour, he himself decided that it should be removed at the hint of an English ship approaching. He was also prepared — overeager in the opinion of a subsequent Isle de France governor — not only to renew the capitulation with visiting enemy ships but also to win further advantages for the Seychelles, such as the right for the island's ships to sail unmolested by the English under a "capitulation flag".

But all this was still in the future. The immediate need was to repatriate the French soldiers and sailors left behind by the English squadron. Quinssy's latest count put them at 190, and he asked the settlers, despite their meagre resources, to contribute as much rice, maize, sweet potatoes, chicken, tortoises, coconuts, and vegetables as they could spare. Assuring them that they would eventually be well paid by the Isle de France authorities, he added: "I cannot stress too often, fellow citizens, in the need of sacrifice at a time like this, and the importance of looking after the French prisoners and sending them off as soon as possible to the Isle de France."

The danger of having hungry soldiers turning to robbery and worse was all too obvious to the settlers, even though Quinssy assured them that he was to form a detachment of 20 men under an officer and three National Guard sergeants from the *Duguay Trouin* to maintain order.

Luckily, it appeared the Seychelles would not have to play host to the French visitors for long. A 60-tonne brig, the *Utilité*, on a fishing trip from the Isle de France, was at that moment anchored at Praslin, having escaped the attention of the English squadron. It was Quinssy's intention, readily endorsed by the settlers, to put it into service for transporting the ex-prisoners to the Isle de France. Collet was dispatched to Praslin with a written order from Quinssy commandeering the ship. The captain, Marchand, leaving behind three barrels of salted fish in Vaulbert's store, sailed immediately for Mahé, where he was persuaded by Quinssy to retain, command of the *Utilité* and sail her with the troops back to the Isle de France.

But first repairs had to be carried out on the ship, and it was not until 24 June that she finally sailed. With the ex-prisoners went Collet and the surgeon Maury to care for the wounded. The ship also carried dispatches from Quinssy to the administrators and the Isle de France Assembly detailing the events of the past weeks, asking for food, arms and other stores to replace those taken by the English, and seeking advice on the question of restoring the French flag.[7]

Quinssy rightly foresaw that his act of surrender would not be well received, particularly by the more extreme Republican elements in the Assembly, who expected the war against the English to be pursued vigorously at all times. Quinssy's action had left him dangerously open to the charge of having royalist sympathies. In his dispatch to the Assembly president, he offered to return to service with his regiment, where, he argued, he might be more usefully employed, as with the capitulation he was now no longer military commandant. He said he had agreed to the settlers' request to continue as civil agent, but only for the sake. of the colony's welfare and until he heard from the Isle de France. If it was considered essential that he continue in his post he would do so. The salary of 1,200 livres did not meet his expenses however, and his position had become a real burden. In any case, he asked that he might return to the Isle de France on leave.

To the president of the local Jacobin club, the *Chaumière,* Quinssy stressed that he had surrendered only after holding out for more than 24 hours against a superior force. The documents he was sending, including the act of capitulation, were, he said, proof of his conduct. "I submit to your justice and that of all my fellow citizens, to whom I shall always regard it as a duty and an honour to merit their esteem," he wrote.

The Assembly, angered by the apparent ease with which the English had seized the Seychelles, was in no mood to listen to excuses. It decreed that Quinssy should be recalled forthwith and a replacement sent who would raise the French flag again over the islands. But Malartic and Dupuy were more understanding. They pointed out in a letter to the Assembly that the capitulation had been endorsed by all the settlers, and that unless a sufficient force was sent to defend it, the raising of the French flag would put the settlers in a highly dangerous position if the English were to return. "Although they might argue that they had been reconquered (by the French), the enemy would not regard this as a valid excuse and would accuse them of violating the treaty."

As for the Assembly's demand that Quinssy be recalled, they considered that this would be not only a personal injustice but would be against the inhabitants' wishes, Quinssy being highly respected by all. Malartic proposed, instead, that Quinssy be granted the leave he requested, and that the Assembly choose a commissioner from among its own members to assume command provisionally in the Seychelles.

This latter suggestion was clearly a barb that Malartic hoped would effectively deflate the Assembly. For whoever was sent to take command in Seychelles and restore the Tricolour would have the unenviable task of justifying his conduct when he had to lower it again on the almost certain reappearance of the English. Quinssy's predecessor, Enouf, had also argued the case for the Seychelles remaining without a flag. He told the Assembly that the capitulation had assured the inhabitants of their liberty and security, while "your decree deprives them of this unique chance that Newcome's humanity has given them to escape the misfortunes of war". The result would probably mean the destruction of the colony, for the English might not be so generous the next time. Enouf suggested also that there could be advantages in having a neutral harbour where French ships might seek rest and repairs.

Passions were running too high in the Assembly for it to listen to such face-saving arguments. The flag must be restored; that was final. However, on the question of a replacement for Quinssy, the Assembly, predictably, avoided Malartic's challenge and quietly dropped the matter. Quinssy, so nearly deposed after only one year's service, would remain commandant of the Seychelles until the end of the war.

If the Isle de France Assembly was determined the Tricolour should again fly over Seychelles the settlers were equally adamant that it should not. Summoned on 7 September to the Établissement to hear the results of the mission to the Isle de France, they decided that there would be no flag until there was a strong enough garrison on the island "to maintain the dignity of the Seychelles". They expressed appreciation of the efforts of their former commandant, Enouf, but declared that Maury, who may have been ready to compromise over the flag, had no right to represent them.

There thus began what one French writer described as "a sort of capitulation" for Seychelles, where "all flags could be flown without any running the risk of being insulted by another". This latter assertion, however, was far from the case. On almost every occasion that an English warship called at Seychelles it seized whatever enemy ships it found there. Nor were Quinssy's military stores exempt from confiscation. At each renewal of the capitulation Quinssy had to hand over to the English commander whatever arms and ammunition he had, although no doubt much was hidden from the enemy's eyes.

Before he left Seychelles Newcome had told Quinssy that he would recommend to the Council in Madras that it acquire the islands for the East India Company, and that he would be back the following October. But Newcome never returned, and of the three ships of his squadron only the *Centurion* resumed the blockade off the Isle de France, this time in company with the 44-gun *Diomède*. Unfortunately for Captain Osborn, he was soon forced to lift the blockade and limp back to Madras having been badly mauled in a brief and spirited sortie by the French.

On that day, 22 October 1794, there had been great rejoicing in the Isle de France when Commodore Jean-Marie Renaud's two frigates, the *Cybèle* and the *Prudente*, together with the *Courier* corvette, returned to Port Louis after driving off the English ships. The French had fought splendidly, getting the better of an English squadron of similar strength, though they had undoubtedly been assisted by the reluctance of *Diomède's* captain Matthew Smith to give close support to the *Centurion*. Smith, whose lack of ardour was apparently due to some grievance rather than want of courage, was subsequently court-martialled, and although the finding of guilty was later repealed and he was restored to rank he was never again called into service.

Among those who celebrated the French victory was a young seaman not long out from St Malo, Robert Surcouf. Master of a small ship engaged in the East African slave trade, Surcouf was to sail for the Seychelles the following year to become, in due course, one of France's most celebrated privateers.

As for the *Centurion*, she returned to the Seychelles four years later, in September 1798, this time under the command of Captain John Spratt Rainier, nephew of the East Indies commander-in-chief, Rear-Admiral Peter Rainier.[8] Although Rainier's log does not mention the capitulation, it seems he found no difficulty in getting the supplies he needed from Quinssy, including six bullocks which for a few days provided the ship's company the rare luxury of fresh beef. Some days after his arrival Rainier ordered a boat to row guard round the ship as it lay off Sainte Anne. The log does not disclose whether this was because Rainier feared, despite the complaisant attitude of the Seychellois, a surprise attack on his ship or, more likely, in order to prevent members of the crew swimming ashore and disappearing into the interior.

Desertion was common enough among English sailors. After months cooped up in the fetid atmosphere of a warship in the tropics, living off salt pork and hard, weevily biscuit and subjected to all the harshness and brutality deemed essential for the maintenance of discipline in one of His Majesty's ships, it would have been surprising if the cool, green slopes of Sainte Anne had not appeared for some an ideal refuge.

Nor were there necessarily ties of kinship or patriotism to keep the sailor with his ship. With the increasing difficulty of finding crew replacements, captains were little concerned about the nationality of those they pressed into service. Any British ship might have Portuguese, Spaniards, Scandinavians, even French, on its muster roll. African slaves might be recruited (it is recorded that an African fought in the *Victory* at Trafalgar), as well as Malay seamen.[9]

Life on the *Centurion* was probably no worse than in the average warship. On the day Rainier ordered a boat to row guard round the ship, three floggings had been carried out: two seamen received 18 and seven lashes respectively for theft and one 12 lashes for drunkenness and neglect of duty.

When, on 7 September, Rainier sailed for Bombay and Ceylon he took with him a slave ship, the *Louisa*, which he had found moored off Cerf island under Danish colours, and with 260 slaves on board. It was not, however, to be a particularly lucky find, for when the *Louisa* was later being sailed under a prize crew to the Cape, her master, a resourceful Frenchman named Baudin, managed with some of his men to regain control of his ship. Instead of making for the Cape the *Louisa* sailed for the Isle de France, where 20 crewmen from the *Centurion* became prisoners of war.

Since its capitulation the Seychelles had increasingly been recognised by the British as a convenient port of call not only between the Cape and India but also for ships bound for the Red Sea and the Persian Gulf, areas that had assumed a new importance since Napoleon's invasion of Egypt in 1798. Records show that while ships called at Mahé for water and provisions they were also checking on what shipping they might find there. According to Baudin, the *Centurion* had hoped to intercept at Seychelles a Danish ship that was believed to be carrying bullion for the French in India.

On average about one English warship a year called at Mahé, and most were able to take away one or more prizes, brigs and sloops usually, and, on one notable occasion, a newly built French frigate. The Isle de France authorities, unable to send sufficient forces to defend Seychelles, could only rage impotently when news arrived from Mahé of yet another ship lost to the enemy. It was natural that they should accuse Britain of breaking the terms of the capitulation. "The English, as soon as it was in their interest to do so, ignored this treaty as so many others," wrote one French observer.[10]

The accusation is unfair, for neither in the document recording the initial surrender nor in the subsequent renewals of the capitulation by Quinssy is there a clause offering immunity to French or other enemy ships found in Mahé harbour. The French, in any case — and particularly General Decaen, last governor-general of the Isle de France — scarcely recognised the existence of the capitulation. It was only with great difficulty that Quinssy could argue his case, on each occasion, for having surrendered to the English without a fight.

As a result of the capitulation Quinssy succeeded not only in protecting the Seychelles from the worst ravages of the war, he was also able to negotiate advantageous terms with the enemy, notably the right of some Seychelles vessels to sail and trade freely across the Indian Ocean under a flag of capitulation. The flag consisted of the letters "Seychelles capitulation" stitched in white on a blue background. To Quinssy each capitulation was an inevitable act of surrender, but surrender with honour. To the settlers it was, more realistically, an act of surrender with profit, something which they saw fit to commemorate by naming one of their vessels the *Seychelles Capitulation*.

9

Envoys from India
1796-1799

Depuis quelque temps nous avons eu ici bien des fracas.
Jean-Nicolas Leboucq Santussan, October 1799

Until the airport opened in 1971 the only way to reach Seychelles was by sea.[1] Cargo ships accommodating up to a dozen passengers called only infrequently, and most travellers to the islands booked a berth in the BI liner that put in at Mahé twice a month on its regular run between Bombay and Mombasa.

The liner's arrival was timed usually for daybreak, and from early morning a crowd would gather at the Long Pier to watch passengers come ashore. There would be joyful reunions, with relatives being welcomed home after long years of absence abroad. For others, the occasion was tinged with the sadness of impending departure; a friend, perhaps, would be sailing that evening, leaving the islands for ever.

In the town visitors from the ship would stroll through the narrow streets, examining the produce of the handicraft stalls, or relax with a drink on the verandah of the Pirates Arms hotel. But the hours pass quickly, and soon it is late afternoon. A final purchase of tortoiseshell napkin rings, and the last visitor is in the launch going back to the ship. Passengers joining here are already on board and, like those who disembarked that morning, their names and the grade of their cabin accommodation will have been recorded for display at the town post office, and in the next issue of *Le Seychellois*. Thus, in style and subject to scrutiny, did one come and go.

Today all that has changed. The big jets from Europe and Asia arrive daily at Mahé airport, depositing swarms of anonymous tourists, who throng the streets of Victoria and the beach at Beau Vallon, bringing a carnival air to what was once a sleepy, colonial retreat. Many visitors venture beyond Mahé, travelling by the inter-island air service to Praslin, where several new hotels have opened in recent years; or they make the sea crossing by schooner or the high-speed catamaran ferry. Other outlying islands are also linked by small plane to Mahé, while for the more affluent visitors there is a helicopter to take them to the exclusive island of their choice. Although hotel accommodation is increasingly available on the smaller, isolated islands, the Seychelles government's declared policy is to avoid uncontrolled development in order to protect the outlying islands from the environmental trauma of mass travel.

The island of La Digue, the fourth largest of the main granitic group, lies close to Praslin, but despite this has managed to retain much of its old world charm. Here the pace of life appears as tranquil and unhurried as it must have been for the island's first inhabitants, who arrived from Bourbon to settle there some 200 years ago.

The sending of Bourbon families to the Seychelles had been advocated as far back as 1775, but Versailles, fearing a repetition of the Brayer du Barré débâcle, had insisted that only those with means should be allowed to go. As it is usually the needy who are most eager to seek a better life elsewhere, this precaution amounted to a virtual ban on emigration,[2] and it was not until the 1790s, as the disruptive effects of the Revolution in France spread through the island communities of the Indian Ocean, that some Bourbon families found themselves sailing to the Seychelles. Most went unwillingly, only agreeing to the journey in order to be reunited with their husbands and fathers, who had been deported earlier for their part in a rebellion against the island's Revolutionary government.

Although France had officially enunciated the principle of man's equality irrespective of colour or class, it recognised the need for caution in dealing with its colonies, and had allowed them to draw up their own constitutions. Predictably, all endorsed the retention of slavery, the mainstay of their agricultural economies.

Yet the issue continued to torment the minds of the settlers. Paris looked with disfavour on the colonies' failure to repudiate slavery, and even some voices in the colonial assemblies were urging abolition, or at least gradual emancipation, fuelling anxiety among the settlers that one day all the slaves would be freed. By 1794 these fears seemed to have been realised when the National Convention in Paris passed the decree of 26 Pluviôse, abolishing slavery throughout the French territories and recognising the rights of all men to citizenship.

It was a year before the decree reached the Isle de France, where it was promptly rejected by the Colonial Assembly; those who protested too loudly in its favour were sent back to France. A year passed, and with the Directory now in power in Paris two commissioners were sent to the Indian Ocean colonies to enforce the 26 Pluviôse decree. Baco and Burnel,[3] who sailed with Admiral Sercey's squadron, had been armed with dictatorial powers, and on their arrival at the Isle de France on 18 June 1796 they made it clear that they intended to abolish slavery on the island. However, they had misjudged the reaction of the settlers, who fomented a general uprising that forced the two commissioners to seek safety in one of Sercey's ships. The ship was promptly ordered by the Colonial Assembly to sail for Manila.

This brief but successful defiance of Paris was greeted with relief in Bourbon (now renamed Isle de la Réunion des Patriotes, or Réunion for short), where the slavery decree had caused similar consternation. Two years later, in 1798, some Réunion inhabitants staged their own rebellion. This time the issue was not slavery but increased taxation, financial extravagance by the authorities, and rumours that reactionary elements in their Colonial Assembly planned to hand the island over to the English. The leader of the insurrection was a former army sergeant, Étienne Alexandre Belleville, although its guiding spirit was a radical priest, Jean Lafosse, president of the St Louis *Chaumière*. Belleville commanded the National Guard in the south and, with ready access to arms, including artillery, was able to muster a fairly formidable force for a march on the capital.

When news of the uprising reached St Denis the governor, Jacob de Cordemoy, mobilised all available troops while the

Assembly sent an envoy, Joseph Hubert, to intercept the insurgents and try to talk them out of their enterprise. In an address to the rebels, the Assembly denied that it had invited the British to land or that plans had been made for mass arrests of troublemakers. "You have allowed yourselves to be misled," the rebels were warned; even Belleville, they were told, was being manipulated by the real power seekers, who would sacrifice him if necessary.[4]

This statement failed to impress the rebels. Hubert was brushed aside and the march continued. By now troops from St Denis had been deployed to block the advance, and when the rebels found that they were surrounded they gave in with hardly a shot fired. A dozen ringleaders, including Belleville and Lafosse, were arrested.

Having crushed the rebellion so easily, the Assembly was prepared to be lenient. Recalling that Réunion was held in high regard "in the eyes of humanity for never having spilled a drop of blood in the Revolutionary cause", it decreed that the punishment should be simple deportation for the leaders of the attempted coup. Although they would not be allowed to take their families with them, they would be given time to prepare for their departure and they could take one slave each. The only question that remained was the deportees' destination.

While the administration debated this, the rebels made their preferences known. Belleville wanted to go to France; at least that was the destination favoured by his wife, who asked the Assembly not to condemn her to death by separating her from her husband. Some mentioned the Seychelles where, it was pointed out, there had been a demand for a priest for many years. Sending Lafosse there would satisfy both the demands of justice and religion. Lafosse was agreeable, as was Célestin Payet, who petitioned the Committee of Public Safety to allow his wife, child, and slaves to accompany him to "the island of Chechel".

There were difficulties, however, in sending rebellious citizens to another French colony without permission, and in the end when the brig *Laurette* sailed with Lafosse, Belleville, and others on 8 June 1798 (20 Prairial Year VI), it was left to the captain to land them at any suitable spot on the Indian coast.

The deportees never reached India, but landed instead in Seychelles. As to how it happened, there is only the explanation given in a sworn statement by Captain Loiseau and his crew, and a brief note written by the deportees themselves. According to Loiseau several days of rough weather after leaving Réunion forced him to seek temporary refuge at Mahé to carry out repairs to the ship and replace provisions that had been contaminated by sea water. Once in Seychelles waters, the deportees rose against the crew.

"They threatened us and abused us with outrageous words of all kinds, which would have revolted the most patient of men," wrote Loiseau. "In vain did we remonstrate with them; that only made their rebellion worse."

With Loiseau and his first officer helpless in the hands of the deportees, the second officer, with a knife at his throat, was forced to sail the ship to La Digue. All this took place on the evening of 1 July 1798 (13 Messidor Year VI). In the darkness, it seems no-one was able to see who was holding the knife. At La Digue, six of the deportees lowered a boat to transfer their belongings to the shore. The next day the *Laurette* was allowed to sail to Praslin where Loiseau reported the previous day's happenings to the municipal agent, François Savy.

Loiseau's account of how he lost command of his ship is so patently false that it can only be assumed he was persuaded or bribed by the deportees, or their friends, to land them in the Seychelles instead of India, from where they would probably never have been able to return. A brief note written by the deportees simply states that La Digue appeared to them as a suitable refuge, and nothing Captain Loiseau did could dissuade them from landing there.

Savy was not pleased at the arrival of deportees from Réunion. Writing later to the president of the Committee of Public Safety in the Isle de France he pointed out that "it is of great importance to the inhabitants of Seychelles that their small colony should not become a place of deportation". His fears were well-founded. Lafosse and his companions were to be the first of a succession of political dissidents deported to the Seychelles over the next 150 years by French and subsequently British administrations.

Some of La Digue's new inhabitants would have been content to remain there provided their families joined them.

Others wanted to escape as soon as possible. Two, Vincent Robert and his son-in-law Lucien, managed after some months to find a ship to take them to the Isle de France, and from there another vessel landed them secretly at Réunion. They were soon discovered by the authorities, however, hiding in the house of an Assembly member, Jean-Nicolas Leboucq Santussan.

Two months later, in December 1798, eight more deportees turned up. After being put ashore at Pays Brûlé by an American slave ship, the *Betsy*, they reported their arrival to the municipal agent at St Joseph, and were then taken under escort to the capital. One told the authorities he had returned because of ill-health, the others said they had come back only to collect their wives, children, and slaves and were ready to return to La Digue with them. Unfortunately they had arrived too late, as their families, as already noted, had sailed with the permission of the government to join them on La Digue. Records show that of the original deportees more than half eventually were to make their permanent homes on La Digue.[5] The two ringleaders were not among them. Lafosse, who had managed to reach France, returned to Réunion after the Peace of Amiens in 1801 to resume life as a parish priest, while Belleville was also back home at about the same time.

The Belleville uprising was not the end of the troubles on Réunion. At the beginning of 1799 the authorities had another insurrection on their hands, this time among National Guardsmen in St Denis. The governor succeeded in reasserting control over the soldiers before they marched on the Assembly, and the rebellion fizzled out.

In the purge that followed 62 people were listed for deportation. Madagascar was selected as their place of exile, but few if any reached there as the ship transporting them was sunk in an action with an English frigate. Some of the deportees may have had little to do with the insurrection, being simply victims of personal spite or jealousy. There is evidence to suggest that the family of at least one, François Mellon, received compensation from the government as some years later a widow Mellon and her six children left Réunion to join other families on La Digue with a land grant made on the orders of the governor-general, Decaen.

Of all the deportees from Réunion the most prominent was

Leboucq Santussan. Not only was he a deputy in the Colonial Assembly, he was also a public notary and a man of substance and influence. Leboucq had been suspect at the time of the Belleville uprising, but it was only after he was found to have hidden at his home the two deportees Vincent and Lucien on their return from Seychelles that he was arraigned before the Assembly on a number of charges. As a result Leboucq was himself ordered to be deported, but he managed to thwart the carrying out of the sentence by hurriedly leaving for the Isle de France. Imprisoned for a time there, he eventually arranged for his family to join him. He then sought, and obtained, permission for all of them to go to France.

Writing later to a friend, Leboucq said he had been told he could sail in the corvette *Surprise*, which had just arrived from India with two envoys of Tippu Sultan, the ruler of Mysore, who were travelling to Paris to seek further assistance for their master in his protracted struggle against the English.[6] But as Leboucq prepared to leave, he was informed that instead of sailing to France he was being sent to the Seychelles. Despite his protests, he and his family were put aboard another vessel bound for Mahé.

A cool reception awaited Leboucq in the Seychelles, where there was by now strong suspicion among the inhabitants that their islands had been earmarked as a convenient dumping place for undesirables. According to Leboucq attempts were made to prevent him landing, but Quinssy intervened with his usual courtesy on behalf of the new arrivals and Leboucq, not being short of money, was soon able to install himself comfortably on Mahé.

He bought a house near the harbour for 5,000 piastres and had sufficient slaves to assure his family the leisured existence to which they were accustomed. Good food, other than fish, was in short supply, but Leboucq had brought his own stock of rice, maize, and flour. He was content to stay aloof from "the rather difficult society" in which he now found himself, and if life was somewhat monotonous in "this little isolated country", he had always his books to entertain him, and the regular exercise he took kept him in good health. His family, too, seemed to cope with the discomforts of their new life. Indeed, thought Leboucq, if it had not been for the fact that he had had to leave most of his effects behind, he could have made a comfortable living for himself in Seychelles as public notary.

Leboucq had been in Seychelles for several weeks when the ship in which he had hoped to travel to France called at Mahé. The *Surprise* had already visited Réunion and Madagascar and was now making its way with the two Indian envoys to the Red Sea coast. Once there they would be able to cross overland to the Mediterranean and continue their journey by another ship. As Egypt was at the time under Napoleon's control, the route seemed to offer — wrongly, as it turned out — a quicker and safer passage than sailing round the Cape.

Was it just cruel coincidence, a coincidence that was to recur more than once in the same harbour and cost France several valuable ships, or was it secret orders from Madras based on foreknowledge of the *Surprise's* movements that brought an English ship, two ships in fact, to the Seychelles while the French corvette was still there? A few more hours might have saved her, but the *Surprise* was still at anchor, hurriedly preparing for departure, when the British frigate *Braave* and the brig *Amboyna* rounded Sainte Anne on Friday, 20 September 1799.

Captain Thomas Alexander of the *Braave* noted: "At 11 came too in Mahé or Seychelles Roads in 12 fathoms ... Found laying here a ship under French colours. Hoisted out the Boats and sent them armed to take possession of her. On the Boats approaching nearer, observed her fire at them. Fired two guns shotted from the ship when she struck. Proved to be a French Republican corvette called *la Surprise* — Monsieur Barbier commander — having on board Monsieur Dubricq, Cheik Abouram Saib and Mehmet Bismila, Ambassadors from Tippoo Sultan to the Executive Directory of France."

What Alexander did not record was that before his men could board the *Surprise* the envoys had escaped ashore, together with their French companion, General Dubuc. Later, as the crew of the *Surprise* were transferred as prisoners to the *Braave*, a party of marines set off after the fugitives.

Unknown to the envoys their mission to France was already pointless, as Tippu Sultan's capital, Seringpatam, had fallen four months earlier to a British force under General Sir David Baird and Colonel Sir Arthur Wellesley (the future Duke of Wellington). The Tiger of Mysore had fought valiantly, until cut down in the final assault.

Tippu Sultan had been one of England's most astute and determined opponents, but his attempt to forge a productive alliance with France — his first emissary was sent to Paris in 1792 — had never been rewarded with the troops and arms he needed, the French being unable or unwilling to offer much more than messages of support. The last of these had emanated from Cairo, where Napoleon held out the vague hope that his "numerous and invincible army" would march from Egypt to deliver "his greatest friend" from the iron yoke of England.

The previous year, on 9 January 1798, two envoys had turned up at the Isle de France with a request from Tippu for troops - and also clove and nutmeg plants for his gardens. The mission was cordially received, but the envoys were told that the Isle de France had no troops to spare as a contingent had recently been sent as reinforcements to the Dutch East Indies.

It was agreed, however, that Malartic would issue a proclamation inviting the island's residents to come forward for service under Tippu Sultan's banner. The response was not encouraging and in the end only a small, ill-assorted group of volunteers sailed for India in the privateer *Preneuse*. Tippu Sultan, who had been hoping for thousands of regular French troops, hid his disappointment as best he could when this negligible reinforcement to his army arrived at Mangalore in April 1798.

"Accounts vary with respect to their numbers," wrote Bengal's new governor-general, the Earl of Mornington, "but the most probable intelligence is that it does not exceed two hundred. Whatever may be its amount, the whole force has been received into Tippu's service with public marks of favour and honour." Mornington, who was Arthur Wellesley's elder brother, said he had learnt that the officers in the Isle de France force were mainly without experience and the private soldiers "the refuse of the lowest class of the democratic rabble".

Surprisingly no attempt was made to conceal their arrival in India, and the text of Malartic's proclamation was in due course published in a Calcutta newspaper for all to learn of Tippu's duplicity. Its terms clearly committed the Mysore ruler to waging war on the English, providing Mornington with the pretext he had been looking for to crush the troublesome

Tippu once and for all. With war now a foregone conclusion, Tippu Sultan decided to make one last desperate appeal to France for help; nothing less than 10,000 European troops and naval support would be needed if he were to resist the English successfully. Two envoys would take the request to Paris, accompanied on their journey by a former French navy captain named Dubuc, who had been a member of the Isle de France volunteer force and who now bore the title of General of Maritime Affairs in Mysore.

Described by a contemporary as a preposterous liar given to committing all sorts of foolishness, Dubuc was hardly the type to ensure the secrecy of his mission. Leboucq Santussan claimed that information about the *Surprise* must have been leaked to "traitorous inhabitants of Réunion" who relayed it back to the English at Madras. The leisurely progress of the corvette, which spent 40 days at Madagascar after leaving Réunion, certainly gave ample time for news of Tippu Sultan's mission to reach Madras before the departure of the *Braave* on 17 August.

Alexander's orders referred only to the delivery of dispatches to the Red Sea squadron, but it is possible he was told to keep a look-out for the *Surprise* in the area of the Seychelles, as Admiral Rainier's orders referred to the navigational hazards he would meet on taking "the southern passage". Whatever the motive that made him call at Mahé, Alexander's satisfaction at finding the *Surprise* was immediately followed by disappointment at Tippu Sultan's ambassadors having eluded him. The marines he had sent after them returned empty-handed. The next day an armed cutter went to Pointe Larue, where it was said the envoys were hiding, only to find that they had already fled, leaving a quantity of baggage behind.

Alexander's frustration was understandable. It was obvious the inhabitants were hiding the fugitives and even Quinssy, who, ever sensitive to the terms of the colony's capitulation, had professed readiness to help track them down, was suspect. The result was an ultimatum from the English commander to the inhabitants: surrender the envoys or have your property pillaged and destroyed. Two days later the Mysore envoys and their suite gave themselves up.

Leboucq, who had been all for holding out against

Alexander, angrily wrote to Quinssy: "Captain Alexander must have a very poor opinion of the French who inhabit the Seychelles islands to have the maintenance of the capitulation dependent on their surrendering their honour."

Leboucq had been in touch with the fugitives from the start, although he denied ever receiving them in his house. He accused Quinssy of putting the English against him by saying that he had lent them a boat to escape. Three times his house had been searched and once he was taken on board the *Braave* to be questioned. "The English admired me," he wrote later with a characteristic lack of modesty. "I showed to all the Englishmen the firmness of a loyal Frenchman who would not break the capitulation, but neither would he betray his country." Leboucq's attempt to uphold the honour of France was of no avail, for the day after his visit to the *Braave* General Dubuc, together with the Indian envoys, "had the baseness to give himself up after having given his word that neither he nor his companions would surrender".

With the envoys and their suite on board and the necessary repairs to the *Surprise* complete, the two English ships and their prize sailed from Mahé at noon on Sunday, 29 September. Alexander's log makes no reference to the eventual fate of the envoys, who were probably returned to India in the *Surprise* while the *Braave* and the brig *Amboyna* continued their way to the Red Sea.

Alexander had left behind on Mahé several sick crew members of the *Surprise*, and had given authorisation to Captain Charles Picard of the *Diligent* schooner to fetch assistance for them from the Isle de France. The English had also to leave behind, hidden somewhere on Mahé, a set of jewels that were to have been presented by Tippu Sultan's envoys to the Directory on their arrival in Paris. Despite Alexander's threats and blandishments the Indians refused to disclose the location of the jewels. For all one knows, they may still be there.

One officer of the *Braave* had a personal reason for regretting his departure from Seychelles. According to Leboucq this officer, whom he had been told was a man of honour and substance, had formed a romantic attachment to one of Leboucq's daughters. Captain Alexander was agreeable to wait for the marriage to be concluded, but the patriotic

Leboucq recorded, with satisfaction, that "my daughter had no more desire to have this Englishman as a husband than I had to have him as my son-in-law".

From officers of the *Braave* Leboucq had also received news of his son, captured earlier in the year while serving in the frigate *La Forte*. The English had been full of praise for the young Leboucq who had been injured while nailing the Tricolour to the main mast during *La Forte's* fatal encounter off the Bengal coast with the English frigate *Sybille*.[7] Happily he had now recovered from his wounds, Leboucq was told, and would soon be reunited with his father under a prisoner exchange.

His mission in the Red Sea completed, Alexander sailed for India at the beginning of November, leaving behind the *Amboyna* with Admiral Blankett's squadron. He had as a passenger a young Scots lieutenant, Charles Adam, who at Mocha had handed over the sloop *Albatross* to one of the *Braave* officers and who was now on his way to Calcutta to assume command of the *Sybille*. Adam must have listened with interest to the account of the capture of the *Surprise*, little dreaming that before long he himself would take an even finer prize in the same harbour.[8]

With the *Braave* forced to put into Trincomalee to have a leaking hull sealed, Adam continued his voyage by coastal ship to Calcutta. His impatience was understandable. Only a few weeks previously he had been celebrating his 19th birthday and now here he was about to put up a post-captain's single epaulette and take command of a 40-gun French-built frigate, known to be one of the finest to come from a Toulon yard.

But on arriving at Calcutta Adam found to his disappointment that the *Sybille* was still at sea, guarding the approaches to the Ganges. She was expected any day, but until then he would have to pass the time as best he could as a guest of his brother John, a writer with the East India Company.[9]

While Adam kicked his heels at Fort William, likely enough indulging a weakness he had developed for the gaming table, the *Sybille* came almost within cannon shot of ending the career of one of France's most famous privateers. The log entry for Monday, 30 December 1799, by the *Sybille's* temporary commander, Lieutenant John Batt, reveals little of the drama of the occasion.

"Sailed in morning (from anchor off the Sandheads), saw a strange sail bearing East. At 9 set the royals and t. gt. studd. In chase of the sail bearing East ... trimmed ship by taking the shot from the after lockers and placing them abreast the main hatches. An American ship in sight to windward ... at Noon strange sail SE. Light breezes and hazy. Lat Obs 20.56."

After another hour or so of pursuit — "all sail set that would draw in chase" — the entry concludes: "Returned shot." The *Sybille* had lost her quarry and Robert Surcouf sailed away to fame and fortune.

* * *

The day after their narrow escape from the *Sybille*, the crew of the *Clarisse* drank their captain's health with a double ration of spirits which had been spared from going the way of the water casks, cannon and spare masts, all thrown overboard at the height of the chase. Already some of this lost gear had been replaced thanks to the conveniently timed capture of the English company ship *James*, outward bound from Bengal with a cargo of rice.

A year had now passed since Surcouf's return from France, where he had taken command of the *Clarisse*, a 14-gun brig. A celebrity on the Isle de France, he was becoming known in Bengal not only for his successful attacks on English shipping but also for the chivalry he showed to those who fell into his hands, especially passengers and, above all, women passengers. Commenting on one of his early exploits in the Bay of Bengal, the *Madras Courrier* drew attention to "a young man called Surcouf who treats his prisoners with courtesy and humanity", even to the extent of returning to them personal objects of value.

This mixture of ruthlessness and gallantry was common to many of the privateers, men such as Lemême, Dutertre, Hodoul, and Ripaud de Monteaudevert, whose interceptions of British shipping caused occasional panic among the merchants of Bengal and Madras. The English, from their position of naval strength, could afford to regard privateers as little better than pirates, conveniently overlooking that the French corsairs were little different in their ways from those Elizabethan heroes Drake and Raleigh.

First to use privateers as part of a grand strategy was La Bourdonnais during the War of the Austrian Succession, and the practice was extended in subsequent wars by the Comte d'Estaing and De la Pallière. In the American War of Independence, during which 29 privateering expeditions were made from the Isle de France, the corsair Deschiens Kerulvay brought back from his first cruise off Ceylon cargoes valued at over one and a half million livres.

But it was during the period 1793 to 1810 that privateering reached its peak in the Indian Ocean, with a total of 193 cruises by ships fitted out at the Isle de France. Such was their success that the colony was so overstocked with manufactured goods and the staple crops of the East that American vessels would look to pick up their cargoes there at advantageous prices rather than go all the way to India.

Yet despite the great profits it brought the participants, the *guerre en course* could never seriously threaten Britain's position in the East. The privateers were no more than a series of pinpricks, and if they forced England to build up a powerful fleet in the Indian Ocean in order to combat them that, inevitably, brought disaster to French and allied possessions in the East, and the eventual surrender of the Isle de France in 1810.

An activity that so conveniently combined patriotism with the pursuit of personal gain had attracted the young Surcouf. At the outbreak of war in 1793 he was captain of a small ship trading between the islands and the African coast. He was eager to play what he hoped would be a profitable role in the war, but his first attempts to convert his ship, the *Emilie*, to a privateer were not successful. So many others had similar ideas that Malartic was reluctant to issue any more *lettres de marque*, and he easily found reasons for refusing them to Surcouf. His ship, after all, was armed with only four cannons, and obviously too small to be a successful privateer.

But Surcouf was not to be deterred by administrative obstacles. The opportunity to bypass Malartic's regulations came — or was it, even at this early stage, contrived? — when he was directed in September 1795 to fetch a cargo of tortoises from the Seychelles. If the inhabitants had none available in their parks he was to purchase what produce he could, such as maize and cotton, and complete this load with tortoises from the neighbouring islands. Setting off in the *Emilie,* Surcouf first called at Réunion, where he added to his crew as a result, apparently, of several citizens of that island slipping aboard his ship unnoticed, only declaring themselves after it was well out to sea.

According to the record, Surcouf severely reprimanded them and gave them something to eat. Soon all on board the *Emilie* would know that this was to be no ordinary voyage, that their captain had much more ambitious plans than bringing back wood and tortoises from the Seychelles. Surcouf stayed at Mahé for three months. He was unable to find any tortoises and he failed to cut and load a cargo of wood, but he did manage to recruit additional crew. Then, with the *Emilie* provisioned for a long voyage, he set off to hunt enemy ships in the Bay of Bengal.

There was, however, one small difficulty. When he returned to the Isle de France, how could Surcouf explain his switch from straightforward trading to a privateering campaign in the Eastern seas? Without the all-important *lettre de marque,* any explanation would be useless if he were captured by the English for they would regard him simply as a pirate. Moreover, the authorities at the Isle de France — assuming he managed to return there — would need written testimony from the crew to justify the changed circumstances of his expedition.

In a document which was endorsed by about half the crew, Surcouf described how, on the afternoon of 7 October, as the *Emilie* lay off Sainte Anne, he sighted two strange sail approaching the anchorage from the south-east. "Because we were expecting none from the Isle de France, we were suspicious of them and made sail immediately", he wrote. This precaution seemed to have been justified, for, without hesitation, the two strangers were seen to be in pursuit under a full press of sail.

Throughout the afternoon Surcouf made for Praslin, with one of the pursuers gaining perceptibly on him in the light airs. Steering between the Cayman reefs and Les Cheminées rocks, he then slipped through the channel between Praslin and La Digue, and then, just before dark, executed a dangerous manœuvre round the Ave Maria reefs. It was a moonless night. When morning came there was no sign of his pursuers.

Only then, according to Surcouf's account, did he make his

fateful decision. As they could not return to the Seychelles because the English ships would be there, and as he had no desire to go back to the Isle de France without a cargo, he would make for the Malaya or Sumatra coasts to load with rice before setting course for home. Significantly, Surcouf noted that he and his men were ready to defend themselves against enemy ships "if we encounter any on the way".

Despite the 30 signatures or personal marks on this document — none of his officers signed — Surcouf's account of how the *Emilie* became a privateer is obviously false. Everything points to his having planned the move from the start, by taking on extra crew at Réunion and Seychelles and provisioning his ship for an extended voyage. As for his sudden departure from Seychelles, the flight before an enemy reads like pure invention. There is nothing in British records to suggest that any warships were near Mahé on that particular day.

It is perhaps not surprising that Surcouf was unable to find a port where he could load rice. However he quickly captured his first prize. She was the *Penguin*, which, according to Surcouf, fired on him, forcing him to defend his ship. With the *Penguin* seen away under a prize crew to the Isle de France — she was loaded with wood — Surcouf continued northwards towards that prime killing ground for French privateers, the mouths of the Ganges.

There he captured a pilot brig, the *Cartier*, to which he transferred as she was a better sailer than the *Emilie*, which returned to the Isle de France with two other prizes, the *Russel* and *Sambollasse*, both heavily laden with Bengal rice. Some weeks and one prize later Surcouf encountered the Company ship *Triton*, "a fine vessel, whose long, black hull has as its only ornamentation a yellow centre band, marked ... by the sombre gunports of a lower battery of twenty-six pieces of 12". Seeing that the *Triton* could easily outsail him, Surcouf hoisted English colours and waited for the larger vessel to approach. She turned out to be a more formidable opponent than Surcouf had imagined, and it was only after 75 minutes of desperate fighting that the *Triton's* crew was overcome.

After this victory by the narrowest of margins, Surcouf decided it would be appropriate to return to the Isle de France, where large crowds gave him a hero's welcome.

Governments, however, look less admiringly on heroes who openly defy their regulations, and Surcouf found all his prizes had been confiscated. Surcouf and the owners of the *Emilie* vigorously contested the administrators' ruling and, faced with a popular outcry, the administrators eventually agreed that Surcouf could return to France to put his case to the government there.

The Directory had the good sense to recognise the arguments in Surcouf's favour — could it afford to discourage anyone who had scored such success against English shipping? — and it admitted the prizes, although Surcouf had to be content with less then their initial value.

Some months after his escape from the *Sybille*, Surcouf exchanged the *Clarisse*, in which he had returned from France to the Indian Ocean, for a bigger ship, the *Confiance*. It was in this vessel that he made perhaps his most spectacular capture in the Bay of Bengal, that of a powerful Indiaman, the *Kent*. According to some reports Captain Rivington of the *Kent* was so confident in the outcome of his encounter with the *Confiance* that he invited the ladies on deck to view the battle. Fatally, and despite the warnings of the officer of the watch on the danger of being boarded, Rivington allowed Surcouf to close. Soon the French were aboard, fighting desperately for possession of the ship.

The English had the advantage of having troops on board, and it was only after two hours of fierce hand-to-hand fighting that the crew of the *Kent* surrendered. Among the passengers was a German princess accompanying her husband to India, who with the other women was treated to Surcouf's traditional courtesy.

With the Peace of Amiens, Surcouf returned to France in April 1801. Honoured by Napoleon, he nevertheless refused a naval command, too independent to put himself under the orders of another. Eventually, restless with years of inaction in St Malo, Surcouf returned to the Indian Ocean in the appropriately named *Revenant*, in which he soon showed that he had lost none of his skill as a privateer. In vain, the English offered 250,000 rupees for his capture.

By 1808 Surcouf wisely decided to retire for good. The wheel of fortune was turning against the privateers. Many of his contemporaries such as Lemême, L'Hermitte, Dutertre, had been killed or captured, and the others would fight on against ever increasing odds.

The privateer most closely associated with the Seychelles was Jean-François Hodoul, who not only used the islands as a base during his operations in the Indian Ocean, the Persian Gulf and the Red Sea, but spent the remainder of his days there in quiet retirement until his death in 1835, when he was buried in the now disused cemetery at Bel Alr on the outskirts of Victona.

Unlike Surcouf and many others who sailed the Indian Ocean, Hodoul was not a Breton. He came from the small fishing port of La Ciotat, near Marseille, and for years commanded a small ship trading among the islands of the Indian Ocean. Three years after losing his brig *Olivette* to Captain Newcome's squadron, he took command of the 16-gun *Apollon* on a privateering expedition.

His successes were numerous, the extent of his wealth unknown, and his generous spirit indisputable. The inscription on Hodoul's tomb, *Il fut juste,* is a tribute that, unfortunately, has not been matched in recent times by the state of his grave and its surroundings. The broken, scored and vandalised appearance of the tomb is a remarkable injustice to the memory of a brave and resourceful Seychellois.

10

Exiles from France
1800-1801

Ils n'étaient pourtant pas les vrais coupables.
Las Cases, 1815

24 December 1800. Christmas Eve. Except in France, where officially it is the 3 Nivôse in the Ninth Year of the Republic.[1] Nivôse, the month of snow, but that evening in Paris it is just dark and cold, with some slight, intermittent rain.

Napoleon Bonaparte, dozing comfortably in his private salon at the Tuileries Palace, would have remained by the fireside had it not been for the importunings of his womenfolk. Josephine and his step-daughter Hortense were impatient. It was to be the first performance at the Opera of Haydn's *Creation of the World,* and already they were late.

"It will distract you," suggested Josephine. "You have been working too hard recently." Napoleon closed his eyes. Why did they not go on without him, he ventured. At once he realised his mistake as, perversely, Josephine offered to stay with him. Reluctantly, the First Consul got to his feet, took the sword, hat and coat that were handed to him, and went out to the waiting carriages. He would go with Lannes, Berthier, and. Lauriston; the ladies would follow in the other coach.

Was it pique at being forced from the fireside that prompted him at that moment to pass a critical comment on Josephine's new shawl? A discussion started among the women, delaying the departure of their coach by a few moments, which almost certainly saved Josephine's life. Had she been following closely behind Napoleon when the small cavalcade turned into the

Rue St Nicaise her carriage would have received the full blast of the explosion. Instead, it was only thrown against the railings of the Tuileries, its windows shattering with the impact. Josephine fainted. Hortense was bleeding from a cut hand. Caroline, Napoleon's sister, heavily pregnant, was unhurt.

In the front coach Napoleon had an equally lucky escape. Because of the lateness of their departure and because, so it is said, César the coachman was a little drunk, the horses were being driven with more urgency than usual. When he suddenly saw the small cart and horse that were blocking his way, César swerved past without any hesitation. Two seconds later, with a tremendous blast that some claimed was heard all over Paris the stationary cart exploded. The horse and the young girl holding its head were blown to bits; others in the vicinity were killed outright or left horribly injured in the roadway. One of Napoleon's escort was thrown from his horse, but otherwise the small procession escaped with only a shaking. Napoleon ordered César to drive on.

Reporting the incident the following day the official *Moniteur* said: "It appears that this cart was loaded with a type of infernal machine." It was, to be precise, an iron-bound barrel of gunpowder packed with nails and metal scrap similar to an experimental bomb the Jacobin Chevalier had demonstrated almost fatally to his co-plotters the previous October.[2]

First reports put the number of those killed at eight, with about 26 injured. Later estimates of dead and injured went as high as 60. Several people were blinded by the explosion, others found that their clothes had been ripped away. The wife of the owner of the Apollo cafe, who had run to the door to see the First Consul pass, had her breasts sliced off by part of a cauldron which hit her obliquely. She died three days later.

At the Opera the explosion was heard just as the Oratorio began. Junot, who was waiting for Napoleon, wondered why cannon was being fired at that hour. He was about to inquire, when the First Consul arrived. As news of the assassination attempt rippled through the audience clapping broke out, and the programme was interrupted as Napoleon acknowledged the applause. "The commotion was so loud and vibrant that the great hall trembled and one feared that it was going to collapse under the general rejoicing," noted one observer.

Napoleon did not sit through the performance. Soon he was back at the Tuileries where, Bourrienne observed, "the grand salon, on the ground floor, was filled with a crowd of functionaries eager to read in the eye of their master what they were to think and say on this occasion".[3] The police had already offered a reward to anyone who could give information about the owner of the cart, but Napoleon had no doubts about the identity of the culprits. "It is the Jacobins, the terrorists," he told the gathering. "It is those rascals who are always in revolt, opposed to every government."

Napoleon's police chief Joseph Fouché was an obvious target for the First Consul's wrath.[4] Already the crowd were distancing themselves from the ex-Jacobin, who described in his *Mémoires* his confrontation with Napoleon: "'Well,' he said to me, as he advanced, his face burning with anger. 'You still tell me that it is the royalists?' 'Without doubt, I will say it,' I replied, adding coolly, 'and what is more I will prove it.'" Fouché asked for eight days to produce the evidence.

Plotting against the consular government had become almost a fashionable pursuit, with several groups, royalist and Republican, engaged independently in devising ways of ridding themselves of Napoleon. Fouché had been correct in attributing this latest attempt to the royalists. Only recently his agents had lost track of a party of Chouans, insurgents from Brittany, who had been sent to Paris by their leader Georges Cadoudal.[5] As there was little doubt about their intentions Fouché had warned Napoleon that an assassination team was at large, but as such reports were frequently received no special precautions had been taken.

It was not until two weeks after the attempt that Fouché's men caught up with the Chouans. One of their number, Jean Carbon, also known as le Petit François, who had bought the cart and the old mare from a grain dealer, was arrested. Under interrogation he named his two accomplices: the Chevalier Joseph Picot de Limoélan, alias 'For the King', and 'Pierrot' Saint-Régent. Limoéan's task had been to signal the approach of Napoleon's carriage. Saint-Régent, a former naval officer, described by Fouché as "one of the most feared of the brigand leaders", had callously offered the young Pensol girl — her mother sold rolls on the Rue du Bac — 12 sous to hold the horse's head before he lit the fuse and disappeared. Both

Carbon and Saint-Régent, the latter discovered in hiding some weeks later, were executed.

While his agents were tracking down the authors of the crime, Fouché had been drawing up a list at Napoleon's insistence of known Republican sympathisers who, if not responsible for the bomb blast in the Rue St Nicaise, were considered quite capable of carrying out such an act. As betrayer of the principles of the Revolution, Napoleon sensed that the Republicans posed the most immediate threat to his ambitions.

"I was not long in understanding that this latest attempt against the life of the First Consul had irritated his dark and haughty soul and that, determined to crush his enemies, he wanted the powers that would make him master," observed the prescient Fouché. "His first essay in military dictatorship was to decree an act of deportation beyond the seas against a number of individuals chosen among the most despised demagogues and anarchists of the capital ..."

Fouché, with a blood-stained past he preferred to forget, was well qualified to put his finger on those dangerous to Napoleon and some, perhaps, who were a threat to himself. He claimed, however, that he managed to have 40 names deleted before the final list of 132 to be deported was agreed.

Who were the unfortunates rounded up by the police, while the Press created a suitable atmosphere of anxiety with reports of continued plotting against the First Consul? Some, such as Monneuse, Dufour, Saint-Amant, Joly, Marlet and Quinon, were *septembriseurs,* the dreaded stigma given to those who were rumoured, correctly or not, of having participated in the prison massacres of September 1792.

Others had been members of the Revolutionary tribunals whose judgements had sent hundreds to the guillotine. Among those *enragés* were the lemonade seller Chrétien, Delabarre, the lawyer Pépin-Desgrouettes, and Métevier, the latter said by his colleagues "never to have condemned except with regret, and to have acquitted with great joy". Also prominent on the list was the name of the former Jacobin general Jean-Antoine Rossignol.

A silversmith at the outbreak of the Revolution, Rossignol had been in the forefront at the taking of the Bastille and the massacre of the Swiss Guards at the Tuileries on 10 August

1792. However, he had earned his place as a minor Revolutionary figure by leading a military campaign against the royalist uprising in the Vendée. It was guerrilla warfare, in which both sides committed atrocities. Initially successful against the rebels, Rossignol started to suffer reverses and by 1795 was in prison accused of incompetence. Freed under an amnesty a year later, he next was suspected of plotting against the government, but was eventually acquitted.

Arrested, and again freed in September 1800 for lack of evidence to connect him with a plot to assassinate Napoleon at Malmaison, he readily became a prime suspect when the bomb went off in the Rue St Nicaise.

Rossignol was by reputation a *septembriseur*, said to have been one of the 'judges' supervising the massacre at La Force prison;[6] as such, he was easily characterised as one of Fouché's "despised demagogues". Others on the list were more difficult to label. "Humble patriots, who had not reached any prominence during the Revolution" was how some observers viewed them. The architect Lefranc may have fitted this description, or Cardinaux, theatre owner and one of the founders of the Société du Panthéon;[7] also, the journalist Eon, Chevalier, the brother of the bomb-maker, and a whole posse of police spies whose names had been submitted by those eager to put them out of circulation. Fouché himself was said to have been particularly interested in including anyone from Lyon, scene of one of his most notorious episodes during the Revolution.

There were others who were victims of personal spite or who found themselves on the list because of a hasty word overheard in public. There was at least one case of mistaken identity, that of Claude Flamant, 40-year-old carriage maker living at 39 Rue Poissonière in Paris. The police mixed him up with another of the same name, from the same canton. His wife, Louise, wrote several petitions to have him freed. "The one who was denounced, Flamand, is a wine merchant at the White Horse, at Nouvelle France," she wrote. "He figured in all the clubs, while the one who was deported is a carriage maker who was never involved in any political business."

Bourienne, who claimed he succeeded in having several names erased from the list, commented: "I shudder to think of the way in which men utterly innocent were accused of a revolting crime without even the shadow of proof. The name of an individual, his opinions, perhaps only assumed, were sufficient grounds for banishment."

A word from a woman had been enough to secure the arrest of the handsome ex-cavalry subaltern Georges Laurent Derville. As for Jean-Baptiste Pradel, a food merchant from Aurillac, it was unfortunate that he should have travelled to Paris to press the government for payment of supplies. In a heated moment "he spoke some words which might have rendered him suspect". Both Jean-Marie Gosset and his brother Louis were, according to their respective wives, victims of falsehoods spread by ill-intentioned comrades, while it is said that Jean-François Barbier, a former priest, was put on the list after being found visiting an old school friend, the suspect General Pichegru.[8]

On 20 Nivôse (10 January 1801) the Consuls of the Republic issued a decree officially listing the names of the 132 deportees. They were described as "perpetrators and accomplices in the explosion in the Rue Nicaise and other attempts at assassinating the First Consul Bonaparte", and to give a judicial tone to what was purely an administrative act, the decree at the same time confirmed death sentences passed the previous evening by the Criminal Court on four Jacobin conspirators who had plotted the assassination of Napoleon at the Opera in October.

To justify this wholly unwarranted "act of government", Napoleon had first approached the Senate and, after arguing that the Constitution was silent on the extraordinary means that might be taken to safeguard the lives of the three Consuls, he persuaded the senators to endorse the order of banishment as a measure taken to preserve the Constitution. It was a brilliant piece of manipulation, for Napoleon now had within his grasp a weapon that would give a semblance of legality to any arbitrary act in the future. Unfortunately for the victims of that first decree, their banishment could never be revoked as that might endanger the sanctity of the Senate decision on which Napoleon's dictatorial powers rested.

It having been decided that the deportees should be sent "outside the European territory of the Republic", it was left to the Minister of Marine to decide where that should be. There seems to have been an effort by the Minister, Forfait,[9] to select a colony that, while far enough away, would not condemn the deportees to an overly harsh environment. Cayenne was considered unsuitable for such a large number. Madagascar was rejected because of its climate and the fact that there was no French settlement there; likewise Senegal, where there were only a few French settlers. In the end the Seychelles was chosen as being sufficiently remote to make escape unlikely, but with a good climate and a settlement thought large enough to accommodate the deportees. Napoleon may have felt a twinge of conscience over the deportations, for Forfait, in a letter to Quinssy, instructed the Seychelles commandant to treat the deportees kindly as long as they behaved and did not upset the morals and usages of the colony.[10]

Quinssy was also told to give them land, and the means to cultivate the soil and maintain themselves. Anticipating objections from the settlers at having deportees among them, Forfait told Quinssy that if the settlers were dissatisfied they could always return to the Isle de France, where orders had been given that they should be resettled if they wished.

Having decided on where to send the deportees, Forfait's next problem was to find ships to transport them. He was reluctant to commit anything as valuable as a frigate for this task, and gave orders for the store ship *Rhinoceros* and two smaller vessels, the corvette *Flèche* and the brig *Arabe*, to be made ready. Each would be loaded to capacity, for in addition to the deportees there would be a detachment of soldiers on board as escort. To make more room the main armament of the corvette and brig would be stored in the hold.

Meanwhile, the deportees, incarcerated in a prison ship in Nantes harbour, waited daily in expectation of their release, as by now word had reached them that the perpetrators of the 3 Nivôse explosion had been found. Their hopes had been boosted also by an instruction to their families not to send them clothes or money on the pretext that these would add unnecessarily to their possessions and might easily be lost.

But the weeks passed and no release order came. Despair replaced hope, followed by the awful realisation that there was, after all, to be no reprieve when 38 of the deportees were taken from their cells in the *Cayenne* and moved by barge downriver to St Nazaire, where they were put aboard the *Flèche*. The corvette sailed on 6 February 1801. In command was Lieutenant Eustace Bonamy, appointed at the last minute because of his knowledge of eastern waters.[11]

No-one on board knew where they were bound, and it was only when the ship was well out in the Atlantic that Bonamy, as instructed, opened his triple-sealed orders and learned he "was to make route towards the isle Mahé, the largest of the Séchelles" and there "disembark the persons detained in his ship and put them at the disposal of the commandant". These orders, he was informed, were not to be communicated to anyone, including the ship's officers. Bonamy was also instructed to avoid all sails and to make no stops on the way unless absolutely necessary. As to what action he should take in the event of encountering a superior force, an unfinished sentence, subsequently deleted, at the foot of the document indicated that it would be better if Bonamy ensured that nothing of the sort occurred.

After the departure of the Flèche, there was no further movement of deportees for several weeks. Forfait found that neither the *Rhinoceros* nor the *Arabe* were any longer available and, in desperation, he was forced ultimately to assign a brand-new frigate, the *Chiffonne*, to the task. The *Chiffonne* sailed for Seychelles on 14 March with 32 deportees. They were the last to be sent; the 60 or so remaining in France were held in various island prisons off the Atlantic coast for about two years, when 40 were then transported to Guyane in Central America.

An account of the voyage of the *Chiffonne* and the fate of the deportees after their arrival in Seychelles was recorded by Jean-Baptiste Lefranc, who was one of about ten deportees who managed to get back to France. Two books appeared based on Lefranc's experiences. The first, *History of the Double Conspiracy of 1800*, which was published in Paris anonymously in 1819, was written by a Monsieur Fescourt, with whom Lefranc had left his notes. Later Lefranc dictated his own book, *The misfortunes of several victims of the tyranny of Napoleon Bonaparte,* but written without the benefit of his notes it is less precise than Fescourt's work.

Lefranc, described by Fescourt as observant, inventive and hard-working, had been associated with various factions from the start of the Revolution. "I walked along the side of a precipice without noticing the drop," he wrote later. Repelled by the excesses of the Terror, he had welcomed the fall of Robespierre. Later, disillusioned with the Directory, he was, by his own cryptic admission, "carried perhaps beyond the bounds of prudence and sagacity". The result was that he was named as an accomplice in the Babeuf plot, but, like his friend Rossignol, was acquitted.[12]

At the time of the 3 Nivôse explosion Lefranc was working as an architect for General Lefebvre, the Duke of Danzig. He claimed he was arrested after being denounced by "a few old-time revolutionaries who remembered I had thanked God for the catastrophe of 9 Thermidor".[13] After spending a month in St Pélagie prison in Paris he was sent with the other detainees to Nantes and eventually put on board the *Chiffonne*.

The mouth of the Loire had been under constant blockade by the English and for eight days after the embarkation of the deportees Captain Pierre Guieysse had to wait until the weather drove the blockading squadron from the coast before he could slip away past Noirmoutier island and reach the open sea. Such was his haste that he cut his cable and had to leave behind 11 of his crew. In addition to the deportees Guieysse had a detachment of soldiers on board to guard them, making a total complement of 269. Quarters were inevitably cramped, and as there had been no time to provide ventilation between decks where Lefranc and his companions were confined conditions were extremely uncomfortable.

"The honest captain executed punctiliously the orders of his master by submerging our existence with all that the most refined cruelty could conceive," commented Lefranc somewhat unfairly, for Guieysse was a kindly enough man although, apprehensive of having his ship seized by men of the violent reputation of the deportees, he had enforced a strict regime for his charges, allowing them only a minimum time on deck for exercise.

"They were fed like the crew, and those whose age or infirmities made it necessary for them to have some extra care were accorded this on the advice of the medical officer," Guieysse recorded. Each deportee had a mattress and blanket provided by the government, but with inadequate clothing they were lucky to get whatever Guieysse could find for them in the ship's store. Lefranc complained bitterly about the food, and with typical March weather in the Bay of Biscay there was

*Charles d'Arzac Ternay
Governor-general of Isle de France and
Bourbon, 1771-76*

*François Magallon de la Morlière
Governor-general of French establishments
east of the Cape of Good Hope 1801-03*

*Jean-François Hodoul
Seychellois corsair*

*Robert Surcouf
French corsair*

By Henry Newcome Esqr.
Captain of his Britannic Majestys
Ship Orpheus & Senior officer of his
Britannic Majestys Ships employed
on a particular Service &a &a &a

I Do in his Britannic Majestys Name, demand
an instant Surrender of the Island of Mahé, and its
dependencies with every thing in and belonging thereto.

I give you one Hour from the
delivery of this Message to decide, if any Resistance
is made, you must abide by the Consequences
thereof.

Given under my hand on Board his
Britannic Majestys Ship Orpheus
16.th day of May 1794.

(Signed) Henry Newcome.

Pour copie conforme à l'Original en dépôt
entre mes mains, aux Archives de Seychelles. Le 10.
Juillet 1794. J.ⁿ B.^{te} Quéau de Quinssy.

A copy of the ultimatum sent by Captain Henry Newcome of HMS Orpheus to the French commandant, Quéau de Quinssy, demanding the surrender of Seychelles, 16 May 1794.

Captain Charles René Magon   *Tippu Sultan*

View of Pondichéry, French settlement on India's Coromandel coast.

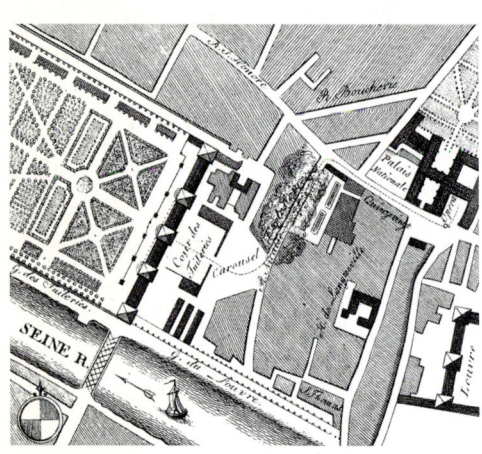

(Top) Artist's impression of the assassination attempt against Napoleon Bonaparte in the Rue St Nicaise, Paris, December 1800.

(Above) Map showing route taken by Bonaparte's cortège on leaving the Tuileries Palace for the Opera House.

(Right) Bonaparte as First Consul.

> « À bord de *La Chiffonne* », le 23 messidor, an IX
> « de la République française. »

> » Recevez, citoyen capitaine Guieysse,
> » Tous les remerciments que chacun vous adresse.
> » Moins, il est mérité, plus le mal est terrible :
> » À notre état cruel vous parûtes sensible.
> » Nous remercions aussi les officiers du bord,
> » Qui, pour nous soulager, furent d'un même accord.
> » Redoutable marin, votre mâle courage
> » A stimulé l'ardeur de tout votre Equipage :
> » Fière de vous porter, « la Chiffonne » pucelle
> » A soumis, par vos lois, l'orgueilleuse « Hirondelle ».
>
> » Canonniers et soldats, par leur zèle héroïque,
> » Battent nos ennemis : Vive la République !

B. Guilhémat, déporté

The deportee Bertrand Guilhémat, on board the Chiffonne, writes to thank Captain Guieysse for his humane treatment of the deportees and congratulates him on the capture of a Portuguese corvette.

(Right) The Chiffonne and the British frigate Sybille in close combat in Mahé harbour.

Two British naval officers who fought successful actions in Mahé harbour Captain Charles Adam of the Sybille, and (right) Commander Collier of the sloop Victor.

(Below) Blair Adam house, Kinross-shire, Scotland, ancestral home of Captain (later Admiral Sir) Charles Adam.

General Charles Decaen, Captain-general of French settlements east of the Cape of Good Hope, 1803-10.

Admiral Charles Alexandre Durand de Linois, Commander of East Indies Naval Division, 1803-06.

Jean-Baptiste Quéau de Quinssy, who was the last French commandant of Seychelles, 1793-1811.

Below: Quinssy's tomb in the grounds of State House, Victoria.

much seasickness on board. Instructed to keep well to the west of Madeira and the Cape Verde islands on his run south, Guieysse was some way off the coast of Brazil when, on 9 May, he engaged a Portuguese corvette, the *Andorinha*, which he captured after a running fight. Unable to spare a prize crew, he let her go after taking the cables, spare rigging and sails he needed.

A month later, after rounding the Cape well out of sight of land, the *Chiffonne* made an even more valuable capture, an English company ship the *Bellona*, bound for London with a cargo that Guieysse described as one of the richest to leave Bengal. In both engagements the deportees, led by Rossignol, had offered their services to the captain, but according to Lefranc "he did not consider us worthy enough to share in his glory".

There could be no question of Guieysse allowing the *Bellona* to go free, and a small prize crew under Midshipman Mahé was detailed to take the captured vessel to the Isle de France. Unfortunately as the *Chiffonne* came alongside the prize, a false swing of the helm brought the *Bellona* under the *Chiffonne's* bowsprit, snapping it off and bringing down with it the foremast in a tangled mass of rigging and spars. Guieysse, anxious now to reach his destination to replace the mast, had to continue his journey at a reduced pace.

The *Bellona* reached the Isle de France without mishap on 7 July. Its arrival was the first indication to the authorities that a French ship was in the Indian Ocean on a special mission, a piece of news that caused some uneasy speculation. For although Mahé was not able to state the *Chiffonne's* destination, he undoubtedly gave a full report on the type of passengers she was carrying.

Later, a Danish ship, the *Hercule*, brought more news of the *Chiffonne*. She had been seen off the coast of Madagascar on July (12 Messidor), with her masts in bad shape. Guieysse had not disclosed his destination to the Danish captain but, as instructed in the event of meeting a Danish or Swedish ship, had warned him to be on the look-out for English cruisers now that Denmark had entered into a protective maritime alliance against Britain.[14]

Another month was to pass before the Isle de France governor-general Magallon de la Morlière was informed not only of the *Chiffonne's* destination and the purpose of her voyage but also that another French ship was in the Indian Ocean on a similar mission. This startling news came in dispatches sent by Captain Bonamy of the *Flèche*.

Although Bonamy had left France almost a month before the *Chiffonne*, he had fallen far behind, his progress hampered by storms and damage from an encounter with an English ship. Ill-luck continued to dog him after rounding the Cape and, short of provisions and with many of his crew sick, he had put in at Réunion. Before sailing from there he had left his dispatches for delivery to the Isle de France authorities.

Magallon was shocked when he read them. It was almost unbelievable that France would send 32 of the worst Jacobins to live among the settlers. What of the dangers these outcasts would present to the safety and way of life of the inhabitants? These rascals would preach the libertarian ideas of the Revolution; they would incite the slaves to revolt as had happened in St Domingue.[15] All the excesses of the Paris Terror would be re-enacted in the Indian Ocean colonies.

The Isle de France inhabitants had sent the Directory envoys Baco and Burnel packing when they had tried to impose the decree abolishing slavery. Who was to say what their reaction would be to the arrival of deportees in the Seychelles? Only recently Magallon had assured the inhabitants that, under the Constitution of 1800, the consular government would permit each colony to retain its customs and traditions. Now it seemed that all this meant nothing. For the moment Magallon decided to keep Bonamy's dispatches to himself. It would be prudent not to disclose the whereabouts of the *Flèche* until she had completed her mission. It would also give him time to think how best to break the news about the deportees to the inhabitants of the Isle de France.

When he eventually did so, the reaction was as he had feared. To Forfait on 25 September (3 Vendémiaire) he wrote: "It is my duty, Citizen Minister, to inform you that the dispositions ... for the men destined to be deported to the neighbourhood of these colonies has caused serious and lively alarm; it is seen in the approach of such men the endorsement of a principle which will be the cause of their inevitable loss ... at this moment the confidence which had begun to be restored thanks to the benign and encouraging influences of the new government has disappeared. One must know the men and the passions of this country in order to be able to judge the immediate effects that this news has produced. I will not hide from you that these two colonies are only held and will always be held so by no more than a thread, so much do they fear the application of that principle about which the slightest allusion provokes a crisis."

Magallon also referred the Minister to the Seychelles capitulation — of which he seemed to have been unaware — pointing out that in a sense the islands were no longer under French rule. It would be embarrassing for Quinssy to have to receive the deportees, and it could be argued that once they had landed there they were free men.

By now there was serious concern about the fate of the *Chiffonne*, which, as the ordonnateur-general Chanvalon noted, was long overdue "whatever call it had to make in the archipelago". He expressed the wish that the *Flèche* would "be more fortunate and complete her voyage before long and return to this colony". Several weeks would have to pass before he knew his hopes had been in vain.

A week after his meeting with the Danish ship *Hercule*, on 7 July (18 Messidor) Guieysse was off Remire island, thought to be the most northerly of the Amirantes, when he sighted two small islands to the north-east which were not marked on the *Neptune Oriental*. He noted that these islands (subsequently named the African Banks) were "very dangerous; some trees, but can be seen only in good weather. Very slight elevation".

Four days later, on 11 July, the *Chiffonne* moored in Mahé harbour. The friendly reception the island always accorded to visiting French warships quickly turned sour when the settlers learned of the passengers it had brought to the colony. "They wanted to send them to some deserted island," Guieysse reported. For three days he was forced to keep the deportees on the ship while the settlers argued about what should be done with them.

On 14 July, Bastille Day, the deportees were landed. The anniversary of the triumph of liberty, Lefranc remarked bitterly, "but for us the triumph of tyranny".[16]

Malavois was particularly bitter about the decision to allow the deportees to land. He reproached the inhabitants — and

Quinssy — for contravening the capitulation with the English and warned them that they were exposing themselves to reprisals. "You do not realise that you are taking to your hearts your worst enemies," he wrote, hinting that the deportees were already planning a slave uprising so that they could seize the settlers' properties. Malavois, who had already planned to retire to the Isle de France, was to continue his campaign against the deportees on his return there, with fatal results for many of them. Quinssy promised the deportees that he would make their stay as pleasant as possible, and urged them to behave and "not to do anything against the morals" of the place. He gave each of them what spare clothing he had and lodged them temporarily in one of the government buildings until he could persuade the settlers to take one or more into their homes.

Reluctantly the settlers agreed, but would consider only those who appeared the least troublesome. Lefranc referred to "a veritable market" on the ship, "where we were like beasts of burden up for sale to the highest bidder. Each of the settlers came on board, examined all of us, stopping in front of any who appeared more suitable to them, and interrogating him on his age and calling".

Lefranc, too resentful to submit politely to questioning, was not chosen and had to be lodged in town by Quinssy. According to the reluctant guest, the government rations consisted of bad rice "and the most detestable sort of fish"; presumably he was savouring for the first time the local variety of *poisson salé*. But the food must have improved, for Quinssy listed a balanced diet of potatoes, turtle meat, fresh and dry vegetables, fresh as well as salted fish, fat and a little bread for the sick.

An additional sombre note to the unhappy scenario of disembarkation was the death two hours after he had been landed of one of the deportees, Pierre Richon, who had been ill during the last two months of the voyage. None of the others seems to have been seriously affected by the rigours of their journey. Quinssy, writing a few months after their arrival, noted that all were in excellent health. "There is no country as healthy as Mahé," he informed Forfait. "Both Europeans and Blacks live to a good age here." It was not a prospect that necessarily appealed to the deportees.

About a month after his arrival Lefranc was taken in by a settler called Mincé, living at Anse aux Pins, who was interested in making use of his knowledge of architecture. Gradually others accepted deportees into their homes as they saw the advantages of the extra labour, or for companionship or, with the better educated, as tutors to their children.

Captain Guieysse's sole concern had been to carry out the necessary repairs to the *Chiffonne* and get under way to the Isle de France. The main task was the cutting, trimming, and stepping of a new foremast, and for this Quinssy had persuaded several inhabitants to lend their slaves. "I was very happy to give to the French government proof of my attachment and that of the inhabitants of this archipelago by helping to put the frigate in a state of repair," he wrote. He had estimated that it would take about a month to complete the work, a dangerously lengthy period for the *Chiffonne* to remain disabled in harbour. Guieysse had taken what precautions he could. A battery of four 12-pounders was set up on Pointe Launay (today's Pointe Conan) to cover the harbour entrance, and a look-out was maintained on Sainte Anne to give warning of an approaching ship.

On the morning of 9 August work on the ship was almost complete. The bowsprit was in place and the foremast was about to be taken on board when the look-out on Sainte Anne signalled that a three-masted ship had been sighted.

The approach of the frigate *Sybille*, for such was the identity of the stranger, galvanised the *Chiffonne's* crew into action. The main battery of 12-pounders and the six 6-pounders on the quarterdeck were run out, but the scaffolding set up on the foredeck to receive the new mast meant that no guns in that part of the ship could be brought into use. A detachment of soldiers under Captain Cudenec set off to man the land battery, while an armed cutter was prepared for use should the need arise.

Captain Adam, who had left Trincomalee on 27 July with orders from Admiral Rainier to cruise in Seychelles waters, had never been to Mahé, nor had any of his officers, and there were several anxious moments as the *Sybille* entered the channel to the harbour, guided solely by the changing colour of the shallows as seen by a man stationed at the masthead. Fortunately there was no harassment from armed enemy boats, for the *Sybille* was flying French colours and, although Guieysse was suspicious, he noted through his glass the French lines of the frigate.

As the *Sybille* came within hailing distance, Guieysse saw that the frigate had dropped anchor. He called her to send a boat across, and a reply came readily enough. If this was reassuring the effect quickly evaporated as Guieysse observed that the newcomer was swinging round to bring her broadside to bear. In an instant the Tricolour was hauled down and replaced with a Union flag. Both ships opened fire simultaneously. According to Adam his was the first broadside, it being instantly returned by the Frenchman. Guieysse reported that he fired as soon as he recognised the identity of the other. The enemy's reply, he said, was almost as prompt.

The ensuing battle was watched from the shore by Quinssy and a crowd of settlers, slaves and deportees. The *Chiffonne's* 12-pounders were no match for the heavier armament of the *Sybille*, and although Cudenec's battery, which after a slight delay had opened fire on the enemy's stern with heated shot, reduced the advantage, it was all over after only 17 minutes.

There was no lack of courage by Guieysse (he was later cleared at a court-martial in France), but the *Sybille*, with only her second broadside, dealt the *Chiffonne* a blow from which the French frigate could not recover. The shot, cutting right through the ship, killed or disabled about 50 men and caused dreadful havoc. In all ten cannons of the main battery and two on the quarterdeck were immediately silenced.

"Without this unfortunate happening, the enemy, despite his superiority, would have had to pay for his hardihood," Guieysse remarked. As it was, firing continued in "tolerable spirit" for some more minutes until a lucky shot from the *Sybille* cut the *Chiffonne's* cable, causing her to veer away so that her guns could no longer bear. Noting that "in this position the whole crew suffered greatly from the fire raining down on us", Guieysse cut the remaining cable so as to drive the *Chiffonne* on to the reef, and hauled down his flag.

The land battery continued the fight for a while longer, but with the *Sybille* now turning all her firepower on Cudenec's position, and seeing an armed boat approaching from the English frigate, the Frenchmen abandoned their guns and fled. From the *Chiffonne* many of the seamen escaped to the shore although Guieysse remained on board to surrender formally his ship to a boarding party under the *Sybille's* first lieutenant, Nicholas Mauger.[17]

The *Chiffonne's* casualty list was substantial, as about one-fifth of the ship's company had been killed or wounded. Among the dead were two of Quinssy's slaves. In contrast, the *Sybille* had got off lightly, with only two seamen, Benjamin Johnson and John Jones, killed and a midshipman, Mr Phillimore, slightly injured. The French wounded were sent ashore to the hospital and the dead were buried on Sainte Anne. Quinssy noted that all who had to have limbs amputated survived, which he attributed not only to the skill of the surgeons but, as he was wont to point out, the healthiness of the Seychelles climate.

The *Chiffonne* now required further extensive repairs and it would be more than a month before she was ready to sail. Fortunately her hull under the water line had not been damaged on the reef, and Adam had no difficulty in refloating her at high tide. In addition to the French frigate Adam also had as prizes the sloop *Sophie* and the ketch *Petit Gustave*. A third vessel, the *Paracti Pacha*, a Portuguese prize of the *Sophie's*, had been sunk during the action and could not be refloated.

Like his predecessors, Adam renewed the Seychelles capitulation, but in addition Quinssy succeeded in having him extend the terms to cover five small vessels which would sail under a plain blue flag with the inscription "Seychelles Capitulation" in white lettering.

"I got agreement that three of these brigs would be sent to the Isle de France with the crews of the *Chiffonne* and the private vessels, with a passport from M. Adam, and as a *parlementaire*," Quinssy noted. The French commandant, old enough at 50 to be Adam's father, seems to have taken a liking to the Scotsman, whom he described as "a very upright man, who spoke French well".

Although Adam was a humane and popular captain, it would have been surprising if the crew of the *Sybille* had not grown restless with their prolonged stay and all the joys of freedom that the proximity of land might conjure up in a sailor's mind. Yet there is no record of desertions from the ship, and only once during their month at Seychelles did

Adam order punishment for three seamen, their crimes being respectively drunkenness, theft, and disobedience of orders. The most severe sentence was the fairly common three dozen lashes, the least a derisory two lashes, all carried out on 26 August.

The day before there had been a flurry of excitement when an unsuspecting schooner sailed into the harbour. "Fired a gun shotted to bring her too," Adam recorded. "Sent the boats to board and found her to be a schooner from the Isle de France; brought the prisoners on board and left an officer with a party of men to take charge of her."

By the end of August the *Chiffonne's* foremast had been finally erected and the rigging run. Adam had maintained the land battery as a precautionary defence but now it was time for the four guns to be brought off. On 2 September the *Sybille*, followed by the *Chiffonne*, were moved out of the inner harbour in preparation for departure. The captured French schooner, *Sophie*, would also be making the voyage back to India.

A final consignment of provisions had been sent ashore for the sick and wounded at the hospital when, at 11 o'clock, unexpected visitors arrived in a small boat. They were led by a Lieutenant Campbell, who two weeks previously had been in command of the sloop *Spitfire* carrying mails from the Red Sea to the Cape. His ship was now lying a half-submerged wreck on one of the African Banks, the miniscule reefs at the northern extremity of the Amirantes which Guieysse had noted the previous month as being "very dangerous". Luckily for Campbell he had managed to get his crew and the best part of his stores on shore and, with some of his men, had set off in the ship's cutter to seek help at Mahé, 150 miles to the east. Adam agreed to relinquish the *Sophie* so that Campbell could return in her to pick up the rest of his crew and resume his voyage to the Cape. Two days later, on Friday, 4 September, with nothing else to detain Adam, the *Sybille* and the *Chiffonne* sailed for Madras.

Adam now had time to relax and savour his success. It had been a remarkable piece of luck to have come across the *Chiffonne*. Writing to his father on 7 September, as the *Sybille* passed through the Maldives islands, he pointed out that although other British ships had taken prizes at the Seychelles, "ours is the best, both honour and profit". Adam knew that capturing a frigate in a single-ship action was an event in one's career that augured well for future advancement; but of more immediate interest was the prize money it would bring. He estimated that his share would be about £3,000, some of which he probably had to allocate to paying off his gambling debts.[18] His satisfaction, however, might have been diminished slightly had he realised that by staying one more day at Mahé he would almost certainly have had a share in another prize, that of the corvette *Flèche*.

On the day the *Sybille* and the *Chiffonne* left the Seychelles, the French ship was only 70 miles away running for the doubtful safety of Mahé harbour with His Britannic Majesty's sloop *Victor* in hot pursuit.[19]

For Captain Bonamy the encounter with the *Victor* when so near his destination was the final misfortune in a long and tiring voyage of delay and frustration. First there had been the necessity of twice putting into small ports in northern Spain, Ribadeo and then Rivadesela, to repair damage suffered in a running fight with two English ships and later to replace a foremast lost in a storm. The deportees, too, had been troublesome, particularly during the enforced stay in Spanish ports. There had almost been a revolt at their continued detention when a rumour started circulating that Napoleon was dead, and there had also been attempts to escape.

Having eventually rounded the Cape, Bonamy had then run into adverse winds which drove him much further east than his projected course. With provisions running low and, worse, with almost every officer sick, he had been forced to put in at Réunion. By then he had himself been keeping watch for 25 days, with only a cadet who remained untouched by the fever to share the duty.

Bonamy was not well received at Réunion, where there was an initial fear that he wanted to land his passengers on the island. It was only reluctantly agreed that the most seriously ill officers — three ensigns, the commander of the military detachment, and the assistant surgeon — could be landed for hospital treatment. Bonamy was able to find in Réunion only one replacement, a ship's surgeon, before he sailed. During the three-day stay one of the deportees, Jean-Baptiste Delrue, died. Bonamy stubbornly refused to disclose his ultimate destination — which put him even less in favour with the Réunion authorities — but, as we have seen, he left this information in his dispatches for onward delivery to the Isle de France government.

On 12 September (15 Fructidor), eight days after leaving Réunion, the *Flèche* was in sight of Frégate island when, shortly after one in the afternoon, a sail was seen to windward "which appeared also to be making for Mahé or to be chasing us".

Commander George Collier of the *Victor* sloop had sighted the *Flèche* some hours previously and was making all sail on a converging course to intercept her. The *Victor* was on most points the better sailer and although Bonamy set as much canvas as he could the gap between the two ships steadily decreased.

Unluckily for the Frenchman strong currents prevented him clearing the western extremity of Frégate, and being forced to put about a confrontation became inevitable. Bonamy, calling his crew aft to explain the position, was gratified to find them eager enough for a fight. He must have regretted, however, that so many of his eight-pounders were in the hold, stored there in order to make room for the 40-man escort from the 2nd and 68th demi-brigades of infantry which he had on board to guard the deportees.

Yet Bonamy did not yet realise how unequal the contest would be, for the *Victor*, which was slightly smaller than the *Flèche*, carried an armament of sixteen 32-pound carronades, in addition to two 6-pounders, which made her an exceptionally well armed ship. Although first introduced in British ships about 20 years earlier, the short-barrelled carronade, known as the smasher because of its short-range destructive effects, was still an unpleasant surprise for an adversary. Collier, who referred to the "disguised state" of the *Victor*, noted that in the opening exchanges with the *Flèche* his second broadside was sufficient to have her break off the engagement.[20]

Bonamy's "feeble broadside of four cannons" had, however, mangled much of the *Victor's* rigging, so that he was able to turn and flee, leaving the English ship half-a-mile to windward before Collier could have new braces and bowlines rove to the lower and top sails. The *Flèche*, too, had suffered some damage to sails and rigging but not enough to impede her progress. The galley was completely wrecked, but fortunately no-one had been killed.

The *Victor* had suffered two casualties — one seaman hit by two musket balls and the master's mate, Mr Middleton, slightly hurt. Collier's log also recorded that two seamen, Peter Cruze and Antonio, had "departed this life", but these deaths were not, it seems, the result of enemy action.

"Night fast approaching added to the chagrin I felt on observing the enemy sail better than the *Victor* on a wind," Collier noted. The chase continued throughout the night and all next day, with the two ships sometimes within gunshot range. But the *Flèche* maintained her sailing advantage and by sunset on 4 September she was a full four to five miles in front. That night she disappeared completely. Collier surmised correctly that the *Flèche* must be making for Mahé, and setting a course for there himself he was rewarded towards sunset on the following day by seeing the French ship standing in for the harbour.

"I kept under easy sail till dark, when the *Victor* was anchored; and at daylight I had the satisfaction of seeing the enemy moored with springs in the basin, or inner harbour, with a red flag at the fore."

Bonamy had lost no time in preparing for the decisive action he knew must follow. First, the deportees, many in pitiful condition after the seven-month-long voyage, had been quickly disembarked despite the renewed protests of the settlers who must have regretted that this particular French ship had managed to evade capture.

The cannons were brought up from the ship's hold so that the *Flèche* was now fully armed. Bonamy positioned his batteries on one side, facing the harbour entrance, and with springs on the anchors he could swing the ship round to ensure the effectiveness of his fire. He was determined that it would be a fight to the end, and all boats had been cut away to prevent anyone leaving the ship.

It was an overcast morning and matched Collier's mood as he surveyed the narrow channel where a moderate wind, whipping the grey water into a choppy turbulence, obliterated signs of where the reef lay. Like Adam, he had no knowledge of the entrance to this harbour which he would have to negotiate if he were to get to grips with the Frenchman. At first light he had dispatched a boat to sound the channel; the master, James Crawford, volunteering for this task despite an attack of fever. Bonamy, however, was not prepared to allow such activity to proceed undisturbed and promptly sent a cutter to fire on the English boat which was forced to retire.

Now, with a minimum of canvas set, Collier cautiously got under way, bringing the *Victor* slowly into the harbour until, at 11.18 a.m., a ranging shot came from the *Flèche*. It fell far short. Eight minutes later, with the *Victor* about 100 yards away, Bonamy opened "a lively fire".

In his account Collier reported that "the extreme narrowness of the channel, added to the wind not being very favourable, compelled me to use warps and the staysails only, which exposed the ship to a raking fire for some minutes, till shoaling our water, I was obliged to bring up. Having two springs on the cable, our broadside was soon brought to bear; and at 11.45 a.m. a well directed fire was opened, which was kept up incessantly from both vessels ..."

The battle went on for almost two and a half hours. Quinssy, who had been on board the *Flèche* until just before the firing began, noted that from "the way in which the guns of the *Flèche* were being served we were very much hopeful of a glorious conclusion for the French flag".

But the *Victor's* carronades had given the *Flèche* a terrific pounding. The French ship's hull was holed in several places below the waterline, damage that could not be patched up, and as the water gained on the pumps the magazine began to flood. Frantic efforts were being made to transfer powder to the wardroom, but with the supply to the guns running out Bonamy decided to abandon ship. On shore, where the *Flèche's* plight was now evident, boats were sent to take the crew off, a hazardous undertaking as the *Victor* kept on blasting the *Flèche*, where a defiant and tattered Tricolour continued to flutter. Just before leaving the ship Bonamy ordered the cable to be cut and a fire was started in three places.

"I plainly perceived the enemy was going down," wrote Collier. "In a few minutes her cable was cut, she cast round and her bow grounded on a coral reef. Mr McLean, the first lieutenant, with a party of officers and men were sent aboard, though scarce had they put off ere we discovered the enemy to be on fire. Lieutenant Smith and other officers were then sent with proper assistance; but just as they had succeeded in extinguishing the fire, she fell on her larboard bilge into deeper water and sunk."

Quinssy received Bonamy as he came ashore, congratulating him on the gallant and prolonged defence of his ship. "If there is anything that can diminish the loss of this corvette," he wrote later to the Minister, "it is the manner in which Commandant Bonamy conducted himself, earning the general admiration of all the inhabitants and of his enemy."[21]

Although the *Victor* had suffered considerable damage a general muster showed, surprisingly, that no-one had been killed or wounded. In comparison, reports of the number of dead and dying his officers had found on the *Flèche's* forecastle led Collier to believe that there "the carnage was great, though only four are acknowledged by the French captain". Collier concluded that most of the casualties had been among the 20 or so men from the *Chiffonne* who had assisted in manning the *Flèche's* guns.

Although Collier spoke highly of Bonamy's fighting skill and bravery — he attributed the Frenchman's obstinate defence to a mistaken belief that the *Victor* was a privateer — he did not overlook the part played by his own men. "I feel I should do an injustice to every officer and man on board did I neglect paying a just tribute to the cool and determined bravery they evinced," he informed the Admiralty. "Even men labouring under a lingering fever, of whom I had unfortunately 30 felt a proportionate zeal ..."

If Collier had any misgivings about failing to capture the corvette or even force her surrender, these were eventually dispelled when Earl St Vincent directed that he should be given a post-commission, antedated to give him precedence over all officers included in the general promotion of April 1802. Collier was also appointed to command the 50-gun ship *Leopard*, in which he returned to England the following year.

The day after the action, having spent the night at quarters in the enemy harbour, Collier signalled for a parley and Quinssy and two officers went aboard the *Victor*. As was now customary, Quinssy presented the copy of the Seychelles capitulation for Collier's endorsement, and asked for a safe conduct for the *Flèche's* crew back to the Isle de France.

Collier told Quinssy that as the *Flèche* had not surrendered he did not think he could do this, but he gave an equivalent authority for the passage of Bonamy and her crew under the Seychelles Capitulation flag.

Having warped the *Victor* clear of the shoals, Collier worked up to Sainte Anne, where he spent a week carrying out repairs to his ship. He left Mahé on Sunday, 13 September, for Praslin where he found the brig *Diligente*. Although she showed both French and Portuguese colours and claimed the status of a dispatch ship, Collier took her as a prize having found that she carried a cargo.

Three days later he sailed from Praslin to join the blockading squadron off the Isle de France.

11

Death at Anjouan
1801-1811

Je ne puis exister plus longtemps loin de mon epoux.
Wife of deportee Bertrand Lacombe

Despite Quinssy's efforts to calm their fears, the reaction of many inhabitants to the presence of the deportees was to leave Seychelles. "Our hearts recoil from being amongst them," wrote the Savy brothers to a friend in the Isle de France. Their anxiety was understandable. All they knew of the strangers was that they were violent revolutionaries, their hands stained by the blood of countless victims; it would only be a matter of time, surely, before the newcomers, who outnumbered the settlers, roused the slaves to revolt.

Malavois played on these fears. He had already decided for reasons of his own to retire to the Isle de France, and he was happy enough to see others leave with him. Hodoul was also going, for he wanted to pursue his career as a privateer. "They do not think themselves capable of living in a place where there are deportees," wrote Quinssy. Another intent on leaving was Le Boucq Santussan, who insisted that he was not a deportee and could leave the island with his family whenever he wished. Quinssy agreed that he had no authority to stop him.

At the Isle de France feelings were also running high. Many still believed that more than 100 Jacobins had been landed in Seychelles, and that more were on the way. The local Press added its voice to the general alarm by publishing brief but lurid biographies of those arrested after the bomb blast of the

3 Nivôse. It mattered little — certainly *le Nouvelliste* failed to point it out — that only one or two of the 'monsters' who were listed had actually been sent to Seychelles, the majority being still imprisoned in France and awaiting deportation elsewhere.

In this atmosphere of fear, with the threat of disorder on their doorstep, the Isle de France Assembly drew up an address to the consular government complaining that France had seen fit "to vomit from her body the murderers of September, the conspirators of 3 Nivôse and the executioners of the Loire and Avignon ... transporting them not far from these islands, close to a population that has up to now conserved its health and sanity". And in a tart response to the reported instructions of Bonaparte that the deportees should be treated with kindness and consideration, the Assembly warned that if any should set foot in the Isle de France he would be summarily executed.[1]

Three weeks later, with the arrival of the brig *Espérance* from Seychelles, the Assembly was able to hear an account of the situation there from the captain. This, apparently, was so alarming that it decided there and then to send an armed expedition to remove the deportees from Mahé. Réunion was invited to take part, but before a ship could be fitted out word came that Hodoul had called there and was now on his way back to Seychelles.

"This circumstance gives us reason to believe the expedition is known of in Seychelles and that it would now necessitate something more considerable than we have," the president of the Isle de France *Commission Intermédiaire* pointed out. As it was impossible just then to muster a stronger force, he suggested the mission be postponed. Several months passed, and then at the beginning of February 1802 word reached Réunion that the expedition was on again. The Isle de France wanted men and supplies urgently. The situation in Seychelles was causing the greatest anxiety and there was no time to be lost in getting a rescue operation under way.

Most of the news about the disturbed state of the islands was being spread by Seychelles inhabitants who had fled their homes there, and it is likely that, to justify their departure and perhaps provoke government intervention to pave the way for their eventual return, they tended to exaggerate.

The impression they gave was of a reign of terror: of

inhabitants harassed by truculent, contemptuous Jacobins, women insulted, properties invaded and weapons seized. Worse — the very mention of it was enough to send shivers through the good citizens of the Isle de France — the deportees were threatening to implement the decree of 1794 which had abolished slavery throughout the French colonies. As their apologist Destrem put it, the deportees "were surprised that eight years after the Convention's decree, slavery still existed, and the least prudent of the Parisians ... took no pains to hide their astonishment".

Yet it is doubtful if any of the deportees seriously considered stirring the slaves to revolt. Their only wish was to escape from the island, and in this they had the ready cooperation of the settlers, who, despite Quinssy's disapproval, were already negotiating the sale of a 60-tonne vessel to take all the deportees to the African mainland. The deal was to be financed partly by the wealthiest of the deportees, the radical businessman Vanheck, with the rest of the money raised in loans from the settlers. Connant of La Digue was prepared to sail the ship to an African port if it then became his.

This scheme, interpreted in the Isle de France as an attempt by the deportees to steal a ship, was later quoted as one example of their bad behaviour, but it was an even more trivial incident that provided the final proof that a slave uprising was imminent. It began innocently enough with the former cavalry officer Laurent Derville, who lived at the house of Vola-maëffa, receiving a visit from a fellow deportee, Joseph Maignant. While there Maignant saw some slaves dancing, and on his return to the Établissement he described the festivities to his friend Serpolet, who the following Sunday went with some others to Vola-maëffa's to see for himself, and was soon joining in the dance. "The Blacks, impressed by having a White man in their midst, offered him refreshment. Serpolet, ignorant of the customs of the colonies, accepted and accompanied them in their revelling."

All this drunken merry-making might have passed unnoticed, but word of it reached the inhabitants either from their own slaves or through an indiscretion by one of the deportees. Soon Serpolet's evening of fraternisation was being condemned as a seditious orgy where slaves and deportees, inflamed by drink, had called for the take-over of the colony.

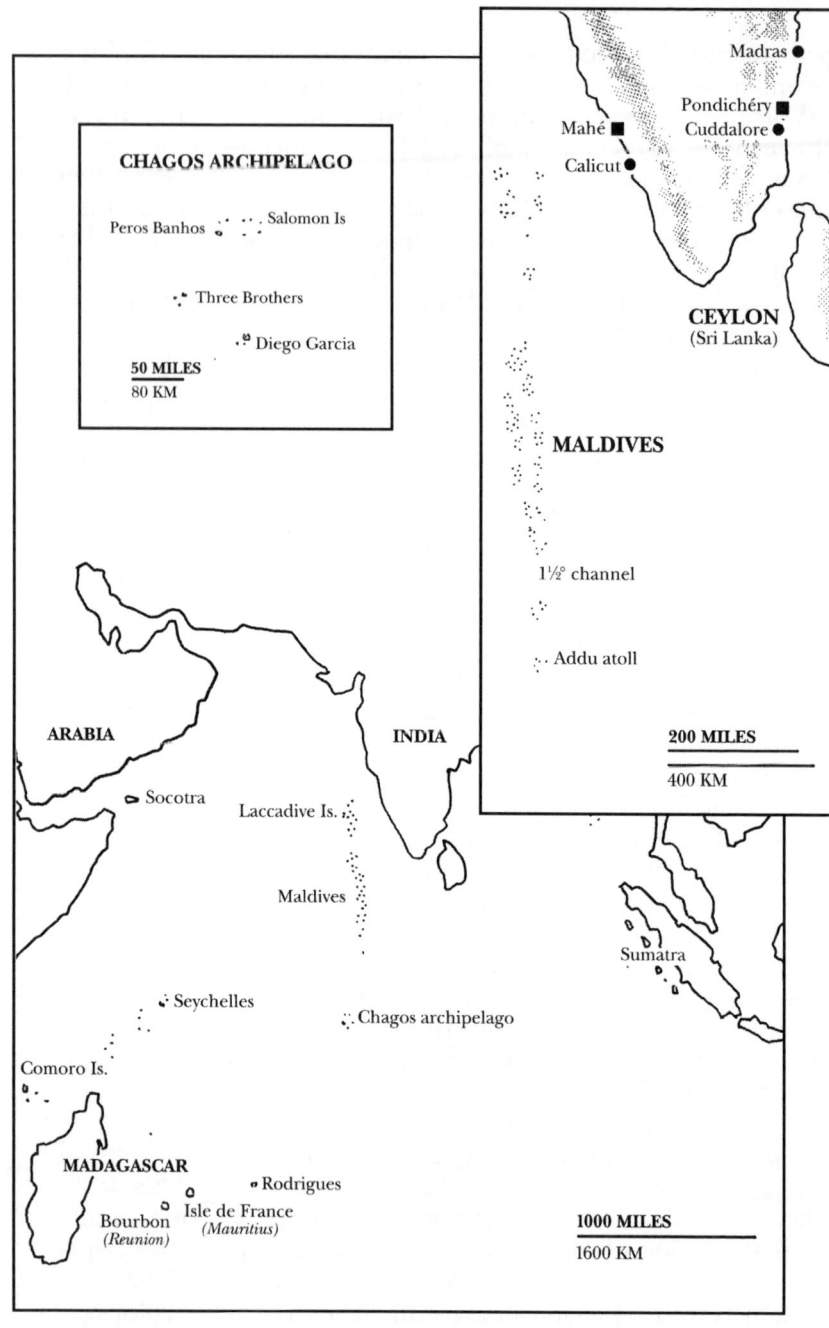

MALDIVES, CHAGOS ARCHIPELAGO & INDIA

If Quinssy had had his way nothing would have happened after this "involuntary lapse in good behaviour" by Serpolet. He would have been confined to a cell for a few days and the slaves given a flogging. Some of the inhabitants, however, particularly the Malavois group, insisted that the affair be considered by the municipal committee. This body, under the chairmanship of the municipal agent, Mondon, decreed that Serpolet and four of the slaves should be banished forthwith to Frégate island.

Several deportees were persuaded to sign a paper endorsing what had been done and this document,[2] together with a highly coloured report of the affair from the inhabitants, was dispatched to the Isle de France, where Malavois saw to it that the alarm bells rang loudly.

France's worst enemy could not have made a more "disastrous decision" than send deportees to Seychelles, he told the *Commission Intermédiaire.* All his predictions were coming true. There had been "a horrible orgy of Blacks, presided over by a deportee", where liberty had been openly proclaimed and "atrocious disorders" planned. He added that Quinssy, "who is very far from enjoying the confidence of all the inhabitants", was largely to blame by being too soft with the deportees. Malavois admitted that the deportees might not all be equally dangerous, some might even be worthy of pity, but who could identify those from the others? The only solution was to remove all of them from the Seychelles without delay.

The Isle de France Assembly agreed, but it still had the problem of finding a ship to carry out the task. Suddenly this last detail was solved by the arrival at Port Nord-Ouest (as Port Louis was now renamed) of the corvette *Bélier.* Almost as if expressly summoned from over the horizon, here was a fully armed ship from France capable of quelling any resistance the deportees might offer. Magallon agreed to the ship being used to remove the deportees and as the *Bélier's* captain, Hulot, was himself a Creole of the Isle de France there was no reluctance on his part to the planned expedition.

The dispatches brought from France by Hulot confirmed the news of two weeks earlier, from an English ship that had sailed in under a flag of truce, that peace negotiations had started between England and France. But even more welcome was the report that Bonaparte, after apparent indecision, had come down firmly for the retention of slavery. In a letter to Magallon, the Minister of Marine Denis Decrès,[3] who had succeeded Forfait the previous October, affirmed the consular government's resolve to see slavery maintained as the basis of the colony's economic and social life. In this instance the First Consul was as good as his word, as four months later slavery was re-established throughout the French colonies.[4] To Magallon it might have read as an endorsement of his precautionary actions in the Seychelles.

He had given command of the expedition to an artillery captain, Joseph Lafitte, who, with the title of government commissioner, was to carry out an ostensibly judicial assignment. He was to inquire into the settlers' complaints against the deportees, and remove those who were proved to be troublesome. The place chosen for their disposal was Anjouan, one of the Comoro islands at the northern end of the Mozambique Channel. Of the four islands in the group it was the best known to both French and English as a place of refreshment for ships making the traditional inner passage voyage to India, and Magallon was confident that, if bribed sufficiently, the Anjouan sultan would be agreeable to accepting the deportees.

The *Bélier* sailed on 20 February, arriving at Seychelles 19 days later. She fired a cannon to announce her arrival, but made no attempt to enter the harbour. Some boats set out to where she lay off North-East Point, but when she again fired most of them, puzzled and apprehensive, turned back. It was observed that those that went on and reached the *Bélier* did not return. Lafitte, fully expecting armed resistance, was taking no chances. Among those who boarded the *Bélier* were three deportees, who were promptly put in irons, as were two soldiers of the detachment who were unable to show good reason for being there. Lafitte's intention was to keep the island guessing as to the identity and purpose of the *Bélier* until enough settlers could be assembled to ensure that the deportees were rounded up in one quick operation. If possible, there were to be no arduous manhunts across the island.

The *Bélier's* behaviour worried inhabitants and deportees alike, and several of the latter went to Quinssy's house to offer their help in defending the island. The commandant, apparently, was not there but "Madame Quinssy thanked them, telling them there was nothing to fear". It is probable that Quinssy was aware of the Isle de France's intention to remove the deportees from Seychelles; if not, he learned of it that evening when Lafitte was able to pass instructions to him to summon the leading inhabitants and prepare them to arrest the deportees at dawn.

At first light, as the *Bélier* stood in to the harbour and landed troops, Savy, Mondon, and some others, with a supporting posse of armed slaves, began arresting the deportees. There was little or no resistance. One by one they were secured in a barn belonging to Mondon, while detachments of soldiers were sent to bring those living on outlying habitations or on the other islands. When the Isle de France Assembly's proclamation was read to Rossignol, he said he could only obey the government and that he would advise his comrades to do likewise. It took a few days to bring in all the deportees and there then began the task of deciding who were to be sent to Anjouan.

If the inhabitants had had their way all would have been included, but it seems Lafitte's brief was to select only about half of the deportees, those considered the most troublesome and dangerous to the peace and security of Seychelles, and indirectly to the Isle de France. "I left it to Lafitte, the task of implementing the plan that had been adopted," commented Quinssy, obviously reluctant to be associated with what was to be done.

Lafitte formed a commission of inquiry, consisting of himself and two inhabitants, and one by one the deportees were brought before it for interrogation. For some the proceedings must have recalled earlier judicial appearances when, roles reversed, they had condemned many an unfortunate to the guillotine. They were allowed to speak in their own defence and, according to Lefranc at least, were able to disprove the accusations against them. But if enough voices were raised against any particular deportee from among the settlers who crowded into the makeshift courtroom Lafitte had little option but to mark him down for Anjouan.

At the end of several days' deliberation, Lafitte pronounced the names of 33 who "should be transported immediately outside this colony, being by their past conduct and their beliefs susceptible of disorganising the Seychelles islands". The list included almost all who had been of any note in the Revolution, such as General Rossignol, acknowledged leader of the deportees, Pierre-Jean Lefebvre, a former gendarmerie officer whose name was linked to various atrocities, and Jean-Baptiste Vanheck (he of the ship purchase scheme), who had been among the leaders at the mob invasion of the Convention on 12 Germinal, Year III, and that rebellious spirit, the architect Jean-Baptiste Lefranc.

Also included were René Joly and Louis Moreau, both 'judges' at the prison massacres in Paris in September 1792, Jacques Saint-Amand, Jean Petit-Mamin, and Pierre Chrétien, known *septembriseurs* or Revolutionary jurymen, and Bertrand Lacombe, in the same category and once described by Babeuf as "purest of patriots". Any who happened to have featured in *Le Nouvelliste* were, of course, condemned. Rossignol and Lefebvre were there, also two former Conventional deputies, Antoine Laporte and Jacques Taillefer; the former said to have embezzled five million francs as a supplier to the Army of Italy, the latter put down simply as being "always very extreme in his opinions".

There were others, however, without the slightest trace of notoriety; men from the lower strata of urban society, such as Maignant and Serpolct, whose 'orgy' with the slaves had prompted the Isle de France government to act. Uncouth and uneducated, they had nothing to offer in the way of useful skills to the Seychellois, or as tutors to their children, and consequently no-one spoke up for them when they appeared before Lafitte.

In addition to the deportees, the commission declared that the four slaves involved in the Serpolet affair, Moutons, Jolicoeur, Fernando, and Étienne, who had already been banished with him to Frégate island, should be transported to Anjouan. Three Seychelles inhabitants, who had protested over the arrest of the deportees, were given one month to leave the colony. They were the surgeon Diarieux, the bosun of the *Chiffonne*, Richard, and Jean Laporte, who had been deported from Réunion some years previously for stealing.

Diarieux did eventually leave for the Isle de France, but Laporte (no relation to the Anjouan deportee of the same name), was still in Seychelles in 1808, when it was recorded that he had been granted a piece of land on La Digue. Quinssy must have made the concession reluctantly, for he described Laporte as a bad character whom he would have dearly liked to get rid of.

Lafitte's final pronouncement was to forbid the remaining deportees to leave Mahé without permission, and to warn that any who misbehaved in future would be banished to Isle Denis. In accordance with the instructions he had been given he left behind 11 soldiers who, with nine from the *Chiffonne*, brought the Seychelles detachment up to its original strength.

The *Bélier* sailed on 13 March, calling at Frégate island to pick up Serpolet and the slaves before bending course for Anjouan. The deportees were at first confined below deck until conditions became so intolerable that they overpowered the sentry and confronted Captain Hulot, demanding air or death. If we are to believe Lefranc, the crew defied the captain when he ordered the deportees to be put in chains. "We wept on their protective arms," says Lefranc, "and emotion was so great in all our hearts that we were on the point of killing the captain." After this the deportees were allowed to spend two hours a day on deck, in groups of four, for the remainder of the voyage. On 3 April, the *Bélier* arrived off Anjouan, and the deportees caught the first glimpse of the place that for most of them was to be their last abode on earth.

"Send them to Anjouan and there will not be one left in three months' time; I know the climate." These words, attributed to a Seychelles settler, were to prove prophetic; of the 37 men who were landed from the *Bélier* all but 11 were dead within a few months. Almost certainly, they were victims of an outbreak of cholera or typhus.

Anjouan's climate is, in fact, no harsher than that of Seychelles. English visitors to the island, which they knew as Johanna, described it as about the size of Madeira and not unlike it in appearance, where "the scenery is on a grand scale and highly picturesque". It was generally considered to be healthy and fertile, and because of the friendliness of its inhabitants — of mixed Sinhalese, Arab and Persian origin — it was, as we have already noted, a favourite place for stopping-over by English ships on their way to India. These would be unlucky if during their stay they did not bring off several boatloads of goats, ducks, fowls, pineapples, coconuts, oranges, limes, pomegranates, guavas, and onions, together with a variety of handsome straw mats used by the natives for sleeping.

But Anjouan had its less pleasant aspects. With a population of perhaps three or four thousand and a much longer history of settlement, it was not the pristine island that Mahé could still claim to be. One English visitor to the island's capital, Mutusamudu, referred to "the miserable, filthy hovels forming the town there, ill becoming the beautiful country around". In such a setting epidemics, particularly of water-borne diseases, would not be uncommon.

Lafitte received a courteous welcome when he went ashore, and was immediately conducted through a maze of narrow alleys to the royal palace, where he presented a letter Magallon had prepared explaining to Anjouan's "most sublime prince" the purpose of the *Bélier's* mission.

"We are confiding to you," wrote the governor-general, "in the spirit of friendship that has all along existed between Your Excellency and the most sovereign Republic of France ... some Frenchmen sent by our government to the Seychelles islands, where the impossibility of keeping them and providing them with sustenance has obliged us to leave them for the time being on some other island or kingdom of the archipelago." No mention was made of the political status of the 'Frenchmen', and with equal lack of candour there was an assurance that they would not be staying long as France was expected to send ships in the near future to remove them elsewhere. Finally, there was a promise that France would reimburse Anjouan for any extra expense incurred.

The sultan, Seyyid Abdullah bin Mohamed, could hardly be but suspicious of this peremptory request to leave 30 or so French citizens with him, and had he been aware of exactly who they were he might well have demurred. But there was, after all, the gifts Lafitte had brought — two 8-pounder cannons, with 100 cannon balls, 16 bales of red cloth, 12 barrels of powder and 40 new muskets — as well as Magallon's suggestion that the Frenchmen would be useful in practising the arts and trade appropriate to the island. Abdullah knew that one thing Europeans were good at was waging war, a skill in which his own people required a great deal of tuition.

From time to time the sultans of Anjouan had sought

England's protection from raids by Malagasy tribesmen, and it was only a year or two since Abdullah had written to Bombay appealing for the company's help against the marauders from Madagascar. He repeated an offer that his predecessor had made in 1796, to cede the whole or part of the island in return for peace and security under the English, but nothing had come of it.

The French gift of arms and munitions, and the men who were to be left on the island, of whose usefulness Abdullah was now highly suspicious, were a poor substitute for the military and naval assistance that he had been hoping for from the English, but he set aside his disappointment and dictated a letter to Magallon expressing his joy at "receiving the troops you have had the goodness to send to us ... whom we will always regard as our brothers and friends". The only stipulation he made was that they should not interfere with the customs of the country, nor, more especially, show an interest in the women. By way of a postscript, Abdullah mentioned that a ship bringing goods for him from India had been taken by Monsieur Surcouf and, as he believed they were now at the Isle de France, he would be grateful to have them forwarded to him.

Rossignol, instructed by Lafitte not to disclose that he and his companions were deportees, gave an undertaking to the sultan that all would be of good behaviour. However, Lefranc was convinced Hulot had informed the sultan they were dangerous men, with the result they were not allowed to enter the town and had to make what shelters they could on the beach. Later, under Lefranc's guidance, the deportees built a large hut to accommodate all of them, consisting of a dormitory, with a kitchen and a covered verandah as a refectory. Lefranc also had a notion to construct an obelisk which would carry the names of the deportees and a legend recording the cruel and tyrannical rule of Napoleon Bonaparte.

He claimed that his skills as an architect so impressed Abdullah that the sultan commissioned him to build him a new palace. But just as the construction was beginning the fatal epidemic broke out and within a matter of weeks only a handful of deportees remained alive. Rossignol was among the first to die, his parting words a prayer that Bonaparte would suffer the same pain and misfortune as he had. "I myself was awaiting death," wrote Lefranc. "A thousand times day and night I had risked my life in order to preserve those of my comrades, but all my nursing had been in vain. My strength was at an end ... I prepared to appear before my supreme judge." In the event Lefranc did not keep the appointment; he and eight other deportees survived, as well as three slaves, one of whom, Fernando, owned by Quinssy, was mentioned as having been especially caring towards the sick deportees.

Another who showed concern for the Frenchmen's welfare was an Anjouan dignitary known to French and English alike as Bombay Jack. Described as of short stature with a dark mahogany complexion, Mubarak Kumba Bomboxak dressed "in the Moorish style of long, flowing robes, slippers and turban".[5] He was a person of considerable influence at the sultan's court, spoke English intelligibly, and undertook more than one mission abroad seeking military aid for the island. An English visitor noted that he displayed "much shrewdness of remark and more knowledge of the world than could possibly be expected".[6]

It may have been Bombay Jack who persuaded the sultan to allow the surviving deportees into the town. But their stay there was of short duration. First to escape, probably with the tacit approval of the sultan, were Vanheck, Laporte, André Corchant, Pierre Vauversin, and Jean-Marie Gosset (his elder brother Louis had died in the epidemic). After crossing to Grande Comore island, where the slaves who had accompanied them disappeared, they made for Zanzibar, but their boat was wrecked on the African coast and they were held prisoner by Arabs for almost two months. During that time Vanheck died, before they finally reached Zanzibar. But Corchant and Laporte were already desperately ill and both died soon after their arrival. The two survivors went on by dhow to Muscat, where Vauversin, passing himself off as a ship's captain, with Gosset as his servant, persuaded an English ship to give them passage to Bombay.

There, almost on the final stage of their journey back to France, Gosset died. Vauversin travelled on alone, first in a Danish ship to the Cape and then to England, from where, after being detained for some time, he crossed over to France. He was arrested immediately on his arrival, but on 21 August

1804 (three and a half years since leaving France), he was released and given a passport to reside in Lyon. The last recorded word we have of Vauversin is a letter he wrote to the government asking for a pension. "My three children and my wife want the barest essentials," he pleaded. "Tears drop from my pen as I contemplate our sad situation." The response of the government is not known.

When Vauversin and his companions left Anjouan only four deportees remained on the island, and they were soon to leave for Grande Comore. According to Lefranc, Abdullah lent them a boat and gave them a letter of introduction to the neighbouring sultan. "I am sending you four Frenchmen who were left with me," he wrote, adding, with what seems an ominous ambiguity, "dispose of them in a manner convenient to you." But fate intervened. Two of the deportees, Chrétien and Joly, drowned when their boat was wrecked off Grande Comore, and Lefranc and Charles Saulnois only just managed to struggle ashore. After some months on the island they continued their journey to Zanzibar, where they heard that Vauversin's depleted party had passed through. Eventually both men succeeded in getting back to France (by way of England, having been captured by an English ship after rounding the Cape), and, like Vauversin, they were promptly arrested.

Undaunted, Lefranc protested to Bonaparte (his letter was intercepted by Decrès), complaining that they had returned to France in the belief that they had been amnestied. This seems to have had some effect, for he was released from prison, although placed under surveillance at Montpellier, with an allowance of 40 francs a month. Seven years later all restrictions were lifted, except for a ban on his going to Paris, and he was able to resume work as an architect at the small town of Lunel, near Montpellier. Some years later he was again under surveillance, until finally freed at the Restoration. Sad to relate, Lefranc was back in prison in 1816, accused of conspiring against the Bourbon government, and it is there that we leave him, the perennial rebel.

The first of the two books attributed to him appeared that year. The second, based on notes he gave to Fescourt, was published three years later. Although the accuracy of much that was written was challenged, he was alone as far as is known in recording at first-hand the deportations to Seychelles and Anjouan. The result is to give him today more substance than any of his companions, whether villain or victimised innocent. Lefranc may have been a rogue, but he was a likeable one, with a stubborn spirit that marked him out as a survivor.

At the Isle de France the overall mood had been one of relief when Lafitte returned to report the success of his mission. The Assembly congratulated him on his "prudent, firm and wise action", and felt confident that having removed the worst of the deportees to far-off Anjouan the rest would be sufficiently intimidated not to cause any more trouble.

"May the fervour of revolt no longer excite them." wrote *Le Nouvelliste*. "They must realise that the government of the Isle de France and Réunion will crush them if they dare rise again." Even Quinssy, who seems to have had more misgivings than most about the way the list of those for Anjouan had been drawn up, admitted in a letter to his friend Jacob, the Réunion governor, that with the trouble-makers removed the others would probably settle down.

A few months later Magallon's satisfaction evaporated when the corvette *Diligent* arrived with news that there were no longer any deportees on Anjouan, that they were either dead or had escaped. How, Magallon must have wondered, was he going to justify the outcome of the operation to the Minister. It had been the Assembly's idea, but he had acquiesced in it and the responsibility was his. The deaths were bad enough, but that 11 should have escaped.

In a letter dated 20 Nivôse Year XI (10 January 1803), he dwelt mainly on the deaths, which, he assured the Minister, had been due to an epidemic and were not caused by any ill-treatment by the sultan, who was "a humane, upright man and a friend of the French". A few weeks later he had what must have seemed slightly better news. A letter written by Lefranc from Zanzibar to a friend in Seychelles and intercepted by Quinssy disclosed that of the 11 escapees, only four were now alive. Perhaps, after all, none would succeed in getting back to France.

Decrès was furious when he learned what had happened at Anjouan. His was the unenviable task of explaining Magallon's blunder to Bonaparte, and he wrote off angrily to the governor-general demanding to know why it had been decided to send the deportees to Anjouan in the first place. Magallon defended his action as best he could. His letter to Decrès implied that Paris was partly to blame, for it had deprived his administration of the means to ensure that the deportees were properly housed and fed in Seychelles. It was almost inevitable that they should cause unrest, and as a result he had had to protect the inhabitants from "the dangers with which they were threatened by certain of these individuals". It was to be hoped, he added, that he would receive in future the supplies that were much needed by all branches of the service.

As far as his choice of Anjouan was concerned, it was the only island that was inhabited and governed where the deportees could be looked after. He pointed out, with unconscious irony, that had he sent them to Madagascar they would almost certainly have escaped or died of misery, whereas "to have jettisoned them on some deserted African coast, more or less into the mouths of the lions, would have been a cruel and criminal action". To have sent them to India would have been like opening the backdoor to them.

Magallon blamed the sultan of Anjouan for having failed to follow the instructions he had given him. He had now written to the Imam of Muscat asking him to detain and return the four escapees should they be found in Zanzibar or on the African coast, but, alas, he feared that they had already left there for India and would probably succeed in reaching France. The only thing to do, Magallon advised somewhat lamely, was for the Minister to place a watch on their families and arrest them when they showed up there.

But already there was more bad news to pass on to the Minister: the escape of four deportees from the Seychelles. Previous to this there had been only one disappearance, that of Claude Richardet, lodging with an inhabitant called Darquier at the Établissement, who towards the end of 1802 was believed to have slipped aboard a ship bound for India. Now, seven months later, four others had escaped: the Linage brothers, Christophe and Jean-Pierre, both artisans from the St Antoine district of Paris,[7] a printer named Jean Tréhaut, and one of Fouché's former police agents, Jean Lesueur, who had persuaded the captain of a ship to take them to Mozambique.

Although there was only a slender chance of recapturing them Magallon sent a ship to Mozambique, with a letter to the

Portuguese governor requesting him to carry out a search for the four and hand them over for return to the Isle de France. Magallon also wrote to Quinssy, expressing his displeasure at what had happened. "I cannot hide the fact from you that you, and even your colony, have shown yourselves neglectful in this matter," he admonished. Did the deportees not realise that their families in France would suffer as a result of their action, which also "can only be to the detriment of those who have remained faithful to their place of exile".

The governor-general was particularly concerned over the attitude of the Seychelles settlers who, he believed, were determined to make the lives of the deportees as miserable as possible so that they would be all the more eager to escape. He ordered Quinssy to reprimand any inhabitant who insulted or threatened a deportee. "Tell the citizens Charles Savy, Calais, Hérisson, and Robert that I am very displeased with their conduct and that if I were to do my duty I should report them ... they should take this as a warning for the future."

The settlers resented the Isle de France's neglect of the deportees and the fact that they had to provide food and clothing for them as Quinssy never had any supplies. They were promised payment but it never materialised. Magallon's only response was to plead his own poverty. "Everyone is in arrears, and one pays when one can," he told Quinssy. Even the soldiers of the garrison were little better off. "These fine fellows must have more patience," replied Magallon, when Quinssy passed on their complaints about lack of pay and rations. "Assure them that I think kindly of them, and whenever I can, and that things can hardly last as they are much longer."

But things were, if anything, to get worse. Unknown to the governor-general peace with England had been broken on 18 May, and for the past six weeks France had been at war. Soon the enemy's blockade would tighten again around the Isle de France and even fewer supplies would reach Seychelles. Towards the end of 1803 Quinssy had to cut the deportees' rations to six ounces of rice a day, two cassava roots, plus an occasional piece of fresh beef and salt. The soldiers had no tobacco and little soap (Quinssy made a substitute soap out of coconut oil), and there were never sufficient vegetables to ensure a healthy diet.

Quinssy by now had an administrative assistant, named Beguignon, who fulfilled the duties of notary, court official and registrar of births, marriages, and deaths. Beguignon was appalled at the condition of the deportees, whom he found "in a deplorable state, without the basic necessities such as shoes, clothing or hats".

But despite the little they had, the deportees' behaviour was, according to Beguignon, exemplary and he urged the Isle de France to allow them to go there to follow their trades, which they were unable to do with profit in Seychelles. He also raised with the administration the deportees' right to marry. Several had formed liaisons with women of the island, but because of settler hostility they rarely expressed their affections openly. When Antoine Boniface, formerly concierge at the Temple prison in Paris, announced that he and the widow St Jorre, who employed him as tutor to her children, wanted to marry, the inhabitants denounced the affair as a public scandal and only Quinssy's intervention saved Boniface from being abandoned on Isle Denis. As long as the authorities prevaricated, settler pressure was sufficient to dissuade Quinssy from performing any marriages.

Six months after Beguignon's first inquiry, the deportee Derville himself wrote to the Isle de France seeking a ruling. He told the *Préfet Colonial* that his request to marry had been shelved by Quinssy on the ground that it had to be referred to the Isle de France. "I can hardly imagine that marriage, an act regarded most favourably by the laws of all people, which even the Code Noir assures to slaves, can be refused to us." He was sure that the failure to reply to Beguignon's inquiry was due to pressure of government business, or simply that the deportees' right to marry was so obvious that a reply was considered unnecessary.

But the marriage issue had by now been passed to Paris, and almost a year and a half were to elapse before Decrès finally ruled that there was no objection to the deportees marrying. The decision was of little use to Derville, who had died at the beginning of 1805, soon after his 40th birthday.

The former medical officer of the *Flèche*, Louis Poupinel, who had stayed on and assumed the duties of surgeon in Seychelles, had been called to Vola-maëffa's on Monday evening, 21 January, to attend Derville. He looked in again the following morning and found the deportee seized by a fit. He died two hours later. Poupinel carried out an autopsy, but found nothing to confirm his suspicions of poisoning and concluded that death was due to apoplexy. The burial took place at the common cemetery, and was attended by Quinssy, Poupinel, and several of the deportees. "I am really upset at the death of citizen Laurent Derville, who despite some small faults was an honest man," wrote Pépin-Desgrouettes.

By the deportees' standards Derville had been fairly well off and the sale of his effects (Vola-maëffa swore she had taken nothing) raised over 200 piastres. They included a 16-year-old boy slave (bought by Quinon for 70 piastres), a pirogue and a double-barrelled shotgun; also, as one might expect to find in the possession of the handsome Derville, two china shaving bowls, a case of razors, and many fancy waistcoats.

There is no record to identify the woman who won Derville's heart, only a hint dropped by Pépin-Desgrouettes, who, in a letter to Quinssy, referred to his having lent Derville five piastres when he was staying with a Madame Larcher.

Quinssy's continuing efforts to improve the lot of the deportees evoked little sympathy in the Isle de France, where Magallon had now been succeeded by General Charles Decaen. When Quinssy and Beguignon sent four deportees to the Isle de France for medical treatment they were sent back, accompanied by a curt note from Decaen informing Quinssy that the cost of their passage would be to his account. "However commendable the feelings of humanity that have prompted your letters in favour of these deportees, we cannot but point out to you that the government having given precise orders that they be kept under surveillance in Seychelles, you cannot make changes to this without having been duly authorised," Quinssy was told. Decaen, formerly one of Napoleon's brigade commanders, was a stickler for the rules.

If the prospect of the deportees marrying their womenfolk was anathema to the settlers, the making over of land to them was resented just as fiercely. Soon after their arrival in Seychelles Quinssy had, in accordance with the Minister's instructions, allocated land to be cultivated jointly by the deportees living at the Établissement, but the settlers were opposed to their being given any more. Quinssy, as usual, sought a ruling from the Isle de France, the ultimate authority on land concessions, and Decaen agreed that land grants could be made. Incensed, the settlers began threatening again to send the deportees to the outlying islands, and when two of them fled into the interior they were tracked down and badly beaten before being returned to the Établissement. Quinssy, forced to placate the settlers, agreed reluctantly to the absconders being sent for a time to Silhouette, after refusing a demand that they be abandoned on one of the Amirante islands.

Quinssy's relations with the settlers were now at an all-time low. He deplored the greed, envy, and spite that seemed to be their sole motivation and, in an uncharacteristic lapse into despair, denounced the colony as a "miserable little country" where all he found were "malign interpretations, calumny, ill-founded reproaches and injustice". He refrained from naming the worst offenders, contenting himself with the hope "that they will change their ways for their own happiness and that of others".

Quinssy's feelings towards the Isle de France administration were hardly less bitter. He resented its neglect of the small colony, and the lack of support he had received in arranging the capitulations during the war and in coping with the large influx of deportees from France. Now they were at war again, and he sensed that he was to experience difficulties with the new ruler in the Isle de France. Decaen had withdrawn most of the garrison, but had also made it clear that he expected the French flag to fly defiantly over the Seychelles.

Quinssy's letters at this time read almost like those of Gillot 25 years earlier. He complained that he had never received any pay for the extra duties of municipal officer and notary that he had undertaken before Beguignon's arrival, that he had received no land nor the wine and salted meat normally given to the commandant. He had had to deprive himself of basic necessities in order to ease the hardships of the deportees and soldiers of the garrison, and found himself subsisting on a diet of cassava "which is neither proper to my station, nor suitable in view of my age (he was now 55) and state of health".

Yet Quinssy was not completely without support. He had a loyal and competent colleague in Beguignon. Unfortunately, the administrative assistant was unable to live apart from his family and soon sought to return to the Isle de France on the ground of ill health. His stay in Seychelles had lasted barely seven months, but in a memoir dated 25 November 1803 (4 Frimaire Year XII) he gives us an insight into the state of the colony at the time.

Turtles and tortoises, that valuable source of food and wealth for the first settlers, were by now virtually wiped out. When Beguignon, seeking to vary the diet of the deportees and soldiers, sent an expedition to Isle du Nord and Silhouette it returned with only five turtles and eight tortoises. Only on the distant islands of Agaléga, Coëtivy, and Diego Garcia were these creatures to be found in any number. Unfortunately Beguignon had no means of halting their continued destruction by visiting ships. Even on Mahé, and on the other islands close by, the cutting of trees and other damage to the environment went on unhindered; Beguignon, with only one pirogue at his disposal, could do little to prevent it. Crocodiles were by now much scarcer on all the islands; they were killed out of hand whenever they were encountered. Louis Garneray, one of Surcouf's lieutenants, who visited the Seychelles in 1802, recalled an incident when the cry of *'Caïman'* was raised as they were filling barrels of water on the beach. About a hundred steps away a large crocodile was advancing. Asked if they ate humans, one of the slaves replied: "I well believe so, master ... especially when they have already tasted human flesh ... then they become incredibly greedy." Attracting the attention of the crocodile, he then ran and climbed into a tree. When the beast attempted to follow him it fell over, and was quickly dispatched.

Beguignon reported that most crops were not doing particularly well, but rice and cotton, especially the latter, were showing promise, and he correctly predicted that within two or three years cotton would be the Seychelles' most valued product. As to the spice garden, still surviving despite its repeated 'destruction', a few clove bushes, two feet of nutmeg and some citrus plants remained. The slaves, according to Beguignon, were well looked after and few ran away, although sometimes pirogues were taken to neighbouring islands.

He noted that the administration building required reflooring as the wood was completely rotten, and he appealed to the Isle de France for nails and tools to carry out much needed repairs. He had taken over the office of the surgeon, but as the house was not habitable he had had to depend on

Quinssy to find him somewhere to live. Many of the deportees and soldiers were lodged in the hospital as there was nowhere else for them to go. Ever since Romainville and his soldier-tradesmen constructed the Établissement in 1779 failure to maintain the buildings or put up new ones had been a common fault of Seychelles administrations. There was always a lack of tools or building materials, and perhaps also of skilled labour, yet it still seems a surprising and inexcusable shortcoming by Quinssy and his predecessors.

Beguignon commended to the attention of the Isle de France authorities the naval surgeon Poupinel. "It is he who looks after the state of the buildings ... who treats the sick on behalf of the government; this honest citizen merits ... that you cast a favourable eye on him," he wrote. One of Poupinel's tasks was to visit the slave vessels "which, almost without exception, call at this archipelago". It was a dangerous undertaking, for the risk of being infected by some fatal disease was very real. Yet despite it all Poupinel was acting without pay. He was a public-spirited volunteer who, Beguignon urged, should be appointed formally as the colony's surgeon, which eventually he was. He married the daughter of the widowed Madame Nageon de l'Étang, and became one of Seychelles' most respected citizens.

Among his patients were the deportees, but they remained generally in good health despite their deprivations; yet another testimony to the salubrious climate of the Seychelles. Only two, François Dufour and François Fourgeon, died during the first year of their stay on the island. The cause of Dufour's death is not recorded, but Fourgeon, who at 68 must have been the most elderly of the deportees, contracted appendicitis and died a few days after being moved to the hospital from Ramalinga's house, where he lodged.

A master wigmaker before the Revolution, he had grieved inconsolably at being separated from his only daughter and his sole wish was for her to join him in exile. On his death Ramalinga handed over his effects to Quinssy: a pair of old shoes, some worn shirts and trousers, an old waistcoat, two handkerchiefs, and a pair of stockings.

In contrast, Dufour, a cabinet-maker from the Poissonière district of Paris, and a man of no particular note in the Revolution, left possessions worth more than 200 piastres.

Dufour had set up in business at the Établissement with Claude Flamant, a carriage maker, and they seem to have prospered. Quinssy found among his effects a bag containing several gold and silver coins, and arranged for the value of his estate to be paid to his widow in Paris.

On 17 April 1803 Pierre Anathase Pépin-Desgrouettes died. Unlike Dufour and Fourgeon, Pépin-Desgrouettes was a travelled and educated man. Before the Revolution he had spent some time in the Bastille for writing inflammatory pamphlets. Later he went to America, but returned to France, became a lawyer and entered wholeheartedly into the spirit of the Revolution. He had been a member of the Cordeliers Club and the insurrectional Commune.

In Seychelles he lodged with Madame Nageon de l'Étang (Poupinel's mother-in-law), and it was there that he died after an attack of fever. He seems to have kept himself apart from the other deportees, and many of the settlers were wary of his reputation as a vitriolic writer. At the time of his death he had been planning to set up a *Maison d'Éducation* at the Établissement. Several tributes were paid to "this honest man and excellent citizen"; his behaviour, Madame Nageon affirmed, had always been that befitting a gentleman. Pépin-Desgrouettes's effects amounted to little: some clothing, a tortoise-shell snuff box, with the portrait of a lady, and a wooden chest, the whole raising 69 piastres at an auction.

As the years passed, Decaen modified his attitude towards the deportees, allowing several in 1806 to go to the Isle de France or Réunion (at that time it had been renamed Isle Bonaparte) on medical grounds. By June 1809 only five remained in Seychelles. Most of the others were in the Isle de France, where Decaen reported that they were employed and behaving well.

With the invasion and capture of the Isle de France by the English the following year the deportees there, along with the other inhabitants, were given the choice of either swearing allegiance to George III or returning to France. The records show that at least five went back home, although, like Lefranc, Vauversin, and Saulnois, they, too, were to spend some time in French prisons or under surveillance.

As for the five deportees who remained in Seychelles, we have a brief description of a meeting a British naval surgeon had with one in Mahé in 1811. The visitor found him to be "chatty, bustling and good-humoured", of robust build and with a full, round face that belonged more to the traditional figure of John Bull than that of an assassin. His home was a modest dwelling of bamboo poles "fixed in the ground an inch or two apart, and connected here and there by wicker work. The roof was scantily thatched, and the door divided in the centre like that of an English barn, with a wooden sunshade over it".

The English visitor was given refreshment, and as they talked he learned that his host had once been an officer of dragoons. Before leaving he bought some shells, "not indeed for their value, but rather as a return for the civilities of the collector, who, equally pleased, amused us with the gaiety of a mind at ease, in sallies of pleasantry on his present situation". Of the five deportees we know were still in Seychelles in 1809, who was the "jolly looking man" who entertained an English surgeon two years later?

It is unlikely that he was Bertrand Guilhémat, a Paris printer and member of the Revolutionary Committee during the Terror, who was described in Seychelles as "a difficult character" and who, in any case, was living at La Digue. If it was Étienne Jalabert, formerly master wigmaker at the Palais Royal, or Pierre Maurice Cardinaux, a Swiss noted for his Revolutionary theatre in Paris, one might have expected them to have told the Englishman that one ran a hairdressing establishment in the town and the other kept a tavern of sorts.

Of the remaining two, Claude Louis Chevalier, brother of the designer of the prototype for the *machine infernale* that almost killed Napoleon, was regarded latterly in Seychelles as being half-mad. The other was Joseph Quinon, a name that survives in Seychelles today. Quinon in 1811 was 53, and best fits the Englishman's description of being "robust and good-natured". Before the Revolution he had been a baker's labourer in Paris, but that would not necessarily inhibit him from describing himself to a visiting Englishman as a former officer of dragoons.

12

The Rivals
1803-1810

" ... dans une petite colonie cela est plus
dangereux qu'ailleurs."
Quéau de Quinssy, 1805

The Peace of Amiens signed by Britain and France in March 1802 lasted just over a year. With both protagonists reluctant to implement all the treaty's provisions it was inevitable that sooner or later the conflict would be renewed. In Seychelles the deteriorating relations with the English had gone unnoticed, and it was several months after Britain's formal resumption of hostilities in May 1803 that the colony was rudely awakened to being once more at war.

The last hostile act by the English in Seychelles had been the sinking of the *Flèche* in Mahé harbour in September 1801. Subsequently raised from the seabed, the corvette was still in harbour undergoing repair when it became the first victim of renewed enemy action. A naval force consisting of a frigate and a brig had arrived off Sainte Anne on the evening of 4 October 1803. Neither ship wore colours, nor did they offer any communication with the shore. At three in the morning Quinssy was informed that the strangers had set fire to the *Flèche*, and he immediately went out in his pirogue to find out, as he put it, the reason for their hostility. However the ships, which, as suspected, were English, sailed away before Quinssy could reach them. Fortunately there had been heavy rain during the night, and the fire on the *Flèche* was doused before much damage was done.

An officer from one of the small ships in harbour who had been taken aboard the British frigate, the *Minerve*, and told that the two countries were at war had tried to dissuade its captain from setting fire to the *Flèche*. He had argued that the ship was covered by the Seychelles capitulation, and that in any case it had been sold to a Portuguese merchant, whose country was neutral. But the Englishman replied that Captain Collier had no right to sell the *Flèche*, which could sail as a privateer and ruin many English families, and that the capitulation had expired with the Treaty of Amiens.

A few weeks later, news of the war was confirmed when Captain Hulot of the corvette *Bélier* arrived at Mahé with dispatches from the Isle de France. After its mission to Anjouan the previous year the *Bélier* had sailed back to France, but the signs of impending war had prompted its urgent return to the Indian Ocean with new orders for Admiral Linois's squadron, which was on its way to the East Indies. Sailing with Linois was General Charles Isidore Decaen, recently appointed to replace Magallon as governor-general at the Isle de France. Decaen's instructions were to call first at Pondichéry, where he would take formal possession of the settlement from the English as agreed under the Treaty of Amiens. But with war likely to break out at any time Pondichéry could become a trap, and the amended orders sent by the *Bélier* were that Linois should sail directly to the Isle de France. Hulot had hoped to overtake the squadron before it reached the Cape, but when he arrived there he found that Linois had departed two days previously. There was nothing else for it but to go on and rendezvous with the squadron at Pondichéry.

Decaen had been reluctant to accept the post of governor-general, which under a reorganisation of the colonial administration was now styled captain-general of the French settlements east of the Cape of Good Hope. His ambition and natural ability had seen him rise rapidly through the ranks of the Revolutionary army, culminating in the command of a brigade under Bonaparte. However exalted the appointment of captain-general might be, the Isle de France was still only a colonial backwater, and if war were resumed, as surely it must, the advancement and honours he could hope for would go to others. Bonaparte had tried to allay Decaen's anxiety, stressing the importance of the Isle de France both politically and militarily. If he did well there, Bonaparte told him, "the First Consul ... will perhaps give him the opportunity to earn one day the greater glory which perpetuates the memory of men beyond the centuries".

Decaen knew that to turn down the offer would be fatal to his career prospects, and so with that vague promise of future reward he sailed on 5 March 1803 with Linois's squadron. It must have been a proud sight to see the most powerful force dispatched to the Indian Ocean since the Revolution leaving the port of Brest. Headed by the flagship *Marengo* (74), there were three 40-gun frigates, the *Belle Poule*, newly built successor to Grenier's ship of the same name, the *Atalante*, and the *Sémillante*, and two transports with 1,100 troops. But on board the *Marengo*, where Decaen and Linois had taken an instant dislike to each other, all was not well. Even before sailing there had been a row over Decaen's accommodation in the ship. It was a trifling matter of pique and prestige, but it was the start of a feud that was to last throughout the two and a half years of Linois's operations in the Indian Ocean.

Charles Alexandre Léon Durand de Linois was of the pre-Revolution nobility and it may be that he failed to treat Decaen with the deference the general felt was his due. The two men were certainly of contrasting, if not conflicting, personality; Linois was cool and aloof, Decaen arrogant, hot-tempered, and sensitive to any imagined slight. Perhaps the soldier was jealous of the sailor's reputation, for Linois, a slight, Nelson-like figure, his missing left eye testimony to his courage in battle, had previously scored a brilliant victory over the English at Algeciras. Although his later exploits in the Indian Ocean were flawed by over-cautiousness and indecision, he was at that moment one of the few naval heroes France had.

As Decaen had not yet been sworn in as captain-general and was therefore, strictly speaking, travelling in a private capacity, Linois had been reluctant to surrender to him his suite aboard the *Marengo*, and instead had had the *Marengo's* captain vacate his quarters for Decaen. It was, in Decaen's eyes, an insult he would not forget.

In his journal Decaen, observing that the sea was rough on leaving Brest, noted with an implicit sneer that both Linois and Captain Larue kept to their bunks during the first day out. "As for myself, I had only some slight twinges of indisposition because I went up frequently on deck to see what was going on," he wrote. But shipboard life soon bored Decaen, and there was another row with Linois when the squadron arrived at Réunion and the admiral refused him permission to land. Later, observed Decaen, "the direction taken was through the Seychelles archipelago, a voyage made less boring by the sighting of the islands. We approached close to that of Agaléga. From there, we went on to pass the Maldives by the Nine Degree Channel" (between the Maldives and the Laccadive islands).

The long voyage left Decaen with little liking for naval officers; only Commander Joseph-Marie Vrignaud, the *Marengo's* first officer who was soon to succeed Larue as captain, earned his approbation. For the moment the general could indulge his prejudices by criticising the poor fare of the admiral's table, and later he was to accuse Linois of being too intent on enriching himself and his crews by prize-money, instead of furthering the fortunes of the Isle de France.

If we are to believe Decaen, Linois was so mean about the hospitality he had to offer his passengers that he could hardly contain his joy at the prospect of their leaving the ship on arrival at Pondichéry. But Decaen stayed on board. Finding that the Union flag still flew over the town he refused to go ashore until it had been replaced by the Tricolour. Both he and Linois were, in fact, suspicious, justifiably as it turned out, of English intentions. Although 250 soldiers had already been landed by the *Belle Poule*, which arrived ahead of the main squadron, there was an all-too-obvious reluctance by the English commander to relinquish the colony's strong points. Was Wellesley deliberately stalling in anticipation of word from London that war had broken out again? To Decaen and Linois it appeared so, as they looked across at the English fleet that had come out from nearby Cuddalore. Lying at anchor to windward of the French squadron, forming a menacing half-crescent, were four ships of the line: the 74-gun *Tremendous*, the *Trident* and *Lancaster* both of 64 guns, and the 50-gun *Centurion*. There were also four frigates, the *Concorde*, *Sheerness*, *Dédaigneuse*, and *Fox*, and the sloop *Victor*.

Decaen's doubts as to whether he should go ahead and reoccupy Pondichéry or insist first on an English withdrawal were solved by the arrival of the *Bélier* and the orders for Linois to sail directly to the Isle de France. Although it was not yet a rupture with England, Decrès informed Linois that the British government was arming to such an extraordinary degree that "this throws a shadow over its intentions". In fact, although neither side at Pondichéry was as yet aware of it, the two countries had been at war for almost two months.

Linois was apprehensive that the English force might find some excuse to detain him if he showed signs that he was preparing to leave. So for the rest of the day the French maintained the appearance that all was well. It was decided that the troops already in Pondichéry would have to be abandoned (they eventually surrendered to the English), as well as the families of the military and civilian administrators. Among them were the wife and children of Louis Léger, who had been appointed to serve with Decaen as *préfet colonial,* or intendant, at the Isle de France. Léger came aboard the *Marengo* in the evening, ostensibly to dine with the captain-general, but to avoid raising suspicions left his family behind.

The deception was a complete success. In the darkness, and maintaining perfect silence, the French ships cut their cables and made for the open sea before the English realised they had gone. Only one of the transports, the *Côte d'Or,* was intercepted, and after protests from the French at Pondichéry the order came from Madras to release her. Admiral Rainier was reprimanded by the governor, Clive, at Fort St George for jeopardising by his action Britain's peaceful relations with France, but later Rainier was commended by the Admiralty.

Linois's squadron arrived at the Isle de France on 14 August and a month later Decaen formally took over from Magallon, who had agreed to accept the lesser post of governor of Réunion. The shake-up Bonaparte had ordered the previous February in the colonial administration meant that all post-Revolutionary assemblies, committees, and other bodies set up in the Isle de France were now abolished. Decaen was to enjoy all the powers of a governor-general under the monarchy and there was no longer any Colonial Assembly that needed to be placated or cajoled to do his bidding. Likewise, Léger, as *préfet colonial,* managed the colony's financial affairs and internal security with all the authority of a royal intendant. The new style of colonial government applied equally to Seychelles, and in his dispatches sent by the *Bélier* to Quinssy, the captain-general expressed confidence that "the spirit of patriotism and zeal which has always existed among the inhabitants of these interesting colonies" would guarantee obedience to his orders.

He informed Quinssy (who already knew thanks to the *Minerve's* visit) that war had broken out again with England, and he promised he would do all he could to diminish the harm this would do to the islands' prosperity. A corollary to this pledge, it seemed, was to ensure the colony would be completely defenceless, for Quinssy was ordered to return by the *Bélier* the remaining soldiers of the garrison in case they should be captured by the English. When the soldiers came aboard, however, Hulot refused to take three of them because of their age and infirmity. The rejected fusiliers, together with an elderly corporal who had been sent previously by Quinssy to Curieuse island to keep an eye on a slave ship in quarantine, would now form the colony's sole police force.[1]

Decaen had been briefed about the capitulation the Seychelles had negotiated with the enemy during the last war. It was not an arrangement that greatly pleased him, and he warned Quinssy against assuming that the Seychelles could quickly revert to the same comfortable state of neutrality. While conceding that Seychelles vessels might fly a flag of capitulation to avoid the unwelcome attention of English cruisers, he insisted that the Tricolour fly over the colony, which, on the signing of the Treaty of Amiens, had "returned under the absolute domination of France".

Decaen, however, avoided giving Quinssy precise instructions on what he should do when an English ship arrived at the colony. It was, he admitted, "an unfortunate and delicate position, about which I cannot at this moment give you any other instructions". But he went on to suggest that Quinssy should ensure he got the most favourable conditions from the enemy. "I trust in your zeal and courage," Decaen concluded, "convinced that you will not subscribe in any way to anything that would be harmful to the inhabitants or dishonourable to your nation and its flag". In other words, Quinssy was to use his own initiative and take the blame for the consequences.

On 28 October, Quinssy assembled the inhabitants and announced the changes in the colony's administration. He read out his renewed commission as commandant (he was no longer also civil agent), and announced the appointment of the newly arrived Beguignon as civil administrator. He formally dissolved the Colonial Assembly, the municipal council, and all other bodies set up since the Revolution, and instructed inhabitants who held titles and documents issued by those authorities to surrender them without delay. Quinssy later reported to Decaen that the new order had been established without difficulty "to the satisfaction of the inhabitants, as it was before 1789".

The geographical area of the colony over which Quinssy symbolically raised the Tricolour included the Amirante islands, the *prise de possession* of those sand and coralline cays having been made on Quinssy's orders the previous year by Captain Michel Blin of the schooner *Rosalie*. Documents relating to this acquisition had been forwarded to Paris by the Isle de France government, which thus recognised for the first time the territorial ambitions voiced by the Seychelles settlers in 1790 when, in a burst of revolutionary fervour, they had claimed the right to rule themselves and all island dependencies "which are more than 300 leagues from any other French colony".

During the last few months of 1803 Quinssy seems to have been too involved with internal matters to worry about the war. It was not until 1 January 1804. that he issued a proclamation advising the inhabitants on the action to be taken should enemy ships appear off the islands. Two cannon shots fired from the Établissement would signal their approach, on hearing which all able-bodied men would report, armed, to the commandant. Those living further away would be summoned to the assembly by letter. At night flares would be fired to warn the inhabitants at Praslin and La Digue.

As with his wartime instructions of 1793, Quinssy gave no indication how, if at all, he would resist. There is little doubt that he had already decided to capitulate as soon as an enemy force arrived. The last war had shown the advantages of such a course, and the recent attempt by the English to burn the *Flèche* had been a timely reminder of the ruthlessness of the enemy should he be opposed. Quinssy knew that the main concern of the inhabitants was to safeguard their property and their lives, possibly even in that order, and that, despite their patriotism, they favoured capitulation. His problem was how to achieve this in a manner that would be acceptable to the captain-general.

Fortunately, for almost the whole of that year, the problem did not arise. The war passed Seychelles by. No English ships were sighted and the Tricolour flew undisturbed over Mahé. But there were plenty of other problems for Quinssy; among them lack of food, complaints by the deportees, slaves escaping, and the normal squabbling among the inhabitants. Excessive drinking was causing frequent fights and disorder and as a result Quinssy restricted the sale of liquor at the Établissement to a canteen run by a former soldier, Claude Gilles. Gilles could offer billiards as a recreation to his customers, but no games of chance. He was forbidden also to sell liquor to slaves, or to visiting soldiers or sailors without the commandant's permission.

Theft of mail was also a recurring problem, and instructions were issued that all letters were to be taken from the ships by the health officer to Gilles's canteen for distribution. A post box, constructed in such a way that letters could not be taken out, was placed outside the canteen.

News of the war that reached Seychelles was not always reassuring. General Rochambeau's defeat in Saint Domingue (Haiti) and the subsequent loss of France's richest Caribbean colony to its slave population had been an unwelcome reminder to the settlers of their own outwardly subservient but potentially explosive labour force. In Europe, it seemed to be a military stalemate. There were no sparkling feats of French arms to offset the reverse in the Americas. Instead the large army assembled by Bonaparte at Boulogne grew bored as it waited for the right combination of diversion, tide, and weather to make the invasion of England possible. Meanwhile Britain was busy mustering another coalition of powers that would take the field against France.

The most noteworthy happening was the creation of the Empire in May, and the crowning of Bonaparte as Napoleon I at the end of the year. Nearer home, the British had renewed the blockade of the Isle de France. But no blockade can be total. The English cruisers had at times to raise their siege in order to re-provision at Madagascar, and even when they were on station there were plenty of opportunities to slip past the squadron when it was looking the other way.

French privateers continued their depredations on the English company's shipping, and the merchants of Bombay and Bengal also suffered markedly from the marauding presence off their coasts of Linois's squadron. But the admiral's failure early in the year to capture the homeward China convoy of more than 20 Indiamen near the Strait of Malacca had been a bitter disappointment.

Instead of breaking and fleeing on sighting Linois, the convoy had anchored in defensive formation, while the English commodore, Nathaniel Dance, audaciously manoeuvred some of his largest vessels towards the French as if they were ships of the line. After an overnight standoff, and some desultory fire at long range the next morning, Linois decided that he was faced with a greatly superior force and broke off the engagement.[2] The casualty list for both sides was one killed and two wounded. Linois later claimed that he had been misinformed about the numbers in the convoy. Three additional ships that were sighted he took for men of war, which meant that "there was no longer any question but to avoid the consequences of an inequal engagement". Some writers were later prepared to excuse Linois, but the hero of Algeciras received little sympathy at the time from Napoleon.[3]

"He has made the French flag the laughing stock of the world." he complained to Decrès. "Write to Linois, make him realise the gravity of his fault; how mistaken he is if he believes that he is the mainstay of the French navy. You will tell him that he lacked spirit, something I admire in a chief, and which he needs much of." Inevitably, Linois's performance drew contemptuous comment from Decaen, which embittered even further that difficult relationship.

Later that year, during his second cruise from the Isle de France, Linois experienced further chagrin, when he had to withdraw before a spirited defence of a convoy by the *Centurion* off Vizagapatam on the Coromandel coast. Although the French managed to cut out one laggard ship, the *Princess Charlotte*, it was all in all a poor showing by the *Marengo* and the frigates *Atalante* and *Sémillante*. The veteran *Centurion*, ending her long service in eastern waters, shepherded the remaining ships of the convoy safely back to England, where, on the last day of 1804, she came to anchor in St Helens Bay, off the Isle of Wight.

On the same day that the *Centurion* had been battling the *Marengo*, the frigate *Concorde*, under the command of Captain John Wood, was lying in the channel between Praslin and Curieuse islands with her crew busy refilling water casks and cutting firewood. A small Portuguese schooner, on passage from Mozambique to the Isle de France, also lay in the roadstead. She had been visited by a boarding party from the *Concorde*, but otherwise had been left unmolested. In his log Wood does not record her cargo, but it must almost certainly have been slaves.

A few days later a French schooner, also from Mozambique, was sighted and brought in as a prize by one of the *Concorde's* boats. She had 70 slaves in her hold, 15 of whom were immediately pressed into service in the *Concorde*. It was a common enough recruitment, for captains, both English and French, were always short of hands. For the freed slaves it was an exchange of one form of servitude for another, although with better prospects of freedom if they survived the hazards of sea warfare. It would be some time before they learned the ways of life aboard ship, but Wood was pleased enough to get them. Already, during his stay at Praslin, several seamen had deserted, slipping away from shore parties into the thickly wooded island interior. Wood had sent an armed detachment after them, but it returned empty handed. The same day, 23 September, the *Concorde* sailed with her prize for Mahé.

Word of the English ship's visit to Praslin had reached the main island, so it was no surprise when she was sighted slowly approaching the anchorage that Wood persistently described in his log as Maha Roads. Two ships were already moored there. "At 4.45 sent the cutter manned and armed to examine the strange vessels," Wood noted. "At 6.30 shortened sail and came to with best bower in 13 fms in Maha Roads."

By the time the cutter returned, darkness had fallen. It reported that the two vessels were indeed French, one a slaver, the brig *Zephyr* and the other a small schooner. Their crews, however, had been busy in anticipation of the Englishmen's arrival. All the slaves and other cargo in the *Zephyr* had been moved ashore, while the schooner had been holed and sunk. Wood had to leave it like that for the night. As a normal precaution against attack, a boat rowed guard around the *Concorde* until morning.

"AM: At 8.30 came off a Flag of Truce," noted the ship's log for 25 September, its only reference to the capitulation by the Seychelles that was to take place during the morning. But the document Wood signed shows that the English captain agreed to conditions much the same as those of the previous capitulations, with similar rejections or modifications to Quinssy's proposed clauses. It was no doubt at the suggestion of the commandant, to show that he was submitting under duress, that Wood gave the colony a one-hour deadline to comply or face the consequences. On the expiry of this time limit, at 10 o'clock, Quinssy went on board the *Concorde* and signed the surrender document. The witnesses were Poupinel and Captain Sausse.

Under the terms of the capitulation Wood took the *Zephyr*, which he insisted should have all its slaves and cargo put back. He agreed that the colony might keep two schooners, duly authorised to sail under the capitulation flag. Sausse was captain of one of the favoured vessels, a fact that seemed to give some substance to Decaen's later accusation that Sausse, who had apparently gone aboard the *Concorde* at Praslin, assisted the frigate to negotiate the entrance to Mahé harbour.[4]

The *Concorde* stayed a further two days at Mahé, during which time the *Zephyr* was warped out of the harbour and provisioned, along with the schooner prize, for the voyage to India. Before setting course for Bombay, Wood called briefly again at Praslin, where he recovered from the Portuguese vessel four of his deserters. These unfortunate men, who had been hoping to escape in the neutral ship, were sentenced to 36 lashes each.

Wood's prizes at Seychelles had hardly been spectacular, but the following month, while cruising about 240 miles southwest of Bombay, he was lucky enough to capture the renowned corsair, Thomas Lemême. When Lemême first sighted the *Concorde* he had taken her for a merchantman, and immediately bore down on her in his fast-sailing corvette *La Fortune*. With both ships closing under a full press of sail it was not long before they were almost abeam of each other. Only then did Lemême realise his mistake and hauling his wind, he made off with the *Concorde* in pursuit. It was by then just after noon. The chase continued throughout the rest of the day, pursued and pursuer exchanging shot whenever they thought they might be in range. Lemême, courageous and resourceful to the last, tacked repeatedly to elude the frigate, but after Wood managed to get off a couple of broadsides with telling effect on the *Fortune's* rigging, the French ship surrendered.

"This capture may be considered as a peculiarly fortunate one, for Monsieur Le Même has not hesitated to declare that it was his intention to have swept the whole Malabar Coast previous to returning from his cruise," wrote the *Bombay Courier* of November 1804, the day after the *Concorde's* return to Bombay with her prize.[5]

"The *Fortune*," the paper noted, "is a remarkably fine vessel mounting 24 guns, built after the construction of *La Révolutionnaire*, lately coppered and a prime sailer." As for Lemême, after being brought to Bombay with all honour by Captain Wood, he was shipped to England later, but died from illness during the voyage.

The loss of *La Fortune* was keenly felt at the Isle de France, where Decaen described it as posing "a very real danger to the supply of essentials on which we have been existing." For despite the successes of the French privateers against English shipping and the huge emporium of products of all descriptions that the Isle de France had become as a result of their captures, the English blockade was beginning to tell. Lemême was only one of several privateers to fall victim to enemy cruisers, a trend that would quicken with the departure of Linois's squadron towards the end of 1805.

The day the *Marengo* left the Cape and sailed into the South Atlantic, Trafalgar had only just passed into history. Linois, of course, knew nothing of Nelson's crushing victory over a combined French-Spanish fleet. Only later would he realise that his withdrawal from the Indian Ocean had been but one more shadow in France's total eclipse in the struggle against the English at sea. Napoleon continued to send out frigates to bolster the Isle de France defences, but it was a futile gesture. Only one last blaze of glory need be mentioned, the victory of the French at the Battle of Grand Port, a few months before the Isle de France capitulated, in December 1810. It was brief, bloody and spectacular - four English frigates were taken - but an encounter which came too late to affect the final outcome.[6]

Linois's last cruise had been relatively successful, so why did he quit when he did? He could justify his withdrawal by pointing to crew shortages, the exhausted state of his men, and the storm damage suffered by his ships. But all these were subsidiary to a single factor, that of his personal relationship with the captain-general. The antagonism of that first day, when Decaen boarded the *Marengo* in Brest harbour, was now such that neither man could stand the sight of the other.

The break came in May 1805 as Linois was preparing to leave on what was to be his last expedition. He had been ordered by Decaen to sail first to Seychelles to nullify the effects of Quinssy's capitulation to Captain Wood by restoring the French flag. It had also been agreed that he would then sail to the Far East to bring back cordage from Manila that was badly needed in the colony. Soon, however, it became apparent to Linois that his plans were common knowledge in the Isle de France, not only as regards his proposed route but also on the state of his crews, many of whom were in hospital and whose numbers he was having to make up by recruiting slaves. He attributed the leak to Decaen or his officers, and just before he sailed in the *Marengo*, with the *Belle Poule* in company (the *Atalante*, still undergoing repairs, was to join the squadron later), he left a letter for Decaen in which he informed him that he would not now be going to the Far East.

"The extraordinary publicity that has been given to my proposed operations, which were several times the subject of discussion at our meetings ... determines me to change my plan of campaign," he wrote. "I will direct my course first to Mahé, where I shall stay for the shortest possible time. From there I will make for the Malabar coast, cruise next off Ceylon where not only do I hope to make several captures, but I wish to be seen and recognised in the several ports of that island."[7] He would then go into the Bay of Bengal and cruise there awhile. From there he would turn back, but instead of making for the Isle de France, he would recross the ocean to the Cape and reprovision his ships there. No mention was made of when he would return to the Isle de France.

Decaen was furious at this obvious snub. Unfortunately, instead of allowing his anger time to subside, he immediately composed a bitter response, in which he not only denied having had anything to do with the disclosure of Linois's plans, but suggested that the admiral himself was responsible for the leak. He admonished Linois for changing his plans without reference to him, and accused him openly of neglecting the good of the colony in order to satisfy his own greed. Two days later the brig *Hippolyte* sailed from the Isle de France for Seychelles. Among its dispatches it carried Decaen's letter.

The following day, an English squadron consisting of the *Tremendous* (74), the *Grampus* (50), and the frigates *Pitt* and *Terpsichore* arrived off the island. Sent to renew the blockade by the new commander-in-chief East Indies, Sir Edward Pellew, bt, the squadron was under the command of the *Centurion's* old captain, Commodore Samuel Osborn. As he looked at the enemy ships through his glass, Decaen surmised correctly that they intended a lengthy stay, and in fact two months were to pass before the English ships repaired to Madagascar to replenish their water supplies, allowing the frigate *Atalante* to leave port to rejoin Linois.

The *Marengo* and the *Belle Poule* had arrived at Mahé on 10 Prairial Year XIII (30 May 1805). Decaen had warned Linois that he would find the English flag flying, but Quinssy, uncertain of the identity of the visitors, played safe and showed no flag at all. Only when he received a letter from Linois suggesting he raise the Tricolour, and inviting him to come aboard the *Marengo*, did he respond. Quinssy found the admiral ready to sympathise with him over the predicament of the capitulation. Together they discussed the unpleasant letter that Decaen had given Linois to deliver to the commandant, in which he ridiculed the ease with which Quinssy had surrendered the island to Captain Wood. He should have bargained with the enemy after hearing their demands, insisted Decaen, and then made the best possible terms for the colony.

The English should have been told that their flag could fly over the Seychelles only for as long as they kept sufficient forces there to protect their conquest. But in any case, Decaen told Quinssy, the capitulation was null and void as it had not been ratified by him. With this, he gave Quinssy a formal warning that, as he was likely to receive further visits from *Messieurs les Anglais,* he hoped that the commandant would "act in such a way that I shall not be obliged to criticise your conduct, because a repetition would force me to treat you more severely".

Linois, who saw the futility of the Seychelles trying to treat or wring concessions from the enemy, wrote to Decaen justifying Quinssy's actions. From what he had seen of the colony, he told the captain-general, it would be difficult to imagine it opposing even an enemy corvette. There were only about 60 Whites on the island, most of them aged and scattered along 15 to 20 leagues of the coast. There were also about 2,000 slaves, but as these were mainly from warrior tribes in Mozambique it would be too dangerous for the settlers to arm them. He praised the zeal and goodwill Quinssy and all the inhabitants had shown to his squadron, commenting that he had paid only 15 piastres for a bullock and five for a turtle. By feeding his crews on fresh meat throughout their six-day stay he had been able to conserve his salted beef.

A day or two before the ships sailed for Ceylon, the *Hippolyte* arrived with supplies for Quinssy. In due course Decaen's letter to the admiral was delivered on board the *Marengo*.

"I have received ... your letter of 3 Prairial, in which you dare to allow yourself to claim that my personal interests are of more concern to me than those of the State," wrote Linois in reply. "You should, when you have such disobliging observations to transmit to me, wait until you are able to say them to my face, so that I may thus have the means of correcting your false accusations." In an oblique comment on the ill-mannered tone of Decaen's letter, Linois reminded the captain-general that he had always shown proper respect in his correspondence.

As regards the planning of his operations, Linois insisted that he would change these as many times as he saw fit. This was his prerogative and within the latitude given him by the Minister of Marine, who, "in the name of His Majesty, confirms the confidence in which I am held".

The letter concluded with the blunt announcement that Linois would not return again to the Isle de France, even if ordered by Decaen, unless "the security of the vessels under my command, the health of the crews, and the good of the service impose on me that necessity". This was Linois's last word. Decaen did not reply, but he was already urging Paris to recall his adversary. Some months later we find him writing to the Minister, with a copy of Linois's letter enclosed, appealing again for the admiral's removal. "If, against my expectations, this decision has not yet been taken, I am once more obliged to request it, besides which the service of His Majesty requires it."

But by now Linois had left the Indian Ocean. Unable to provision his ships properly at the Cape, and determined not to return to the Isle de France, he had had no alternative but to sail on to France. His final cruise had restored some of the lustre to his reputation, and he was no doubt confident that he would be able to win Decrès's support for his actions.

But Linois did not reach France. Intercepted by a superior force off the Cape Verde islands, both the *Marengo* and *Belle Poule* were taken and Linois, who was wounded in the engagement, was to spend the rest of the war as a prisoner in England.

The departure of his squadron from Seychelles had been marked by a minor drama involving the loss of a pirogue belonging to Hangard. The elderly settler had been supplying the ships with turtle during their stay, but not, apparently, in sufficient quantity to satisfy Linois, who requested Quinssy for a further consignment before he sailed. Hangard was reluctant to send his slaves out again, complaining that he lacked a strong enough cable for his pirogue in the heavy seas, but eventually, with a show of bad grace, he ordered his crew to make one last trip to the Isle du Nord for turtles. The next morning, the pirogue set off from Hangard's habitation on North West Bay with a load of turtles for the squadron, which was even then preparing to leave its anchorage off Sainte Anne. By the time the pirogue, named the *Mille Pattes* because of its extraordinary length, had rounded North Point the *Marengo* and *Belle Poule* were under sail. The frigate, sighting the pursuing craft, hove to until it came alongside. Unfortunately, due either to the heavy sea or bad handling by Hangard's *commandeur,* the 38ft pirogue smashed against the side of the frigate, split down its entire length and tumbled the crew of 13 into the sea. All were safely brought aboard the frigate, which, because of the delay that would have resulted from returning the slaves to the shore, immediately got under way again.

Linois was in a few weeks able to transfer the slaves off the coast of Ceylon to a French ship bound for the Isle de France, where they were entrusted to Hangard's lawyer for eventual repatriation to Seychelles. Quinssy, rarely on good terms with the ill-tempered Hangard, showed scant sympathy over the loss of the pirogue. He denied a claim by Hangard that the weather had been too rough for going out, and attributed the accident either to the negligence of the crew or the rotten state of the pirogue. Only when ordered by the Isle de France did he arrange for a valuation of the *Mille Pattes*, which was carried out almost a year later by four inhabitants, Blin, Mondon, Lacour, and Hodoul.

At Hangard's request, they left the compensation to be fixed by the *préfet colonial,* Léger, but pointed out the difficulty of finding a tree of similar length to that from which the pirogue had been fashioned. A figure of 1,000 piastres as compensation was mentioned, but Quinssy, in a letter to Léger, scoffed at this, saying the pirogue had been hollowed out without the use of fine tools and that its value had been greatly exaggerated "by those people who like to interfere in everything". For 1,000 piastres, he claimed he could buy a small brig at the Isle de France.

Many months after this incident we find Hangard complaining that his slaves had not been returned, and that with the cotton crop ready he needed them for his ginnery, as he was now too old and infirm to do much himself. Quinssy blamed Hangard's own representatives at the Isle de France for the delay in shipping the slaves back.

Some weeks after Linois's departure from Seychelles, the frigates *Pitt*[8] and *Terpsichore* arrived, having been detached from Commodore Osborn's squadron to scout for signs of the French admiral. They wore French colours, although it is doubtful if Quinssy was deceived by this ruse. Mindful, however, of Decaen's instructions about flying the Tricolour, he raised the French flag. When the enemy did declare himself there was no formal capitulation. Captain Walter Bathurst[9] of the *Terpsichore* merely seized the colony's Tricolour, made Quinssy a prisoner during his one-day stay and, after visiting an American ship that he found in the harbour, sailed off, with the *Pitt* in company. Quinssy noted that the English ships, which had recently provisioned at Madagascar, did not even bother to take on wood or fill any water casks.

Having maintained the flag until forced to lower it and

avoided a formal capitulation without damage to the colony, Quinssy repeated the same tactics just over two months later, on 7 November 1805, when another English frigate, the *Duncan*, sailed into the harbour. This time, he was to pay dearly for not negotiating at once the colony's surrender.

Captain Clement Sneyd, in temporary command of the *Duncan*, was intent on making as many prizes as he could, and destroying enemy shipping he was unable to take with him. He already had a prize in company as he stood in towards Mahé's north-west shore: a small privateer, the *Emilie* (somewhat larger than Surcouf's ship of the same name), which he had captured after a fierce fight off the island of Réunion. Sighting a sail lying between the islands of Conception and Thérèse, Sneyd sent the *Emilie* to investigate while the *Duncan* continued round North West Point to the main anchorage.

The next day the *Emilie* arrived in the harbour, with the slave brig *Courrier des Seychelles* in tow. It was a prize that had been stripped of much of its assets, for the nearly 200 slaves who had been aboard were now hidden somewhere on the island, having been put ashore as soon as the captain had sighted the English ships' approach. He had also removed all the ship's cables and anchors.

Quinssy protested to Sneyd over the taking of *the Courrier des Seychelles*, pointing out that it was one of the colony's vessels allowed to sail unmolested under the capitulation flag. But Sneyd was not interested in previous capitulations or the formal surrender of the colony. Angered by the loss of the slaves and the defiant attitude of Quinssy and the settlers, he sent an armed party round to Port Glaud to retrieve everything that had been taken from the brig.

According to reports that Decaen was to receive, the English pillaged the estates of Blin and Dupont, proprietors of the *Courrier des Seychelles*. The settlers and their families had fled into the interior, leaving their property at the mercy of the English sailors, who took all they could, but there were still no slaves. Sneyd sent a further party to assist in the search, and eventually it returned with the brig's anchors, cables and sails. The slaves were still missing and Sneyd was furious, nor was his temper improved on being told that four seamen in the landing parties had deserted, taking their muskets and ammunition. Although a search was mounted they were never found, and the *Duncan* had eventually to sail without them.

Sneyd stayed six days at Seychelles. During that time his men carried out several punitive raids along the west coast. A brig coming in from Madagascar was fired on, severely damaged and forced to run aground in Anse Boileau. Another small vessel, the *Rosalie*, was found undergoing repairs at Anse à la Mouche and was set on fire. Having with that destroyed what he could along the west coast (Sneyd seems to have left the Établissement unmolested), the *Duncan* sailed off with her two prizes in company.[10]

The settlers, angered and frightened at the damage the enemy had caused, turned on Quinssy. Why, they demanded, had he not ensured the safety of their property through the usual act of capitulation? When he quoted Decaen's orders that he should not voluntarily surrender the colony, but wait until this was demanded, they insisted he write to the Isle de France to have these annulled. To back this up they drew up a petition asking Quinssy to intercede with Decaen and Léger, pointing out that the colony was without defence and exposed to all the misfortune of war.

"The inhabitants are in constant fear as soon as an English ship arrives," they wrote. "Their families have to seek refuge in the woods, with their belongings and Blacks, while the husbands are obliged to report to the Établissement." Not that they could offer even token resistance to an enemy landing; the lack of roads made it virtually impossible to concentrate their forces at any threatened part of the coast. Most of the damage this time had been done to shipping, but surely if the enemy "should not be able to satisfy his greed with plunder from ships he will devastate the islands and ruin everyone".

But Decaen did not share the settlers' anxiety. When informed of the *Duncan's* visit, he felt the outcome had been quite satisfactory and the important thing was that Quinssy had not formally surrendered and could therefore continue to fly the French flag as if the enemy had never been. "Which leaves matters where it seems to me natural that they should be," he told Decrès.

Quinssy, however, never again attempted to defy an English ship. When the *Duncan* returned in June 1806 he quickly arranged a capitulation with its captain, Lord George Stuart.[11] The day after her arrival the *Duncan* was joined by the 74-gun

Russel. The ships stayed several days, carrying out repairs to sails and rigging, and taking on water and provisions. The *Duncan's* log records several desertions during the stay. Three seamen took the opportunity of being in a shore party to slip away on the second day. Another deserted the following day, and shortly before the *Duncan* and *Russel* sailed for Bombay the purser's steward jumped ship. There is no mention of any of them being found.

Two months later Quinssy renewed the capitulation when a squadron led by the *Albion* (74), under the command of Captain John Ferrier,[12] arrived at Mahé. The others were the *Pitt*, another frigate, the *Drake*, and two sloops, the *Psyche* and *Seaflower*.[13] Ferrier stayed only a few hours, sailing as soon as he had loaded firewood and refilled his water casks.

Anticipating renewed criticism from Decaen at his surrendering the colony first to the *Duncan* and then to the *Albion*, Quinssy wrote to Paris to justify his actions. He recalled the pillaging and burning suffered at the hands of Captain Sneyd and his crew, as a result of which, on the next visit by an enemy ship, "I thought it prudent to renew the same capitulation that I had earlier made with Captain Wood of the English frigate *Concorde*." He expressed the hope that the Minister would approve his actions, which had protected the inhabitants from further harm, and cited the opinion of Linois that the Seychelles, because of its precarious position, should adhere to the capitulation agreed on with the enemy.

Decrès, it seems, approved Quinssy's action, for the capitulation, scrupulously renewed each time an enemy ship called, continued in force until hostilities ceased with the fall of the Isle de France at the end of November 1810. Decaen made a half-hearted attempt to provide Seychelles with a defence by setting up a National Guard in May 1807, and sending a detachment of army veterans as reinforcements the following year.[14] But he never again pressed his views on how he thought Quinssy should treat with the enemy.

Communication between the two islands was always uncertain; at one point Quinssy complained that of eight ships that left Seychelles for the Isle de France over a period of six months with dispatches for Decaen, not one had returned. With such delays, any decision that Decaen might take about Seychelles had most likely lost its relevance by the time it reached Quinssy. It was perhaps, in part, a realisation of this that induced Decaen to forgo further interference with the colony's series of surrenders to enemy ships.

Thanks to this, particularly the Seychelles ships' right to unmolested passage under a flag of capitulation, the colony's economy bounded ahead during the last years of the war. The number of slaves working on the islands, always a reliable indicator to economic activity, rose from 2,414 in 1807 to more than 3,200 within two years, while the acreages under cotton, now the islands' principal crop, sugar-cane, coffee, and cloves, increased substantially.[15]

When the end came, with Decaen's surrender of the Isle de France and its dependencies, the Seychelles brig *Favorite* happened to be in port there and was seized by the English. But because she flew a capitulation flag, she was allowed to leave, and sailed in haste to Mahé with the news. Three weeks later an English merchant ship, the *Brothers*, called at Mahé and confirmed the *Favorite's* sad tidings.

13

Human Bondage
1804-1810

> Je suis bien fâché, Monsieur, des farces que ce gueux
> D'aza vous a fait ... je vous prie de [le] vendre.
> > *Pierre Hangard to M. Masse of Isle de France, 1805*

Even today it is a lonely place, dark and gloomy, with suggestions of menace. On each side of the road the trees whisper uneasily among themselves. Occasionally, there will be a crack, and then a thump. A falling coconut? The ear remains alert as one hurries along.

The sound of the sea is muffled up here, on the squat spur of land that separates Anse aux Poules Bleues from Baie Lazare. On the map, Mahé resembles a crumpled boot – this is the heel. The small road along its ridge divides as it descends towards the blunted point, eroded in places by several sandy coves. To the right lies Anse Soleil, while the left-hand fork twists down through the palms to Petite Anse.

In September 1804 there was no road here, only a path perhaps, along which the negress Anna strolled one morning to watch over her master's turtles. Whether she was accompanied to Petite Anse, where the turtles were penned, is not known but by the afternoon she was dead, her naked body found by a passing herdsman at the edge of the beach. There were signs that she had fought for her life for her head was cruelly battered and her body marked by multiple cuts and contusions.

First it was thought that as her clothes had been taken some runaway slaves were responsible, an opinion held by her master, Bruneau la Souchaire. Later investigation, however, pointed to the possible guilt of two slaves owned by the settler Avice, whose habitation was at Anse Royale, on the other side of the island. When they were interrogated, each slave accused the other. Fournier, who was already chained at the block for some other offence, claimed that Céphale had killed Anna because she had been the cause of his brother's death. In trying to catch some fruit bats for her he had fallen from a tree and broken his neck. Céphale, however, said Fournier had been enamoured of Anna, and that when she rejected his advances he had killed her.

The tribunal appointed to look into the affair was unable to determine where the guilt lay. Perhaps both slaves were innocent, or again, perhaps they had together killed Anna. The result was that both were kept in prison. Three weeks later Fournier was dead. Poupinel, visiting the prison, noted the untouched food amid the filth of the cell and concluded that he had starved himself to death.

Céphale survived for another eight months. A diary entry by Poupinel dated 2 Messidor Year XIII (20 June 1805) records that when the cell door was opened by the prison corporal "we saw and recognised the said Black to be dead, and exterior examination and his previous illness being sufficient proof that death was the inevitable result of what is known as jail fever. Blacksmith called to break off the irons".

For the slaves, death was a sure way of ending their miserable existence, and far from being a penalty to fear it was welcomed by many of them. Under the Code Noir, promulgated by Louis XIV in 1685 to regulate the conditions of slavery, the death penalty was mandatory where a slave had run away three times. Many years passed before the authorities realised that slaves considered death a risk worth taking.

Writing to Ternay in 1775 the Bourbon commandant, De Bellecombe, pointed out that the Caribbean colony of Martinique had obtained permission to replace the death penalty in cases of repeated escape with a life sentence in a chain gang. He suggested that the King's authorisation to Martinique should be assumed to apply to all French colonies. Ternay agreed, but evidence suggests that the death penalty continued to be exacted for persistent escaping and for other offences, such as striking a master in the face or causing him injury. Despite the obvious brutality of its punishments, the Code Noir had, in fact, been introduced to improve the conditions of slavery and restrict the punishments masters could impose. In 1723 letters patent were issued forbidding, for example, the torture and mutilation of slaves.

Unfortunately many of the law's stipulations were ignored or, at best, complied with in a perfunctory manner. The code laid down a minimum scale of rations and rest periods, but who was to gainsay a master if he rejected the granting of such luxuries? That many failed to observe the compulsory rest day can be deduced from Léger's instruction to district commandants in the Isle de France to ensure that slaves had Sundays free, or a compensatory day of leisure.

Generally, however, Léger noted that slaves who worked well and submissively were treated humanely. Certainly their treatment in Seychelles and the other French colonies in the Indian Ocean compared favourably with conditions in the Caribbean, particularly in the post-Revolutionary period when the spectre of a general uprising of the Blacks loomed large.

But if some slave owners treated their charges relatively well, others were cruel and vindictive. One English visitor remarked that slaves he saw there seemed better fed and had less work to do than the poorer peasantry of Europe.[1] Another visitor expressed disgust at the masters' lack of consideration for his slaves. Writing some years after the end of the war, when British curbs on slave trading had made it more difficult to obtain fresh supplies from the African mainland, the latter observed that it was "extraordinary that the proprietors of the slaves ... should pursue the same line of policy respecting their moral conduct as when they (the slaves) were both numerous and cheap".[2]

The loss of a slave who died either from neglect or the effects of punishment was to the master the loss of an essential commodity, and to be without a slave was to be impoverished. Gillot was only expressing the view of the ordinary settler when, on his return to the Isle de France in 1775 and finding that he had lost all his slaves, he described the possession of just one personal slave "as the only means left for me to live".

During the war years the slave population of Seychelles rose steadily and by 1809, the year before the surrender of the Indian Ocean colonies to Britain, there were more than 3,000 or an average of ten slaves to each white inhabitant. Numbers continued to rise so that by the time peace was formally restored in 1818 there were more than 6,000 slaves in the colony, employed principally in the cultivation of the main cash crops at that time, namely, cotton, sugar-cane, coffee, and cloves.

Although the Seychelles administration owned few slaves, Quinssy himself had a substantial number: about 80 were working for him in 1807 on the 480 acres he owned on Mahé, about a quarter of the land producing vegetables, cotton, and sugar-cane. Other big landowners such as Hangard, Blin, Lebeuze, and Mondon owned more than 100 slaves. Slave-owning was not confined to Whites and almost all the free Blacks had slaves, the most noteworthy being Vola-maëffa, of whom mention has already been made.

The islands' black or coloured inhabitants had either been born of free parents, or had been freed by their master, usually for loyal service. In such instances it was customary for the freed slave to be given a slave of his own, to ensure that he did not become a charge on the state. But sometimes the conferring of freedom was motivated by the master's self-interest. If the slave was old and infirm, chronically unwell, or his trouble-making meant it was impossible to sell him, the master might decide to free him and thus rid himself of the responsibility of feeding, clothing and housing, and paying the head tax on someone who was no longer an economic asset. Such acts of giving liberty were frowned on by the administration, and Decaen had to warn Quinssy that all manumissions must be approved first by the government.

Slaves in the Seychelles were of four main types. First there were the Créoles, those of African or mixed parentage who had been born on the island (the term was by now losing its original designation of Europeans who had been born in the colonies). The Créole was regarded as more intelligent than the others and it was from their ranks that the foremen, or *commandeurs,* were drawn.

Next there were those from Madagascar, the Créoles Malgaches; a particularly proud and often fierce people, who regarded work in the fields as fit only for women. They made excellent carpenters, cabinet-makers and blacksmiths. Third and largest group were the Africans. Captured perhaps somewhere in the interior of East or Central Africa and brought to the Mozambique coast for shipping to the islands, they were known simply as Mozambiques, a term that continued to be used, derogatorily, in Seychelles. These tribesmen settled in badly on the White man's island, and were quickly dubbed less intelligent than the others. Because of their natural strength and stamina their labour was exploited to the full in the plantations. Lastly, there was a small number of Indians and Malays, the Créole Malbar, who were often employed indoors as domestic servants.

Given their different languages and customs, there was little mixing between the groups. Although all in time adapted to the ways of the White man, their style of living and dress reflected the background from which most of them had been cruelly uprooted. The Créole and the Indian were usually materially better off. In the slave camps, the house of a Créole would have a wooden bed, cupboards, mattress, pillow and sometimes curtains round the bed and window. The African, on the other hand, cared little about his clothes or the comfort of his home. According to one observer he would readily sell his clothes for a temporary mistress or a bottle of spirits, for the chaffing of shirt and trousers irritated him and he much preferred wearing a waistcloth, or *langouti.*

"To have their hair plaited or cut according to the style of their people, the skin well polished, their tribal marks prominently displayed, and a langouti round them; that's the costume that suits them. Add to that an iron pot, a knife, a calabash, a vacoa bag to cover their shoulders in the rain, a little haversack slung from the langouti to hold pipe and tobacco, and the Mozambique considers himself well dressed and fitted out. Anything he might be given over and above that is hardly of any value in his eyes, except for the arak that it might be exchanged for." Drink, unfortunately, was a means of forgetting at least temporarily one's miserable condition, and despite regulations controlling the sale of liquor it was always easily obtainable at little cost.[3]

The redeeming feature of the Black was his carefree nature, his fondness for his master's children (although he might well neglect his own) and the absence of any real wickedness. The worst that might be said of most slaves was that they were lazy - natural enough in one who is forced to work at the crack of a whip. And if a slave preferred singing, dancing and sitting around talking to working, his inclinations were not dissimilar from those of his master. This easy-going life style of the Seychelles settler had always been a source of irritation to the French administration and it was equally a matter for comment by the English who visited the islands after the war.

They noted that although the Seychellois had the manners and speech of a Frenchman, he lacked the restlessness and impatience that seemed to them a predominant characteristic of the French. They praised the warm hospitality and strong parental and filial affection of the Seychelles settler, and deplored his "want of all public spirit, indolence and ignorance".

"They profess the Roman Catholic religion, but their conformity to this or any other faith is very lax," affirmed one visitor. "In society there is little or no distinction of class, beyond that of colour, but those who are the most wealthy or intelligent are regarded with most attention and respect."[4]

Understandably the Seychelles inhabitant suffered from his isolation and the restrictions to his moral and material development. There was no formal schooling, education where it was provided being in the hands of family tutors, a role, as we have seen, that was fulfilled by several of the deportees from France. Lack of religious observance was hardly surprising, given that throughout the French colonial period — and until well into the 19th century under English rule — there was no resident priest. As a result the Seychellois followed his own simple code of conduct which, though natural to the circumstances in which he lived and which was free of any viciousness or depravity, was readily dubbed immoral by the early Victorian visitors from England.

One such visitor, whose eye did not miss the graceful manners and "many personal attractions" of the women of Mahé, regretted that morality was not amongst their leading virtues, and expressed surprise that divorcees were received without scruple by families where the women were of chaste reputation.[5]

Despite a generally tolerant view of breaches of the marriage vow there were, as another writer noted, "some very respectable French families scattered over the islands".[6] This particular commentator has left us a description of the houses in which some of these families lived. Usually they were built no more than 100 paces from the sea, "some even with taste and elegance". With shingle roofs, and with the spaces between the wooden frame filled with broken stone and mortar, they were then plastered and whitewashed. Other houses were built of square blocks of coral, which was also frequently used for making lime.

There were in the town two billiard rooms, but no regular tavern "for very few strangers visit the island and the hospitality of the inhabitants renders such an establishment unnecessary". Billiards and card-playing, as well as dancing, were the favourite pastimes of the Seychellois. The wild, hypnotic rhythms of Africa were strong and pervasive, and the slaves' impact on the music of the islands persists to this day in such dances as the *séga*.

According to one observer "among all the dances of the Blacks the most lascivious [is] the *Tschiega,* which they dance only on special occasions and for some unusual amusement". Today the hip-swivelling *séga* is the unofficial national dance, popular with inhabitants and tourists alike. More evocative of the dark, magical rites of Seychelles' African ancestry is the *moutia,* performed, perhaps, in some moonlit forest clearing to the steady throb of a drum. Such dances would go on throughout the night until the dancers fell to the ground exhausted.

The main holiday on the island was New Year, when the celebrations went on for two full days. It was customary for the master to hand gifts of clothing to his slaves, trousers, shirt, and a waistcoat in blue cotton to the men, and a skirt, shirt, and mouchoir to the women. Occasionally a blanket was also given.

Some of the barriers between master and slave were relaxed on such occasions, with the master and his family joining in the dancing of the Créole servants. The festive mood, however, was always liable to turn ugly, and concern over the behaviour of some of the slaves prompted Quinssy to issue an instruction that they must have a permit from their master to be away from their habitation during the holiday. "Every Black slave who is not provided with a letter from his master ... or who causes trouble or disorder shall be arrested and consigned to prison at the Établissement, where he will be severely punished and whipped there and then," he warned. Although this restriction seems to have applied to African slaves only, there was also a general ban on slaves going out with arms or sticks, and the inhabitants were forbidden to sell liquor in bulk to any slave during the holiday period, or to sell small quantities to Blacks (again the discrimination against the Mozambique) except with the permission of the commandant.

To supervise the conditions and disciplining of slaves, Quinssy set up in July 1806[7] a *conseil de commune* of four inhabitants, with himself as chairman. Although an unofficial body, the *conseil* lasted throughout the French administration, being concerned not only with slaves but also with the upkeep of roads and the supervision of the treasury accounts. Its first members were Charles Savy, Langlois, Mondon, and Blin, each being responsible for a particular area of the island. To finance the costs of maintaining detachments to hunt down runaway slaves Quinssy had the proceeds of a slave tax that had been authorised by Decaen, amounting to 50 centimes, or one-tenth of a piastre, for every slave owned.

Runaway slaves were a perennial problem, despite the rewards for their capture that had been introduced by Quinssy and Beguignon at the beginning of 1804. Depending on how long the slave had been at liberty, the reward ranged from half-a-piastre to 20 piastres. For simply bringing back the head of a slave, a flat rate of three piastres was paid.

Beguignon left Mahé early in 1804, after no more than six months' service in Seychelles, and Quinssy remained without an assistant until December 1806, when his replacement, a naval under-commissioner named François Le Roy, arrived. This event, as with the arrival of Beguignon, was quickly followed by the issuing of new directives and regulations whose authorship, although published jointly under the names of Quinssy and his administrative assistant, it was not difficult to recognise.

Quinssy invariably praised the work of his assistant in his dispatches to the Isle de France, although one suspects he resented any disturbance to the leisurely manner in which he had been accustomed to conduct the colony's affairs. He readily agreed to Beguignon's recall (the official reason for this was ill-health, although it would be more accurate to say that Beguignon could not accept being separated from his family). Quinssy's relationship with his successor, Le Roy, was soon soured by differences on how they thought the colony should be administered. Quinssy was no longer as energetic as he had been, and what in the early years of the war had been accepted as a calm and conciliatory leadership by the settlers now seemed to many to lack control and direction.

One of Le Roy's first actions was to set up, as decreed by Decaen, a *tribunal de paix* with power to impose fines of up to 200 francs without appeal. Quinssy, appointed to preside over the tribunal, assured Léger in a letter that he would carry out his duties with "justice, probity, correctness, and frankness".

As if in response to some criticism by Léger, he added: "I will employ to the best of my ability my modest knowledge and experience to fulfil the functions of this post, as I have always done as an officer in the service, since 1775." Later, Quinssy received, to assist him in his task as *juge de paix,* three copies of Napoleon's new *Code Civil* and three copies of the order setting out the privileges and honoraria of the court officers.

The administration of justice seems to have been almost at a standstill since the suppression by Decaen of the assemblies and tribunals set up during the Revolution. Le Roy, for one, was appalled by the apparent lawlessness in the colony, which is not surprising considering that Quinssy had still only three elderly soldiers to enforce his orders.

Records relating to the punishments meted out to slaves are scant. The most common punishment was a whipping, which varied from a few casual blows for negligence or momentary absence, to up to 30 lashes for theft or blatant insubordination as permitted by the Code Noir. For mutiny, continual absences, or the wounding of another slave the culprit would be chained by the neck and feet before the punishment was administered, usually by a *commandeur.* Some *commandeurs,* it has been noted, would not be permitted to give more than 20 lashes because of the damage they could inflict on a slave's back, while others might give up to 100 lashes "and hardly mark the skin". This last statement, it must be said, was made by an unabashed apologist for slavery.[8]

The death penalty was imposed for serious crimes such as murder and arson, but as the accused had to be sent to the Isle de France for final judgement and execution of sentence, it was not unusual for a prisoner to die or escape before he could be transferred.

In October 1809 Quinssy sought to speed the judicial process by establishing a Special Tribunal to try slaves accused of murder. The idea of the tribunal, to which Decaen agreed, had been prompted by the murder two months earlier of a white overseer, Pierre Michel Inard, who had been employed by the medical officer, Poupinel, to look after his estate. Several slaves were accused in the killing, but it was a 'Mozambique' named Pompé who, it was said, struck the fatal blow.

Pompé had managed to escape, and it was not until July 1810 that he was interrogated by Jean-François Hodoul, as *commissaire rapporteur* of the Special Tribunal. Eight days later, on 28 July, Pompé was unanimously found guilty by the tribunal. Sentence of death was passed, but as no-one was able or willing to carry out a beheading, the tribunal ordered that Pompé be burned. This act was carried out at half-past three the following morning, on a beach near the Moussa river.[9]

The increased lawlessness on the island was reflected in the behaviour of the deportees, whom Le Roy considered as the most troublesome and unruly characters he had ever met. This was obviously a biased opinion, understandably so as Le Roy soon after his arrival had been a target for thieves. He must have had a considerable wardrobe, for he complained that 60 articles of clothing were stolen from him by his servant, adding: "A few days later some of them were found in the house of two of the deportees, who have been ordered by the justice of the peace to compensate me for those not found."

At this time 23 deportees still remained in the colony. Only one or two had been allowed to go to the Isle de France for medical treatment. The others — those not already dead or who had escaped — were becoming increasingly frustrated by their continued detention and the settlers' resentment over their being given many of the rights of inhabitants. A petition to the Minister of Marine had been drawn up by the deportee Niquille and signed by 16 others, complaining about their treatment in "this hot and arid archipelago, subject to deprivations of every kind".

"The silence that ... we have maintained up to this day is being broken only through necessity," they told the Minister. Six long years had passed since the true authors of the assassination attempt against Napoleon had been identified, arrested and condemned, and yet there was still no sign from Paris that those who had been unjustly banished to Seychelles were to be allowed to return to France. An exile without apparent hope of release had become unbearable.

Although Le Roy was unsympathetic — he had also been incensed to find an anonymous pamphlet that set out the deportees' grievances circulating in the Établissement — Decaen was moved by the justice of their case and soon allowed those who wanted to, to change their place of exile for the more acceptable conditions of the Isle de France.

Another aspect of lawlessness in Seychelles, which was apparent on the outlying islands, was the wholesale destruction of tortoises and turtles. Le Roy had been appalled when he saw the great heaps of flesh and shells left rotting on the beaches, fouling the air and even driving away turtles that were about to come ashore to lay their eggs. The slaughter might have been done just for a few casks of oil, for nothing deterred the greed and rapaciousness of the sailor and the settler.

The green turtle and the hawksbill — the latter usually taken for its tortoiseshell carapace — were defenceless on the beach, and had little protection in the sea, for they were caught easily enough as they foraged in shallow water among the reefs and rocks.

Early attempts by royal administrators to regulate the slaughter, faint-hearted though they had been, had represented a curb of sorts, but this had passed away during the Revolutionary period into an unrestrained licence to kill. Le Roy now persuaded Quinssy to issue a directive banning the taking of any tortoises or turtles over the next five years. Quinssy probably realised it was an impracticable measure, for how could he enforce, with the resources at his disposal, the prohibition of something that had been going on unabated for almost 40 years, bringing profit to powerful and unscrupulous interests in the Isle de France? The government might be aware of the long-term effects of hunting the tortoise and turtle, but it was too appreciative of the additional supplies of meat they provided for ships and hospitals during times of food shortage to interfere seriously. Not surprisingly Decaen annulled Le Roy's initiative by informing Quinssy that any banning order could come only from the Isle de France.

During the next 100 years the green turtle became almost

extinct in the Indian Ocean. A few rookeries exist today in the Arabian Sea, and occasionally a Seychelles family may dine off some stray turtle caught off the islands by a local fisherman, an act that is illegal as turtles of all species are now protected under Seychelles law. The hawksbill still survives precariously; the sale of tortoiseshell souvenirs at handicrafts shop in Seychelles has been banned for several years, but there are signs that the hawksbill is now being hunted by poachers for its flesh, despite this being considered poisonous.

As for the giant tortoise it was virtually extinct by 1830 throughout the Seychelles except for the remote atoll of Aldabra. In this last refuge, they managed to evade the hunters, although by the early years of the 20th century it was said one could live on Aldabra for years without seeing a single tortoise. Darwin had expressed concern over the future of the Aldabra tortoise, and successive British colonial governments did try to provide some form of protection in the terms of the leases they gave for fishing, hunting turtles, and wood-cutting on the island, but it left much to be desired.

Then in the late 1960s, just when it seemed that *Geochelone gigantea* was to be finally sacrificed to the needs of Western defence strategists who had earmarked Aldabra for development as a military base, rescue came at the insistence of conservationists from around the world. In 1976 the atoll was declared a Strict Nature Reserve, a pledge of protection for all the animal and bird life of the island which the Republic of Seychelles, on its attainment of independence the same year, readily agreed to honour.

By 1983 the giant tortoise was not only flourishing on Aldabra — today a World Heritage Site — with an estimated population of around 152,000, but it had been returned to one of its former homes in the main Seychelles group, the island of Curieuse, where because of the low population density and abundance of food its numbers were expected to increase rapidly. Despite several setbacks, the Curieuse project has been making steady progress.

And so the story ends happily for the giant tortoise. Yet it could so easily have gone the other way, which would have left the giant tortoise on the Seychelles coat of arms the only reminder of one of the islands' first inhabitants.

14

Rule Britannia!
1810-1827

Grand Dieu, sous quel gouvernement sommes nous!
Louis Henri Dumont, March 1812

As he paced the quarterdeck of the becalmed frigate, testing for sign of a breeze that would see them under way again for the Seychelles, Captain Philip Beaver[1] could think back with satisfaction to the dramatic events that had brought the whole of the Indian Ocean under his nation's now unchallenged dominion. One by one, the French islands had been taken: first Rodrigues, then Bourbon, and finally the main stronghold Mauritius, known to the French as the Isle de France, had fallen to powerful forces dispatched from Madras and the Cape.

What a spectacle that had been, watching the armada of boats, packed with British infantry and Indian sepoys, pulling away from the transports towards the shore, each keeping station according to the pace he, Beaver, had decreed as naval officer in charge of the landing. There were some who would carp at his insistence on a rigidly timed approach through the narrow passages in the coral reef fringing the Mauritius shore, "with nothing in the shape of an enemy to be seen for miles", but Beaver, although he readily subscribed to the notion that one Englishman was equal to several Frenchmen, had been in charge of the landing at Aboukir, in Egypt, ten years earlier, and was not going to take chances with a risky enterprise. Fortunately everything had gone smoothly, most of the troops reaching the shore with their boots as well as their powder dry.

Later, when the march on Port Louis began, there had been some skirmishing with the enemy, but it was little more than a token defence, and Decaen, realising the hopelessness of his situation, soon capitulated. At noon on 3 December 1810, five days after they had stepped ashore, British troops marched in to occupy Port Louis. Their losses had been some 160 dead or wounded.

Under the terms of the surrender the French gave up the Isle de France and all its dependencies. As the British already held Bourbon and Rodrigues, it only remained for them to take formal possession of the Seychelles islands and the French trading posts in Madagascar. It was to the main settlement of the former that Beaver was now bound in the 46-gun frigate *Nisus*. There he would land a marine lieutenant as temporary representative of British authority before sailing to India to pick up a cargo of gold coin urgently needed in Mauritius. The French had succeeded in carrying away most of the gold on the island (under the surrender terms Decaen and his troops had been allowed to return to France with their baggage in English transports), and what coin remained was being hoarded by the inhabitants, who lent it to the British at exorbitant interest.

The *Nisus* had left Mauritius on 5 April 1811, with Beaver hoping for a quick passage that would allow him to be back in time to intercept a French squadron that was known to be on its way out from Brest, unaware that the Isle de France was in English hands. Now, here he was, many days later, caught in calms somewhere north of Agaléga island, with the Seychelles still some 400 miles away. "The ship rolled, without making any progress, seeming to bask very contentedly beneath the beams of a scorching sun," noted Prior, the Irish surgeon.

As he sweated and fretted at the prospect of the French ships being taken by his junior Schomberg of the *Astrea*, who had temporarily replaced him at Mauritius, Beaver's only consolation was that he had insisted before leaving that Schomberg[2] should share the proceeds of any prizes he took. Accumulating riches was a common ambition among frigate captains and for Beaver, now aged 45 and despairing of ever achieving flag rank, it had become an obsession.

Perhaps he regarded prize-money as a just balance to the lack of patronage that had curbed the advancement of his career, for he pursued it with a dedication and perverseness that would eventually draw severe and sardonic criticism from his superiors.

On 17 April the *Nisus* sighted Frégate island, but soon the wind died away again and with night falling Beaver anchored. For several days lack of a breeze and contrary currents prevented the *Nisus* making headway, and it was not until 23 April that she was able to enter Mahé harbour. Beaver, determined not to waste time, sent a party ashore to cut wood and replenish the water casks, at the same time sending a note to Quinssy informing him that he was taking possession of the island in the name of His Majesty King George III.

Quinssy, who had been expecting the arrival of the English for some months and was worried that the colony would now lose all the benefits it had enjoyed under the Seychelles capitulation, argued in a letter to Beaver that the surrender of the Isle de France did not affect the Seychelles as it had already surrendered. He enclosed for Beaver's perusal a copy of the agreement he had made with Captain Wood in 1804 and subsequently renewed by visiting British ships on six separate occasions.[3] He also appealed to Beaver to recognise all the inhabitants' land titles, even those that had not been confirmed by the Isle de France authorities.

Beaver replied that while he had no objection to admit all the articles of that capitulation to remain in full force, he had not come to ratify the neutrality of the Seychelles but to take possession of the archipelago as a permanent colony of the King of Great Britain. The inhabitants therefore would be subject henceforth to any regulations the British might impose.

The next day the British flag was raised on Mahé. A detachment of marines formed the honour guard at the brief ceremony and as the Union Jack unfurled they discharged three volleys with their muskets and the *Nisus* fired a salute of 15 guns.

Beaver's log notes that the marines brought back to the ship three prisoners. Although these unfortunates are not further identified, they were most probably deserters, for Beaver was an unbending disciplinarian, whose severe and frequent punishments would eventually be brought to the unfavourable notice of the Admiralty.

The next day, with the reprovisioning of the *Nisus*

completed, Beaver was ready to depart. According to Prior, the fresh beef that would supplement their diet for several days on the way to India was better than anything they had had since leaving England. Beaver, who had assured Quinssy that all land titles he had conferred would be respected, was pleased to know that none existed on Sainte Anne, Cerf, or the other islands enclosing Mahé harbour. They remained government property and, in Beaver's view, were thereby subject to be acquired as prizes by himself and the officers and crew of the *Nisus*. He would lodge his claim as soon as he returned to Mauritius.

The position of the marine lieutenant, Bartholomew Sullivan, who was being left behind on Mahé as representative of British authority, was somewhat ambiguous. Beaver told Quinssy that Sullivan did not hold any official position, and that the French should continue administering the colony. Only later did Sullivan assume the post of commandant. Prior noted that he had been "appointed to this situation by General Farquhar, as a slight compensation for a severe wound received in the unfortunate action at Grand Port". Sullivan had been on board the *Iphigénie* – one of four frigates destroyed or captured by the French that day – and had been freed with other British prisoners on the surrender of the Isle de France. For an officer who was convalescing, his posting to Seychelles was hardly an enviable one. Resented by the French officials, he could expect little co-operation from that quarter, while having no troops, he had to rely on his natural gifts of command and persuasion in the exercise of the slender authority he had been given.

Many of the settlers were friendly and helpful enough. Sullivan remarked that, except for those in official positions, he never found any of the inhabitants inclined to be insolent or troublesome, although later he was to complain of frequent attempts to deceive him. Even Beaver recorded having received valuable information from the inhabitants on the course he should lay for India.

Grenier's discoveries of 40 years earlier were still largely unknown to the English, and Beaver had intended, on quitting Seychelles, to sail north as far as nine degrees of latitude in order to pass between the Maldives and the Laccadive islands. Then a chance encounter gave him the opportunity to cut about 1,000 miles off his route by taking the one-and-a-half degree channel at the southern end of the Maldives chain. "I had never heard of this channel," he admitted, "till a gentleman at Seychelle gave me a manuscript chart, by which it appeared to be about 15 leagues wide; I therefore determined to take it."[4]

Beaver had not been misled. He recorded that soon after daybreak on 6 May the masthead sighted to the north the palm trees of the Haddunmathi atoll of the Maldives. "We passed them 15 or 16 miles distant, and never saw the land to the southward though the weather was very clear. I should therefore pronounce the passage to be spacious and most eligible for ships that are bound to the Bay of Bengal, in the south-west monsoon."

The day after Beaver's successful transit of the Maldives, the French squadron he had hoped to intercept at Mauritius was sighted off that island by a patrolling frigate. Unfortunately for Captain Charles Schomberg he was stuck in Port Louis harbour without a wind that would take him quickly to sea. By the time he had warped his frigate, the *Astrea*, out of harbour to join the rest of the English squadron the French had disappeared. Thinking that they might have made for Seychelles, Schomberg sailed northwards, but after some days without sight of the enemy he returned to Port Louis.

The commodore of the French squadron, Captain François Roquebart, had taken the precaution on his arrival off the Isle de France to send two boats ashore under cover of darkness to confirm if the island was still held by the French. One boat, supplied by the frigate *Clorinde*, was wrecked on approaching the shore and the crew were taken prisoner. The other succeeded in bringing back the dismal news of the island's surrender. According to his instructions, Roquebart should now have sailed on for Java, but he knew his ships were in no state to do so. They were desperately low in food and water (each frigate carried about 200 soldiers, who were to have reinforced the Isle de France garrison), while the crew strengths had been seriously depleted by an outbreak of smallpox, the result of having brought aboard as supplementary hands negroes from a captured Portuguese slaver. Roquebart had to find a safe port quickly to rest and reprovision.

"I proposed Seychelles to him," noted the *Clorinde's* commander, St Criq, "but it was too distant, he said. Also he did not think that they would be able to provide for the needs of three frigates." Roquebart and his captains decided that they would try, first, Isle Bonaparte (as Bourbon was known under the empire), and, if that failed, Madagascar. Arriving off the eastern coast of Isle Bonaparte, Roquebart sent boat parties ashore at Sainte Rose, but discovered by the English they were forced to withdraw. After an ineffectual call at the capital, St Denis, which he found firmly in enemy hands, Roquebart sailed for Madagascar. It was there, off Foulepointe, that Schomberg's squadron caught up with him.

The French tried to escape, and for several hours the weather prevented the English from closing. It was almost dark when the frigate *Phoebe* began to engage with some effect the nearest French frigate, the *Néréide*. She fought back bravely, but with the *Galatea* frigate coming up to assist the *Phoebe* the French ship was soon disabled. The *Néréide's* captain had already been killed and more than 100 members of her crew were dead or wounded when she retired from the contest. *Galatea*, too, was temporarily out of action, having received a severe mauling.

In the *Renommée* Roquebart fought off the English for about 25 minutes, but with Schomberg joining the action in the *Astrea* he, too, was eventually overwhelmed. With Roquebart dead, the *Renommée* struck.

Accounts vary as to the behaviour of the third frigate, the *Clorinde*, commanded by Captain Jacques St Criq. According to Schomberg, the *Clorinde* closed in the action and then struck. Almost immediately afterwards, and having received a warning shot from Roquebart, she made off. Chase was given by the English ships, but as the small *Racehorse* sloop was the only one likely to catch up with the Frenchman Schomberg decided during the night to break off pursuit.

St Criq was to tell his court-martial in Paris that the weather had prevented him from closing with the enemy, and that he lost touch with the other two frigates. One English historian was inclined to accept St Criq's version that he never engaged the English, noting that it "perfectly agrees with his behaviour on a former occasion, [when] M. St Criq abandoned his commodore in March 1806 off Puerto Rico". The writer added, however, that "if some glory was lost to the French navy by the misconduct of the *Clorinde*, more was gained by the acknowledged good conduct of the *Renommée* and the *Néréide*".

Once St Criq had lost his pursuers he set course for Seychelles. He had learned about conditions there from a member of the crew who had lived on Mahé for almost two years, and it appeared to St Criq "to be the least dangerous place" to make for. Perhaps he thought that he would find the other ships of the squadron there, if they had succeeded in eluding the English. The *Néréide* did, in fact, manage to slip away in the confusion of the battle despite its having been disabled, but it was captured some days later without a fight at Tamatave.

Leaving St Criq to make the best of his way to Mahé, we must jump ahead a few weeks to 27 June to rejoin Beaver as he returned to Mauritius, where he found lying in the harbour Schomberg's two prizes, the *Renommée* and the *Néréide*. It had been a bitter blow to the inhabitants when the two captured frigates were brought in, for, according to Prior, there had been high hopes on the island that Roquebart's squadron would drive the English from the Isle de France. "After this accident, as they termed it, a new play at least was required to restore the good-humour of the town," Prior observed maliciously. For Beaver the sight of the captured frigates would have been hardly less of a disappointment had it not been for the share he had assured himself in the prize-money they represented. There was also, to cheer him up, the prospect of even greater financial reward from the sale of Sainte Anne and the other Seychelles islands he had earmarked for himself and the crew of the *Nisus*.

This claim was in due course rejected by the Mauritius governor, Sir Robert Farquhar, bt, but for the moment the *Nisus's* captain was simply told that his request would be considered by the government, and with that he went off satisfied to take part in the reduction of the Dutch colony of Batavia.

The *Nisus* was back at Mauritius by the end of 1811. In the following year Beaver sailed to Cape Town, where he received on board as a passenger Bombay Jack, the befriender of the Frenchmen deported to Anjouan ten years previously.

Bombay Jack had been sent to the Cape to put the familiar Anjouan plea for help against Malagasy marauders, and was now on his way home. Prior found "his sable excellency" an entertaining companion. "We all felt a strong partiality toward this man of nature," he wrote. These were feelings Bombay Jack apparently reciprocated, for at the end of the voyage he took his leave of the *Nisus* crew "with unaffected sorrow". During the ship's stay at Anjouan Prior conducted a clinic, treating among his patients several women and the nephew of the sultan. He remarked on the islanders' attachment to the English, which extended even to their assuming English names that had taken their fancy, such as Duke of Hamilton, Lord Rodney, and Lord Howe.

"We were not a little surprised to be so unexpectedly introduced to so much good company," commented Prior, adding that the illustrious titles did not, however, inhibit the Anjouannais from asking for the crew's castoff shoes and stockings.

From Anjouan the *Nisus* sailed to Zanzibar and then eastwards to Seychelles, where it arrived on 19 November. Prior was of the opinion that the island was much livelier than on their first visit 18 months previously. "But where is the place that does not improve by the commerce and capital of England?" he asked.

Although the final years of the French regime had seen increasing prosperity for the Seychelles, Prior was justified in commenting on the apparent boost the English connection had conferred on the island's economy. For a few more years cash crops, particularly cotton, would prosper, while continued illicit trading in slaves brought its own ill-gotten rewards. The Seychelles bubble was to burst, however, before the end of the decade when cheap American cotton began to arrive in Europe.

If Prior was pleased with the changes he saw in Seychelles, not so Beaver. He was in fact furious to find that the islands of Sainte Anne and Cerf, which he had claimed on behalf of the King, were now in private hands "in virtue of a grant most illegally made". He noted that new buildings had been erected on Cerf island and a plantation laid out, and when he landed there he was told that Sainte Anne and the other islands had been leased to a British naval surgeon about a year earlier. To add insult to injury, Beaver was informed that he was not allowed to cut wood there for his ship. As he sailed back to Mauritius, Beaver vowed that he would "represent this arrogance in such a light, to the commander-in-chief, as I trust will teach these Eastern civilians that they are not at liberty to violate any of our national engagements with impunity".[5]

There was more to annoy Beaver on his return to Port Louis. While he had been away the authorities had disposed of some of the arms and stores taken from the two captured French frigates amounting to some 22,000 dollars' worth, and of this the governor had taken 10 per cent as tax.

To Beaver this "extraordinary and illegal" act undermined the prize-money rights of the whole navy, which were never subject to duty. An indignant letter was immediately dispatched to the commander-in-chief at the Cape station seeking redress for "this attempt to deprive the officers and crew under my command of the trifling and hard-earned money justly due to them". Rather unwisely Beaver went on to compare this niggardly action by the authorities with their own lavish expenditure of public money "as would make the heart sicken and strike the world with astonishment". It was a direct attack on Farquhar; there was little doubt as to who would get the better of the exchange.

The governor, who had been away at the time on a visit to Bourbon, received a copy of Beaver's letter on his return. He penned a lengthy letter justifying his actions to the Cape commander-in-chief, Rear-Admiral Sir Robert Stopford, asking that his comments be transmitted to London.

He pointed out that it had been expedient to continue granting land to the Seychelles settlers, and he had done so only on condition that the land would be cultivated, otherwise it reverted to the Crown after two years. He ridiculed Beaver's claim to all uninhabited and unleased islands — of which, he said, there were nearly 70 — as something "perfectly novel and unprecedented, I believe, in the history of colonial conquest". As to Beaver's reference to a hard-earned reward for himself and his crew, Farquhar pointed out that all the *Nisus* had done was to carry out a nominal seizure of mainly uninhabited islands.

The French settlers there, "as Your Excellency must be aware," he wrote, "not only cheerfully furnished water, firewood, provisions and refreshment for payment to His Majesty's ships on all occasions, but this friendly intercourse was actually confirmed on the spot some years since by a written convention between the chief of that island and several captains of His Majesty's navy".

As for the tax he had imposed on the sale of the effects from the captured frigates, he had been acting in accordance with French law, but had immediately suspended this when it was pointed out to him that such a levy on prize-money was contrary to an Act of the British Parliament. He assured Stopford that he had no wish to deprive Schomberg of the fruits of his victory, adding, with a hint of malice, that Beaver would have known nothing of the matter had not Schomberg's officers complained about the share Beaver was getting in the frigates while they were debarred from benefiting from his profitable freighting of gold coin from India.

Farquhar's comments were forwarded to London, and in due course Rear-Admiral Tyler, who had by then succeeded Stopford at the Cape, received a letter from the Lord Commissioners of the Admiralty in which they directed the commander-in-chief to inform Beaver that the conduct of Governor Farquhar in the matter of the Seychelles archipelago and the captured French frigates — "so very different from that of Captain Beaver" — had received their approbation. But Beaver never knew that he had been rebuffed. He had died two months earlier at Cape Town, his death said to have been caused by an illness contracted during the Batavia campaign.

His rival Schomberg assumed command of the *Nisus*, and sailed shortly afterwards for Brazil to escort a convoy back to England.

In resisting Beaver's claims to the unleased islands of the Seychelles, Farquhar was following the cautious and largely conciliatory policy he adopted in all his dealings with the conquered French islands. Apart from the inhabitants' language and religion, nothing was of a more sensitive nature to them than the land and their slaves. Neither could be abruptly interfered with without serious repercussions on the economies and social stability of the former French colonies. Farquhar rightly realised that the allocation of land to the settlers must continue if the colonies' economic activity was to be sustained. As for slavery, he did the best he could to enforce Britain's ban on the trading in slaves but did nothing to interrupt the system of forced labour in the homes and plantations of the settlers. That freedom for the slaves would come there was no doubt, but not yet awhile.

Whatever the English did, however, it was natural that in Seychelles as elsewhere the French would resent the presence of the conqueror. Even when there was only one Englishman, in this case Sullivan, they would thwart him whenever they could. Sullivan was soon informing his superiors in Mauritius that "from the little opportunity I have had to judge of these persons, I am confident that no sense of honour, shame or honesty will deter them from endeavouring to practise upon Englishmen any species of deception, as indeed they consider us a people easily duped". He numbered Quinssy among them, expressing the suspicion that the French commandant had antedated documents relating to land grants to prevent them falling to the Crown.

Yet, although Sullivan felt vulnerable without troops to buttress his authority he was made of durable stuff, and by adopting a policy of firmness and fairness he eventually won from most of the French settlers their respect if not affection. The first real challenge to his authority — one that he could not oppose — came about a month after the *Nisus* landed him in Seychelles, when the frigate *Clorinde* arrived from its unhappy encounter with Schomberg's squadron off Foulepointe. Once more, Sullivan found himself a prisoner of the French.

St Criq reached Mahé on the morning of 30 May, approaching the coast near Anse aux Pins, from where he noted that the harbour was empty of shipping. He raised a red flag and fired several cannon, but as there was no apparent response he continued up the coast and anchored off Sainte Anne, where a fishing pirogue gave him the news that an English officer was on the island, flying the British flag. At some time during the afternoon Sullivan and Quinssy's administrative assistant Le Roy went out to the *Clorinde*, believing, according to Quinssy, that it was an English ship. Once he stepped on board Sullivan was made prisoner, but after accepting parole he was allowed to return to his house, with instructions to stay there and remove his flag.

Le Roy, too, was taken prisoner. Since Sullivan's arrival he had collaborated eagerly with the Englishman, and Quinssy noted bitterly that his administrative assistant now ignored him, recognising Sullivan as commandant — "contrary to that desired by Monsieur Beaver" — and offering him slaves and property. St Criq had found some of Le Roy's letters to Sullivan, which made clear what their relationship was, but Le Roy seems to have persuaded the *Clorinde's* captain that he was still a loyal Frenchman, for Sullivan later accused the administrative assistant of having broken the terms of the capitulation by procuring supplies for the French frigate. Dismissing him "as one of those wretches to whom the Revolution has given birth", he returned Le Roy to Mauritius under guard.

While the Seychelles inhabitants must have been pleased to see a French ship in the harbour, past experience made them reluctant to offer any help or sustenance for fear of English reprisals. Most likely it was Quinssy who solved their dilemma by insisting, just as he had with Commodore Newcome and his squadron in 1794, that St Criq furnish proof that the colony's assistance had been obtained only under duress. This would explain the "strongly worded letter" St Criq said he wrote to Quinssy, a letter which a Mauritian historian later described as "menaces of the most odious nature",[6] and which clearly left the Seychellois with no alternative but to help the French ship.

During the seven days of St Criq's stay the inhabitants worked unstintingly to get the *Clorinde* ready for sea. A total of 650 barrels of water and enough food and firewood to last three and a half months were loaded on board, while slaves carried out necessary repairs to the ship. As a precaution against the arrival of an English ship St Criq set up a battery on shore. Later, he boasted that even if a fleet of ten ships had attempted to enter the harbour he would have sunk all of them, as they would have had to approach the anchorage one at a time, and endure his enfilading fire for at least a quarter of an hour before they could bring their broadside to bear on the *Clorinde*.

When he wrote this St Criq was awaiting court-martial in Paris accused of disobeying orders in face of the enemy, an offence punishable by death, which would explain his brief display of bravado. He also outlined for the benefit of the judges a plan he said he would have employed to attack the island had he found it in effective enemy hands.

Whatever St Criq really thought about his chances of holding off an English squadron, Quinssy, for one, must have been greatly relieved to see the *Clorinde* sail out of harbour at sunset on 7 June, "in circumstances happier than those attending the *Chiffonne* and the *Flèche*". St Criq had lost 13 men during his stay – one had died of wounds received at Foulepointe, another had been killed by falling into the ship's hold, eight were left behind in the hospital at the Établissement, and there were "three wretched deserters".

Despite the orders given to Roquebart, St Criq had no intention of sailing to Java, where it was believed the English had already launched an attack. He elected instead to return to France but, diverted from his course by unfavourable winds and currents, he made first for Diego Garcia, where he had noted from his *Neptune Oriental* that he could expect to find tortoises and coconuts. He was surprised, however, to discover that two inhabitants of the Isle de France had been living there for the past 40 years, trading in coconut oil and tortoiseshell. There were, unfortunately at that time, few tortoises and St Criq had to sacrifice his cabin curtains in barter for 13 of the huge creatures.

On 24 September, more than three months after leaving Seychelles, the *Clorinde* sailed into Brest harbour, having narrowly eluded capture by a blockading ship of the line. News of St Criq's return reached Napoleon at Antwerp, where, according to Decrès, the Emperor read his report "with interest". In a letter to St Criq, the Minister questioned him, somewhat ominously, about the fate of the rest of Roquebart's squadron. "Tell me, quite honestly in your next dispatches, what you think had happened to the two other frigates," he asked. St Criq could reply only that he did not know.

Napoleon was never noted for his attachment to naval officers, but Roquebart, who had accompanied him on some of his campaigns, was a favourite, and Napoleon was convinced that he would have won a victory as spectacular as that of Grand Port had it not been for St Criq's failure to engage Schomberg's squadron. "I did my utmost to have St Criq shot," he is said to have remarked, but the court-martial that tried St Criq in March 1812 decided by six to two that his disobedience had not occurred in face of the enemy, and sentenced him only to cashiering and three years' imprisonment.

St Criq served two years in prison, and was then released and restored to the service on Napoleon's abdication. His freedom was short-lived, for after escaping from Elba Napoleon remembered the case of St Criq and personally ordered his re-arrest. The unfortunate St Criq had to stay in prison until Napoleon's fate was finally sealed at Waterloo.

As soon as the *Clorinde* had left Seychelles Sullivan restored the Union flag to the staff outside his house, an action that marked the beginning of 165 years of uninterrupted British colonial rule. Yet few of the inhabitants envisaged at the time that they would be under the English for long. Captured colonies were frequently returned to their owners on the conclusion of peace, and most of the Seychellois took the required oath of allegiance to King George III confident that they would soon renounce it, once the Tricolour again flew over Mahé.

In the event, of all the French possessions in the Indian Ocean only Bourbon — or Réunion, as it was, finally, to be renamed once more — was returned to France under the Treaty of Paris, the British having noted that it lacked a natural harbour and was, consequently, of little use as a base.

Much to his chagrin, Quinssy was soon removed from all his official functions. Sullivan became commandant of the colony and, as one of his first acts, summoned the inhabitants to choose a new *juge de paix*. Before the selection was made Sullivan discovered that Quinssy had put his name forward for re-election, and "was obliged to tell him that while he held a commission in the French service and until he had received the permission of the government to remain here as an inhabitant his claim was utterly inadmissible".

Eventually Jean Loiseau was appointed justice of the peace, and Lablache filled the position of administrative assistant previously held by Le Roy. But Quinssy, from now on in perpetual conflict with Sullivan and his successors, scored an important triumph. Having gone off to Mauritius to complain of Sullivan's cavalier treatment of him, he succeeded in getting the authorities to restore him as *juge de paix*. Sullivan's understandable annoyance was further inflamed when Quinssy, on his return to Seychelles, presented himself to take the oath of office "dressed in a sort of French uniform, with side-arms".

If the settlers did not seem perturbed about changing their allegiance — Sullivan noted that only one refused to take the oath — they were anxious that nothing should disturb their lifestyle or the prosperity of their slave-based economy. Now that Britain was giving more attention to enforcing its ban on trading in slaves, the remoter islands of the Seychelles had become increasingly important to ships coming from Africa for there they could land and revive their human cargoes out of sight of the prying eyes of authority.

Slaves that were not shipped off to more distant destinations could be absorbed surreptitiously into the local population or, under a system of transfer permitted between islands, they could be dispatched to Mauritius or Bourbon. Sullivan, with no regular force at his command, was usually powerless to interfere with these arrangements. As he pointed out to Mauritius, he could "expect but little aid from the inhabitants, the public being unfortunately interested in its [slave trading's] favour". He assured Mauritius, however, that "no exertions will be wanting on my part in putting a stop to a traffic contrary to law, and so disgraceful to humanity".

In June 1812 he had one notable success. Word had reached him that a slave ship had just landed a consignment of slaves at Madame Pasquier's habitation on Praslin, and Sullivan began immediately preparations to surprise the culprits. He mustered a force of eight government slaves and one free Black and, having armed them with pistols, cutlasses, and muskets, set out quietly at night in a pirogue for Praslin.

The raid, which was launched at dawn and carried out with all the dash and daring that was to mark subsequent anti-slavery operations of the British navy in African waters, was a complete success.

Sullivan found chained in huts near the beach 37 slaves, "newly introduced, or rather their skeletons, as they appeared to have been nearly starved during the voyage". Their owner, François Romarf, who insisted he was an inhabitant of Praslin, "made use of language towards me the most insolent", noted Sullivan, who chased after Romarf when the latter tried to escape into the interior with seven of the best slaves. They were soon recovered. Another two slaves, left by Romarf with a settler, were given up, and these, along with two seamen slaves from the ship, the *Virginie*, brought the total to 41.

It was a commendable effort by Sullivan, but he was to be thwarted in bringing the affair to a satisfactory conclusion by the machinations of the settlers. Quinssy being absent, the acting *juge de paix,* François Marchais, convened a sitting of the tribunal, which decided that Romarf should have an opportunity to appeal to a higher authority. In the meantime, it suspended the confiscation of the slaves. Sullivan, who protested that he was not given a chance to appear before the tribunal, was unsure of the legal position, and consequently did not prevent Romarf's being set free. It was, he complained, the second time that the tribunal had interfered in a matter which he considered outside its competence.

By now completely frustrated, Sullivan had already offered his resignation as commandant, and a month after the Praslin raid he was replaced by an army officer, Lieutenant Bibye Lesage, who himself was succeeded in 1815 by the first British civilian administrator, Edward Madge. Madge's term as commandant is remembered mainly for his bitter feuding with Quinssy, culminating in 1816 in the arrest of the latter and his remand as a prisoner to Mauritius charged with helping the captain of a slave ship to evade justice.

The *Marie-Louise* had been seized by Madge when it put in at Praslin with 48 slaves on board, but the part-owner, Jean Sausse, managed to slip away in another brig, taking 11 of the slaves with him. Madge was furious. He was convinced that Sausse had been helped to escape, and immediately offered a reward to anyone who named his accomplice. "This notice was dangerous to the public peace," observed Quinssy, "and had the effect of implying that it was a boat of mine that had aided Monsieur Sausse."

In vain, Quinssy protested his innocence. He challenged the credibility of an accusation which he said had been induced by money and drink, pointing out that Sausse had canoes and a pirogue of his own, as well as the ready help of the crew of the *Hirondelle*, in which he had escaped. But Madge was impervious to argument. "He made what he wanted of the statement to satisfy his own passions," Quinssy noted bitterly, after he was told he was a prime suspect and that he must not leave the island without permission.

Later Madge accused him of being drunk and disorderly in a public place, and Quinssy was put under house arrest until he was shipped off as a prisoner for trial at Mauritius. On his arrival there he was immediately freed on bail, and after some months the authorities decided there was no case against him.

Quinssy never forgave Madge for the humiliation he had suffered. Although he returned to Seychelles completely vindicated, and had the satisfaction of being reinstated as *juge de paix,* he was unsuccessful in his repeated attempts to bring an action against Madge, although he went to the extent of seeking permission from the Prince Regent to sue. Madge emerges from the affair with little credit. He was deceitful, vindictive, and lacking in judgement. His behaviour hardly augured well for the future of British administration in the Seychelles.

He appears to have been one of the largest slave owners in Seychelles, with almost 200 slaves, and he certainly used his position shamelessly for personal profit, engaging enthusiastically in the very trade his duty obliged him to stamp out.[7] Yet despite everything, he succeeded in prolonging his term as commandant of Seychelles until 1826. The year following Madge's retirement, Quinssy died.

In his later years Quéau de Quinssy had become increasingly feeble and forgetful, neglecting to sit as *juge de paix* and, with the judicial process virtually halted, obliging the principal inhabitants to petition Madge to have him removed from office. The signatories to the petition were Nageon, Hoareau, St Jorre, Humbert, and Loiseau; its wording was almost as much a tribute as a complaint. "He is very old," they wrote, "he has exercised many public functions for a long time; he has need of a rest."

Quinssy was by then well over 70. He had had a remarkable career, first as a soldier in India and then as a colonial administrator, serving successively the monarchy, the Republic and the Empire, and finally the English. His ultimate loyalty, however, was to Seychelles, to the islands he loved and at times hated, and to the people for whom he exercised his talent as a negotiator to shelter them from the worst ravages of war.

No-one served continuously for so long in any of France's Indian Ocean territories, yet today, sadly, one looks in vain in the libraries of France for the briefest biography of Jean-Baptiste Quéau de Quinssy. His death on 10 July 1827, at the age of 79, effectively marked the end of the French period in

Seychelles. Henceforth, under the English, the islands would pass into a lengthy period of economic decline.

The most important cash crop, cotton, had already disappeared in the wake of the cheap American product flooding Europe. Many of the settlers, accompanied by their slaves, abandoned the islands for Mauritius. Those who remained continued to cultivate the rice, maize, tobacco, cocoa and cloves that had first fired the imagination of Brayer du Barré, but all with scant success. Only coconut oil, which largely replaced cotton, and towards the end of the century vanilla, brought any notable return to the islands.

Cinnamon bark, too, was to become an important export, restoring some of the strands of Poivre's shattered spice island dream. The destruction of the giant tortoise and the turtle that had been carried out so wantonly by the French continued under the English, who, in addition, were willing accomplices in the wholesale slaughter by the Americans of the sperm whale. Fortunately the fabled Coco de Mer of Praslin was rescued from extinction thanks, in part, to the intervention of General Gordon, of later Khartoum fame.

Politically, the century was one of stagnation. The few highlights in Seychelles were the emancipation by stages of the slaves in 1835 and 1839, the naming of the capital of Victoria in 1841 (the year in which Queen Victoria gave birth to her first son, Edward, Prince of Wales), and, in 1903, the granting of full colony status to Seychelles, ending the Mauritius dependency.

The French experiment of utilising the islands as a place of exile was continued, and the Seychellois had as a result to play host to a succession of Britain's political undesirables, from an Ashanti chief and fiery Egyptian nationalists to, as last of the line, a Cypriot archbishop, in 1956.

The French ruled the Seychelles for just over 40 years, during which time they fixed the cultural identity of the islands, which has been hardly blurred by a subsequent century and a half of British administration. The manners and customs of the people today recall their French connections. The principal spoken language is a French-based Creole, and their religion, promoted by France in the 19th century as a symbol of nationalism, is predominantly Roman Catholic.

In the early years of the colony the bulk of the population, mostly of African and Malagasy origins, lived and died in bondage and anonymity. Later there were further injections of African blood to the population as men, women and children, freed from Arab slave ships by British warships patrolling the Indian Ocean, were landed in Seychelles to begin a new life as indentured labourers and apprentices.[8]

From this mix of African and European, with additions of Indian and, later, Chinese blood, the people of the Seychelles Republic were formed. Today they live in racial harmony, which must make them the envy of much larger, richer, and more troubled countries.

SEYCHELLES ROLL-CALL

Biographical notes on some of those who feature in the Seychelles story. Sources consulted include: Dictionary of National Biography, Dictionary of Mauritian Biography, *Michaud's* Biographie Universelle, Dictionnaire de Biographie Française, *St Elm Duc papers,* Dictionnaire de la Noblesse *(M. De la Chenaye-Desbois),* O'Byrne's Naval Biography, Marshall's Royal Navy Biography, Naval History of Great Britain *(Wm James) and private archives.*

ADAM: Sir Charles Adam. b. 1780. British naval officer. Son of William Adam, Lord Chief Commissioner of Scottish Jury Court, and great-nephew of the architect brothers James and Robert Adam. Entered navy in 1790 as captain's servant. In 1793 transferred to the *Robust* (74), commanded by his uncle, Captain George Keith Elphinstone (later Viscount Keith). Was present as acting lieutenant at siege of Toulon. Commanded gunboat at capture of Cape Town from Dutch in 1795, and mentioned in dispatches. Lieutenant, 1796; post-captain, 1799. In April 1801, while commanding the frigate *Sybille,* captured the French frigate *Chiffonne* in Seychelles harbour. Returned to England in the *Sybille* in 1803, and on renewal of war the same year was given command of his prize, the *Chiffonne.* Served in North Sea and along Spanish coast. In command of *Invincible* (74), took part in defence of Tarragona. In June 1814, commanding the *Impregnable* (98), bearing flag of the Duke of Clarence, brought the Emperor of Russia and King of Prussia to Dover for state visit. Commander of royal yacht. Rear-admiral, 1825; vice-admiral, 1837; admiral, 1848. Commander-in-chief, North America and West Indies, 1841-45; First Sea Lord of Admiralty, 1835-41 and 1846-47. Knight Commander of Order of the Bath (KCB), 1835; Member of Parliament for Kinross, 1831-32 and for Clackmannan and Kinross, 1833-4. Appointed Governor of Greenwich Hospital 1847. Married, 1822, Elisabeth Brydone. Their son William was MP for Kinross, 1859-80. Adam died at Greenwich on 16 September 1853.

ALEXANDER: Thomas Alexander. British naval officer. Lieutenant, 1790; post-captain, 1796. Appointed in succession to the *Sceptre* (64), *Sphynx* (20), and *Braave* (40), the latter having been captured from Dutch at Cape Town in 1795. In September 1799, sailing from Trincomalee to the Red Sea, captured in Seychelles harbour the French corvette *Surprise,* which had two envoys of Tippu Sultan on board. In 1800, in the *Braave,* took part in attack on Batavia. Returned in ill health to England, June 1802. Rear-admiral, 1819.

BOUGAINVILLE: Louis-Antoine de Bougainville. b. Paris, 1729. French mariner and explorer. After serving with army in Canada joined navy in

1763. Attempted to form a colony in the Falkland islands. The account of his voyage round the world in the *Boudeuse* and the *Étoile*, 1766-69, helped to popularise the concept of the Noble Savage. Visited the Seychelles and in two reports to Versailles, in 1772 and 1773, stressed the strategic importance of the islands. Secretary to Louis XV, 1772. Commodore of French squadron in North America, 1779-82. Survived the Revolution; made a senator by Napoleon. Named after him are the largest of the Solomon islands, a strait in Vanuatu (formerly the New Hebrides), and a tropical plant. Died in 1811.

COLLIER: Sir George Ralph Collier, bt. b. 1774. British naval officer. Son of clerk in navy's victualling department. As a lieutenant in the *Isis* (50) was at capture of Dutch squadron off Texel, 1799. Sent to England with dispatches and given command of the *Victor* (18). In September 1801, after a fierce battle in Seychelles harbour, sank the French corvette *Flèche*. Post-captain, 1802. Returned to England in command of *Leopard* (50), 1803. In 1807, commanding the *Surveillante*, took part in expedition against Copenhagen, and brought back Admiral Gambier's dispatches announcing surrender of Danish capital. Made Knight Commander of Order of the Bath (KCB). Served in War of 1812 against United States. Baronet, 1815. In 1818 appointed commodore on coast of West Africa for suppression of slave trade. Elected honorary life member of Africa Institution, 1820. His annual reports to Admiralty on slave trade printed by order of House of Commons. Groom of the Bedchamber to Duke of Gloucester. Collier was skilled astronomer and marine surveyor, and spoke French, Spanish, and Italian. Married, 1805, Maria Lyon, daughter of a Liverpool doctor. Died 1824.

DA GAMA: Vasco de Gama. b. Sines, c. 1469. Portuguese admiral and viceroy. Ten years after discovery by Bartolomeu Dias of route round the Cape of Good Hope, King Manuel commissioned Vasco da Gama to sail with four ships to Indies. Left Lisbon on 8 July 1497, arriving at Calicut, south India, in May the following year. Returned to Portugal in September 1499 and was raised to nobility. Three years later Vasco da Gama was sent on punitive expedition to Calicut, where ruler had massacred Portuguese inhabitants. Sailed in 1502, with 20 ships, and founded on way the Portuguese colonies of Mozambique and Sofala. Bombarded Calicut and extorted reparations. On return voyage to Portugal in 1503 his ships made sightings of the Seychelles islands. Vasco da Gama made his third voyage to India in 1524, with title of viceroy. Died at Cochin in December 1525.

D'APRÈS: Jean-Baptiste Nicolas d'Après de Mannevillette. b. Le Havre, 1707. French mariner and hydrographer. Produced in 1745 hydrographic atlas *Neptune Oriental,* with second edition in 1775. In 1750, commanding the *Glorieux,* he took the astronomer De la Caille to the Cape of Good Hope to make astronomical revision of the southern sky. Appointed in 1762 director of the *Dépôt des Cartes et Plans de la Navigation des Indes* in Paris. Closely associated with various expeditions to the Seychelles, notably that of Grenier and Rochon. He was first Frenchman to employ method of measuring distances of sun and moon to determine longitude.

DECAEN: Charles Mathieu Isidore Decaen. b. 1769, at Caen, Normandy. French soldier and administrator. Joined marine artillery in 1787, leaving three years later at request of parents. In 1791 enlisted in the Calvados Volunteers. Fought in the Vendée and with the Army of the Rhine. Was present at battle of Hohenlinden against Austria, 1800. Captain-general of French establishments east of Cape of Good Hope, 1803-10. Opposed Queau de Quinssy's capitulation of Seychelles. On surrender of the Isle de France returned to France. Commanded French army in Catalonia and, in 1813, the army in Holland. At Restoration given a divisional command, but rallied again to Napoleon during the Hundred Days. Imprisoned in 1815, but amnestied two years later. Reserve general until 1830. Died at Egmont, near Paris, 1832. Decaen's name is inscribed on the Arc de Triomphe in Paris.

DUFRESNE: Marc Joseph Marion Dufresne. b. St Malo, 1719. French mariner and explorer. Naval lieutenant, 1746. Commanded the St Malo privateer *Prince de Conti* (30), which, with the *Heureux* (36), brought away Prince Charles Edward Stuart from Scotland after failure of 1745 Jacobite rebellion. In 1752 Marion Dufresne joined the Compagnie des Indes, and subsequently traded in the East on his own account. In 1768 he fitted out the expedition of the *Digue* (20) and the *Curieuse* to the Seychelles. Three years later, accompanied by Julien Crozet, he left the Isle de France in the *Mascarin* and the *Marquis de Castries* to explore the southern ocean. On 13 January 1772 discovered, 1,500 miles south-east of the Cape, the Marion islands (later renamed the Prince Edward islands by Cook; main island retains name Marion). Sailing eastward, discovered on 24 January another group of islands. Crozet landed and took possession for France. Called Isles Froides, later renamed the Crozet islands. Reached Tasmania in March, and two months later sailed into the Bay of Islands, on New Zealand's South Island. On 12 July, Marion Dufresne and shore party attacked by Maoris. Only one survivor, the others having been killed and eaten. Crozet, who avenged the deaths, took possession of New Zealand, not knowing that Cook had already done so. Geographical contribution of voyage considered slight, but Crozet's observations on the Maoris and natural features of New Zealand were valuable. Marion Dufresne is sometimes confused with a relative, Nicolas Thomas Marion Dufresne, who was also a mariner.

GILLOT: Antoine Nicolas Benoît Gillot. b. Metz. French administrator and commandant of Seychelles. Officer in Battalion de l'Inde and subsequently captain in Isle de France militia. In October 1771 sent by Poivre to Seychelles to prepare ground for spice plantation. Chose site at Anse Royale. Leaving others to complete the work he returned to the Isle de France in April 1772. Ship foundered, and Gillot lost all his possessions. Returned to Seychelles with spice plants and Poivre's instructions for their cultivation. Spice garden was not a success, and in 1779 Gillot's appointment was terminated. Allowed to keep the garden, which was destroyed the following year in error by Seychelles commandant Romainville. In 1781 Gillot married, at Pamplemousses, Isle de France, Cécile la Roche du Ronzet. Appointed commandant of Seychelles in 1783, and served until 1787, when he was removed from the post.

GRENIER: Jacques Raymond de Grenier. b. Martinique, 1736. French mariner. Joined navy at age of 10 as honorary lieutenant; captain, 1778; commodore, 1786. In the *Heure du Berger* (1768-70) he surveyed Seychelles waters, studied action of winds and currents in Indian Ocean, and reconnoitred direct route to India. After bitter and protracted quarrel with astronomer Rochon over safety of the route, the French Marine Academy and Academy of Sciences pronounced in Grenier's favour. Returned to Indian Ocean in the *Belle Poule* (30), in which he again visited Seychelles. During the War of American Independence Grenier commanded the frigate *Boudeuse* (1778-80), and captured an English frigate. In addition to excellent charts, he published *Mémoires de la campagne de découvertes du Chevalier Grenier,* 1772, and *L'Art de la guerre sur mer,* 1787. Died, as Vicomte de Giron, in Paris, 1803.

GUIEYSSE: Pierre Guieysse. b. Nant, Aveyron, 1766. French naval officer. Joined merchant marine at 17, and rose to rank of first officer. Second-in-command of the ship *Trajan,* captured in 1793. Managed to escape after five months in England, and on return to France joined the navy as sub-lieutenant. Lieutenant, 1794. Served in frigate *Gloire,* and again became prisoner when his ship was captured in April 1795. Freed in exchange. Commander of frigate *Méduse,* June 1796, and promoted to rank of frigate captain. After wreck of *Méduse,* was appointed second captain of the *Harmonie,* subsequently lost in combat off St Domingue. Commanded the corvette *Enfant Prodigue,* 1797-99, and captured English corvette the *Charlotte* in October 1798. In January 1801 appointed to command of frigate *Chiffonne,* and two months later sailed from France for

Seychelles with 32 deportees. Landed deportees at Seychelles on 14 July 1800. A note left by one deportee, Bertrand Guilhémat, testified to Guieysse's humanity. On 19 August the *Chiffonne* surrendered to English frigate *Sybille* after fierce combat in Seychelles harbour. Guieysse subsequently cleared of blame by court-martial. Member of *Légion d'Honneur*, 1805, and Chevalier of the *Ordre Royal de la Légion d'Honneur*, 1821. Retired from service, 1807. Married, 1800, Marie Renée le Gallic. Two sons, Eugène and Armand, became, respectively, commissioner-general of marine and director of naval construction at Lorient. Guieysse died on 24 February 1853. (The author is indebted to members of the Guieysse family in Paris for providing the above material).

HODOUL: Jean-François Hodoul. b. La Ciotat, near Marseilles. French privateer, and later Seychellois planter and businessman. Arriving in the Indian Ocean in the early 1790s, he engaged in several trading and slaving voyages between the Isle de France and Madagascar, also calling at Seychelles, where he married in 1794 Marie Corantine Olivette Jorre de St Jorre, the daughter of a settler. Hodoul embarked on his career as a privateer two years later, spending several months off the Malabar coast and taking many prizes. On his return to the Isle de France he purchased the *Uni*, in which he captured on 28 May 1800, close by Sainte Anne island, the English privateer *Henriette* (Captain William White). This action gave rise to several of the reports of buried treasure in Seychelles. Hodoul continued to pursue a successful career as a privateer in the Indian Ocean, Red Sea, and the Gulf. He settled in Seychelles after the Peace of Amiens in 1802, built a house at Les Mamelles, south of present-day Victoria, and established a plantation on Silhouette island. Writing in October 1829, a former British naval officer, James Holman, described Hodoul as "one of the oldest and most wealthy, as well as one of the most respectable inhabitants of the place". Hodoul, he said, spent much of his time improving his extensive property, where he had lately introduced the cultivation of cocoa. Hodoul died on 5 January 1835, and was buried in the town cemetery.

JOURDAIN: John Jourdain. b. Lyme Regis, Dorset, where father was mayor. English merchant. Traded on his own account with Azores. Engaged as a factor by East India Company for the Fourth Voyage, to Arabia and India in the ships *Ascension* and *Union*, 1608-09. His journal of the voyage, which contains the first known description of the Seychelles islands, lay unnoticed for about 250 years until a manuscript copy was found in the Sloane collection at the British Museum. On the arrival of the *Ascension* at Aden, Jourdain and a companion, Philip Glasscock, travelled to Sanaa, becoming the first Englishmen to venture into the interior of the

Yemen. When the *Ascension* was wrecked off the Malabar coast Jourdain went to Agra, before joining a ship of the Fifth Voyage at Surat, sailing for Sumatra. Jourdain spent several years trading in pepper, and in 1613 was given command of the *Darling* for an expedition to the island of Amboyna. He returned briefly in 1617 to England, where he seems to have separated from his wife, having excluded her from his will. He became the company's chief merchant in the Moluccas, where Dutch actively opposed the English presence. Jourdain was killed in 1619 in a fight with a Dutch ship. It was typical that Jourdain, with his flair for diplomacy, should have been attempting to arrange a truce when he was cut down by a musket ball.

LA BOURDONNAIS: Bertrand François Mahé de La Bourdonnais. b. St Malo, 1699. French mariner and administrator. Went to sea at age of 10, made several voyages to East Indies. In 1725, as first lieutenant of the *Badine*, took part in capture of Mayyazhi (Mahé), France's only settlement on the Malabar coast. Traded on his own account in Bengal and Arabia, and later served for two years in Goa under Portuguese crown. Governor-general of Isle de France and Bourbon, 1735-46. In 1742 he sent Picault and Grossin on the voyage that resulted in the discovery of the Isles Mahé, later renamed the Seychelles islands. During the War of the Austrian Succession, La Bourdonnais led a naval squadron to the coast of India, where his campaign culminated in the capture of Madras in 1746. After quarrelling with French commander Dupleix, La Bourdonnais was recalled to France and imprisoned in the Bastille on charges of corruption and maladministration. He was eventually acquitted. Died at Paris in 1753.

LA PÉROUSE: Jean-François de Galaup, Comte de la Pérouse. b. near Albi, 1741. French mariner and explorer. Entered navy 1756 and served in North America, where he was wounded and made prisoner. Ensign, 1764. Transferred to Indian Ocean, where, as captain of store ship *Seine*, sailing to Pondichéry in 1773, he put in at Seychelles and reported great disorder at French settlement. Lieutenant, 1777. Commanding a frigate in squadron of d'Estaing in the Caribbean in 1779 he captured two English warships. Captain, 1780. Destroyed English settlements at Hudson Bay in 1782. In 1785 commissioned by Louis XVI to make voyage of discovery in frigates *Boussole* and *Astrolabe*. After extensive sailing in the Pacific both ships foundered off Vanukoro, in Solomon islands, in 1788. Circumstances of loss remained a mystery until vestiges of the wreck of the *Astrolabe* were found by an English ship in 1826, and by the French navigator Dumont d'Urville the following year. Remains of the wreck of the *Boussole* were found in 1962. Channel between northern Japanese island of Hokkaido and Soviet island of Sakhalin is named La Pérouse strait.

LESAGE. Lieutenant Bibye Lesage. British army officer. Civil Agent, Seychelles, 1813-15. b. 1779, London. Lieutenant, 22nd Foot (later the Cheshire Regiment); was at capture of Isle de France (Mauritius), 1810. In 1815 granted concession of Denis Island and, later, Desroches. Sent by Governor Farquhar to Madagascar in 1815 to negotiate a treaty with Radama I. In 1819 Lesage was a passenger in the ill-fated *Six Soeurs* (Captain Raymond Hodoul) from Seychelles, and was among survivors from the burning ship who reached La Digue after ten days in an open boat. Lesage continued to live in Mauritius as a commercial agent.

LINOIS: Charles Alexandre Léon Durand de Linois. b. Brest, 1761. French naval officer. Served as volunteer in American War of Independence. Sailed to East Indies as lieutenant in fleet of Marquis de St Félix, 1784-85. In May 1794, while commanding the frigate *Atalante*, was captured by English outside Brest, and spent 11 months in captivity. Captain, 1795. The same year, commanding the *Formidable* (80) at battle of Groix, off French coast, lost an eye. Again made prisoner; freed in an exchange some months later. Took part in expedition against Ireland, 1796. Rear-admiral, 1799. In 1801 achieved brilliant victory over English fleet at Algeciras; awarded sabre of honour. In command of East Indies division, 1803-06; made several valuable prizes throughout campaign. In 1805, in flagship *Marengo* (74) and with supporting frigates, he visited the Seychelles. Linois backed Quéau de Quinssy over the capitulation of the islands. On homeward voyage encountered a British squadron off Cape Verde islands; French ships taken after fierce fight. Linois, wounded in leg, remained prisoner until exchanged in 1814. Made Count of the Empire, 1810. Appointed governor of Guadeloupe at Restoration. Rallied to Napoleon. Surrendered Guadeloupe to English in August 1815. Acquitted at court-martial of revolt and insubordination. Died at Versailles, 1848. Linois's name is inscribed on the Arc de Triomphe in Paris.

MADGE. Edward Madge. British army officer. Civil Agent, Seychelles, 1815-26; b. 1776; commissioned 1794; lieutenant, 19th Foot (Green Howards); captain, 1802. Assistant Registrar of Slaves at Mauritius, 1826; removed from government service as result of parliamentary inquiry, 1828; died at Pondichéry, 1850. Group of rocks near Praslin formerly named Madge Rocks.

MAGALLON: François Louis Magallon de la Morlière. b. 1754, l'Isle Adam, near Paris. French soldier and administrator, son of a general. Ensign in Bourgogne Regiment, 1769; captain, 1786. Subsequently served in Revolutionary armies. Divisional general, 1795. Commander of troops in Admiral Sercey's squadron which carried Directory's agents Baco and

Burnel to the Isle de France to implement the 1794 decree abolishing slavery. In ensuing disturbances Magallon refused to march troops against the inhabitants, and approved expulsion of the two agents. Remained commander of troops on the island until appointed in July 1800 governor-general of French establishments east of Cape of Good Hope. Replaced by Decaen in August 1803, and became governor of Réunion island. As governor-general Magallon was faced with problem of the deportees sent to Seychelles, and he authorised transfer of some 30 of them to Anjouan, where most of them died. Strongly criticised over this by Minister of Marine. Magallon returned to France in 1806, and commanded a division until 1814. Retired, 1815. Married at Pamplemousses, Isle de France, 1797, Louise Marguerite Josephine Merven. Died at Paris, 1825.

MAGON: Charles René Magon. b. Paris, 1763. French naval officer. As commander of the frigate *Amphitrite* in 1788, he retook Diego Garcia from the English, destroying their fortifications. In 1791, commanding the corvette *Minerve*, called at the Seychelles on way to Bengal with the government commissioners Yvon and Gautier, and formally raised the Tricolour at the Établissement. Captain, 1795. Subsequently moved to the *Cybèle* (40). During the disturbances at the Isle de France over the arrival of the Directory agents Baco and Burnel in 1796, Magon was temporarily imprisoned on charges brought by the popular assemblies. In command of the *Mont Blanc* (74) under Admiral Villaret de Joyeuse in West Indies. Rear-admiral, 1803. Had reputation in navy of being a 'fire-eater'. Commanded the *Algéciras* (80) at Trafalgar, 1805, and was fatally wounded while leading an attempt to board an enemy ship.

MALARTIC: Anne-Joseph Hippolyte de Maurès, Comte de Malartic. French soldier and administrator. b. Montauban, 1730. Entered army at 15 as ensign in the Sarre Regiment, later transferring to the Béarn Regiment. Served in Flanders and Italy during War of the Austrian Succession. Sent to Canada in 1755 and took part in Montcalm's campaign against English. Returned to France in 1763 at the end of Seven Years' War. Appointed governor of Guadeloupe, 1769. Field marshal, 1780. Governor-general of French establishments east of Cape of Good Hope from June 1792. Malartic was a wise administrator who, during the early years of the Revolution, averted serious disorder in the Isle de France. Although his authority was severely curtailed by Colonial Assembly he retained confidence of inhabitants. Approved removal from the Isle de France of the Directory agents Baco and Burnel in 1796. Appointed Quéau de Quinssy commandant of Seychelles in 1793, and supported him against Assembly over the capitulation of Seychelles the following year. Died at

Port Louis, 28 July 1800. British admiral Sir William Hotham described Malartic as "a fine old soldier, with very intelligent countenance". As mark of respect on his death, the British blockading squadron ranged close in to Port Louis harbour with flag of truce at half-mast.

MOREAU DE SÉCHELLES: Jean Moreau de Séchelles. b. Paris, 1690. French administrator. Father, Pierre Moreau, was treasurer at Invalides. Entered law and became a magistrate. Employed in government finance. Compromised in fall of Finance Minister Desmarets and War Minister Le Blanc, and imprisoned in the Bastille. Married in 1712 Marie-Anne Catherine d'Amoreyan. Two years later he acquired the *seigneurie* of Séchelles, and took that name (recorded sometimes, incorrectly, as Vicomte Moreau de Séchelles). In 1727 named intendant of Hainaut on sponsorship of Le Blanc, who had returned to War Ministry. During War of the Austrian Succession, 1740-48, was acting intendant to army of Bohemia. He was said to have displayed great concern for welfare of the troops, even if at expense of the ordinary people, which may be why Frederick the Great described him as a model military administrator. Rewarded by appointment as state counsellor and given the intendance of Flanders. In following years he was intendant to the armies of Flanders and Alsace. Appointed *contrôleur-général des finances* to Louis XVI in 1754. In disgrace over his personal behaviour, he retired in August 1756 at the urging of his family. Died, "with great piety", in 1760. His eldest daughter, Marie-Hélène, married the Intendant of Paris, René Hérault; youngest daughter, Marie-Jeanne-Catherine, married the Marquis de Moras, who succeeded Moreau de Séchelles as Finance Minister in 1756 and became Minister of Marine the following year.

MORPHEY: Nicolas Corneille Morphey. b. 6 January 1729. French mariner. Son of an Irish immigrant, Corneille O'Morphey, and his French wife Jacqueline. Joined the French East Indies Company. Sailed for the Isle de France, where in 1754 he married Anne Perrine Houdman, daughter of a French settler. Morphey's wife died in May 1756. Two months later Morphey was dispatched by the Isle de France governor-general, René Magon de la Villebague, to establish French sovereignty over a group of islands that had been discovered 12 years earlier by Lazare Picault.. He sailed on 16 July 1756 in the frigate *Cerf*, arriving on 6 September off the main island, named Mahé by Picault. Three days later, on 9 September 1756, the Feast Day of Saint Anne, he entered the sheltered anchorage which Picault had named Port Royal. Morphey spent several weeks travelling over the island, taking formal possession of it under the name Isle de Séchelles. Morphey eventually returned to France, where he married again. He died in 1774.

OWEN: William FitzWilliam Owen. b. 1774. British naval officer. Entered navy in 1788, and served with Channel fleet in the first years of the war. In July 1803 appointed to command the brig *Seaflower*, in which he went to East Indies. In August 1806 visited the Seychelles with a squadron under the command of Captain John Ferrier, in *Albion* (74). Sailed for Maldives and then Sumatra, where off the west coast discovered the Seaflower channel between the islands of Si-buru and Si-pora. In November 1806 piloted Sir Edward Pellew's squadron into Batavia roads and shared in operations resulting in destruction of Dutch ships. Taken prisoner by French in September 1808 and detained at Isle de France until June 1810, when he was exchanged. Employed as superintendent of transports at Madras for expedition to take the Isle de France. Returned to England in 1813. Appointed to survey Canadian lakes, 1815. In 1821 appointed to the *Leven* and *Barracouta* to carry out survey of African coast. Visited Seychelles and left description of islands in published memoirs, 1833. Died at St John, New Brunswick, in 1847.

PICAULT: Lazare Picault. b. Toulon. French mariner. Sailed for India in November 1735 as third officer in the *Apollon*, returning to France two years later. In November 1739 arrived at Isle de France as second officer of the *Thétis*. In 1742 Picault, commanding the *Elisabeth*, and Jean Grossin, in the *Charles*, sailed from Isle de France to explore the waters to the north-east of Madagascar. They discovered the islands that were to become known as the Seychelles. Picault visited the islands again in 1744, naming the main island Isle Mahé after the Isle de France governor-general Mahé de La Bourdonnais. Picault died in 1747, at Pamplemousses, Isle de France.

POIVRE: Pierre Poivre. b. 1719, at Lyon. French administrator and scientist. Travelled to China in 1740, intending to be a missionary. On returning to France Poivre's ship was attacked by an English ship, and in the action he lost an arm. Taken to Batavia, he observed for the first time spice cultivation by the Dutch. Later he joined Mahé de La Bourdonnais in India, and returned with him to the Isle de France. On the voyage back to France Poivre's ship was taken in the Channel, and he spent seven years as a prisoner in Guernsey. In 1749 he returned to the East to establish a trading post for the Compagnie des Indes at Fai-Fo in Cochinchina (near Da Nang, in present-day Vietnam). From there he brought to the Isle de France several spice plants, with which he started the royal garden at Pamplemousses. Later he travelled to the Philippines, and charted the Moluccas, or Spice islands. Returning to Isle de France with 3,000 nutmeg seeds and other spices and fruit trees, he distributed these to the settlers, but almost none of the plants survived. The governor-general, Magon de la

Villebague, was hostile to his projects and, in disgust, Poivre returned to France. Taken prisoner a third time by the English, he was kept at Cork until April 1757. He retired to Lyon, and was given letters of nobility. On the Crown's taking over from the Company at the Isle de France and Bourbon, Poivre was brought out of retirement and appointed, in 1767, royal intendant. During the six years of his administration the island colonies prospered. Poivre encouraged the arts and sciences, promoted marine exploration, and attempted to turn the Seychelles into spice islands for France. In 1772, frustrated in his conflicts with the home government, he returned to France. Rewarded for his services with a pension of 12,000 livres. He died at Lyon in 1786.

QUÉAU DE QUINSSY: Jean-Baptiste Quéau de Quinssy, or Quincy. b. Paris, 1748. French soldier and administrator. Son of Jean-Charles Quéau de Quinssy, nobleman, and Jeanne le Flamand. Gentleman in household of Monsieur, brother of Louis XVI and the future Louis XVIII, 1775. Ensign in Corps des Volontaires Étrangers de la Marine, 1778. Served in Suffren's campaign off Indian coast and Ceylon. Wounded at Negapatam. Also served in India with the Marquis de Bussy. Transferred in 1784 to the Pondichéry Regiment. Captain, 1789. Commander of the Grande Rivière region, Isle de France, 1791. Appointed commandant and civil agent of Seychelles, 1793. Remained commandant of the colony until final surrender of Seychelles to Britain in 1811. *Juge de paix,* 1806. In 1816 the English governor Madge suspended him as *juge de paix* for his alleged complicity in escape from seizure of the slave brig *Hirondelle* and its captain, Jean Sausse. Arrested and sent to the Isle de France, Quinssy was freed on bail. Insisted on trial before Court of Admiralty, which judged him innocent. Attempted unsuccessfully to bring civil action against Madge for damages. Addressed a memoir on the subject to the Prince Regent in March 1817. Reinstated in Seychelles as *juge de paix.* Chevalier of St Louis, 1815. Married at Isle de France in July 1786 to Marie Madeleine Antoinette Duval, from whom he was divorced in July 1793. Married for a second time in Seychelles in October 1794 to Marie Joseph Dubail, daughter of a former captain in the Isle de France Regiment, who had been divorced by her husband, Auguste Vaulbert, at Mahé four months earlier. Quinssy's tomb is in the grounds of State House, Victoria.

ROCHON: Alexis-Marie de Rochon. b. Brest, 1741. French marine astronomer. Destined originally for religious orders, he adopted the title of abbé. Librarian, Royal Marine Academy, Brest, 1766. Sailed to Morocco in 1767, and to the Isle de France, Madagascar, and Seychelles in 1768-70, in the *Heure du Berger.* Made numerous scientific observations, but missed, as result of near-shipwreck, the passage of Venus across the sun, 2 June

1769. Was assigned to join Kerguelen's expedition to southern seas in 1772, but left expedition at Isle de France after a quarrel. Subsequently asked by Poivre to accompany Marion Dufresne on his voyage of exploration, but governor-general refused him permission. Back in France, Rochon was appointed in 1774 in charge of King's cabinet of physics and optics. Credited with being the first to utilise in scientific research the principles of double refraction; he invented the micrometer, and, in astronomy, perfected a method of determining longitude. Appointed member of the Institut de France and of the Academy of St Petersburg. Lost all his positions at outbreak of Revolution, and retired to Brest. In 1791 he published first volume on his travels to Morocco, Madagascar, and Seychelles. In 1802 he returned to Paris and, three years later, obtained official lodgings at the Louvre. Died in Paris, 1817.

SARTINE: Antoine de Sartine, Comte d'Alby. b. Barcelona, Spain, 1729. Lieutenant-general of police, 1759-74. Introduced street cleaning and lighting in Paris, making it a model European capital. Minister of Marine, 1774-80. Took the decision in 1778 to end the Brayer du Barré settlement in Seychelles, and put islands under a military commandant. Also approved the emigration of Bourbon settlers to Seychelles. In an attempt to win Sartine's favour, Brayer du Barré sent him a map of Mahé with a bay on the west coast marked "Port Sartine". The name did not survive. Sartine retired in disgrace in 1780 after disclosure by Finance Minister Necker that his Ministry was 20 million livres in debt. He emigrated to Spain at the outbreak of the Revolution and died there in 1801.

SNEYD: Clement Sneyd. b. 1773, Staffordshire. British naval officer. Entered navy 1786; lieutenant, 1793. Served in *Suffolk* (74), flagship of Rear-Admiral Peter Rainier, in East Indies. In December 1796 moved to the *Russel* (74) and took part in action at Camperdown off Dutch coast, October 1797. Appointed in 1801 to the *Culloden* (74), fitting for flag of Rear-Admiral Sir Edward Pellew, by whom he was appointed acting commander. Governor of Madras Hospital. At Seychelles from 8 to 13 November, 1805, in temporary command of the *Duncan* frigate; took the *Courrier des Seychelles* slave ship as prize, burned another and pillaged several estates along Mahé's west coast. Sneyd was subsequently acting captain of the frigate *Sir Francis Drake* before returning to England in the *Albion*, commanded by Sir John Ferrier. Post-captain, 1811. From 1811 to 1813 in command of the *Myrtle* (20) off the coast of Portugal. Rear-admiral, 1846.

SOUILLAC: François, Vicomte de Souillac. b. Château de Bardou, Périgord, 1732. French naval officer and administrator. Entered navy in

1749, after serving in cavalry for two years. Distinguished service during Seven Years' War. Lieutenant, 1763; Chevalier of St Louis, 1770. In 1775 appointed governor of Bourbon, and on death of Guiran Labrillane in 1779 became governor-general of the Isle de France and Bourbon. Captain, 1777. Souillac was a popular governor-general. In 1784 he was appointed to rank of commodore, and the following year succeeded the Marquis de Bussy as governor-general of French establishments east of the Cape. Faced with the increasingly troublesome administration of Gillot in the Seychelles he sent, in 1786, an Isle de France official, Malavois, to Mahé with secret orders to inquire into Gillot's conduct. He also drew up a set of regulations for the colony which became, in effect, the first Seychelles constitution. Souillac returned to France in 1788. In 1790 took command of the Brest fleet but was forced to retire; lived as an *émigré* in London from 1792 to 1801. Died at Château de Bardou, 1803. There is on Mahé's west coast a small bay called Anse Souillac.

SURCOUF: Robert Surcouf. b. St Malo. 1773. French privateer. Sailed in 1780 for the Isle de France and India. Made several slaving voyages to Mozambique, and on one occasion was wrecked on the African coast. Given command of the brig *Modeste*, which he renamed *Emilie*. Sailed in 1795 to Seychelles to load with tortoises after Governor-General Malartic had refused to authorise his sailing as a privateer. Claiming that at Seychelles he had been chased by two English warships Surcouf began his career of sea raider off the coast of India. He captured several English ships, including the East Indiaman the *Triton*, the first time a capture had been made in the Bay of Bengal. Returned to the Isle de France in March 1796. Because he had no *lettre de marque* all his prizes were confiscated, but Surcouf successfully appealed against the decision on his return to France. In February 1798 Surcouf sailed for the East again in the *Clarisse* (14) to resume his attacks on English shipping, becoming as a result one of the richest and most renowned privateers of the Indian Ocean. Changed the *Clarisse* in 1800 for the *Confiance* (16), of Bordeaux, in which his noteworthy prizes included the East Indiaman the *Kent*, taken after fierce hand-to-hand fighting. Surcouf, who visited Seychelles several times during this period, returned to France in 1801. He was honoured by Napoleon, who offered him a naval commission to return to the Indian Ocean with two frigates. Surcouf refused, and remained in retirement in France until 1807, when he went back to the East in the *Revenant* (18). The following year, however, he retired finally to France. His career was notable for his audacity as a privateer and the gallantry he showed his prisoners. At one point the English had a reward of a quarter-million rupees on his head. Surcouf was a modest man who rarely spoke of his exploits. He died in 1827.

TERNAY: Charles Louis D'Arzac de Ternay. b. Ternay, Vienne. French naval officer and administrator. Entered navy 1738 and took part in several operations in Mediterranean. Ensign, 1746; lieutenant, 1756. Served with distinction in North America, commanding in succession the *Mutine*, *Pomone*, and *Zéphyr*. In 1759, was in the *Inflexible* (64) at the battle of Les Cardinaux (Quiberon Bay), off the French coast. Captain, 1761. The same year led a squadron against English fishing settlements in Newfoundland. Appointed governor-general of the Isle de France and Bourbon in 1771, and served until 1776. Observers described him as of small stature, aloof, active, and given to frequent inspection tours of island. In 1772, on receiving unfavourable reports about Brayer du Barré's settlement in Seychelles, he ordered the return of the commandant and most of the inhabitants. Commodore, 1779. In February 1780, with his flag in the *Duc-de-Bourgogne* (80), Ternay escorted Rochambeau's army of 6,000 men to fight alongside the American colonists. Disembarked at Newport, Rhode Island, where a few months later he died on board his ship. Monument erected to him at Newport. The most westerly point of Mahé island was called Cap Ternay (renamed Pointe Matoopa). There is also Baie Ternay, and between Mahé and Conception island, Ternay Strait.

SOURCES AND NOTES

Bibliothèque Nationale, Paris	BN	The British Library, London	BL
Archives de France, Paris	AF	India Office Library, London	IOL
Institut de France, Paris	IF	Mauritius archives	MA
Musée de la Marine	MM	Réunion archives	RA
Public Record Office, Kew	PRO	Seychelles National Archives	SNA

INTRODUCTION

1   While it was for long assumed that the islands were named after Moreau de Séchelles, it seems more likely that the honour was conferred on his family, represented by two daughters both of whom had contracted influential alliances. According to French historian Marcel Emerit (*L'Information Historique*, 1973) Moreau de Séchelles had been forced by his family to resign in 1756 as *contrôleur-général des finances* on account of his scandalous behaviour. His successor was the Marquis de Moras, husband of Moreau de Séchelles' younger daughter and a powerful figure in the Compagnie des Indes. The elder daughter, Marie-Hélène, widow of René Hérault, Intendant of Paris, also had powerful connections through her son, Colonel Jean-Baptiste Hérault de Séchelles, whose wife was a cousin of the Isle de France governor-general, René Magon de la Villebague, and niece of the influential Marshal de Contades. After the Colonel's death in battle, the upbringing of his son, the future revolutionary, Marie-Joseph Hérault de Séchelles, was undertaken jointly by Marie-Hélène, her daughter-in-law, and the Marshal de Contades.

CHAPTER ONE

Albert-Auguste Fauvel's *Unpublished documents on the history of the Seychelles anterior to 1810,* first published in 1909 and subsequently reprinted by the Seychelles government, and *The Journal of John Jourdain, 1608-1617,* published in 1905 by the Hakluyt Society, London, have provided most of the material for this chapter. Manuscript sources include logs and reports on Picault's two missions to the Seychelles, filed under 4 JJ86 AF and 4 JJ87 AF, an undated memoir on the Isles Mahé, C4/145 AF, and another on French colonies, under Colonies F 3/48 AF. Copies of the document affirming the act of possession of the Seychelles islands, signed by Corneille Nicolas Morphey and others on 1 November 1756, are filed at the Mauritius and Seychelles archives.

1   In some references the name of the ship is given as the *St Charles*. Documents from the archives of the Dutch East Indies Company suggest that the vessel had once been the property of Jacob van der Stoel, commissioner to the governor of the Dutch East Indies.

2   Baie Lazare, on Mahé's south-west coast, recalls Picault's landing in

Seychelles although his ships are believed to have anchored further up the coast in Boileau Bay. The distance from the ships to the shore, given as a quarter-league in the log, would be less than a mile. A league was about three and a half miles.

3   Discovered by the Portuguese navigator João de Nova, or Jean de Nove, the island has been identified as the Farquhar atoll, although Picault's description would seem to match better Aldabra – still renowned for its giant tortoises – which lies 350 miles further west. João de Nova discovered the Atlantic islands of Ascension and St Helena. There is in the Mozambique Channel a small island named after him.

4   The cayman, found in Central and South America, is of the alligator family. The creature that lived in the Seychelles was believed to be the true African crocodile, *Crocodylus niloticus,* although later research has suggested that it was in fact the even larger Indopacific estuarine or saltwater crocodile, *Crocodylus porosus.*

5   Comment by Jean-Baptiste Nicolas Denis d'Après de Mannevillette, author of the hydrographic atlas *Neptune Oriental,* 1746, quoted by Charles Grant in *History of Mauritius,* 1801.

6   Madagascar's racial composition is evidence of there having been a mass migration westwards of people of Malay-Polynesian stock, and it has been suggested that some of those travellers made a halt at Seychelles. Guy Lionnet, in *The Seychelles,* 1972, refers to some of the conflicting theories on migratory movements across the Indian Ocean, including a "rather tenuous piece of circumstantial evidence" that the Indo-Malayan casuarina tree was found growing in the Seychelles and Madagascar, but nowhere else in the Indian Ocean.

7   The Dutch named Mauritius after their head of state, Prince Maurice of Nassau. The Mascarene islands of Mauritius, La Réunion, and Rodrigues derive their communal name from Pedro Mascarenhas, captain of one of the ships of Garcia de Noronha's fleet, which sailed from Lisbon in 1511.

8   Quoted by J.F. Thomazi, *Un millionaire au service du Roi: La Bourdonnais* (Paris, 1963).

9   Writing to the Minister of Marine in 1740, D'Après de Mannevillette criticised French dependence on Dutch and English charts, which "mark a prodigious number of islands and sandbanks, put, as it were, by chance, and which have for long made navigators tremble".

10   It has been suggested that La Bourdonnais had earlier received a report from Picault of a group of islands the latter had sighted in December 1741 when blown off course during a return voyage from Pondichéry. – "A short history of Seychelles", *Seychelles Phone Book,* Cable & Wireless, 1999.

11   Vasco da Gama's biographer, João de Barros, refers to "a Moor from Guzerat called Malema Cana (who), because of the pleasure he found in conversing

with our people and in order to please the king of Malindi, he agreed to sail with them". *Malemo Cana,* however, means "master of astronomical science", from the Arabic *Mu'allim* and a Tamil word *Kanajan.* It has been claimed that the guide was Ahmed ibn Majid, an Arab from Oman who, between 1468 and 1489, produced sailing instructions known as *Al-Muhet.*

12   Reference to islands seen by Vasco da Gama appears in a Pedro Reinel chart of c. 1517 (which disappeared from Munich at the end of the Second World War) and in subsequent Reinel charts. The first cartographic representation of the Seychelles islands, however, is accorded to the Cantino Planisphere, dated 1502. It is largely Ptolemaic and Arabic in conception, and the Seychelles identification is not obvious. The planisphere takes its name from Alberto Cantino, agent of the Duke of Ferrara, who was sent as a spy to Lisbon to acquire knowledge of the latest Portuguese discoveries. The chart, after disappearing for many years, was found in 1860 being used as a screen in a butcher's shop in Modena, northern Italy. It is now in the Biblioteca Estense in Modena.

13   This account of Vasco da Gama's voyage, written in Flemish and entitled *Calcoen* (Calicut), was published anonymously in Antwerp in 1504. A duplicate edition, with notes and an English translation, appeared in London in 1874. Thomé Lopes, who sailed in the rear division of Vasco da Gama's fleet, referred to many islands being seen between 24 February and 12 April 1503. *(Navigatione verso l'Indie orientali scritta par Thomé Lopez Portughese,* Ramusio, Vol. 1, 1663).

14   Discovery of the Seychelles is attributed to Fernão Soares by William Foster, editor of *The Journal of John Jourdain, 1608-1617,* although he gives no source. In an anonymous chart dated c. 1510, thought to be by Jorge Reinel, with corrections made by his father, Pedro, and which is in the possession of the Herz August Bibliothek in Wolfenbüttel, Germany, there is a group of six islands named *As Iyoas,* in the approximate position of the Seychelles. As corrupted orthography is not uncommon in old charts, it is possible *As Iyoas,* which has no apparent meaning in Portuguese, should be read as As Irmas, or the Sisters. In later Reinel charts the islands appear as As Sete Irmas (the Seven Sisters).

15   There is a St François island in the Amirantes group, named by the Chevalier de Pontevez, in 1730. He also named the nearby island of Alphonse.

16   This was Frégate island, named by Picault presumably on account of the frigate birds he found there. He wrote: "The island must have one league in circumference, and is surrounded by reefs; a heavy sea prevented us from landing on that day." A landing on Frégate is still a difficult undertaking because of the reef and currents.

17   Guy Lionnet, in *The Romance of a Palm,* offers an explanation for Picault's oversight: "What probably happened was that although Lazare Picault saw coco de mer palms on Praslin, he did not see any coco de mer nuts there. This is

understandable, since at the time Praslin was wooded to such an extent that it was almost impossible to penetrate the island." Another possibility mentioned subsequently by Lionnet is that, like Barré some 25 years later, Picault, on first seeing the nuts, may have been unwilling to believe his eyes. The cotton noted by Picault on the palms was "the fibrous material which is found at the base of the coco de mer leaves".

18   Edward Boscawen, British admiral, b. 1711, third son of Viscount Falmouth; rear-admiral, 1747. Commanded in India, 1748-50, with indifferent success, failing to take Pondichéry after siege. Distinguished himself during Seven Years' War, conducting naval operations at capture of Louisburg, Canada, 1758, and blocking French preparations for invasion of England, 1759. Lord of the Admiralty, 1751. Died 1761.

19   In the 16th century spices were as important a commodity as oil is today, being used, along with salt, to preserve and make more palatable the meat that was stored for consumption during winter in Europe (most of the livestock having been slaughtered because of lack of feed). While salt was readily available, spices had to be imported, across the Indian Ocean by Arab or Indian ships to the Red Sea, then by caravan to the Mediterranean ports, from where Venetian galleys transported the spices to Europe. All along the route there were middle men to take their cut, pushing the price up by as much as 10,000 per cent. It was this trade that first the Portuguese and then the Dutch determined to seize for themselves.

20   Thomas Jones, *Relation of the Fourth Voyage,* in *Purchas His Pilgrimes,* Vol. III, Hakluyt Society, London.

21   Identification of the islands as the main Seychelles group was made for the Hakluyt Society by Rear-Admiral Sir William Wharton, Royal Navy Hydrographer, 1884-1904.

22   Remark by William Revett, in *A Journal kept in the Fourth Voyage* (India Office Marine Records). Revett was chief factor in the *Ascension*. A fourth chronicler of the voyage was the ship's steward, Robert Covert, who published in 1612 *A True and Almost Incredible Report of an Englishman that (being cast away in the good Ship called the Ascension in Cambaya, the farthest part of the East Indies) travelled by land threw many unknowne Kingdomes and great Cities with a great Empereur called the Great Mogull, a Prince not till now knowne to our English Nation.* To match this pretentious title, the author described himself as Captain Robert Covert.

23   The *Ascension* reached Aden on 17 April 1609, the first English ship to visit that "famous and strong place", and was joined by the *Good Hope* a month later. The captain of the *Good Hope* had been murdered in a mutiny while the ship was off Madagascar, and two ringleaders were hanged from the yardarm in Aden harbour. On leaving Aden, the *Ascension* visited Mocha before sailing for India.

She was wrecked off the Malabar coast. Although most of the crew were saved, the cargo was lost. The third ship in Sharpeigh's fleet, the *Union*, after surviving the storm at the Cape, reached Sumatra, where a cargo of pepper was loaded. On the homeward voyage she ran aground, and almost all the cargo was lost.

24   Daniel Defoe (Captain Charles Johnson), *A General History of the Robberies and Murders of the most Notorious Pirates, 1717-1724*, London.

25   Astove is also reputed to be the site of treasure from a Portuguese frigate, the *Dom Royal*, which went aground in 1760. (A.J. Venter, *Under the Indian Ocean*, 1973).

26   Professor J. Stanley Gardiner, lecturing to the Royal Geographical Society in London in June 1906 after a scientific mission to the Seychelles, referred to pirates' visits. "The tradition is that there was, in Praslin, a pirate settlement and station for repairs and that one of the bays on the north side, Côte d'Or and Curieuse, was used for this purpose ... where a legend is universally spread, experience leads us to believe that it rests on a basis of truth *(Royal Geographical Society Journal,* Vol. 29). M.J. Moine, in "Essai sur les Îles Seychelles", in *Bulletin de Madagascar,* 1972, mentions the remains of houses, iron, cannon balls, a well with lead cover, and the ruins of a forge being found on Frégate island, indicating a prolonged stay by pirates. Three tombstones in coral, on which were laid sword hilts and copper sabres, were also found.

27   A paper believed to contain Le Vasseur's clue to the treasure, together with other letters in the possession of a Seychelles inhabitant, were deciphered in the 1920s by Charles de la Roncière, keeper of printed papers at the Bibliothèque Nationale in Paris, and subsequently linked to mysterious carvings on rocks at Bel Ombre beach on Mahé island. Early diggings turned up no gold, only two coffins containing human remains and a body buried in the sand. As pirates would kill those who helped to bury treasure in order to ensure its location remained secret, this find spurred the searchers on, but nothing more was uncovered. In the late 1940s a middle-aged Englishman, Reginald Cruise-Wilkins, began the hunt again, raising capital and forming a syndicate to carry out excavations at Bel Ombre. He died some 20 years later, still searching. In 1988 sons of Cruise-Wilkins resumed the search, with 100,000 dollars from an American investor.

28   The stone of possession, its carving now eroded and vandalised, possibly during the Revolution, is on display at the National History Museum in Victoria.

29   The first geographer to enter the name Seychelles in a chart seems to have been the French Hydrographer Royal, Jacques-Nicolas Bellin (1703-73), who noted that it was "the same as the Isles Mahé, visited in 1742". The spelling of Seychelles was always variable. Sometimes the final 's' was omitted, while 'i' frequently replaced the letter 'y'. To countless English seamen during the Napoleonic wars the islands were known as the Seashells.

30 François-Marie Peirenc, Marquis de Moras, who married Moreau de Séchelles' youngest daughter, Marie-Jeanne-Catherine. Moras succeeded his father-in-law as *contrôleur-général des finances* in 1756, becoming Minister of Marine in February the following year.

CHAPTER TWO

The mission of the *Digue* and the *Curieuse* to Seychelles in October-December 1768 is described in detail in the manuscript "Journal historique de la découverte des îles Mahé", MS 1286, IF. The rest of the source material for this chapter was found in printed publications, notably Guy Lionnet's *The Romance of a Palm*, 1972, and *Striking plants of Seychelles*, 1981, and the Hakluyt Society's reprinting of *Purchas His Pilgrimes,* with its accounts of the voyages of Pyrard de Laval, John Huyghen van Linschoten, and Ibn Battuta. The anonymous note on the coco de mer to Sartine, Minister of Marine, dated 1775, is filed under C 4/145 AF.

1 Mayyazhi, renamed Mahé, was first occupied by the French in 1725.

2 The last crocodile on La Digue was killed in 1810. Swiss herpetologist René Honegger photographed a well preserved crocodile skull found in Seychelles (R.E. Honegger, *Beobachtungen am der Herpetolfauna den Seychellen,* Salamanca, 1966).

3 The presence of seals on the Isle aux Vaches was noted in charts drawn up by Alexander Dalrymple in 1780 from a survey by the East India Company ship *Eagle* in 1771. One explanation for the presence of seals could be that the mean sea temperature was then much lower than it is today. Dalrymple, b. Edinburgh 1737, former captain of an East Indiaman, was Hydrographer to the Admiralty from 1795. Friend of D'Après de Mannevillette, he was a firm believer in the existence of a southern continent. Died 1808.

4 The Poule Bleue, or Blue Hen, of Seychelles has never been identified, no residual skin or bone having been found. Guy Lionnet, in *Birds of Seychelles,* suggests that it may have been similar to the flightless rails of Aldabra and Madagascar.

5 Marco Polo. b. Venice, 1254. Crossed Asia via Mongolia and returned by way of the Indian Ocean after 17 years in the service of Kubla Khan. Died 1324.

6 George Everhard Rumpf (1627-1702), known as Rumphius, botanist and merchant of Amboina, in Dutch East Indies. Became blind before his *Herbarium Amboinense* was completed. It was eventually published in 1741-55.

7 The name *Lodoicea sechellarum* was given to the coco de mer palm by the French naturalist J-J.H. de Labillardière in 1801, but was changed to *Lodoicea maldivica* in 1917, in accordance with international agreement on botanic

nomenclature which gave precedence to anterior names. Guy Lionnet *(The Romance of a Palm)* notes that the word *Lodoicea* is thought to derive from Laodice, daughter of Priam, king of Troy, and *Lodovicus,* latin for Louis, given possibly in honour of Louis XV of France.

8   Guy Lionnet, *Striking plants of Seychelles.*

9   The name of this island has been given by some writers, apparently wrongly, as Jeannette.

CHAPTER THREE

In addition to the published memoirs of Grenier and Rochon, source material includes: at the Archives de France, Paris, dossiers B 4/114 and C 2/278; at the Bibliothèque Municipale, Quimper, a memoir by Musson, second captain of the *Vert Galant,* ref 2H, and at the Mauritius archives, Grenier's log, OC 49B, and Lafontaine's log, OF 24A. At the Archives de France there are also undated memoirs, written probably by D'Après, on Duroslan's voyage in the *Heure du Berger,* 1769, filed under C 4/145, Duroslan's log, C 4/112, and Oger's log, 44 JJ 86.

1   Edmund Halley (1656-1742), English astronomer and mathematician, first to calculate the orbit of a comet (1705), which, on its predicted return in 1758, was named after him. His chart of prevailing winds (1686) was first meteorological map.

2   James Cook, b. Malton, Yorkshire, 1728. After serving for eight years in coastwise trade, joined navy. Saw action in Seven Years' War. Made three successive voyages in the Pacific, and first saw south-east coast of Australia in April 1770. Killed by natives in Sandwich islands (Hawaii) in 1779.

3   Dalrymple had insisted on being given command of the ship to Tahiti, but the Admiralty would not agree to appointing any other than a naval officer.

4   Bernard-Marie Boudin de Tromelin, b. Morlaix, Brittany, 1735. Joined navy at St Denis, Isle Bourbon, 1751, and served in East and West Indies. Director of works at Port Louis, Isle de France, from 1771. Second-in-command to Suffren, 1781-82. Vice-admiral, 1792; retired, 1795. Died 1816. Tromelin island, also known as Île du Sable, 300 miles east of Madagascar, was for long a notorious hazard to shipping.

5   Elisabeth Marie Sobobie Betia, Queen of Sainte Marie and kingdom of Foulepointe. Daughter of Rasimilaho, who was the son of the European pirate Tom Tew. Betia became queen of the whole kingdom on her father's death in 1750. Had as a lover René Charles le François de Grainville Forval, of the Isle de France, who was in her father's service. The name Forval is mentioned in Seychelles census returns from 1791. Forval died at Mahé on 30 August 1815.

6   Pierre-André de Suffren, b. Saint Cannat, south of France, 1729. Fought in American War of Independence. In command of five ships in Indian Ocean, where he inflicted heavy losses on English during 1782-83 at Madras, Negapatam, and Cuddalore. Recaptured Trincomalee from English in September 1782 and saved Dutch East Indies. Given title of Bailli Suffren de Saint-Tropez in the Order of Malta. Died at Versailles on 8 December 1788 from wound received in duel. Described by Admiral Raoul Victor Castex (1878) as "one of the three immortal names that are emblazoned on naval history of the days of sail".

7   Yves Joseph Kerguelen de Trémarec, b. Quimper, Brittany, 1734. Sailed from Isle de France on 25 March 1771 with the *Fortune* and the *Gros Ventre* on voyage of exploration of the southern seas. Discovered the Kerguelen islands on 12 February 1772. Sent the following year, in the *Roland* and the *Oiseau*, to complete explorations. Delayed at Madagascar by epidemic and returned to Isle de France in September 1774. Accused by officers of immoral conduct and negligence. Imprisoned, but later freed. Back in France in 1795 and died two years later.

8   Dominique François Arago (1786-1853), French physicist; discovered principle of production of magnetism by rotation and wave theory of light. Director of Paris observatory. Minister of War and Marine in provisional republican government after 1848 Revolution. Died in 1853.

9   Napoléon Bonaparte. b. Ajaccio, Corsica, 1769. Entered royal military school at Brienne. Distinguished himself as captain of artillery at siege of Toulon, 1793. Commander of army in Italy under Directory. Expedition to Egypt, 1798-99. First Consul, 1799. Reorganised administration of French education, justice, and finance. Consul for life, 1802. Eliminated all internal opposition, with deportation of Jacobins and royalists. Promulgated Civil Code, 1804. Proclaimed himself Emperor of the French under title of Napoléon I, 1804. Although victorious in Europe, he failed to subdue Great Britain. After dissolving his marriage with the Empress Joséphine married Marie-Louise, daughter of Austrian emperor, 1810. Their son, born 1811, proclaimed King of Rome. Series of military disasters culminated in fall of France, 1814. Napoléon abdicated. Escaped from Elba and resumed power, until final defeat at Waterloo, 1815. Exiled to St Helena, where he died in 1821. Body returned to France for interment in Invalides, 1840,

10   The *Belle Poule*, armed with twenty-six 12-pounders and four of 9, was built in 1766, the first of three warships of that name. Returned to France after several years in Indian Ocean in 1777. Captured by the English in July 1780. The second *Belle Poule* was a 40-gun frigate, built in 1803, which served in the squadron of Admiral Durand Linois, 1803-05. Captured on way back to France in 1806 by an English squadron commanded by Sir John Warren. The third *Belle Poule*, one of the last of the great frigates of sail, was built in 1834. Most celebrated voyage, under command of the Prince de Joinville, was to bring back the remains of Napoleon from St Helena, in 1840.

11   Silhouette, the third largest island of the main Seychelles group, was named during the Marion Dufresne expedition of 1768, presumably after Étienne

de Silhouette (1709-67), Finance Minister to Louis XV. Silhouette, appointed to the post in March 1759, was forced out of office after nine months because of the unpopularity of his economic measures. His detractors accused him of turning taxpayers into mere outlines, giving rise to the word *silhouette*.

CHAPTER FOUR

Poivre's correspondence with Versailles on introducing spices into the Indian Ocean islands is quoted by Madeleine Ly-Tio-Fane in *Mauritius and the Spice Trade,* 1958. She also quotes extracts of Poivre's conversation with Malesherbes (Ms 1756, Musée National de l'Histoire Naturelle, Paris) in her article "L'Établissement du Jardin du Roi aux Seychelles" in the *Journal of the Seychelles Society,* No 6, November 1968. Pittman's report to the Bombay Council and an account of the visit of the English ship the *Eagle* to Seychelles in 1771 are contained in Vol. 105 and 110, Home Misc, IOL.

Brayer du Barré's voluminous correspondence, 1771-73, is filed under C 145 AF and C 4/145 AF. This includes his two testimonials, dated Port Louis, 4 August 1771 and 4 July 1773. Sartine's comment on the favourable terms given to Brayer du Barré, 12 March 1775, is filed under CC 3/15 AF. Much of this correspondence is quoted by Fauvel, *op. cit.*

Gillot's report on Seychelles, filed under A 3.1 SNA, appears in *Annonces, Affiches et Avis Divers pour les Colonies des Isles de France et de Bourbon,* Port Louis, No 16, 28 April 1773, MA. There are references to Gillot's mission under C 145 AF. Poivre's instructions to Gillot, 26 June 1772, are filed under TB 10/3 MA.

1   Slave ships bound for Africa from the Isle de France would normally skirt the north of Madagascar, but on the return voyage wind and current would often force them further north, sometimes to within sight of the Maldives. Seychelles was a convenient stopping place on the return voyage. There the slaves could be landed to recuperate. A memoir dated 1772, quoted by J.M. Filliot in *La traite des esclaves vers les Mascaraignes au XVIII siècle,* noted that coconut oil was a substitute for vinegar in disinfecting slaves after a long voyage.

2   Chrétien-Guillaume de Lamoignon de Malesherbes (1721-94), lawyer, secretary of state for the royal household. Defended Louis XVI before Convention. Executed during the Terror.

3   Brayer du Barré's testimonial reads: "We, administrators-general of the Lottery of the Royal Military School, certify that the *sieur* Brayer Pinton du Barré maintained at Rouen the receipts of the said lottery during a period of three and a half years with the greatest exactitude and honesty, to the satisfaction of the public; that he rendered to us all the accounts, and that he left only in order to settle in

Paris, whereupon we delivered to him the present certificate. Signed: Paul de Bresilliers." - quoted by Fauvel. There is some doubt about the identity of the Royal Military School referred to, as of the dozen such schools existing in France in the 18th century none was located at Rouen.

4   The names of those in Delaunay's party were: Anselme, Berville, Drieux, Bernard (surgeon), Parigue (master carpenter), Jean-Jacques Boal, Michel Boul, Jean-Marie Sartel, Charles Aumont, Joseph Bonneavoine, Jean-Thomas Gorineau, Louis Verdière, Claude Givart, and La Rüe. There were also 13 slaves, of whom five were Indian, under a *commandeur* named Miguet. One of the slaves was a negress named Marie.

5   On 7 August 1786 the brig *Petit Cousin* (Captain Louis-François Raquin), from the Isle de France, arrived at Diego Garcia where it found an English settlement. Told by the governor that the English had taken possession for the East Indies Company. After some difficulty, allowed to take coconuts and tortoises.

6   Three of Delaunay's party returned to the Isle de France in the *Étoile du Matin*, having been dismissed for bad behaviour. There is no record of their names, but the slave Marie might have been one, as an English ship that visited the settlement later in the year noted that no women were seen.

7   In June 1771 Poivre had assigned two ships, the *Isle de France* (Captain Coëtivy) and the *Nécessaire* (Captain Cordé) to sail to the Far East for spice plants. The naturalist Pierre Sonnerat (1748-1814) went on this expedition, and also visited Seychelles the same year. He gave the first scientific description of the coco de mer palm, which was read to the Academy of Sciences in Paris in 1773, and was subsequently reproduced in his book *Voyage à la Nouvelle Guinée*, published three years later. Coëtivy discovered the island of that name, which is the most easterly of the Seychelles.

CHAPTER FIVE

The correspondence of Brayer du Barré and of Gillot during the period 1772-77 is reproduced extensively by Fauvel, as well as correspondence between the Isle de France administrators and Versailles on the Seychelles colony. Manuscript sources include material filed under C 4/145 AF, a dossier that includes Ternay's comment, dated 12 October 1772, that it might have been better if the Seychelles islands had not existed; Bellecombe's report to Ternay on Gillot, 31 May 1775, under CC 3/15 AF; and Minister of Marine, at Fontainebleau, 29 October 1775, to Maillart Dumesle, referring to Brayer du Barré's claim to have found silver, C 3/16 AF.

Manuscript material at the Mauritius archives includes Gillot's correspondence, in the series TB 7 to TB 14, and letter from Bellecombe and Chevreau, governor and intendant at Pondichéry, to Isle de France, 5 July 1777, confirming report of Brayer du Barré's death, OA 26 A/1.

Fauvel reproduces memoirs and log extracts written by La Pérouse, Bougainville, and Trobriand. Grenier's letter, dated 7 October 1772, in which he refers to his "enemy Rochon", is filed under B 4/125 AF, and a manuscript account of "Campagne de La Pérouse", under Ms 9413 BN.

The offer of a prize of two slaves to first settler to grow a clove or nutmeg bush successfully was published in *Annonces, Affiches et Avis pour les Colonies des Isles de France et de Bourbon,* No 19, 10 May 1775, MA.

1   Others listed as going to Seychelles were the *sieur* Bellabre, *armateur;* Christopher Sales, bourgeois; and three sailor-workers, Pierre Barrière, Charles Haumont, and Jean Fragnio. *Annonces, Affiches et Avis.* No 30, 27 July 1774, MA.

2   Jean-Baptiste, Comte d'Estaing, b. Château de Ravel, Auvergne, 1729. Served in army in India with Lally. In 1759 transferred to navy, and served with distinction in American War of Independence. Vice-admiral, 1777. In 1789 was commandant of National Guard at Versailles. Guillotined, 1794.

3   Leroux Kermoseven was estimated to be worth 1.5 million livres, and owner of 800 slaves. He supplied Suffren's squadron when it called at the Isle de France on its way to India in 1781.

4   Residence of Mon Plaisir, at Pamplemousses, near Port Louis, had been country home for the company's governors. Purchased by Poivre, who created a magnificient garden there, which he handed over to the Crown on leaving the Isle de France in 1772. Under Jean-Nicolas de Céré, it became world famous for its collection of exotic plants. Known successively as Jardin du Roi, Jardin National des Plantes, and, under the Empire, Jardin Impérial.

5   The Portuguese snow *Diamant* arrived at the Isle de France on 3 January 1773 with the remains of the cargo from the *Thélémaque,* wrecked on the west coast of Madagascar. Reported in *Annonces, Affiches et Avis* ... No 1, 13 January 1773, MA.

6   Sartine to Maillart Dumesle, 29 October 1775. It has been claimed, perhaps wrongly, that Brayer du Barré was himself imprisoned for perpetrating the fraud, notably by Eugène de Froberville, who attributes this information to Bellecombe. It is also quoted by Fauvel.

7   *Annonces, Affiches et Avis* ... No 42, 18 October 1775, MA. The notice reads: "The *sieur* Brayer du Barré who plans to go to the Seychelles islands to put his establishment in order, informs those who have claims on him to be good enough to contact the *sieur* de Launay, commercial agent, who will give them satisfaction." The same issue announced the intended departure for Seychelles of M. Forval de Grainville, Chevalier of St Louis; Quienet and Tayeau, merchant

marine officers; Ducurlabatte, surgeon; Martin, Chabois, and Dupont, White workers; a free Black named Joli Coeur; and 31 Indians.

8   Antoine, Chevalier de Guiran Labrillane, governor-general of Isle de France and Bourbon, 1776-79. Naval captain; commodore, 1779. According to contemporaries he was "gentle, honest, helpful, just and virtuous", but because he feared being thought weak he acted with a severity that soon made him unpopular. He asked to be recalled, but died before this happened on 28 April 1779. There were rumours at the time that he had been poisoned.

CHAPTER SIX

Details of Colonel Charles Frederick's stay at Bourbon are given in a letter from Bourbon governor Souillac to the Minister of Marine, 22 April 1777, filed under C 3/17 AF. Correspondence between Souillac, by then governor-general of Isle de France and Bourbon, and Versailles relating to Romainville's term as Seychelles commandant and destruction of spice garden is also filed at the Archives de France, Paris, under C 4/145, as well as being quoted by Fauvel, and by Froberville in *Découvertes et Colonisation des Seychelles,* Paris, 1846.

Dimensions of buildings at the Établissement du Roi, converted to English measurements, are those given by Quinssy and Beguignon on 22 January 1804, TB 21/2 MA, some of which differ from figures contained in Malavois's memoir, dated 1795, quoted by Fauvel. Reference to surviving masonry near State House was made by the then Seychelles archivist Henri McGaw in an article in the Seychelles government *Bulletin,* 4 September 1975.

Gillot's correspondence with the Isle de France administrators, 1775-86, including the affair of Dr Jacquin, and the account of the voyage from Tranquebar of Senhor Anacleto Gomez, of Porto, is filed in the TB series at the Mauritius Archives and under C 4/145 at the Archives de France. Several of the manuscripts are also held at the Seychelles archives. Gillot's comments on spice growing, and letters from Tromelin and Céré are contained in "Lettres du Jardin de l'Isle de France" (Royal Society of Arts and Sciences of Mauritius). The secret instructions to Malavois, 15 November 1786, are filed under TB 10/3 MA.

Correspondence between the East India Company and the Admiralty in London (Lord Hillsborough), 16 and 24 November 1781, on the advisability of destroying the French settlement at Seychelles, is filed under Home Misc. 155, IOL.

Admiral Laplace's description of Tromelin island is quoted in *Îles d'Afrique,* by M.A.P. D'Avezac, Paris, 1848.

1   Fourth Earl of Sandwich, 1718-92, First Lord of the Admiralty in 1778. Gave his

name to the sandwich, which he could eat without having to rise from the gaming table.

2   The detachment was commanded by Sergeant Julien Abraham and Corporal Joseph la Bretonnière. It included a carpenter, cabinet-maker, cooper, locksmith, blacksmith, mason, gardener, baker, and a tailor. The Isle de France Regiment was formed in August 1772, together with the Régiment de l'Isle Bourbon and the Régiment de Port Louis, for the defence of the Mascarene islands. Its uniform was white, with royal blue facings. In 1775 the three regiments were merged into a single Régiment de l'Isle de France, but a year later the Bourbon Regiment had its separate identity restored. The other colonial regiment known to have served in Seychelles was the Régiment de Pondichéry, raised in December 1772. Its uniform was white, with orange facings. Under the regimental numbering system introduced in August 1791, the Régiment de Pondichéry became the 107th Regiment of infantry and the Régiment de l'Isle de France the 108th.

3   Statement by Sergeant Martin Lequieux, 2 April 1785. TB series, MA.

4   Maurice Augustus, Comte de Benyowski. b. 1741. Hungarian adventurer. Taken prisoner by the Russians in 1769 while fighting for Polish independence and banished to the Kamchatka peninsula, in eastern Siberia. Escaped, and reached France in 1772. Invited to form a colony in Madagascar with French volunteers. Made king by Malagasy chiefs in 1776. Quarrelled with the Isle de France administration, which sent a punitive expedition against him. Killed in battle in 1786.

5   The piastre of Spain and Portugal was used as currency in the French colonies before the Revolution, apparently in the belief that it was necessary to prevent the *louis d'or* being exported. In 1767 the piastre was fixed at 5 livres 6 sols; by the 1780s it was worth 10 livres.

CHAPTER SEVEN

Souillac's regulations for the Seychelles, 5 November 1786 and 30 July 1787, are filed at the Mauritius archives. Malavois's proposals for administrative reform and the defence of the islands are reproduced fully in Fauvel's *Unpublished documents* ... Entrecasteaux's correspondence with Minister of Marine on implementing the reforms, September to December 1788, is filed under C 4/145 AF, and his later advice to Malavois to exercise restraint, 28 April 1789, at the Mauritius archives. Minutes of the Seychelles Assembly, 19 and 27 June 1790, with list of suggested reforms *(cahier préliminaire de doléances,* 29 June 1790), and its response to the Isle de France Assembly's offer to include Seychelles as part of the larger colony are also filed at the Mauritius archives.

Details of the Yvon and Gautier mission are recorded in the Register Yvon, Archaelogical Society of Tarn and Garonne, quoted by J. Moine,

"Les Seychelles et la Révolution française" in *Journal of Seychelles Society,* No 7, November 1971.

Lislet Geoffroy's mission to Seychelles is described in an unsigned manuscript, "Voyage aux isles Séchelles par l'Euphrasie, commandé par M. Amiol", Na 12 098, BN, and in a letter from Lislet Geoffroy to Isle de France, TB 11, MA.

1   Antoine de Bruny, Chevalier d'Entrecasteaux. b. 1737. Naval officer, relation of Suffren. Governor-general of the Isle de France and Bourbon, 1787-89. Rear-admiral. Died in 1793 while on a search mission for La Pérouse in the South Pacific.

2   Few documents have been found by the author relating to Caradec, who succeeded Gillot as commandant in September 1787 (the date given by Jean-Michel Filliot in *Histoire des Seychelles,* Paris, 1982). Filliot quotes Caradec, described as a man of character and ability, deploring the Seychellois habit of holding parties every Sunday, when the settlers would frequently get drunk. Caradec's signature appears on papers concerning the Drancourt succession, dated 27 June 1788. TB 22, MA.

3   Thomas, Comte de Conway. Military officer. Governor-general of French establishments east of Cape of Good Hope, 1789-90. Field marshal.

4   David Charpentier de Cossigny. Colonel, Régiment de l'Isle de France. Second-in-command, Isle de France and Bourbon, 1784-85. Governor-general of French establishments east of Cape of Good Hope, 1790-92. General, second-in-command and commander of troops, 1794-95. Field marshal.

5. André Julien Dupuy, counsellor at the Châtelet of Paris, was *intendant-général* from August 1789 to November 1798. He was, with the exception of Poivre, the only Isle de France administrator to hold the full title of intendant. The others were ordonnateur, acting intendant.

6. Daniel Lescallier. b. Lyon, 1743. Charged with missions for the Revolutionary government to St Domingue, Guyane, India, and Seychelles. In 1810 was appointed *préfet maritime* at Le Havre. Baron of the Empire. In 1811 appointed French consul-general in the United States.

CHAPTER EIGHT

The couplet at head of chapter is from *Ode à M. de Séchelles,* by A.L. Thomas, published in Paris in 1756 as tribute to Moreau de Sechelles. Documents relating to the capitulation of the Seychelles are filed at the archives in Mauritius and Seychelles, and at the Archives de France, Paris. Minutes of the Isle de France Colonial Assembly, 3 to 9 Fructidor Year II (20 to 26 August 1794) are filed at the Mauritius archives, under reference

B 16. Captains logs for the *Centurion* and the *Orpheus* are in Admiralty series ADM 51 PRO.

1   Under France's Republican government the aristocratic 'de' was omitted from names.

2   Comment by François Le Roy, naval sub-commissioner, serving as administrative assistant to Quinssy, in a letter to Léger, *préfet colonial* at Isle de France, 2 December 1806. The two men were soon, however, to be enemies.

3   According to the Seychelles museum authorities the name of the artist is not known, although it is possible that the portrait is of a relatively recent date.

4   Captain (later Vice-Admiral) William F.W. Owen.

5   Captain Henry Newcome, as a lieutenant commanding the fireship *Combustion*, had taken part in Sir Edward Hughes' action against Suffren off Madras in February 1782. The following year, in command of Hughes' flagship the *Superb* (74), he was again in action against Suffren, off Cuddalore. Newcome died in 1799. Of the other captains in Newcome's squadron at Seychelles, only Captain Samuel Osborn reached flag rank. He died, as an Admiral of the Blue, in June 1816. Captain Edward Pakenham, who commanded the *Resistance*, took part in the reduction of Dutch possessions at Malacca on 17 August 1795, along with Newcome in the *Orpheus*. In March 1799 Pakenham and almost all his crew were lost when the *Resistance* blew up after being struck by lightning.

6   It was customary to begin each date entry of the ship's log at midday. Thus the capture of the *Deux Andrés* is described as if occuring over two days, 27 and 28 May.

7   The brig *Utilité* was able to take only about 50 of the ex-prisoners, and another ship was sent from the Isle de France to bring back the remaining 148. - Malartic to Minister of Marine, 25 Vendémiaire Year III (16 October 1794).

8   Peter Rainier. b. circa 1741. Entered navy in 1756 and served in East Indies. Lieutenant, 1768. During War of American Independence, while commanding the sloop *Ostrich*, captured American privateer. He was badly wounded in the action. Post-captain, 1778. Returned to East Indies in command of *Burford* (64) in 1779, and took part in all of Sir Edward Hughes' operations. Returned to England at the peace. Commander-in-chief East Indies, 1794-1804. Rear-admiral, 1795; vice-admiral, 1799. Share in prize money amounted to princely fortune. Admiral, 1805. Member of Parliament for Sandwich, 1807. Died 1808, leaving one-tenth of his wealth towards reduction of national debt.

9   Admiralty dispatch to Rear-Admiral Stopford, Cape of Good Hope, 13 June 1811, refers to "several black men called government slaves" serving in ships under Stopford's command. Says this can be permitted, but on no account should

any be allowed to come to England. In another Admiralty dispatch, dated 18 February 1811, advice is given not to have too many Malay seamen in one ship, and to be careful that they do not carry their 'creeses'. In an earlier letter from the Admiralty, 12 April 1799, to Vice-Admiral Sir Roger Curtis, bt, at Portsmouth, reference is made to ships making up their crews with slaves at St Helena, saying that this practice must stop.

10   J.B.G.M. Bory de St Vincent, *Voyage dans les Q.uatre Iles des Mers d'Afrique,* Paris, 1804.

CHAPTER NINE

Early references to the sending of Bourbon settlers to Seychelles include an anonymous memoir, c. 1775, filed under C 4/145, AF, and a letter, dated 19 July 1778, from Bourbon governor Souillac, informing the Isle de France administration of Bourbon settlers wishing to go to Seychelles if they are assured of assistance. Bulk of the source material for this chapter, however, is from the Réunion archives, including settlers' petitions (L 311), the Belleville rebellion and deportation to Seychelles (L 323), and Leboucq's correspondence (L 323 and L 324). Savy's letter to Isle de France Committee of Public Security, 31 July 1798, is filed at Mauritius archives (TB series), and notification of arrival in Seychelles of immigrants from Isle Bonaparte (Réunion) in the brig *Adèle* (8 August 1807), at Seychelles archives, under A 3.26.

On Tippu Sultan and the affair of the two envoys intercepted at Seychelles source material includes report to Executive Directory in Paris and proclamation by the governor-general, Malartic, 29 January 1798, under C 4/112 AF, and Admiralty letters and logs of Captain Alexander in ADM series, PRO. Description of General Dubuc as "preposterous liar" is contained in anonymous memoir, Home Misc. 572, PRO.

Published works provide almost all the material relating to Surcouf and activities of other privateers, notably C. Cunat's *Histoire de Robert Surcouf,* 1842, and *Vie du capitaine Robert Surcouf,* (Anonymous), 1825.

1   A weekly seaplane service had been started in the 1960s between Mombasa and Seychelles to cater for the United States satellite tracking station on Mahé island.

2   In September-November 1790, Bourbon inhabitants petitioning to go to Seychelles included Elie Payet and his wife, Marie-Louise, of St Pierre, who claimed the land they had was not enough to live off. Pierre Gontier, also of St Pierre, and Paul Hoareau, of St Joseph, who pleaded poverty and referred to the increasing population of Bourbon, were also petitioners, as were three merchants, Jean Olivier Sauvé, Pierre Raymond Marais, and Jean Tremblé, who said they had fallen on bad times.

3   Étienne Laurent Pierre Burnel (1762-1835), b. Rennes; soldier at the Isle de France when the Revolution broke out. He became a journalist and secretary of the Colonial Assembly. Returning to France after expulsion from Isle de France he was captured by English. In 1798 was made Directory's agent in Guyane. Refused to serve under Empire or the restored monarchy. René Gaston Baco de la Chapelle (1741-1800), b. Nantes, lawyer, and a deputy for Nantes at Estates-General in 1789. Mayor of Nantes in 1793 and successfully defended city against royalist attack.

4   Address signed by Gillot l'Étang, president of Réunion Assembly, May 1798, L 323, RA.

5   By the beginning of 1804 there was a total of seven men, five women, 14 children and 26 Blacks on La Digue. In charge of the island's administration was Florent Payet, described as a good farmer who had been compromised in the deportations.

6   Tippu Sultan, ruler of Mysore, son of Haidar Ali, traditional ally of the French. Fought four wars against the British. Cruel, vain, and arrogant. At end of the third Anglo-Mysore war, 1790-92, he was forced back to his capital, Seringpatam, and obliged to pay a huge indemnity. But Wellesley, the governor-general, was intent on destroying power of Mysore completely, and provoked fourth Anglo-Mysore war, 1798-99. Tippu Sultan killed at siege of Seringpatam.

7   The powerful *La Forte* frigate had been flagship of Admiral Sercey's squadron, which arrived in the Indian Ocean in 1796 with the Directory agents Baco and Burnel. The action with the *Sybille* took place in February 1799 off the Sandheads, Bay of Bengal. *La Forte's* magazine was hit and ship blew up. *La Forte's* captain, Beaulieu-le-long, was killed.

8   In much of the literature on the Seychelles, the name of Captain Adam is given as MacAdam. This appears to have been the result of a misreading of a manuscript by Fauvel. See this author's article on Admiral Sir Charles Adam, *Mariner's Mirror,* Vol. 63, No 3, August 1977.

9   John Adam. Writer in Bengal establishment, 1794. Private and political secretary to governor-general, Marquis of Hastings. Acting governor-general for nine months, 1823. Died in 1825, off Madagascar, while on way home. Charles Adam's other brothers were William George Adam, auditor to the Duke of Bedford, and General Sir Frederick Adam, who commanded a brigade at Waterloo.

CHAPTER TEN

There is a considerable volume of published memoirs, letters, and other documents on the Jacobin deportations to Seychelles. Manuscript material consulted for this chapter includes: Minister to Bonamy, 21 Nivôse Year IX (11 January 1801) and Bonamy to Minister, 28 Brumaire Year X (11 November 1801), both under C 4/145 AF; Guieysse to Minister, 2 Ventôse

Year IX (21 February 1801), Quinssy to Minister, 5 Vendémiaire Year X (27 September 1801), on assistance given to Guieysse at Seychelles, and sworn statement by crew of the *Flèche*, 2 September 1801, all under BB 4/158 AF; and Magallon to Minister, 3 Vendémiaire Year X (25 September 1801), reporting on imminent arrival of the *Chiffonne* and the *Flèche*, and the effect this would have on the colonies, filed under C 4/148 AF.

On Quinssy's loss of two slaves in the action of the *Chiffonne*, there is a note from the *ordonnateur-général,* Chanvalon, to Magallon, 2 Nivôse Year X (23 December 1801), saying Quinssy cannot be compensated immediately by the government because of lack of funds. "He will have to await a more happy moment," he wrote (TB 11 MA).

For British descriptions of the actions of the *Sybille* and the *Victor,* the captains logs (ADM 51, PRO) have been supplemented by Adam's correspondence (Adam papers, Blair Adam, Kinross-shire), Marshall's *Royal Navy Biography,* and William James's *The Naval History of Great Britain.*

1   The revolutionary (or Republican) Calendar was in official use in France and its colonies from 22 September 1793 (1 Vendémiaire Year II) to the end of 1805 (11 Nivôse Year XIV). Each month, its name derived from the seasons, was of 30 days, the additional days of the Gregorian calendar being tacked on at the end of the year as *jours sans-culottides.*

2   Chevalier, described by Fouché as "a man of atrocious mind and frightening reputation", was arrested in November after the discovery of bomb materials in his room. He was tried by military court and shot with his principal associates on the Plain of Grenelle on 11 January 1801.

3   Louis-Antoine Fauvelet de Bourienne (1769-1834) was a student friend of Napoleon at the Brienne military school. Became his private secretary and accompanied him to Egypt in 1799. Later Counsellor of State, 1801, and Minister in Hamburg, 1804. After Waterloo Bourienne supported the Bourbons; elected deputy to Assembly. Died in a Caen asylum. His *Mémoires de Napoléon,* 10 volumes, is considered not always reliable.

4   Joseph Fouché, Duc d'Otrante. b. 1758, Le Pellerin, near Nantes. Statesman and organiser of French police. Member of Convention, 1792, and voted for execution of the King. Shifted his allegiance frequently. Served in every government from 1792 to 1815. Proscribed as regicide in 1816, and lived abroad. Died at Trieste, 1820.

5   Georges Cadoudal. b. Kerléano, Brittany, 1771. Notary's clerk. Involved in royalist uprising in the Vendée, north-west France, during the Revolution. Last leader of the Chouan guerrilla bands. Surrendered to Republican forces in June 1796, but continued to plot against Republic and First Consul. Arrested in 1804, he was tried and executed. His family was ennobled by Louis XVIII on the

Restoration. The name Chouan comes from the cry of the *chat-huant,* or owl, used as call-sign by followers of the Brittany smuggler Jean Cottereau, alias Jean Chouan, who fought for royalists and was killed in battle in 1794.

6   In Victor Barrucaud's *Les Mémoires de Jean Rossignol,* 1896, no mention is made of the September massacres. Correspondence relating to this period has since disappeared.

7   Constructed as a church at Sainte-Geneviève in Paris, the Panthéon during the Revolution was converted to a temple for the interment of distinguished figures.

8   Charles Pichegru (1761-1804). Sergeant-major in artillery in 1789; made a general in 1793. First a protégé of the Jacobins, a national hero, and, finally, an agent of counter-revolutionary forces. Resigned from army in 1796. The following year he was elected deputy of the Council of Five Hundred. Supported moves against Directory. Deported to Guyane in 1797, but escaped to England and Germany. As a royalist agent returned to France secretly in 1801 to contact Georges Cadoudal. Arrested, and later found strangled by own scarf in the Temple. It is not certain that he killed himself.

9   Pierre Alexander Forfait (1752-1807). Director of naval construction, Le Havre, 1789; Minister of Marine, November 1799 to October 1801.

10   Bory de St Vincent, *op. cit.,* claimed Forfait did not realise that the Seychelles was relatively prosperous as a result of the capitulation, and thought that living on a barren island would have a corrective effect on the deportees' behaviour.

11   Bonamy replaced Captain Jean-Baptiste Gemon on 19 January 1801 (29 Nivôse Year IX), the latter having been in command of the *Flèche* for only one month.

12   François Noël Babeuf (1760-97), known as Gracchus. His political doctrine was forerunner of Communism. Plotted against Directory; arrested, but fatally stabbed himself before he could be executed.

13   9 Thermidor Year II, or 27 July 1794, the day when Robespierre was overthrown by the Convention and the Terror officially ended.

14   On 16 December 1800 Russia, Sweden and Denmark formed the League of Armed Neutrality to combat the British blockade of continental Europe. Prussia joined the league the following year.

15   A slave revolt which broke out in 1791 in St Domingue, one of France's richest Caribbean colonies, resulted after a bloody and protracted struggle in the independence of Haiti, on 1 January 1804.

16   Rossignol addressed the other deportees as they landed, declaring: "Friends, do not despair, you will again see the soil of the motherland. The monster

who has consigned us to this island is destined for a violent end: a modern Nero, his career will finish sooner than you imagine. France will not remain for long under the shackles of its oppressor. He will perish, and his death will be the signal of our deliverance." (quoted by Destrem, *Les déportations du Consulat et de l'Empire*, 1885).

17   Lieutenant Nicholas Mauger was from Guernsey.

18   In the correspondence between Adam and his father there are references to Adam senior's displeasure at his son's gambling. (Adam papers, Blair Adam, Kinross).

19   The *Victor* had been in the Red Sea, employed in the transport of General Baird's troops from India to Egypt. It had already called at Diego Garcia for water and turtles when it encountered the *Flèche*.

20   The invention of the carronade is attributed to General Robert Melville, who had it cast at the Carron company's ironworks, on the banks of the river Carron, in central Scotland. When first introduced in naval ships, additional gun ports were made in the forecastle, quarterdeck, and poop, and the rating of the ship remained unchanged. A 44-gun frigate, for example, was still rated as such though armed with an additional six carronades. By 1781 more than 400 British ships mounted carronades.

21   Bonamy was later to command the *Lion* (74), of the Toulon fleet. In an action against the English off Sète on 25 October 1809 the *Lion* ran aground and was set on fire.

CHAPTER ELEVEN

The accounts given here of the deportees' stay at Seychelles and at Anjouan, and of their various fates, are based largely on Jean Destrem's *Les déportations du Consulat et de l'Empire,* 1885, and the published works by Lefranc and Fescourt. Neither Lefranc nor Destrem, who was related to Hughes Destrem, deported after 3 Nivôse to Cayenne, can be regarded as unbiased.

Other accounts include reports in the newspaper *Le Nouvelliste des Isles de France et de la Réunion,* Brumaire-Ventôse Year X (October 1801-February 1802). Manuscript material includes letters from Quinssy to his friend Jacob de Cordemoy, governor of Réunion, 10 and 19 Vendémiaire Year X (2 and 11 October 1801), L 311, RA; Malavois's warning to the Isle de France administration about the deportees, 15 Pluviôse Year X (4 February 1802), TB 21, MA; and Magallon's correspondence with Minister of Marine, Imam of Muscat, the governor of Mozambique, and with Quinssy, January-June 1803, TB 21, MA.

Anjouan's appeal to Bombay government for assistance against Malagasy raids is filed under Home Misc 511, 16 August 1796, and Home Misc 473, 12 July 1800, IOL; Quinssy's complaints to Léger about conditions in Seychelles, including reference to "miserable little country", 10 Frimaire Year XII (2 December 1803), at Mauritius archives; his remarks about the deportee Laporte, in letter to Decaen, November 1808, WO 1/721, PRO; and Derville's appeal on right to marry, 2 April 1803, A 3.17, SNA.

The descriptions of Anjouan are by British naval officers, Captain G.L. Sullivan *(Dhow chasing in Zanzibar waters,* London, 1873) and Captain W. F.W. Owen and others of the ships *Leven* and *Barracouta (Narrative of voyages to explore the shores of Africa* ..., London, 1873). The meeting in Seychelles with a deportee was described by surgeon James Prior of the frigate *Nisus (Voyage along the Eastern Coast of Africa, Mozambique, Johanna and Quiloa* ..., London, 1819).

1   Colonial Assembly decree, 4 Vendémiaire Year X (26 September 1801).

2   Signatories were Vanheck, Dufour, Corchant, Lefebvre, Lacombe, Monneuse, Maignant, Thirion, and Pépin-Desgrouettes. Despite their testimony against a fellow deportee, only three of the nine were spared from being expelled to Anjouan. They were Pépin-Desgrouettes and Dufour, both of whom died in Seychelles, and Monneuse, last heard of in the Isle de France, in 1809.

3   Denis Decrès, Duke under the Empire. b. 1761. Served in navy in America and in Indian Ocean under Saint-Felix, 1793. Recaptured French ship from Marathas. On arrival back in France in 1794 was arrested on suspicion of being of nobility. Reinstated. Served with Villeneuve in Irish campaign, 1796, and commanded the frigate *Diane* in Bonaparte's Egyptian campaign. Minister of Marine from October 1801 to end of the Empire. Did much to build up navy after excesses of the Revolution. Died in Paris in 1820 as result of assassination attempt by his valet. His name is inscribed on the Arc de Triomphe in Paris.

4   Law of 30 Floréal Year X (20 May 1802).

5   G. Lenotre, *Les derniers terroristes,* 1932.

6   James Prior, surgeon in the frigate *Nisus.* Prior was a literary figure, and wrote biographies of Burke, Goldsmith, and Marlowe. Knighted in 1858. Died at Brighton in 1869, aged 82.

7   The Linage brothers, one a tinsmith, the other an armourer, settled at the Cape, where they ran a successful business. Later Christophe obtained permission to return to France to attend to his affairs, and was commissioned to transport animals to Madame Bonaparte and the Natural History Museum in Paris. He went back to the Cape in 1804. The same year their widowed mother sought permission for their return to France, which was granted.

CHAPTER TWELVE

A substantial part of the source material for this chapter has been provided by the Decaen Papers at the Bibliothèque Municipale of Caen, and the *Mémoires et journaux du Général Decaen,* edited by Ernest Picard and published in 1911. As usual, Fauvel has also been heavily drawn on. Manuscript sources include C 4/148 AF, C 2/278 AF, and C 3/19 Bourbon AF, and at the Seychelles archives, references 3.20, 3.21, and 3.27. On the British side source material includes Admiralty dispatch to Rainier, ADM 2/937 PRO, and captains logs, ADM 51 PRO. Seychelles' measures against smallpox are referred to in TB 21 MA, and population and produce figures for 1807 and 1809 are filed under TB 27 MA.

1   The slave ship *Ulysses* had arrived at Curieuse on 11 September 1803 with 38 cases of smallpox. Many of them died on the island. The surgeon Samouilhan, recording probably the first vaccinations in the Seychelles (the process had been successfully introduced at the Isle de France some months earlier), noted that after vaccinating a negress sent to him by Sausse, "she has shown, up to today, no signs (of the disease), although I used the pus from a patient with severe smallpox". It was not until 1808 that Decaen ordered compulsory vaccination in Seychelles.

2   Linois' force consisted of the *Marengo* (74), the frigates *Belle Poule* and *Sémillante,* and the corvette *Berceau.* The *Atalante* (40) was absent from the action, its having been assigned by Linois to take the government agent Cavaignac to Muscat to set up a French consulate there. The sultan, however, who had been impressed by Britain's ability if it wished to cut off his trade with India, refused to see Cavaignac, and he had to leave empty-handed. Decaen later criticised Linois for detaching a frigate and thereby weakening his main force.

3   By retiring before what he thought was a vastly superior force Linois did exactly what he had determined not to. Writing to his wife Julie from aboard the *Marengo* on 20 Ventôse Year XII (11 March 1803), after the encounter but when still unaware of the true strength of the China convoy, Linois referred to British Indiamen being easily mistaken for ships of the line, adding that he had not forgotten the experience of "one of our brave admirals" who, with a force of six frigates, had failed to engage six Company vessels for that reason. "In the whole of India one is still talking about it," he wrote. To avoid any such reproach he had decided immediately on sighting the convoy to attack, but, before long, realised that here indeed was a much stronger force. Three of the enemy vessels were manoeuvring to take him in the rear, while the rest encircled him. "It was," he wrote, "a decisive moment for the safety of the division," and so he retired. No professional sailor, he declared, could deny that, just as he had attacked with daring likewise he had retired with prudence.

Later, on his arrival back at the Isle de France, Linois learned the awful truth. Although he continued to justify his action, claiming that he had all his officers and men as well as public opinion in the Isle de France behind him, Linois told his wife that after the humiliating way Decaen had received him he could no longer serve with the captain-general and would ask to be recalled. "The correspondence that has taken place between the captain-general and myself, if one day it should come to the notice of the government, will be sufficient to annihilate my adversary and ensure my triumph. All principles, good will, and agreements have been violated by him, while my conduct has been directed with the greatest of care," he wrote on 27 Germinal Year XII (19 April 1804). – Linois correspondence, Musée de la Marine, Paris.

4   In a letter to Quinssy, 4 Prairial Year XIII (24 May 1805), Decaen ordered the arrest of Sausse, and his return to the Isle de France in the schooner *Hippolyte*.

5   The article was reprinted in the *Calcutta Gazette* of 12 December 1804, a copy of which was sent by Decaen to the Minister of Marine, 30 Nivôse Year XIII (19 January 1805).

6   In a daring attack on a French squadron anchored in the natural harbour of Grand Port, on the Isle de France's south-east coast, two British frigates, the *Sirius* and *Magicienne*, were grounded and destroyed and two others, the *Iphigénie* and *Néréide*, were taken. About 2,000 British seamen were captured. The Battle of Grand Port is the only French action of Napoleonic wars fought in the Indian Ocean that is included in the battle honours inscribed on the Arc de Triomphe in Paris. Today, a small museum at Mahébourg, in Mauritius, contains relics of the battle.

7   The Dutch colony of Ceylon, captured by the British during the Revolutionary wars, had been retained by them under the Treaty of Amiens.

8   The frigate *Pitt* was commanded by Captain Thomas Vashon. It had previously been the *Salsette*, to which name it reverted in 1807 after the death of the British Prime Minister, William Pitt.

9   Captain Walter Bathurst. Lieutenant, 1790; post-captain, 1799. On 20 October 1801 he sailed in the *Eurydice* (22) to the East Indies with dispatches relating to the Treaty of Amiens. Removed successively to *Terpsichore* and *Pitt* frigates.

10   The *Duncan* was renamed the *Dover* in 1807.

11   Lord George Stuart. Lieutenant, 1800; post-captain, 1804. Companion of the Order of the Bath. On 8 April 1806, in the frigate *Duncan*, captured a French privateer of eight guns and 71 crew.

12   Captain Sir John Ferrier. Post-captain, 1790; rear-admiral, 1810; commanded the North Sea fleet, with his flag in the *Bellerophon*, 1810-13; vice-admiral, 1814. Described by Nelson as "a man of sense, and as steady as Old Time himself". Ferrier, who had assumed command of the *Albion* on resumption of hostilities in 1803, fell in with the China convoy under Commodore Nathaniel Dance shortly after its brush with Linois in February 1804. At the request of Dance

he accompanied the convoy on its homeward voyage as far as St Helena.

13   The *Drake* was commanded by Sir Fleetwood Pellew, second son of the commander-in-chief East Indies, Sir Edward Pellew (later Lord Exmouth). The sloop *Seaflower* was under the command of Lieutenant William Owen, who was in the 1820s to become well known for his surveys of eastern waters.

14   The uniform of the National Guard, which was known as the Compagnie de Mahé, was blue, with red collar and cuffs, white trim, yellow buttons, and shako. Officers' commissions were granted in February 1810 to the settlers Savy and Esparon.

15   Seychelles census 1807 and 1809, TB 27 MA and A/4 SNA. Seychelles trade was boosted also by the frequent calls of American ships, which were banned from putting in at the Isle de France if they had previously called at the Cape (recaptured by the British in 1806).

CHAPTER THIRTEEN

Little documentation on slavery in Seychelles during the period of French rule has been found. For the lifestyles of slaves resort has had to be made to the probably favourable description given by Baron d'Unienville in *Statistique de l'île Maurice et ses dépendances,* 1838. Marie-Claude Antoine d'Unienville was registrar of the Mauritius Court of Appeal and Colonial archivist, and a committed advocate for retention of slavery under the British. Documents on the Pompé murder trial are filed under A.23 SNA, while a memorandum on the case of Céphale and Fournier can be found under TB 22 MA. Other source material has been traced under CC 3/15 AF and C 4/148 AF. Additional comments on the condition of slaves are by two British naval officers who visited the islands in the 1820s. Slavery was abolished in Seychelles in 1835. The petition by the surviving deportees in Seychelles to the Minister of Marine, 7 May 1807, is quoted by Destrem in *Les déportations du Consulat et de l'Empire,* 1885.

1   James Holman, RN, FRS. Entered navy in 1798; lieutenant, 1807, While serving in *Guerrière* frigate on North American station in 1810 he was blinded in action. Made a Naval Knight of Windsor. During a voyage round the world he visited Seychelles in 1829, aboard the warship *Jaseur* (Captain Lyons).

2   Captain W.F.W. Owen, who visited Seychelles in December 1824.

3   J.T. Bradley, in *The History of Seychelles,* 1940, notes that *bacca,* fermented sugar-cane juice, was mentioned by Malavois in 1787 as being drunk frequently by the inhabitants at meals. Another common drink was *toddy,* or fermented coconut palm juice.

4   Remark attributed to a Lieutenant Cole, of the army's Staff Corps, by Captain Owen.

5   Captain Owen, *ibid.*

6   James Holman.

7   France officially discontinued the Revolutionary Calendar at the end of 1805, reverting to the Gregorian Calendar as from 1 January 1806.

8   Baron d'Unienville, *op. cit.*

9   The members of the Special Tribunal were Quéau de Quinssy (president), Jean-François Hodoul (rapporteur), François Le Roy, and four prominent citizens: Jean Loiseau, Antoine Maurel, Jean-Pierre Langlois, and Henri Delacour.

CHAPTER FOURTEEN

Supplementing the published works by ship's surgeon James Prior and Captain W.H. Smyth on Captain Beaver's visits to Seychelles, manuscript material includes Beaver's letter to Rear-Admiral Stopford, commander-in-chief at the Cape, dated 19 October 1812, under reference CO 167/15 PRO, and Beaver's journal for 1812, filed under MS 32 at the Ministry of Defence Naval Library, London. There are also Governor Robert Farquhar's letters to the Cape, CO 167/15 PRO, and Beaver's note to Quinssy claiming possession of the Seychelles, filed under BB 4/332 AF.

Accounts of Roquebart's squadron at the Isle de France and Réunion, and its subsequent encounter with Schomberg's force off Madagascar are contained in *Le Moniteur,* Paris, 6 October 1811, filed under BB 4/332 AF, and letters from Major-General Henry Wade, acting governor, Mauritius, to the Cape, 12 April 1811, and Lieutenant-Colonel Henry Keating, St Denis, 17 May 1811, both filed at India Office Library, London. The Le Criq affair is reported in the same issue of *Le Moniteur,* and also in a letter from Schomberg, quoted by Marshall in *Royal Navy Biography,* 1823, and in a report from Quinssy to Decrès, 6 June 1811, filed at Mauritius archives.

Sullivan's term as commandant of Seychelles is described in his correspondence with Chief Secretary A. Barry, of Mauritius, between 28 September 1811 and 22 June 1812, under references TB 29/1 MA and TB 29/2 MA. Quinssy's difficulties with British are outlined in correspondence with Governor Farquhar and the Chief Justice, HA 8 MA, and in notes in the *Dictionnaire de Biographie Mauricienne.* Seychelles settlers' petition for retirement of Quinssy, 26 September 1822, is filed under HA 14 MA.

1   Captain Philip Beaver. b. 1766. Clergyman's son. Entered navy at early age and saw service in West Indies, East Indies, and Mediterranean. Associated with colonisation expedition to island of Bulama, off Sierra Leone, 1792-94. Naval officer in charge of landing General Sir Ralph Abercromby's expeditionary force at Aboukir Bay, Egypt, in March 1801. Commander of the frigate *Nisus*, 1810. Died at Cape Town, April 1813.

2   Captain Charles Marsh Schomberg. b. Dublin. Son of Sir Alexander Schomberg, also a naval officer.

3   Only five visits by British warships, not all of which resulted in renewal of the capitulation, have been identified by the author. They are: frigates *Terpsichore* (Captain Walter Bathurst) and *Pitt* (Captain Thomas Vashon), 22-28 August 1805; the frigate *Duncan* (acting Captain Clement Sneyd), 8-13 November 1805: return visit by the *Duncan* (Captain Lord George Stuart), 14-17 June 1806; ship-of-the-line *Albion* (Captain John Ferrier), accompanied by the frigates *Pitt* and *Drake* and sloops *Psyche* and *Seaflower*, 29 August 1806; and the frigate *Dédaigneuse* (Captain William Beauchamp Proctor), 9-13 June 1807.

4   Quoted by W.H. Smyth, *Life and Services of Captain Philip Beaver*, 1829. In his journal Beaver listed his informants as "Mr Sausse, who has been captain of a French merchant vessel for 35 years, the last 30 of which he has navigated in these seas only", Hodoul, senior, and a "Mr Alberade, a seaman who has made, as mate or captain, 17 voyages to Madagascar".

5   Beaver was so indignant as to be almost at a loss for words. In his journal he noted that the islands he had claimed for the officers and men of the *Nisus* "had been granted to an individual a year back, and that individual, a surgeon of one of our frigates, when I arrived on this station! The annoyance – the injustice – the madness – the folly but language is too feeble for me to express my indignation. Mr Farquhar's conduct is almost inconceivable ... yet to complete the business I was refused to cut wood on these islands ... is not this beyond all sufferance?"

6   Baron d'Unienville, *op. cit.*

7   Evidence given by Commander F. Morseby to committee of inquiry into slave trade at Mauritius, 19 May 1826, British Parliamentary Papers, quoted by Jean-Michel Filliot, *Histoire des Seychelles*, 1982.

8   Although Arab trading dhows frequently called at Seychelles up to recent times, Arab influence on the islands has been slight. It is interesting to note, however, that the Arabic word *salaam* appears in Seychelles Creole, not usually as a greeting but in sentences such as *Fer li salanm*, or "Give him my regards", and *In ale san salanm ni goudbay*, which can be roughly translated as "He went off without saying a word".

BIBLIOGRAPHY

Beamish, Tony. *Birds of Seychelles,* Department of Agriculture, Seychelles, 1981.

Boteler, Thomas. *Narrative of a Voyage of discovery to Africa and Arabia, performed in His Majesty's Ships Leven and Barracouta, from 1821 to 1826, under the command of Capt. F. W. Owen, R.N.,* 2 vol., London, 1833.

Bradley, J.T. *The history of Seychelles,* 2 vol., Victoria, Seychelles, 1940.

Cunat, C. *Histoire de Robert Surcouf,* Paris, 1842.

Dayer, P. L. *Les Îles Seychelles: esquisse historique,* Fribourg, 1966.

Destrem, Jean. *Les Déportations du Consulat et de l'Empire,* Paris, 1885.

Fauvel, A.A. *Unpublished documents on the history of the Seychelles anterior to 1810,* Victoria, Seychelles, 1909.

Fescourt, M. *Histoire de la Double Conspiration de 1800,* Paris, 1810.

Foster, William (ed.) *The Journal of John Jourdain, 1608-1617,* Hakluyt Society, Cambridge, 1905.

Froberville, Eugène de. "Îles africaines de la Mer des Indes", in *Îles d'Afrique,* M. A.P. d'Avezac (ed.), Paris, 1848.

Grenier, Chevalier de. *Mémoires de la campagne de découvertes dans les mers des Indes,* Brest, 1770.

Holman, James. *Voyage round the World,* 4 vol., London, 1834.

Jenkins, E.H. *A history of the French Navy,* London, 1973.

Lefranc, J.B. *Les infortunés de plusieurs victimes de la tyrannie de Napoléon Bonaparte,* Paris, 1816.

Lenotre, G. *Les derniers terroristes,* Paris, 1932.

Lionett, Guy. *The Romance of a Palm: Coco-de-Mer,* Victoria, Seychelles, 1972.
    Striking plants of Seychelles, Victoria, Seychelles, 1981.
    The Seychelles, Harrisburg, Pa, USA, 1972.
    La Geste Française aux Séchelles, La Réunion, 1987.
    Les mémoires imaginés de J.B. Quéau de Quinssy, La Réunion, 1988.

Ly-Tio-Fane, M. *Mauritius and the Spice Trade,* 1 *The Odyssey of Pierre Poivre,* Port Louis, Mauritius, 1958. 2 *The Triumph of Jean-Nicolas Céré and his Bourbon collaborators,* Paris and The Hague, 1970.

Marshall, John. *Royal Navy Biography,* London, 1823.

Parkinson, C. Northcote. *War in the Eastern Seas, 1793-1815,* London, 1954.

Prior, James. *Narrative of a voyage in the Indian Seas on the Nisus frigate during the years 1810 and 1811,* London, 1820.

Rochon, Alexis, *Voyage à Madagascar, au Maroc, et aux Indes Orientales,* 3 vol., Paris, 1791 and 1801-02.

Roncière, Charles de la. *Le Filibustier mystérieux: Histoire d'un trésor caché,* Paris, 1934.

Scarr, Deryck. *Seychelles since 1770,* London, 2000.

Smyth, W.H. *Life and Services of Captain Philip Beaver,* London, 1829.

Thiry, Jean. *La Machine Infernale,* Paris, 1952.

Thomas, Athol. *Forgotten Eden,* London, 1968.

Toussaint, Auguste. *Histoire de l'Océan Indien,* Paris, 1961.
    Histoire des îles Mascareignes, Paris, 1972.
    La route des îles. Contribution à l'histoire maritime des Mascareignes, Paris, 1967.
Unienville, Baron A.M. d'. *Statistique de l'île Maurice et ses dépendances, suivi d'une notice historique sur cette colonie,* Paris, 1838.
Wanquet, Claude. *Histoire d'une Révolution: La Réunion, 1789-1803.* 3 vol., Marseille, 1980.
Webb, A.W.T. *The story of the Seychelles,* Victoria, Seychelles, 1964.

SEYCHELLES CAPITULATION

The following is the text of the document, signed on 17 May 1794 by the Seychelles commandant, Captain Jean-Baptiste Quéau de Quinssy, and Captain Henry Newcome, of the British frigate *Orpheus*, setting the terms for the surrender of the colony. It was renewed several times, with amendments, by Quéau de Quinssy until hostilities finally ended in 1811.

Jean-Baptiste Quéau Quinssy, capitaine au Régiment de Pondichéry No 107, commandant militaire et agent civil pour la République française aux Îles Mahé ou Seychelles, Praslin et autres adjacentes, propose la capitulation suivante au Commodore Newcome, commandant l'Orpheus pour S.M. Britannique, la division et l'expédition particulière composée du Centurion, capitaine Osborn, et de la Resistance, Com. Packenham, d'après sa sommation en date du 16 mai 1794:

Article 1:
La Colonie, place, et la batterie de l'Isle Mahé ou Séchelles, Praslin et toutes ses dépendances, se rendent au Commodore Newcome le 17 mai presente année à 9 heures du matin. La garnison anglaise s'emparera des postes, batteries, bâtiments civils, et le pavillon anglais sera hissé sur la place.
— I shall take possession of the Colony of Mahé and its dependencies.

Article 2:
La batterie de la place tirera trois coups par pièces à boulet; il sera fait trois décharges de mousqueterie avant d'amener le pavillon français
— Agreed.

Article 3:
Les propriétés des habitants seront respectées; Il ne leur sera causé aucun trouble ni dommage dans leurs biens, meubles, immeubles, vaisseaux, marchandises, esclaves et dans leur personne, en aucune manière.
— Private property shall be protected. The inhabitants and their slaves shall remain unmolested. I take the brig Olivette.

Article 4:
Les batteries, munitions, canons, magazines, tous les bâtiments civils et effets appartenant à la République ne seront point touchés, tout restera dans l'état actuel.
— The cannons, military stores and effects belonging to the Republic, in their magazines, shall remain at my disposal. The public buildings will be preserved. The two small pieces carrying 2lb balls, shall only be permitted to remain on the parade facing the governor's house, for the purpose of making signals in case of insurrection amongst the slaves.

Article 5:
Le commandant militaire et agent civil ne sera point fait prisonnier de guerre.
— He shall be prisoner of war during my stay only.

Article 6:
Les registres, papiers utiles aux citoyens habitants et ceux de la République pour la comptabilité seront respectés, non visités; étant intéressant pour les families et pour l'état que des choses aussi nécessaires soient conservées.
— Agreed.

Article 7:
La dite capitulation fait de bonne foi sera garantie par la signature du Commodore Newcome et signée par le commandant militaire et Agent Civil et par trois citoyens habitants des Seychelles représentant le corps des citoyens des Îles Mahé ou Seychelles et Praslin.
— Agreed.

Fait à Mahé, Îles Seychelles, le 17 mai 1794.
Done on board H.B.M. ship Orpheus, in the roads of Mahé
or Seychelles, the 17th May 1794.

    (signed) Jn Bte Quéau Quinssy   Henry Newcome
        Hangard
        Nageon de l'Étang
        Cornier Bellevaut

INDEX

Only ships that are known to have called at Seychelles are listed, under *Ships*. Names of Seychelles commandants are indicated with an asterisk. Abbreviations include: comdt. for commandant and, in some cases, also civil agent of Seychelles; gov.-gen., for governor-general of the Isle de France and Bourbon or, after 1789, of the French establishments east of the Cape of Good Hope.

Abdullah bin Mohamed, sultan of Anjouan, 184-9 *passim*.
Aboukir, battle of, 231.
Adam, Capt. Charles, 145; and capture of frigate *Chiffonne*, 165-7; renews Seychelles capitulation, 167; 167-9, 171; biog., 250.
Aden, 23.
Admiralty, British: endorses plan to attack Seychelles, 88; 173, 240.
Africa: source of slaves, 15, 222-3; influence on Seychelles music and dance, 225; population from, 249; East African coast, 17, 21, 147.
Agaléga (Galéga), 18, 52, 194, 201, 232.
albreolhos (reefs), 18.
Aldabra: *See under* Seychelles islands.
Alexander, Capt. Thomas: capture of corvette *Surprise*, 141; and envoys of Tippu Sultan, 141-4; biog., 250.
Algeciras, battle of, 200.
America, 24, 28; war of independence, 57, 83, 89, 120, 147; shipping in Indian Ocean, 146, 214; whaling at Seychelles, 248.
Amirantes, 12; sighted by Vasco da Gama, 17; 18, 22; reconnoitred by Duroslan and Labiollière, 57-8, 59-60, 66; 76; claimed by Seychelles, 112; 163, 168, 193; Seychelles takes possession, 204. *For individual islands, see under* Seychelles islands.
Anjouan: and French deportees, 181-189 *passim*; climate and inhabitants, 183-4; and Malagasy raiders, 185; attachment to English, and offers to cede island, 185, 237; 199.
*Anselme, acting comdt, 73.
Arabs: in Indian Ocean, 11, 14; Omani, 18; attack English at Pemba, 21; massacred by English, 21-2; victims of pirates, 23; and Anjouan, 183; 186, 248; Arabia, 21.
Armed Neutrality, League of, 161.
Asia: and coco de mer, 41, 42; 135.
Audibert, settler, 108.
Austria, 28, 83; War of Austrian Succession, 18, 24, 147.

Avice, settler, 220.

Babeuf, François, French revolutionary, 160, 182.
Baco de la Chapelle, René, Directory agent, 136, 162.
Baird, Gen. Sir David, 141.
Barré: and discovery of coco de mer, 39, 43.
Bastille Day, 163.
Bataille, surveyor, 98, 99.
Batavia, 237, 240.
Bathurst, Capt. Walter, 214.
bats, 13, 33, 220.
Batt, Lieut. John: fails to catch Surcouf, 145.
Beaver, Capt. Philip, 231; and deal over prize money, 232, 237, 238-9; and Quinssy, 233; criticised by Admiralty for excessive severity, 233; his claim to Seychelles, 234, 237, 238-9; told of short route to India, 234-5; and Bombay Jack, 237; dies, 240; 242.
Beguignon, assistant to Quinssy, 190, 204; report on Seychelles, 174-5; returns to Isle de France, 193, 226; attitude to deportees, 228.
Bellecombe, comdt of Bourbon, 78-9, 220.
Bellevaut, Capt. Cornier, settler, 123-4.
Belleville, Étienne, ex-army sergeant: and insurrection, 136-7; deportation and return, 137-9.
Bengal, 28, 113, 145, 161; merchants of, 146, 206; Bay of Bengal, 150; route to, 16, 50, 234; and Surcouf, 146-50 *passim*; 210.
Benyowski's Volunteers, 96.
*Berthelot de Ia Coste, Lieut., comdt, 88, 89, 93.
Betia, Elisabeth, queen of Ste Marie, 47.
Blacks, free or freed: restriction on settling in Seychelles, 111, 116; 121; as slave owners, 74, 221, 222. *See also* slavery.
Blin, Capt. Michel, settler: and Amirantes, 204; and Hangard, 214; his estate and schooner destroyed, 215; as slave owner, 222, 226.
Boileau, Capt., settler, 93, 108.
Bombay, 134, 186, 206; Council (East India Co.) sends ship to Seychelles, 65; *Bombay Courier* newspaper, 209.
Bombay Jack (Mubarak Kumba Bomboxak): befriends deportees, 186; character, 238; passenger in *Nisus*, 237-8.
Bonamy, Lieut. Eustace, 159; at Réunion, informs Isle de France of deportees, 168, 169; action against *Victor*, 170-3; praised by Quinssy, 193.
Bonaparte, Napoleon, 56; and Egypt, 132, 141; and Surcouf, 150; escapes assassination, orders deportations, 152-8 *passim*, 228; retains slavery,

179-80; and deportees, 176, 185, 187, 188, 197; and Decaen, 192, 199-200; 205; emperor, 205; criticises Linois, 206; 209; his Code Civil received at Seychelles, 227; and St Criq court-martial, 243-4.
Boscawen, Adml, Edward, 20.
Bougainville, Louis Antoine, 45, 58; report on Seychelles, 74-5; biog., 250.
Bourbon, 15, 24; and spice growing, 62-3, 79, 105; settlers to Seychelles, 77, 85, 94, 102, 105, 135; and English spy, 84; representation in National Assembly, 108; and Ramalinga family, 111; 116; renamed Réunion, 136; captured by English, 231; 232, 235; transfer of slaves, 244. *See also* Réunion.
Brayer du Barré, Henri, 63-4; and first Seychelles settlement, 63-8 *passim*, 72-3; complains about Poivre, 67; and Hangard, 72-3; further requests to Versailles, 72-3, 75-6; decision on his removal, 76; attempts fraud, 80; names bay after Sartine, 80; goes to Seychelles, 81; complaints about his behaviour, 81; in India, where death confirmed, 82; 93, 135, 248.
Brazil, 161.
Brest, 45, 56, 200, 210, 232.
Bruneau la Souchaire, settler, 220.
bullion, 132; gold coin, 232, 240.
Burnel, Étienne: *See* Baco de la Chapelle.

Cadoudal, Georges, Chouan leader, 153.
Calais, settler, 190.
Calcutta (Fort William), 28, 145.
Calicut, 17.
Canada, 28, 29, 77.
Cape of Good Hope, 14, 21, 65, 84, 88, 115, 140, 161, 162, 168, 186, 188, 199, 210, 231, 239, 240.
Cape Verde islands, 161, 212.
capitulation, 124, 128-9, 131, 199; and flying of French flag, 126, 129, 211; capitulation flag, 127, 132, 167, 174, 208, 218; English accused of breaking terms, 132; and deportees, 164; renewed, 167, 173, 208, 217; Decaen's attitude to, 203, 216; and settlers, 204; supported by Linois, 211; not renewed, and consequences, 215-6; Decaen acquiesces in, 217; and final surrender, 233.
*Caradec, 106.
Cargados Carajos (St Brandon), 50-2.
Caribbean, 23; loss of St Domingue (Haiti), 205.
carronades: in *Victor*, 170; damage caused to *Flèche*, 172.
Cayenne, 63, 79.

cayman: *See* crocodiles.
Céré, Jean-Nicolas, botanist, 79; advises Gillot, 87-8.
Ceylon, 54, 91, 131, 147, 210, 212.
Chagos archipelago, 18, 66.
Chandernagore, 28, 113.
Charpentier de Cossigny, David, gov.-gen., 112-4 *passim*.
Chevalier, bomb-maker, 153, 156.
Chevreau, Étienne, acting intendant, 88, 96, 100.
Chinese: in Indian Ocean, 14; as Seychelles inhabitants, 249.
cholera, 184.
Chouans, 154.
Chrétien, Pierre, deportee, 156, 182; drowns off Grande Comore, 187.
cinnamon, 66, 68, 88, 103, 111, 248. *See also* spices.
citrus plants, 195.
cloves, 68, 70, 87, 111, 142, 195, 222, 248. *See also* spices.
Coco de mer, 19, 35; legend, 35-7; descriptions of nuts and palm, 37-9, 43, 69; as aphrodisiac, 37, 42-3; discovery, 39; identified by Poivre, 41; find exploited, 41, 65, 68, 72; habitat, 42; Rochon's theory of distribution, 42; specimen for Paris, 54; Crown monopoly, 102; saved from extinction, 248.
cocoa, 76, 111, 248.
coconuts, 14, 22, 23, 58, 76; restriction on collecting, 101, 111; 127; oil, and as substitute for soap, 66, 191, 243, 248.
coffee, 65, 76, 218, 222.
Collet, officer of *Duguay Trouin*, 126-7 *passim*.
Collier, Capt. George: action against *Flèche*, 170-3 *passim*; promotion, 173; renews capitulation with Quinssy, 173; at Praslin, 173; sold *Flèche*, 199; biog., 251.
Columbus, Christopher, 55.
Comoro islands: Grande Comore, 21, 187; Anjouan, 180, 183-4; and deportees, 183-8 *passim*.
Compagnie des Indes, 11, 15, 26, 29.
Conan, surgeon, 108, 114.
conseil de commune, 226.
Conway, Thomas, Comte de, gov.-gen., 106, 107, 111.
Cook, Capt. James, 44.
Cordemoy, Jacob de, gov. of Réunion, 136, 188.
cotton, 65, 103, 147, 194; acreage increased, 218; 222, 238, 248.
Créole: definition, 222; various types, 255-6; language, 286.
crocodiles: described by Picault, 13; Jourdain's allagartes, 22; 25; threat to seamen, 31; and sharks, 31-2; extinction on Mahé, 32; on other

islands, 39, 58, 59, 69; Rochon's comments, 53; 118; scarcity, 194.
Cuddalore, 120, 201.
cyclones, 69.

Da Gama, Vasco, 17; biog. 251.
Dalrymple, Alexander, hydrographer, 44, 52.
Dance, Nathaniel, commodore of China convoy, 206.
D'Après de Mannevillette, Jean-Baptiste, hydrographer, 45; his *Neptune Oriental*, 51, 163, 243; criticised by Rochon, 52; and Duroslan's comment, 59; biog., 251-2.
Darwin, Charles, 230.
De Boynes, Minister of Marine, 72, 74, 75.
Decaen, Gen. Charles Isidore, capt.-gen., 132, 139; and deportees, 192, 196, 228; and Seychelles capitulation, 194, 204, 211, 214, 215, 218; reluctance to accept post, 199; and Linois, 200, 210-2 *passim*; at Pondichéry, 201-2; arrives at Isle de France, 202; 203, 204; and Capt. Sausse, 208; 210, 227; surrenders, 232; biog., 252.
Decrès, Denis, Minister of Marine, 180, 187; and deportees, 188, 191; 202, 207, 217; approves Seychelles capitulation, 217; and St Criq, 243.
*Delaunay, Maj., comdt, 64-6, 67-8, 70; neglects duties, 72; leaves Seychelles, 73; 66.
Deportees: *from France:* arrests, 155; first group sails, 158; second group sails, 159; those who return, 159, 196; arrival at Mahé, 164, 171; 169; tutors for settlers' children, 165; 166; plan to remove, 176-9; half sent to Anjouan, 181-2; their fates, 186-8; escape from Seychelles, 189; ill-treatment and neglect, 190; reports on behaviour, 191, 228; plea to marry, 192; their health and deaths, 195-6; settle in Isle de France, 196, 229; remainder in Seychelles, 196-7; petition to Minister, 228-9; *from Réunion:* 135; insurrection leaders sent to India, 137-8; at La Digue, 138; their return, 139; deportee Jean Laporte, 182; *during British administration,* 248.
Derville, Georges, deportee, 157, 177; request to marry, 191; dies, 192; effects sold, 192.
Desroches, François Dudresnay, gov.-gen., 49, 54, 56, 64.
D'Estaing, Comte de, 74, 147.
Diego Garcia, 18, 59; and English outpost, 66, 97; 194; and French trading post, 243.
D'Offay, settler, 94, 108.
Drake, Sir Francis, 20, 146.
Drancourt, Capt., settler, 93, 108.
Dubuc (Dubriq) Gen., 141, 143, 144.

Duchemin, Capt. Jean, 30-5 *passim*; names La Digue island, 40; 41; annexes Seychelles archipelago, 41; and coco de mer, 41; 49, 68.
Dufresne, Capt. Marc Joseph Marion; expedition to Seychelles, 30-5, 37-41; 56, 67; biog., 252.
Dumas, Col. Jean-Daniel, gov.-gen., 29, 46, 49.
Dumont, Louis, settler: quoted, 231.
Dupont, settler, 215.
Dupuy, André, intendant, 114-5, 121, 128.
Duroslan, Lieut., 54, 57; at Amirantes, 57-8; at Mahé and Praslin, 58-9; usefulness of reports noted by D'Après and Minister, 59.
Dutch, 18; and spices, 20, 62; 65, 88; East Indies, 142, 237.

Egypt, 132, 141, 142.
Elisabeth, Queen, 20.
England (Great Britain): and rebellion of American colonies, 83, 89; 120, 161; peace negotiations with France, 179; renewal of war, 190, 198; 238.
English (British), 18; in India, 18-21 *passim;* ship calls at Seychelles, 22-3; interest in Seychelles, 24, 30, 65-6, 72, 76, 104; and coco de mer, 41; and Seychelles capitulation, 122-9 *passim;* and privateers, 147; 162; and Anjouan, 183, 185, 205; lack of knowledge of sea routes, 234-5; administration of Seychelles, 248-9.
*Enouf, Charles, comdt, 116-8, 129, 130.
Entrecasteaux, Joseph de Bruny, gov.-gen., 104, 106-7.
equator, 50, 52, 73, 103.
Établissement (Victoria), 85; and repairs to buildings, 98, 195; 108, 113, 122, 192, 205, 216, 225, 243.
Europe, 18, 20, 23; war in, 28, 121, 205; 102, 134; and cotton, 238; 249.

Farquhar, Sir Robert, bt, British governor of Mauritius (Isle de France), 234; and Beaver, 237-40 *passim*; and slavery, 240-1.
Fernando, slave, 182; at Anjouan, 185.
Ferrier, Capt. John: renews capitulation with Quinssy, 217.
fish, 13, 22, 25, 33, 40; fish oil, 66; salted fish (*poisson salé*), 66, 164; 140; fishing, 35, 230
Flemish, 14, 21.
Forfait, Minister of Marine, 157-8, 162, 164, 180.
Fouché, Joseph, Minister of Police, 154-6 *passim*; 189.
Foulepointe, 47, 236, 241, 243.
France: and Indian Ocean, 15; and war, 20, 25-6, 88, 179-80, 190, 198, 203, 206; and Seychelles, 25-7, 28, 103, 108, 232; and India, 28,

142-3; finances, 61; and colonies, 83, 115, 135; constitutional monarchy, 115; Directory, 136, 141, 144, 150, 160, 162; Empire, 205.

Frederick, Col. Charles, of Bombay army, 84.

Frégate: and pirates, 23; 37, 103, 111, 116, 170, 179, 182, 233.

French Revolution, 49, 56; impact on Indian Ocean colonies, 107-8, 111-2, 135, 163; and the Terror, 120, 160, 163; 197; fall of Bastille, 155; uprising in Vendée, 156; 227, 242.

Froberville, Eugène de, 16; and coco de mer, 17, 38, 42.

Ganges, Mouths of (Sandheads), 145, 149.

Gautier, Col, of Pondichéry Regt, 113-5 *passim*.

George III, 196, 233, 244.

Gilles, Claude, canteen owner, 205.

*Gillot, Antoine, settler and comdt: and spice garden, 68-70, 73, 78-9, 86-7, 100; at Praslin, 69; saved from drowning, 69; financially ruined, 69; and Hangard, 71-2, 93-4, 98; his haemorrhoids, 78, 89-90, 95; quoted, 83; relations with settlers and soldiers, 87, 89-90, 93-5 *passim*, 98-9, 100; and Quienet, 87, 94, 97-100; and slaves, 69, 78, 79, 94; appointed commandant, 89; quarrel with Jacquin, 95-6; affair of missing piastres, 96-9; reprimanded, 98-9; replaced, 100; 101, 118, 221; biog. 252-3.

Glaud, Capt., settler, 80.

Goate, Lieut. William, 123.

Gordon, Gen. Charles of Khartoum, 248.

Grand Port, Isle de France, battle of, 209, 234.

Grenier, Lieut., Jacques: quoted, 44; commanding *Heure du Berger*, 45; and shorter route to India, 46, 49-50, 54-5, 234; and Madagascar, 46-7; and Poivre, 49; avoids shipwreck, 50-1, 54; criticised by Rochon, 51; study of currents, 52; and Seychelles, 50, 52-4, 57-60 *passim*, 73; return to France, 54-5; commanding *Belle Poule*, 55; appointed to *Boudeuse*, 57; dies, 57; 81, 200; biog., 253.

Grossin, Jean, 11, 13, 16, 19, 23.

Guyane, 159.

Guieysse, Capt. Pierre, 160-2 *passim*; at Seychelles, 163, 165; and action against *Sybille*, 165-6; 168; biog. 253-4.

Guiran Labrillane, Antoine, gov.-gen., 82; dies 86.

Halley, Edmund, astronomer, 44.

Hangard, Pierre, settler, 70; character, 71-2; and Gillot, 72, 93-4, 98, 100; and Brayer du Barré, 71, 72; acquires Sainte Anne settlement, 72;

marriage of daughter 94; 100, 101, 108, 125; loss of pirogue and crew, 213-4; quoted, 219; as slave owner, 222.
Hérisson, settler, 190.
Hodoul, Capt. Jean-François, privateer and settler, 128, 146, 151, 175, 214; member of tribunal trying slave Pompé, 228; biog., 254.
Hughes, Adml Sir Edward, 88.
Hulot, Lieut., 179, cruelty to deportees, 183; 185, 199, 203.

Ibn Battuta, Arab traveller: and coco de mer, 43.
India, 15; route to, 16-7, 20, 24, 30, 45-6, 49-50, 55, 60, 84, 180, 235; Coromandel coast, 16, 19, 50, 206; Malabar coast, 16, 19, 28, 37, 209, 210; 18-21 *passim*, 26; war in, 28, 88; and coco de mer, 35-6, 41, 42, 43, 65; 56, 82, 138, 168, 189, 234.
Indian, 14; troops for Seychelles, 103, 121; inhabitants of Seychelles, 249.
Indian Ocean, 14, 16, 17, 18, 21, 24; areas not charted, 45; theatre of war, 120; 135, 161, 199, 200, 210, 231, 244.
Isle de France, 11; supply of tortoises, 12, 85-6; 13; and La Bourdonnais, 15, 16; 20, 25, 29; and Poivre, 29, 54, 62; spice growing, 29, 62-3, 87, 105; 61, 78, 83, 84, 101; financial constraints, 89; 103, 104; and slave ships, 105-6; and French Revolution, 105, 111, 112-5; proposal to Seychelles, 108-10; National Assembly commissioners, 113-7; smallpox, 116-7; and Seychelles capitulation, 126-9 *passim*; and blockade, 130, 205, 211; abolition of slavery rejected, 136; affair of Baco and Burnel, 136, 162; 139; and Tippu Sultan, 142, 143; 167; and privateers, 147, 148, 149, 150, 209; surrender, 147, 196, 209, 218, 231, 232, 234; and deportees, 162, 170, 175-96 *passim*, 229; 174, 193, 199, 201; Decaen assumes command, 202; battle of Grand Port, 209; Linois leaves, 210; 217.
Isle de France Regt; detachment to Seychelles, 85; 88; withdrawn, 90.
Isle de Palme (Praslin), 19, 26.

Jacobins: club in Isle de France, 128; club in Réunion, 136, 162, 175, 176.
Jacquin, surgeon; quarrel with Gillot, 95-6; and missing piastres, 96-8.
Jardin du Roi (Spice garden), 62, 68, 70, 78, 79, 86-7, 100, 105, 111.
Java, 235, 243.
Jean de Nove atoll, 12, 41.
Joly, René, deportee, 182; drowns off Grande Comore, 187.
Jones, Thomas, bosun: quoted, 11; 21, 22.
Jorre de St Jorre, settler, 108, 110; widow St Jorre, 191; 247.
Jourdain, John, ship's factor, 21, 22; biog. 254-5.
justice of peace (*juge de paix*), 227, 244, 246, 247.

Kerguelen, Capt. Yves-Joseph, 55, 56.

Labiollière, Capt., 57, 59, 60, 88.
Lablache, Quinssy's son-in-law, 244.
La Bourdonnais, Mahé de, gov.-gen., 15, 16, 18, 20, 30; and use of privateers, 147; biog. 255.
Laccadive islands, 201, 234.
Lacombe, Bertrand, deportee: wife quoted, 175; 182.
Lacour, settler, 214.
La Digue, 37, 40, 57; annexed by France, 58; 59; and crocodiles, 59; 76, 117; deportees from Réunion, 135, 138, 139; 148, 183, 197.
Lafitte, Capt Joseph, 180, 183, 188.
Lafontaine, Capt., 49, 51, 52.
Lafosse, Jean, deportee, 136, 137, 139.
Lambert, Pierre, settler, 93, 94, 100.
Lampériaire, Lieut., 30, 35, 37, 38, 39; raises flag at Anse Possession, Praslin, 40; 41, 65, 74.
Langlois, settler, 226.
langouti (waist cloth), 223.
La Pérouse, Jean-François, 45; at Seychelles, 74, 75; biog. 255.
Laplace, Admiral, 92-3.
Laporte, Antoine, deportee, 182, 186.
Laporte, Jean, deportee from Réunion, 182.
Larcher, Madame, friend of deportee Derville, 192.
Laurence, free black, 121.
Lebeuze (Lebeuge), settler, 94, 108, as slave owner, 222.
Leboucq Santussan, Jean-Nicolas; quoted, 134; 139-40; deported, 140; controversy over Tippu Sultan's envoys, 143-4; 145; insists on leaving Seychelles, 175.
Lefranc, Jean-Baptiste, deportee, 156; writings on deportation, 159; role in Revolution, 159-60; complaints against Guieysse, 160, 161; 164; settler employs him as architect, 165; selected for Anjouan, 182; complaint against Hulot, 183; at Anjouan, 185; escape and return to France, 187; letter intercepted, 188; 196.
Léger, Louis, préfet colonial, 191, 202, 214, 216, 221, 227.
Lemême, Capt., privateer, 146, 150; capture and death, 208-9.
Le Nouvelliste, newspaper of Isle de France, 175, 182, 188.
Le Prédou, surgeon, 122.
Leroux Kermoseven, 77.
Le Roy, François, administrative assistant, 226; opinion of deportees, 228-9; attempts to save turtles, 229; and frigate *Clorinde*, 241; 244.

*Lesage, Lieut. Bibye, comdt, 246; biog., 255-6.
Lescallier, Daniel, commissioner, 115-7 *passim*.
lettres de marque, 147.
Le Vasseur, Olivier (La Buse), pirate, 24.
Lewis, Lieut.; reports on settlement, 65.
L'Hermitte, Capt., privateer, 150.
Linois, Adml Alexandre, 199; character, 200; quarrel with Decaen, 200; at Pondichéry, 201-2; at Isle de France, 202-3; failure to take China convoy, 206; withdrawal before *Centurion's* defence, 206; departure from Indian Ocean, 209; final break with Decaen, 210-3; at Seychelles, 211-2, 203; backs Quinssy over capitulation, 212, 217; taken prisoner 213; 214; biog. 256.
liquor: excessive drinking in Seychelles, 205; restrictions on sale of, 205, 225; slaves' liking for, 223; deleterious effects, 223.
Lislet Geoffroy, Jean-Baptiste, surveyor, 117-8.
Loiseau, Capt., 138.
Loiseau, Jean, settler, 244, 247.
Long Pier, Victoria, 134.
Louis XV, 26, 28, 61, 75.
Louis XVI, 75, 115, 118, 120.

Machabée (Domingue), slave, 94.
machine infernale, 197.
Madagascar, 11, 14-7 *passim*; and pirates, 23; visited by Grenier, 46-9; French settlements, 46-7, 49; 50, 56, 65, 88, 92, 96, 139, 141, 158, 161, 189; used by English ships to replenish supplies, 205, 211, 214; 216, 232, 236.
Madeira, 161, 183.
*Madge, Edward, comdt., 246; quarrel with Quinssy, 246-7; character, 247; biog., 256.
Madras, 20, 75, 120, 125, 141, 143, 146, 168, 202, 231.
Magallon de la Morlière. François, gov.-gen., 161-2; and deportees, 163, 179, 184, 189-90; 192, 199; biog. 256-7.
Magon, Capt. Charles, 113; biog. 257.
Magon de la Villebague, René, gov.-gen., 24.
Mahé, 19; site of treasure, 23; Morphey's visit, 24-6; 57; Duroslan's visit, 58; advantage of military detachment, 83; proposals for settlers, 101-2; Malavois' survey, 102-4; land grants, 105; 126; calls by English warships, 132; steamship service, 134; 135, 138; Surcouf's visit, 147-9; 163; healthy location, 164; 169, 170, 171, 184; destruction of forest, 194; visit by Linois, 211; 217; and Isle de France surrender,

218; 219; ladies of Mahé, 224; and British take-over, 233; visit by *Clorinde*, 241-2; British flag restored, 244.

Mahé island: *place names:* Anse Baleine, 117; Anse Boileau, 216; Anse Bougainville, 117; Anse Forbans, 93, 117; Anse Intendance, 117; Anse à la Mouche, 87, 97, 98, 99, 216; Anse aux Pins, 165, 241; Anse aux Poules Bleues, 33, 117, 219; Anse Royale, 62, 68, 70, 72, 78, 86, 117, 220; Anse Soleil, 219; Baie Lazare, 11, 219; Barbarons, 117; Beau Vallon, 93, 135; Bel Ombre, 93; Boileau Bay, 117; Cap Ternay, 118; Grand Anse, 117; Machabée, 93; North Point, 213; North East Point, 180; North West Bay, 93, 113, 213; Petite Anse, 219; Police Bay, 117; Pointe Conan, 165; Pointe Launay, 165; Pointe Larue, 143; Port Glaud, 117, 215; Port Launay, 117; Port Royal, 19, 24, 26; Port St Lazare, 11; Rivière au Caïman, 33; Rivière St Louis, 85.

Mahé, India, 28.

Mahé, Midshipman, 161.

Maignant, Joseph, deportee, 177, 182.

Maillart Dumesle, Jacques, acting intendant, 72, 78, 80, 81.

maize, 65, 105, 127, 147, 248.

Makarios, Archbishop of Cyprus, 248.

Malagasy, hostile to Whites, 46; as slaves, 222; raids on Anjouan, 238; 248.

Malartic, Anne-Joseph, comte de, gov.-gen., 115, 117, appoints Quinssy as Seychelles commandant, 119; and capitulation, 128-9; and Tippu Sultan, 142-3; and Surcouf, 149; biog., 257.

*Malavois, Jean-Baptiste, comdt and settler: mission to Seychelles, 98, 99-100; proposals on administration and defence, 102-3; on tortoises, coconuts, and land, 104-5; appointed commandant, 106; in conflict with settlers, 106-7; and Seychelles independence, 108-10; resigns, 112; 117; and deportees, 163-4, 175, 179; criticises Quinssy, 179.

Malaya: seamen from 131; 149; as slaves, 223.

Maldives islands, 16; and coco de mer, 35-6, 42-3; 55, 168, 201, 235.

Malesherbes, Chrétien-Guillaume, 63.

Mangalore, 142.

Manila, 136, 210.

Marchais, François, acting justice of peace, 246.

Marco Polo, 36.

Marine, French Ministry of, 29, 61. *Ministers of Marine listed under their names.*

Mascarene islands, 15, 18, 47; and spices, 111.

Maudave, Comte de, 47, 49.

Mauger, Lieut. Nicholas, 167.

Mauritius (Isle de France), 15, 89, 126; British landing, 231-2; and shortage of gold coin, 232; 235; disappointment over Roquebart's defeat, 37; 239, 244; slave transfers, 245; 246, 248; Seychelles dependency ends, 248.
Maury, surgeon, 128, 130.
Mellon, François, deportee, 139.
Mille Pattes, Hangard's pirogue, 213-4.
Mincé, settler: and Lefranc, 165.
Moluccas (Spice islands), 20, 62, 63.
Mombasa, 134.
Mondon, municipal agent, 179, 181, 214; as slave owner, 222; 226.
monsoon, 16, 50, 113.
Moras island (Praslin), 26, 35, 38, 39.
Morel Duboil, settler, 108.
Mornington (Richard Wellesley), Earl of, gov.-gen., Bengal, 142, 201.
Morocco, 45, 56,
Morphey, Capt. Corneille, 24-6; annexes Isle Séchelles, 26, 28; 30, 41; biog., 258.
Moslems, 23.
Motais de Narbonne, Augustin, acting intendant, 100, 104.
Mozambique, 189, 207; as term for African slave, 223, 226.
Mozambique Channel, 21, 180.
Muscat, 186; imam of, 189.
Mysore, 142, 143.

*Nageon de l'Étang, settler and acting comdt, 108, 110, 113-4, 117; daughter's marriage, 195; his widow, 195, 196; his son, 247.
Nantes, 158, 160.
National Guard, 127, 136, 139; Seychelles detachment, 217.
Negapatam, 120.
Nelson, Adml Lord, 200, 209.
Neptune Oriental, 51, 52, 163, 243.
Newcome, Capt. Henry: at Seychelles, 123; and capitulation, 124-5, 130; 151, 242.
New Zealand, 56.
3 Nivôse (Rue St Nicaise) bomb plot, 152-3, 154-5, 157-60, *passim*, 175-6, 228.
nutmeg, 66, 68, 70, 87, 111, 142, 194. *See also* spices.

Oger, officer in *Heure du Berger:* takes possession of Silhouette island, 58; and La Digue, 59.

Osborn, Capt. Samuel: at Seychelles, 124; commodore of blockading squadron off Isle de France, 130, 211.
Owen, Adml William: biog., 258-9.

Pamplemousses, 79, 121.
Panthéon, 156.
Pasquier, Madame: and slave trafficking, 245.
Peace of Amiens, 139, 150, 198, 203.
Pellew, Adml Sir Edward, East Indies C.-in-C., 211.
Pemba, 21.
Pépin-Desgrouettes, Pierre, deportee, 155, 192; dies, 196.
pepper, 20, 66, 68.
Peros Banhos, 18.
Persian Gulf, 23, 132, 151.
Philippines, 66.
Phillimore, Midshipman, 167.
Phoenicians, 14.
Picault, Lazare: first voyage to Seychelles, 11-4 *passim*, 18; his Island of Plenty, 13; second voyage, 18-9; death, 20; 23, 24-6 *passim*, 30, 38, 49, 50; biog., 259.
Pichegru, Gen. Charles, 157.
pierre de possession, 26, 41, 65.
Pigafetta, Antoine, 35.
pirates, 23-4, 146, 148.
Pirates Arms Hotel, 134.
Pittman, Capt, Philip, Indian army: and chart of Seychelles, 65.
Plassey, battle of, 28.
Poivre, Pierre, intendant, 29; Spice island dream, 29, 105, 248; and spice growing at Isle de France, 29, 62-3, 105; and shorter route to India, 30; and coco de mer, 39, 41, 49, 54; 56, 59; and Gillot, 68, 70; and spice growing in Seychelles, 63, 66, 70; and Brayer du Barré, 67-8; resigns, 69-70; 73; and Pamplemousses garden, 79; biog. 259-60.
Pompé: trial for murder of overseer, and execution by burning, 228.
Pondichéry, 16, 28, 50, 54, 74, 82, 84, 117, 199, 201-2.
Pondichéry Regt: detachment sent to Seychelles, 90; recalled, 121; commander, 113; Quinssy joins, 120.
Popequin, Pierre-Louis, surgeon, 96.
Port Louis (Port Nord-Ouest), 15, 57, 62, 107, 179, 232, 235.
Portugal, King of, 66.
Portuguese: exploration of Indian Ocean, 14, 16-8; 20, 22; and coco de mer, 36; secrecy of sea routes, 53; 131, 161, 167; *Flèche* sold to,

199; slave ships, 207, 208, 235.
Poupinel, Louis, surgeon, 191, 195; marriage to daughter of Nageon de l'Étang, 195; 208, 220; and his slave Pompé, 228.
Praslin: and treasure, 23; goats left on island, 33; visit by *Curieuse*, 35, 37-40; and coco de mer, 37, 38, 39, 41, 66, 69, 72; crocodiles, 39; French flag raised, 40; 58, 65; visit by *Heure du Berger*, 58-9; Gillot's description, 69; stationing of troops, 102, 103; 108, 111, 116, 121, 127, 135, 138, 148, 174, 204, 207; English seamen desert, 208; Sullivan's raid, 245-6.
Praslin island, place names: Anse Possession, 39; Baie Ste Anne, 59.
Praslin, Duc de, Minister of Marine, 35, 64, 66, 72.
Prévost, Simon, Poivre's agent, 62.
Prince Regent (George IV), 247.
Prior, James, surgeon, 232, 234, 238; comment on Seychelles, 238; at Anjouan, 238.
privateers, 146, 147, 150, 151, 173; depredations against English, 206; victims of English warships, 209.
Prussia, 28.
Pyrard de Laval, François: and nut of Maldives, 36-7, 43.

*Queau de Quinssy, Jean-Baptiste, comdt, 118, character, early career, 119-20; appointed commandant, 120; marriages and divorce, 120; puts island on war footing, 121-2, 204-5; capitulation, 124-5; controversy over flag, 126, 129; 127, 128; renewal of capitulation, 130, 132, 167, 174, 203, 208, 210, 217; 140; and Tippu Sultan's envoys, 143; and deportees, 158, 164, 175, 177-83 *passim*, 188, 190, 192, 195; remarks on climate, 164, 167; and *Chiffonne*, 166, 167; and *Flèche*, 172-3; Madame Quinssy, 181; and Beguignon, 191, 192, 193, 226; relations with settlers, 193; resents Isle de France neglect, 193; quoted, 198; and Decaen, 202-3, 211-12; and Linois, 211-2; failure to renew capitulation and consequences, 214-5; as slave owner, 222; 226; and Le Roy, 226-8, 229, 241; 228; surrender to Beaver, 233; criticised by Sullivan, 241; and *Clorinde*, 242; removed from posts, 244; restored as justice of peace, 244; 246; arrested and sent to Mauritius, 246-7; dies, 247; and settlers' petition, 247; biog., 260.
Quienet, Jean-Baptiste, settler: and Gillot, 87, 94, 96; accused of complicity in theft, 97-100; 108, 110.
Quinon, Joseph, deportee, 155, 297.

Rainier, Capt. John Spratt, 131.

Rainier, Adml Peter, C.-in-C., East Indies, 131, 143, 202.
Raleigh, Sir Walter, 146.
Ramalinga, free black of Bourbon, 110, 195.
Red Sea, 23, 132, 141, 143, 144, 145, 151, 168.
religion: first Seychelles parish, 77-8; call for priest, 111, 137; lax observance by settlers, 224; 240; promoted by France, 248.
Renaud, Capt. Jean-Marie: breaks Isle de France blockade, 130.
Réunion: Isle Bourbon renamed, 136; Belleville insurrection, 136-7; 143, 148; the *Flèche* calls, 169-70; and deportees, 176, 182, 188; 201; Magallon as governor, 202; 215; captured by English, 231; returned to France, 244. *See also* Bourbon.
rice, 19, 66, 105, 126, 127, 140, 164, 194, 248.
Robert, Vincent, deportee from Réunion, 138-9; settler, 190.
Robespierre, Maximilien: quoted, 101; 160.
Rochon, Alexis-Marie: and coco de mer, 37, 42, 54; early years, 44-5; joins *Heure du Berger* expedition, 46; and transit of Venus, 46, 50; differences with Grenier, 46, 51, 53-4, 73; at Madagascar, criticises colonisation, 47-8; blames D'Après, 51-2; comments on Seychelles, 52-4; and Kerguelen, 55; refused permission to sail with Marion Dufresne, 56; return to France, 56; dies, 56; and Rochon Dam, 56; 57, 92; biog., 260-1.
Rodrigues: and tortoises, 12, 14, 30; 14, 18; captured by English, 231.
*Romainville, Lieut. Charles, comdt, 85-6; destroys spice garden, 86-7, 105; recalled, 88; 105, 118, 195.
Romarf, François, slave dealer, 245-6.
Rossbach, battle of, 28.
Rossignol, Jean-Antoine, deportee, 155-6; role in Revolution, 156, 160; 161, 181, 182; at Anjouan, 185; dying curse, 185-6.
Roquebart, Capt. François, 235, 236, 237.
Rudolf II: and coco de mer, 37.
Rumpf, George (Rumphius), botanist, 36.
Russia, 28.

sailors: desertions in British navy, 131, 167, 208, 217; punishments, 131, 168, 208, 233.
Sandwich, Earl of, 84.
Sartine, Antoine de, Minister of Marine, 75, 76-7, 80-2 *passim*; biog., 261.
Saint Benoît, 24, 26.
St Criq, Capt. Jacques, 236; in action off Foulepointe, 256-7; court-martial, 243, 244; at Seychelles, 241-3; returns to France, 243; Napoleon wants him shot, 243.

St Denis, Réunion, 136, 139, 236.
St Domingue, 162, 205.
St Malo, 15, 30, 130, 150.
St Nicaise: *See* 3 Nivôse.
St Pierre, Bernadin de: and coco de mer, 37.
St Vincent, Adml Earl, 173.
Sainte Anne, 26, 40; first settlement, 58, 62, 63, 64, 65; and Hangard, 72, 93-4; Brayer du Barré asks for exclusive use, 76; 103, 105, 106, 117; freed French prisoners landed, 125, 126; 148, 165; burial of seamen, 167; 213, 234, 237, 238, 241.
Sainte Anne feast day, 25.
Ste Marie island, 23; conceded to France, 47.
Sausse, Capt. Jean: accused by Decaen, 208; accused by Madge, 246.
Savy, settler, 94, 97, 108; François, 138; brothers wish to leave, 175; 181; Charles, 190, 226.
Schomberg, Capt. Charles, 232, 235; in action against French off Foulepointe, 236, 240; 237, 240; sails for Brazil, 240.
seals, 32-3.
Séchelles, Château de, 9.
Séchelles island, 26, 28, 39, 40, 41, 49, 53.
Séchelles, Jean Moreau de, 9; biog., 258
séga, 225.
Senegal, 158.
September massacres, 155, 182.
Sercy, Adml, 136.
Seringpatam, 141.
Serpolet, Nicolas-François, deportee, 177, 179, 182, 183.
Sete Irmas (Seven Sisters), 17.
settlers: numbers, 120, 212; 122; and capitulation, 124, 126, 128, 129-30, 216; and deportees, 164, 190-1; relations with Quinssy, 193; petition to Isle de France, 216; life style, 224-5; submit to British authority, 234, 244-5; abandon Seychelles for Mauritius, 248.
Seven Years' War, 24, 28, 77, 83.
Seychelles: animals, 13, 14, 22, 32-3, 59, 75, 95, 118, 248; descriptions of, 13, 19, 22-3, 25, 39, 52-4, 59, 74-5, 103, 118, 194, 225; main island named, 26; climate, 30, 52, 183, 195; archipelago annexed, 41; first settlement, 58, 62-73 *passim*; crops, 64-5, 68, 76, 103, 105, 127, 147, 194, 218, 222, 238, 248; Crown take-over proposed, 73, 82; military detachment, 84-5, 90, 107, 121, 183, 217; hospital, 85, 167, 168, 195, 243; food shortage, 90, 190; and shipwreck survivors, 90-1; administrative reform and defence, 101-6 *passim*; dilemma for

France, 103; effects of French Revolution and declaration of independence, 108-12; territorial claims, 112, 116, 204; Tricolour raised, 113; executive powers, 115-6; population, 120-1, 212; suppression of Revolutionary bodies, 203-4; post box, 205; administration of justice, 226-7; coat of arms, 230; British take possession, 232-3; effects of British rule, 238, 240-1, 244-5, 247; full colony status, 248. *See also* Capitulation, coco de mer, crocodiles, deportees, Établissement, liquor, religion, settlers, Séchelles island, slavery, spices, tortoises.

Seychelles islands: *Inner islands*: Aride, 23, 40; Ave Maria rocks, 39, 148; Baleine rocks, 39; Bird (Isle aux Vaches), 75; Booby (Isle aux Fous), 40; Cachée, 106; Cerf, 26, 86, 93, 103, 105, 106, 117, 131, 234, 238; Chauve Souris, 33; Chauve Souris (Praslin), 40; Cayman reef, 148; Conception, 80, 215; Cousin, 40; Cousine, 40; Curieuse, 39, 59, 65, 76, 203, 207, 230; Denis, 75, 183, 191; Félicité, 39, 58; Longue, 26, 103; Les Cheminées, 148; Mamelles, 33; Marianne, 39; Nord, 91, 111, 194, 213; Recif, 103; Rocher Caché, 39; Ronde, 26; Ronde (Praslin), 39; St Pierre, 40; Sisters, 40, 58; Sud-Est, 26; Thérèse, 80, 215; Vaches-Marines, 33; *See separate entries for* Frégate, La Digue, Mahé, Praslin, Sainte Anne, Silhouette. *Outer islands:* African banks, 163, 168; Aldabra, 18, 230; Astove, 23, 52; Boudeuse, 58; Coëtivy, 112, 194; Cosmoledo, 18; D'Arros, 60; Desroches, 60; Étoile, 58; Marie-Louise, 58; Noeufs, 58; Platte, 57, 112; Poivre (Isle du Berger), 57, 60; Remire, 60, 163; St Joseph, 60.

Seychelles, Republic of, 17, 18, 112, 230, 249.

sharks, 31, 40, 53, 58.

Sharpeigh, Capt. Alexander, 21.

Ships:

French ships of commerce, including slavers: *Bons Amis,* and shipments of tortoises, 104; *Courrier des Seychelles,* slave brig taken as prize, 215; *Deux Andrés,* captured by *Resistance,* 125; *Duguay Trouin,* 123, 126; *Hélène,* and founding of Établissement, 85; *Laurette,* 137, 138; *Louisa,* slaver captured by *Centurion,* 131-2; *Marianne,* 67, 68, lost off Isle de France, 68-9; *Nécessaire,* 70, 71, brings news of the Seychelles settlement, 72; *Olivette,* 122, 124, 125, 126, 151; *Rosalie,* 204, 216; *Sophie,* prize, 167, 168; *Thélèmaque,* 64, wrecked, 80; *Virginie,* slave ship captured at Praslin, 245; *Zephyr,* slave ship, 207, taken by *Concorde,* 208.

French warships, privateers, and Company vessels: *Apollon,* privateer commanded by Hodoul, 151; *Bélier,* 179, removal of deportees to

Anjouan, 180-4 *passim*, carries orders for Linois, 199, at Pondichéry, 202, at Seychelles, 199, 203; *Belle Poule* (I), 55, 57, brings back settlers from Seychelles, 73, 82; *Belle Poule* (II), with Linois' squadron, 200, at Pondichéry, 201, 210, at Seychelles, 211, 213, captured, 213; *Cerf,* 24, 25, 26; *Charles,* 11, 13, 14; *Chiffonne,* 159, 182, 243; to Seychelles, 159-163, repairs to, 165, in action against *Sybille,* 166-7, as prize to Madras, 168, crew members in action against *Victor,* 173; *Clorinde,* 235, action off Foulepointe, 236-7, at Seychelles, 241-3, returns to Brest, 243; *Curieuse,* 30, 65, 69, at Praslin, 35, 37, to Jean de Nove, 41; *Digue,* 30, 31, 35, 41, 65; *Elisabeth,* first voyage to Seychelles, 11-4, second voyage, 18-20; *Emilie,* 147, 148, 149, 150; *Étoile du Matin,* first voyage to Amirantes, 57, second voyage, 59, 68, brings spice plants from East, 62; *Flèche,* 158, 243, sails for Seychelles, 158-9, in Indian Ocean, 162, 163, 169-70, action against *Victor,* 170, 172, 191, raised from seabed, 198, burned by English, 198, 204; *Heure du Berger,* voyages of exploration in Indian Ocean, 45, 46-50 *passim,* 52, 54, at Seychelles, 52, 58-9, at Amirantes, 58, 66; *Hippolyte,* with dispatch from Decaen, 211, 212; *Marengo,* 200, 201, 209, at Pondichéry, 201-2, action against *Centurion,* 206, at Seychelles, 211, 213, captured, 213; *Minerve,* 113, 116; *Seine,* 74, 75, 81; *Surprise,* 140, 141, 143-5 *passim; Vert Galant,* 49, 50, 51, 52, 54.

British ships of commerce, including Company vessels: *Ascension,* 21, at Seychelles, 22-3; *Brothers,* at Seychelles, confirms fall of Isle de France, 218; *Eagle,* 65.

British warships: *Albion,* 217; *Amboyna,* 141, 144, 145; *Braave,* 141, 143, officer's romantic attachment, 144, with Adam as passenger, 145; *Centurion,* 123, 124, 132, 200, resumes Isle de France blockade, 130, returns to Seychelles, 131, and *Louisa* prize, 131, to England, 206; *Concorde,* 217, at Pondichéry, 208, at Praslin and Mahé, 207-8, capture of privateer *Fortune,* 208-9; *Dedaigneuse,* 201; *Duncan,* pillage at Seychelles, 215-6; *Minerve,* sets fire to *Flèche,* 198, 203; *Nisus,* 232, 239, at Seychelles, 233-4, 237, raising of British flag, 233, at Cape and Anjouan, 237-8, at Zanzibar and return to Seychelles, 238, 241; *Orpheus,* 123-5 *passim; Pitt,* 211, at Seychelles, 214, return visit, 217; *Resistance,* 123, 125; *Seaflower,* 217; *Sybille,* 145, 146, 150, 168, 169, action against *Chiffonne,* 166-7; *Terpsichore,* 211, 212; *Victor,* 169, engages *Flèche,* 170-1, in action at Seychelles, 172-3, takes prize at Praslin, 174, at Cuddalore, 201.

Silhouette: annexed by France, 58; and turtles, 58; 90, 76, 91, 94, 111, 116, 193, 194.

Sinhalese, 183.

slavery and slaves: runaway, or *marrons*, 16, 30-1, 94, 205, 226; 26, 47, 62, 68, 77; offered as prize, 79; 92; slave ships, 93, 105-6, 195, 245; 93, 102, 103; drunkenness, 106, 177, 205; fear of uprising, 108, 162, 163-4, 177; numbers, 120, 215, 222; pressed into navy, 131, 207, 210; abolition decree, 136, 162, 177; retained by Napoleon, 180; arming of, 181, 212; 182, 186; Code Noir, 191, 227; living conditions and habits, 194, 220-1, 223, 225; 207, 213, 215; murder case, 219-20, 228; granting freedom to, 222; racial types, 222-3; influence on music, 225; punishments, 227-8; tax on slave owners, 226; British attitude and illicit trading, 238, 240-1, 245-6, 247; 242.

smallpox, 235.

Sneyd, Capt Clement: raids Seychelles ships and plantations, 215-6; 217; biog., 261.

Soares, Fernão: and discovery of Seychelles, 17.

Socotra, 22, 23.

Souillac, François Vicomte de, Bourbon gov., 84; succeeds as gov.-gen., 66; intervenes to remove Gillot from command, 97-8, 100; regulations for Seychelles, 101-2; approves Malavois' proposals, 104; 111; biog., 261-2.

Spain, 83, 121, 169; Spaniards, 131.

spices, 20; cultivation at the Isle de France, 29, 62-3, 105; at Seychelles, 63, 66, 68, 78-9, 86-7, 105, 111, 121, 194, 218; trials at Bourbon, 79, 105; Poivre's dream, 248.

State House, Seychelles, 85

Steinauer, Gen. Jean, acting gov.-gen., 49.

Stuart, Capt. Lord George, 216.

Suffren, Pierre-André, 55, 88, 120.

sugar-cane, 19, 85, 103, 218, 222.

*Sullivan, Lieut. Bartholemew, comdt., 234; and Quinssy, 241, 244; complains over Seychelles inhabitants, 241; made prisoner, 241; acts against Le Roy, 242; restores British flag, 244; appointed commandant, 244; efforts to end slave trading, 245; resigns, 246.

Sumatra, 16, 50, 54, 149.

Surat, 72.

Surcouf, Robert, 130, 146-50 *passim*, 185, 194, 215; biog. 262.

Tahiti, 44.

Tamatave, Madagascar, 237.

Ternay, Charles d'Arzac, gov.-gen., 72-3, 76, 78, 79; proposes Crown takes over Seychelles, 81; returns to France, 82; 83, 103, 220; biog, 262-3.
Tew, Tom, pirate, 23.
9 Thermidor (Fall of Robespierre), 160.
Three Brothers (Seychelles), 12, 18, 19, 64, 81.
Tippu Sultan, 141, 142-3 *passim.*
tobacco, 65, 103, 248.
tortoises, 12, 14, 19, 23, 30, 32; at Aldabra, 32, 230; 41, 61; Bougainville warns of extinction, 75; 76, 80, 81, 85-6; scarcity on main islands, 86, 194; 90, 93; hunting banned, 101, 110; Malavois' plan to conserve, 104-5; 125, 127, 148; at Diego Garcia, 194, 243; wholesale slaughter, 229; five-year ban rejected, 229; on Curieuse, 230; on coat of arms, 230; destruction under English, 248.
tortoiseshell, 66, 134, 229, 243.
Toulon, 16, 145.
Trafalgar, battle of, 131, 209.
Tranquebar, 91.
treasure, 24.
Tribunal de paix, 227, 246.
Trincomalee, 91, 120, 145.
Trobriand, Capt. Denis: annexes Denis island, 75.
Tromelin, Capt. Boudin de, 46.
Tromelin (Isle du Sable), 92-3.
troops: 77, 85, 89, 90, 99, 103; and Indian sepoys, 103, 121; and black militiamen, 121; 184; complaints over pay and rations, 190; partial withdrawal from Seychelles, 193; 195, 202; all recalled, 203; 205; veterans sent to Seychelles, 217; three soldiers remain, 228.
turtles, 19; green turtle, 32; hawksbill (*caret*), 32; at Silhouette, 58; at Curieuse, 59; at Tromelin island, 92; 164, 212, 213, 219. *See also under* tortoises.

vache-marine, or dugong, 32-3.
Vanheck, Jean-Baptiste, deportee, 177, 182; escapes from Anjouan, dies, 186.
vanilla, 66, 248.
Van Linschoten, John, 42.
Vaulbert, settler, 127.
Vauversin, Pierre, deportee: escapes from Anjouan, 186; arrested in France, 186-7, 196.
Venus, transit, 45, 50, 51.
Victoria, Queen, 248.

Victoria, capital of Seychelles, 56, 85, 135, 248.
Vola-maëffa, inhabitant, 94, 97, 177, 191; as slave owner, 222.

Waterloo, battle of, 244.
Wellesley, Sir Arthur (Duke of Wellington), 142.
whaling, 248.
Wood, Capt. John, 207; renews capitulation with Quinssy, 207-8; captures privateer Lemême, 208-9; 210, 211, 233.

Yvon, Louis, 113-5 *passim*.

Zanzibar, 23, 187, 188, 189, 238.